D1544158

For Gary Theurer
With every Good Wish
for studies of our
past
Roger D.
8/10/95

CULTURES IN
CONFLICT

Lithograph of Nauvoo in 1848. From Henry Lewis, *Das Illustrirte Mississippithal* (Leipzig, 1848).

Warsaw in 1848. From Henry Lewis, *Das Illustrirte Mississippithal* (Leipzig, 1848).

CULTURES IN CONFLICT

A DOCUMENTARY HISTORY OF THE MORMON WAR IN ILLINOIS

John E. Hallwas – Roger D. Launius

Utah State University Press
Logan, Utah
1995

Utah State University Press
Logan, Utah 84322-7800

Typography by WolfPack
    Cover design by Michelle Sellers

The paper in this book is acid free.

Library of Congress Cataloging-in-Publication Data

Cultures in conflict: a documentary history of the Mormon War in Illinois / by
John E. Hallwas, Roger D. Launius [editors].
      p.   cm.
    Includes bibliographical references and index.
    1. Mormons—Illinois—History—19th century—Sources. 2. Illinois—His-
tory—1778-1865—Sources. 3. Nauvoo (Ill.)—History—Sources. I. Hallwas,
John E. II. Launius, Roger D.
F550.M8C85 1995
977.3'04—dc20   95-4347
                                                                    CIP

CONTENTS

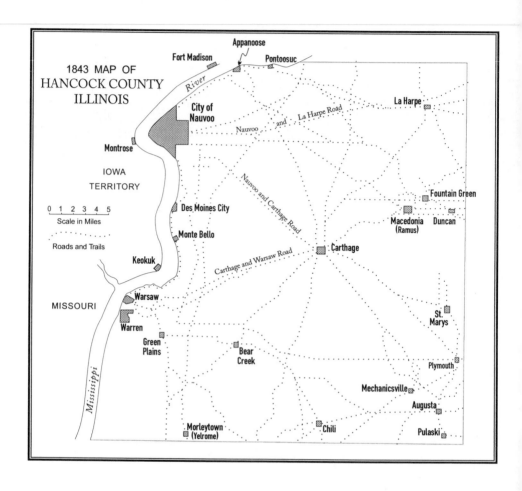

1843 MAP OF
HANCOCK COUNTY
ILLINOIS

Appanoose

Fort Madison

Pontoosuc

River

City of
Nauvoo

La Harpe

Nauvoo and La Harpe Road

Montrose

IOWA

TERRITORY

Nauvoo and Carthage Road

Fountain Green

0 1 2 3 4 5
Scale in Miles

Des Moines City

Macedonia   Duncan
(Ramus)

Roads and Trails

Monte Bello

Keokuk

Carthage

Carthage and Warsaw Road

Warsaw

MISSOURI

St.
Marys

Warren

Green
Plains

Bear
Creek

Plymouth

Mississippi

Mechanicsville

Augusta

Morleytown
(Yelrome)

Chili

Pulaski

PREFACE

This book employs documents to relate and interpret the most broadly significant episode in Illinois during the 1840s—the rise and fall of Mormon Nauvoo. It is a story of cultural clash, of escalating tension, fear, hatred, and violence between two social groups, which climaxed in a miniature civil war.

Despite extensive historical research and writing on Mormonism in Nauvoo, there has been little in-depth investigation of primary documents relating specifically to the conflict between the Mormons and the other settlers in the region. This is especially true of documents written by and about non-Mormons. *Cultures in Conflict* makes available in one place nearly a hundred documents illuminating various sides of the controversy as it develops a thorough, balanced, and probing account of what occurred in early Hancock County. The documents are arranged in six major sections, each with its own introduction establishing the context and providing an overview of that phase of the Mormon era. A headnote at the beginning of each document gives specific information about the people and events discussed in it, comments on that item's significance, and indicates the source. We have avoided the inclusion of explanatory notes in the documents themselves—so much of what passes for this type of scholarship is really pedantry—and have confined such material to the headnotes. The editorial method we adopted for dealing with these documents seeks to preserve spelling, grammar, paragraphing, and use of language as in the original. We have, however, sometimes changed punctuation to enhance readability because so many of these documents were punctuated poorly (or not at all) to begin with. We have used ellipses to indicate sections of a document not included in this book, but we have avoided struck-through words and phrases unless they contribute to an understanding of what was going on in the mind of the writer at the time.

This analysis progresses chronologically through the Mormon period in Illinois, emphasizing the wide variety of perspectives that survive in documents of the Mormon conflict. There were, we believe, not just two kinds of responses to the Mormon presence in Nauvoo and to the violent events which occurred but many kinds of responses—ultimately, as many perspectives as there were people who wrote down their views, and each person's writing is to be valued not just for information about what occurred but as a symbolic structure, an expression of the author's inner self. We would like to help historians and others to read better, to realize that nonfiction writing provides not just facts but fascinating self-revelations. While most Mormon conflict documents are not literary works, they are still valuable as unique views of the world. Our approach to the documents in this way has helped us to discern the critical role of myth in the causation and comprehension of the conflict.

We want to thank many people and institutions who materially contributed to the completion of this project. Several individuals helped locate documents, read all or part of this manuscript, or otherwise offered suggestions which helped more than they will ever know: M. Guy Bishop, Alma R. Blair, Newell G. Bringhurst, Paul M. Edwards, Jessie L. Embry, Lawrence Foster, Relly Fowler, Lois Fowler, Danny L. Jorgensen, Stanley B. Kimball, James H. Lawton, Bill Lionberger, Sally McPherson, Lee Pement, Ronald R. Romig, William D. Russell, Donald R. Shaffer, Jan Shipps, W. B. Spillman, Linda Thatcher, and Edward A. Warner. We also extend grateful thanks to the staffs of the Brigham Young University Library, the Chicago Historical Society, the Historical Department of the Church of Jesus Christ of Latter-day Saints, the Huntington Library, the Illinois State Historical Library, the Illinois State Historical Society, the Missouri Historical Society, the Reorganized Church of Jesus Christ of Latter Day Saints Library-Archives, the State Historical Society of Iowa, the Utah State Historical Society, and the Western Illinois University Library. Finally we appreciate the excellent work of John R. Alley and the staff at Utah State University Press, who contributed so much to the making of this book.

INTRODUCTION

The so-called Mormon conflict that occurred in Hancock County, Illinois, during the 1840s has been frequently discussed by historians but is not well understood. Nevertheless, the main events in that famous frontier episode are easily summarized. Expelled from Missouri in 1839, the Mormons fled to western Illinois, where they soon established the city of Nauvoo under the leadership of their prophet, Joseph Smith, Jr. Situated on a bend of the Mississippi River in Hancock County, Nauvoo grew rapidly during the next seven years as a flood of Latter Day Saints settled in the area.[1] A separatist community with a zionic religious purpose, Nauvoo was a city of over ten thousand people by the time of Smith's death in 1844.

Even as Latter Day Saints gathered there and Smith sent missionaries far and wide to attract converts, relations with surrounding non-Mormons steadily degenerated. Within the city, critics of Smith arose and established a newspaper in the spring of 1844. City authorities at Smith's urging declared the paper a nuisance and sent the local police to destroy it, and that act galvanized non-Mormon opponents, who threatened, and prepared for, violence against the Saints. Smith and his brother Hyrum were arrested, but before they could be tried, a mob stormed the county jail at Carthage and killed them. The accused leaders of the mob, including Thomas C. Sharp, the fiery anti-Mormon editor of the nearby Warsaw newspaper, were tried in the circuit court but not convicted. Frequent intimidation and sporadic violence characterized ensuing relations between Mormons and non-Mormons until the former, by then under the leadership of Brigham Young, agreed to leave the county. Thousands of Saints headed west in the late winter and spring of 1846, but some refused to go. Intimidation and violence again erupted. In September a non-Mormon posse of perhaps six hundred men battled Nauvoo militia, took over the city, and expelled the remaining Mormons.

Why this series of events occurred was, of course, a matter of dispute among the participants. Each side blamed the other, but unfortunately, neither side understood the other very well. The modern explanation of the conflict has been developed primarily by Mormon scholars, most of whom view the conflict in western Illinois not only as historians but also as members of the same interpretive community as the Nauvoo Mormons of the 1840s. That is, many of them assume that the early church was led by divine revelation through Joseph Smith and that the Saints were innocent followers of God, persecuted by enemies who failed to recognize their righteousness. Although using the tools of modern scholarship, those scholars too often view the Mormon conflict only as part of the sacred history of their church—a church whose mission was, and is, to restore erring humanity's true relationship to God, hasten the millennium, and bring salvation to the peoples of the Earth.

But unfortunately, as an explanation for past events, sacred history has serious limitations. Religious scholar Jan Shipps has explained this in a fine short article on Mormon historiography:

> In sacred history, the divine is an actor in the drama, a direct participant, not a supernatural presence. Because the divine is a *natural* part of the process, sacred history inevitably takes on a mythic character, which makes it "truer than true," if by truth one means that which is established and verified according to the canons of historical scholarship. Sacred history has other characteristics as well. It is stripped down—in artistic terms, stylized—so that the story is told in blacks and whites, with no grays. The persecuted and persecutors, the people of God and the people of Satan, good and evil are locked in mortal combat in which compromise is out of the question. All the ambiguity and complexity of human experience is shorn away. Moreover, the context is left ambiguous enough to keep the narrative from being either time bound or culture bound; it functions as scripture. . . . Mormonism's sacred history, like all sacred history, is a part of the mythological dimension of this religion. By its very nature it can only be *retold* and defended; not reinvestigated, researched.[2]

Much Mormon scholarship on the Nauvoo era is essentially sacred history. If not overtly mythic—as Mormon historical writing once was under such scholars as B. H. Roberts—it too often reduces the actual complexity of events, avoids matters that challenge or contradict Mormon myth, views the Mormons as good and their opponents as evil, and ignores the cultural context of the early church.[3] Hence, Mormon scholars too often write history that, if not blatantly, at least tacitly defends the faith. Their work might be of a scholarly nature, but it strives to reinforce traditional Mormon conceptions about the church rather than to comprehend the full complexity of the past.[4]

This is exemplified in the discussions of the Nauvoo experience contained in the two leading modern histories of the church: *The Story of the Latter-day Saints* by James B. Allen and Glen M. Leonard, and *The Mormon Experience: A History of the Latter-day Saints* by Leonard J. Arrington and Davis Bitton. Allen and Leonard provide only brief comments about religion in the United States at the time and otherwise ignore the ideals and values of non-Mormon America, so there is virtually no cultural context for understanding the Mormon conflict in Illinois. Also, they treat the Mormons as idealized figures whose motives are sacred. No action by Smith is ever truly questioned, and no criticism of Smith leveled by others is examined on its merits. For example, the dissenters who founded the Nauvoo *Expositor* to protest theocratic authoritarianism, the secret practice of polygamy, and other intrusions of the church into secular affairs are dismissed as "a disgruntled cabal" that "plotted dissension" with no other explanation offered for their actions, when other reasons are readily apparent.[5] The reader is forced to conclude that they must have been evil men bent on the destruction of the church when such was never the case. In contrast, the good "city fathers," in destroying the newspaper established by the dissidents, are not depicted as violating freedom of the press—much less any other constitutional right—and Smith himself is not viewed as the instigator of that action, despite his complete and unquestioned control of the community.[6] Mormon innocence is thereby sustained by the authors, both professionally trained historians who apparently chose not to move beyond the faith story and ask other legitimate questions.

Even Arrington and Bitton, an exceptionally capable and fair pair of historians, fail to explore seriously the Mormon conflict in Illinois. While they do a somewhat better job than Allen and Leonard in relating the church to its American cultural context—although they omit such pertinent intellectual currents as American millennialism and theories about the origin of the prehistoric mound builders—they still do not investigate seriously the causes of the conflict between early Mormons and their neighbors. Instead they see it as essentially a matter of religious persecution (one of their chapters is even entitled "Early Persecutions"). And Smith is idealized as a sensitive, magnanimous, just, loving, and sincere man, while his critics are portrayed as misinformed and ill motivated. The Mormon dissidents who established the *Expositor*, for instance, are dismissed as "libelers" who simply published "inflammatory allegations about the sex lives of Mormon leaders and members." The dissenters' actual motive—to reform the church—and their well-informed critique of Smith's leadership are never seriously considered. Once again, the destruction of their newspaper is not viewed as a violation of freedom of the press and due process of law. Furthermore, when focusing on developments after the death of the prophet, Arrington and Bitton cover the complex events of the exodus with a simplistic commentary. The "Mormons united under Young's leadership and, under the duress of continuing persecutions, reached westward for the long-sought dream of a Kingdom of God on earth." They were forced to leave Nauvoo only when "persecution began again in the fall of 1844, when Mormon homes in Illinois were subjected to 'wolf hunts'—freewheeling raids."[7] These historians do not mention Mormon intimidation, deception, repression, theft, and violence, or any other matters that might call into question the sacred nature of the Mormon experience. Similarly, they do not make any attempt to portray dissenters or non-Mormon critics of the church as anything but miscreants and troublemakers motivated by religious bigotry.[8]

Historian Klaus J. Hansen has suggested that this historical approach is common because Mormon scholars who are members of the Latter-day Saint faith must overcome years of religious training that predisposes them to view the church, its leaders, and its institutions as righteous and just. "Utah Mormons cannot admit a major flaw in Nauvoo," writes Hansen, "for these were the very practices and doctrines [Brigham] Young transplanted to the Rocky Mountain kingdom."[9] For inheritors of this Mormon legacy, Nauvoo is the first major embodiment of their vision of the world. As Ronald K. Esplin has noted, "Nauvoo was, and is, and will be important to Latter-day Saints because it was *the* City of Joseph. It was the city he built, where he lived and acted, where he died. Above all, it was the city where he fulfilled his religious mission. . . . In a very real sense, his other labors were prologue."[10] With such a perspective, sacred interpretations of the Mormon conflict in western Illinois are not easily overcome.

But modern scholarly history is far different. As Jan Shipps has pointed out, "It is marked by emphasis on context" and "by the inclusion of all the ambiguity and complexity of the human experience—by a recognition that there are two sides to any story."[11] The present documentary history treats the Mormon conflict in western Illinois as a complex episode which we can understand only through sensitive comprehension of both Mormon and non-Mormon ideals, values, and motives. This collection of documents, while far from exhaustive, illuminates significant facets of the conflict, and the commentaries explore the consciousness of those who were caught up in it. The memoirs, letters, speeches, newspaper articles, and other items provide evidence of misunderstanding, narrowness, bigotry, self-glorification, intimidation, criminal behavior, and violence on both sides. Furthermore, the documents in this volume—and many others like them which could not be included for lack of space—demonstrate that the Mormon conflict was not a matter of religious persecution. Non-Mormons did not much care for the oddities of Mormon belief—and some reacted with emotions ranging from curiosity to horror—but they did not try to suppress faith in the Book of Mormon or the prophet's revelations, or prevent the Saints from worshipping as they pleased.

This documentary history suggests that the conflict was essentially an ideological struggle between two cultures—that is, groups with differing social visions. As a recent study has pointed out, the Mormons believed that the good society arose "through a covenant with God that created a people," while non-Mormons felt it arose "through a contract among individuals that created a government." In short, Mormon Nauvoo was "an ambitious theocracy that asserted itself within a Jacksonian social environment deeply devoted to democracy."[12] When Smith extended his religious ideology into temporal affairs—by holding all the important offices in Nauvoo, controlling the political life of his community, directing the voting behavior of his followers, and planning to establish a political kingdom of God on earth (with himself in charge)—he placed Nauvoo on a collision course with the rest of America. Conflict of some kind was inevitable, and when he condemned his Mormon critics as enemies of the people and suppressed their civil rights through institutionalized violence, the non-Mormons—politically frustrated and fearful of despotism—resorted to mobocratic measures. Other causes, such as lawlessness by some Mormons toward the Gentiles (as they called unbelievers) and economic and social strife, contributed to the outbreak of violence, but this ideological struggle was central.

How then did the misapprehension about religious persecution arise? It had much to do with the lack of separation between the government and the church at Nauvoo, a development that was anathema to Jacksonian democracy. Most of those who embraced Mormonism, as Marvin Hill appropriately concluded in

Quest for Refuge, "wanted a society that would exclude unnecessary choices and would exclude pluralism." He wrote that "above all, they wanted to diminish the secular influences that pluralism engendered." The Latter Day Saint movement was founded on a belief that Jacksonian society had gone awry and would subvert or co-opt them if it had the chance. The result was an effort to close off the outside world, "to revitalize this magical world view [of medieval society, to] combine it with elements of more traditional Christianity, and [to] establish a theocratic society where the unconverted, the poor, and the socially and religiously alienated could gather and find a refuge from the competing sects and the uncertainties they engendered."[13] Like their spiritual forebears, the Puritans, the Mormons were engaged in a utopian quest for the kingdom of God, a flight from corruption, and a confrontation with the followers of Satan, all within the context of millennial expectations.[14] Any non-Mormon opposition to this weltanschauung was regarded as religious persecution by Joseph Smith and his associates. Indeed, because he was a religious leader, Smith commonly characterized any criticism of him, for whatever reason, by non-Mormons or disaffected Mormons, as persecution.

In accepting that view, those examining the conflict in Hancock County have failed to explore fully the wide range of available documents and have tended to ignore the crucial influence of myth on the attitudes, perceptions, actions, and interpretations of the early Saints. As James Oliver Robertson observes in *American Myth, American Reality,* "Myths are the patterns of behavior, or belief, and/or perception—which people have in common. Myths are not deliberately, or necessarily consciously, fictitious."[15] Myth in this sense is not a fable or falsehood but a story or understanding about events and situations that have great significance for the people involved. Myths are, in fact, essential truths for the members of a cultural group who hold them, enact them, or perceive them. They are sometimes expressed in narratives, but in literate societies like the United States, they are also apt to be embedded in ideologies. Robertson's book is one of many studies that focus on American myths—such as the myth of the chosen people, the myth of a God-given destiny, and the myth of New World innocence or inherent virtue.[16]

As scholars of Mormon history now recognize, versions of these myths were also held by the early Mormons, who related them to their church experience.[17] In fact, the key figure in Mormon history, Joseph Smith, was almost as deeply influenced by American myth as by Christian myth. As one article has recently pointed out, Smith "asserted that the Mormons alone were the chosen people, not the American public, and that their development of a new social order, amid the apparent disorder of early nineteenth-century America, would hasten the Millennium. The nation would fulfill its divine destiny through the Saints."[18] Such a mythic perspective, which was held as self-evident truth by the early Mormons, bonded them to each other and explained their lives; it was the foundation of their identity.

Mormonism was, in fact, part of a religious awakening aimed at revitalizing the culture from which it emerged. As such, the process of early church development conforms to a common pattern that William G. McLoughlin has described in *Revivals, Awakenings, and Reform.* It includes such matters as loss of authority, individual stress, criticism of society as corrupt, reassertion of a lost or obscured tradition, the creation of a new cultural pattern, and the appearance of a prophet whose experience "epitomizes the crisis of the culture."[19] The proponents of such an awakening escape from their anxiety-ridden situation by placing the burden of corruption on others and viewing themselves as the champions of the new moral or social order. The Mormons did exactly that by appropriating the American cultural myth of God's new chosen people, along with the corollary myth of innocence. Hence, they viewed themselves as inherently virtuous followers of God, the members of his one true church, surrounded by the wicked.

Like other aspects of Mormon myth, this idea was promulgated by Joseph Smith, and it found clear expression in the Book of Mormon, where an angel explains, "There are two churches only; the one is the church of the Lamb of God, and the other is the church of the devil; wherefore, whoso belongeth not to the church of the Lamb of God belongeth to that great church, which is the mother of abominations."[20] The unfortunate results of such a mythic dichotomy are described in the introduction to Part III of this history and are revealed in documents throughout the volume.

Inevitably, the "innocent" Mormons failed to recognize any of their own shortcomings—such as disregard for the Gentiles, abuse of the Nauvoo Charter to prevent Smith from arrest and extradition, coercion and deception in the practice of polygamy, and subversion of democratic government. All of these unfortunate Mormon behaviors were either not acknowledged or rationalized as necessary practices to counteract or respond to the followers of Satan, the enemies of all righteousness, who persecuted them from outside Nauvoo and conspired against them from within. As one might suspect, this mythic mind-set led to intimidation and vilification of nonconformists and eventually to the only documented case of out-and-out religious persecution enacted in Hancock County—against the dissenters who dared to point out Mormon shortcomings in their newspaper and demand reform. It also helped to foster a countermyth, in which the non-Mormons viewed the troublesome religious separatists at Nauvoo as wicked and themselves as the virtuous champions of America's cherished ideology, democracy. But unlike the Mormons, the non-Mormons felt increasingly overwhelmed by their mythic opposites, who had taken control of the county. Frustrated in their quest to defend Jacksonian republicanism from what they regarded as theocratic despotism, some of them resorted to violence.[21] In short, myth begat myth, and the result was bloodshed.

In psychological terms, both sides repressed (and hence ignored) their own potential for evil and projected it onto their ideological opponents. The non-Mormons did it to justify acts of aggression that violated their own deep commitment to constitutional rights and the rule of law. It is not accidental that the leading non-Mormons, Thomas C. Sharp and William N. Grover, were lawyers and later became well-respected judges. The Mormons, whose dichotomous myth was more fully rationalized and deeply held, were actually dependent upon their image of wicked, persecuting enemies for their very identity. Unless the followers of the devil were at the gates, there was no purpose, no defining struggle for the righteous children of God. Hence, the Mormons preferred their mythic vision to the more complex, disturbing reality—that the dividing line of good and evil cut through their own hearts as well as those of their enemies. Of course, when violence finally did erupt, they simply viewed it as verification of their myth. It is because of these mythic ramifications and their psychological underpinnings that Mormon identity remains strongly rooted in the Nauvoo experience.

As this suggests, the Mormon mythic consciousness not only substantially conditioned what took place in Hancock County but also later shaped the church's historical comprehension of what had occurred. Mormons have tended to dismiss all critical non-Mormon documents as ill motivated and therefore untrustworthy, while regarding those by the Saints as unquestionably reliable, both for factual reconstruction of what happened and interpretation of people and events. Through that practice, Mormon myth embedded in the documents has, of course, gone unrecognized and has been used to substantiate the sacred history of the church.

A good illustration of how myth in a Mormon document reshapes and interprets events is the following paragraph from the journal of Joseph Grafton Hovey, a young Mormon living in Nauvoo during the conflict:

> About this time there came among us one, John C. Bennett, with great recommendations from the governor and others, friends of ours standing in high state. Therefore, John C. Bennett, was put in the office of Major General of the Nauvoo Legion. . . . All things were in a prosperous condition until 1842, when the aforesaid Bennett, C. Higbee, and others did go about our city insulting our wives and our daughters, telling them that it was right to have free intercourse with the fair sex. They said that the Prophet Joseph taught that it was the word of the Lord. Therefore, many were deceived. . . . Hence, he [Bennett] had a good opportunity to practice his fiendish designs. He was a man of great talents according to the Gentiles. However, he was brought before the authorities and cut off from the Church. He then went into the other cities and states and tried to bring persecution upon us by telling that we believed in more than one wife and having all things in common; in fact, everything the devil could do to destroy our Prophet Joseph. The newspapers were filled with the most vile and audacious calumnies that could be invented by the enemies of all good.[22]

This account by a Nauvoo resident—who probably never knew Bennett personally—views him as a follower of the devil, one of "the enemies of all good" who was out to destroy the prophet and the church. Therefore, it was the "fiendish" Bennett who originated polygamy—which Hovey denigrates as the "right to have free intercourse" with various women—not the prophet, of whom Hovey says in the next paragraph, "He was as innocent as the angels of heaven." Bennett was, in fact, made the scapegoat for activities that the Nauvoo Mormons did not want to acknowledge in Smith or in the Mormon community generally. However, there is conclusive evidence that Smith originated and engaged in the secret practice of polygamy, which was so upsetting for Hovey and others, and there is corroborative evidence for much of what Bennett asserted in his 1842 exposé. But the myth of persecuted innocence made it impossible for this Mormon to embrace any alternative position, or to record in his journal what had actually happened.

And Hovey's perspective is typical of those present in the county in the 1840s. Both the Mormon and non-Mormon documents in this history reveal the wide-ranging influence of myth. Hence, it is impossible to produce anything other than a simplistic, inaccurate history if documents of the era are not evaluated critically as expressions of myth and ideology and if writings by Mormons, non-Mormons, and dissenting Mormons are not taken seriously. This documentary history seeks to do both. In the process, it depicts a theocratic, expansive, separatist community that would have provoked opposition anywhere in America, and it chronicles the rise of mobocratic violence in reaction to it, which became impossible for authorities on the Illinois frontier to control. With regard to the non-Mormons, the inescapable conclusion is that they had justifiable ideological grounds on which to criticize Smith and oppose the spread of Mormon theocracy. By using violence, however, they breached the very democratic ideals to which they subscribed and committed the most notorious acts of the Mormon conflict—the murders of Joseph and Hyrum Smith in June 1844, and the expulsion of the remaining Mormons from Nauvoo in September 1846. With regard to the Mormons, they perceived non-Mormon opposition as religious persecution. While they can be praised for their religious idealism, hard work, and personal sacrifice, the antidemocratic tendencies of their dogmatic, crusading spirit are equally apparent.

Conflict between these groups arose because of their strikingly different cultural values. The experience of people in Hancock County during the 1840s demonstrates the inevitable conflict between theocratic and democratic government, the danger of demonizing other people, and the self-deceptions fostered by the myths of innocence and political righteousness.

Notes

1. The two major Mormon groups treat the last part of their names differently. The Church of Jesus Christ of Latter-day Saints, based in Salt Lake City, Utah, uses a hyphen and a small *d* in the last part of its name. The Reorganized Church of Jesus Christ of Latter Day Saints omits the hyphen and capitalizes the *D*. In the first generation of the church, evidence suggests that the official name was Church of Jesus Christ of Latter Day Saints, and it will be referred to that way in this documentary history. Individual sources may have different versions and the editors have let these stand as in the original documents.

2. Jan Shipps, "The Mormon Past: Revealed or Revisited?" *Sunstone* 6 (November–December 1981): 57.

3. If there is any doubt about the mythic quality of B. H. Roberts's work, read any of the introductory material to his magnum opus, Joseph Smith, Jr., *History of the Church of Jesus Christ of Latter-day Saints*, ed. B. H. Roberts, 6 vols. (Salt Lake City: Deseret News Press, 1902–12); a seventh volume was published in 1932, and the whole series was reprinted by Deseret Book Company in 1976 and reissued in paperback in 1978. Purportedly written by Joseph Smith, the *History* was edited by B. H. Roberts from various Mormon diaries, journals, and records. For a discussion of the work's compilation, see Dean C. Jessee, "The Writing of Joseph Smith's History," *Brigham Young University Studies* 11 (Spring 1971): 439–73; Dean C. Jessee, "The Reliability of Joseph Smith's History," *Journal of Mormon History* 3 (1976): 23–46; and Dean C. Jessee, "Return to Carthage: Writing the History of Joseph Smith's Martyrdom," *Journal of Mormon History* 8 (1981): 3–21.

4. In recent decades a debate among Mormon scholars has raged over the writing of what has been described as "faithful history." On the multitude of perspectives on it, see Marvin S. Hill, "The Historiography of Mormonism," *Church History* 28 (December 1959): 418–26; Leonard J. Arrington, "Scholarly Studies of Mormonism in the Twentieth Century," *Dialogue: A Journal of Mormon Thought* 1 (Spring 1966): 15–32; Robert B. Flanders, "Writing the Mormon Past," *Dialogue: A Journal of Mormon Thought* 1 (Autumn 1966): 47–61; Moses Rischin, "The New Mormon History," *The American West* 5 (March 1969): 49; Richard D. Poll, "God and Man in History," *Dialogue: A Journal of Mormon Thought* 7 (Spring 1972): 101–9; Thomas G. Alexander, "Toward the New Mormon History: An Examination of the Literature on the Latter-day Saints in the Far West," in *Historians and the American West*, ed. Michael P. Malone (Lincoln: University of Nebraska Press, 1983), 344–68; Thomas G. Alexander, "Historiography and the New Mormon History: A Historian's Perspective," *Dialogue: A Journal of Mormon Thought* 19 (Fall 1986): 25–50; Marvin S. Hill, "The 'New Mormon History' Reassessed in Light of Recent Books on Joseph Smith and Mormon Origins," *Dialogue: A Journal of Mormon Thought* 21 (Fall 1988): 115–27; Paul M. Edwards, "The New Mormon History," *Saints' Herald* 133 (November 1986): 13; Davis Bitton and Leonard J. Arrington, *Mormons and Their Historians* (Salt Lake City: University of Utah Press, 1988); George D. Smith, ed., *Faithful History: Essays on Writing Mormon History* (Salt Lake City: Signature Books, 1992); and D. Michael Quinn, ed., *The New Mormon History: Revisionist Essays on the Past* (Salt Lake City: Signature Books, 1992).

5. In fact, these Mormon dissidents asserted in the *Expositor* that they "know of a surety, that the religion of the Latter Day Saints, as originally taught by Joseph Smith, which is contained in the Old and New Testaments, Book of Covenants, and Book of Mormon, is verily true, and that the pure principles set forth in those Books, are the immutable and eternal principles of Heaven, and speaks a language which, when spoken in truth and virtue, sinks deep into the heart of every honest man." Only then did they condemn the prophet for abuses of his power; for mixing religion and politics, even to the extent of declaring himself a candidate for the presidency of the United States in the 1844 election; and for teaching doctrines such as plural marriage that were contrary to the gospel of God they had accepted in joining the church. See the Nauvoo *Expositor*, 7 June 1844, available on microfilm at the Illinois State Historical Library.

6. James B. Allen and Glen M. Leonard, *The Story of the Latter-day Saints* (Salt Lake City: Deseret Book Co., 1976), 190, 192. Dallin H. Oaks, former justice on the Utah Supreme Court and present apostle in the church, has tried to pound a square peg into a round hole in seeking to legitimate the clearly illegal act of destroying the *Expositor* in June 1844. See Dallin H. Oaks, "The Suppression of the Nauvoo *Expositor*," *Utah Law Review* 9 (Winter 1965): 862–903. This act was considered a violation of "due process" by virtually everyone except the Latter Day Saints at the time, and Governor Thomas Ford—himself an authority on constitutional law and as fair an individual as was present in the Mormon conflict—called it "irregular and illegal, and not to be endured in a free country" (Thomas Ford, *Message from*

the Governor, in Relation to the Disturbances in Hancock County* [Springfield, Ill.: Walters & Weber, Public Printers, 1844], 3–4).

7. Leonard J. Arrington and Davis Bitton, *The Mormon Experience: A History of the Latter-day Saints* (New York: Alfred A. Knopf, 1979), 77–78, 93–94.

8. Not all writing about Mormonism in Illinois has suffered from the myopia of sacred history that has characterized so much modern work on the subject, even by exceptional Mormon historians. Robert Bruce Flanders's 1965 classic study of Nauvoo, incomplete as it is because of its intentional disregard of social and religious issues, opened an avenue of discussion that most others have been unwilling to follow. Flanders, not a member of the Utah Latter-day Saints, and perhaps because of this freedom, said that he wrote of Joseph Smith not as a religious leader but as a "man of affairs—planner, promoter, architect, entrepreneur, executive, politician, filibusterer—matters of which he was sometimes less sure than he was those of the spirit." See Robert B. Flanders, *Nauvoo: Kingdom on the Mississippi* (Urbana: University of Illinois Press, 1965), vi. He also wrote of Mormon Nauvoo as a western boomtown rather than a religious "city on a hill." There is little of the reverence in Flanders's study that most Mormon scholars have displayed in handling the subject. Usually the sacred history approach has created a romanticized and superficial image of Nauvoo and the events that took place there.

9. Klaus J. Hansen, "The World and the Prophet," *Dialogue: A Journal of Mormon Thought* 1 (Summer 1966): 106.

10. Ronald K. Esplin, "The Significance of Nauvoo for Latter-day Saints," *Journal of Mormon History* 16 (1990): 72.

11. Shipps, "The Mormon Past," 57.

12. John E. Hallwas, "Mormon Nauvoo from a Non-Mormon Perspective," *Journal of Mormon History* 16 (1990): 53, 58. The present introduction draws heavily from this article, which explores the ideological underpinnings of the conflict.

13. Marvin S. Hill, *Quest for Refuge: The Mormon Flight from American Pluralism* (Salt Lake City: Signature Books, 1989), 14, 17.

14. On the Puritan outlook and purpose, see Avihu Zakai, "Theocracy in Massachusetts: The Puritan Universe of Sacred Imagination," *Studies in the Literary Imagination* 27 (Spring 1994): 23–31.

15. James O. Robertson, *American Myth, American Reality* (New York: Hill and Wang, 1980), xv.

16. Some of the more important of these studies are Conrad Cherry, ed., *God's New Israel: Religious Interpretations of American Destiny* (Englewood Cliffs, N. J.: Prentice Hall, 1971); R. W. B. Lewis, *The American Adam* (Chicago: University of Chicago Press, 1955); Russell B. Nye, *The Almost Chosen People* (East Lansing: Michigan State University Press, 1966); Richard Slotkin, *Regeneration through Violence: The Mythology of the American Frontier, 1680–1860* (Middletown, Conn.: Wesleyan University Press, 1973); and Ernest L. Tuveson, *Redeemer Nation: The Idea of America's Millennial Role* (Chicago: University of Chicago Press, 1968).

17. Although thorough studies of Mormon myth have yet to be completed, some helpful articles and book chapters for those interested in the subject include Thomas G. Alexander, "A New Approach to the 'Everlasting Covenant': An Approach to the Theology of Joseph Smith," in *New Views of Mormon History*, ed. Davis Bitton and Maureen U. Beecher (Salt Lake City: University of Utah Press, 1987), 43–59; Gustav H. Blanke and Karen Lynn, "'God's Base of Operations': Mormon Variations on the American Sense of Mission," *Brigham Young University Studies* 20 (Fall 1979): 83–92; Melodie Moench, "Nineteenth Century Mormons: The New Israel," *Dialogue: A Journal of Mormon Thought* 12 (Spring 1979): 42–56; and Richard T. Hughes and C. Leonard Allen, "Soaring with the Gods: Early Mormons and the Eclipse of Religious Pluralism," in *Illusions of Innocence: Protestant Primitivism in America, 1630–1875* (Chicago: University of Chicago Press, 1988), 133–52.

18. Hallwas, "Mormon Nauvoo from a Non-Mormon Perspective," 54.

19. William G. McLoughlin, *Revivals, Awakenings, and Reform: An Essay on Religion and Social Change in America, 1607–1977* (Chicago: University of Chicago Press, 1978), 12–16.

20. The Book of Mormon (Salt Lake City: Deseret Book Co., 1981), 1 Nephi 14:10; The Book of Mormon (Independence, Mo.: Herald Publishing House, 1966), 1 Nephi 3:220.

21. Two books argue this case eloquently: Hill, *Quest for Refuge*, and Kenneth H. Winn, *Exiles in a Land of Liberty: Mormons in America, 1830–1846* (Chapel Hill: University of North Carolina Press, 1989). Hill emphasizes that the Mormons rejected American pluralism, strove to establish a theocratic government, and were persecuted for their antipluralism. Winn stresses that the Mormons felt alienated in what they perceived as a corrupt America, strove to reestablish communal republicanism, and were regarded as antirepublican subversives by non-Mormons.

22. Joseph G. Hovey, "Autobiography (1812–47)," p. 17, Archives, Harold B. Lee Library, Brigham Young University, Provo, Utah.

The image of Nauvoo as a pastoral, peaceful place. This painting was done by David H. Smith, the youngest son of Joseph Smith, Jr., in the late 1850s or early 1860s. Titled *Bend in the River*, it shows the southern part of Nauvoo, where Smith's home, office, and store were located. Courtesy of the Library-Archives, Reorganized Church of Jesus Christ of Latter Day Saints, the Auditorium, Independence, Missouri.

PART I

THE COMING OF THE MORMONS

Detail of a profile of Joseph Smith, prophet and president of the Mormon church, executed in Nauvoo by Sutcliffe Maudsley, ca. 1844. Courtesy of the Library-Archives, Reorganized Church of Jesus Christ of Latter Day Saints, the Auditorium, Independence, Missouri.

INTRODUCTION

During the bitter winter of 1838–1839 some five thousand Latter Day Saints crossed the Mississippi River from Missouri and settled in western Illinois. Since the organization of the Mormon Church almost ten years before, this group of religious pioneers, led by Joseph Smith, Jr., had received the brunt of political rhetoric, social ostracism, and in some cases, mob violence. These people came to Illinois in 1838 and 1839 not as ordinary settlers but as refugees from neighboring Missouri, where the state's population had expelled them following a brutal and deadly conflict.

In Illinois during the early 1840s, these people built one of the most impressive and powerful cities in the region, the community of Nauvoo, erected by the Mormons on a limestone flat by the banks of the Mississippi River some fifty miles north of Quincy.[1] Throughout the first half of the 1840s, Hancock County was dominated by Nauvoo, with its wealth, population, cultural achievements, and military and political power. For most of the Saints, the rise of this mighty religious commonwealth was the fulfillment of the shattered dreams of previous church-dominated communities at Kirtland, Ohio, and Independence and Far West, Missouri. They believed that God had finally empowered them to establish his kingdom on earth, which they called Zion.[2]

The Mormons began construction of the city of Nauvoo during the summer of 1839 and continued a massive building program until the church abandoned the site in 1846.[3] By the end of the first year, the Saints possessed what was essentially an overgrown wilderness community of log homes, a few shops, and an infant mercantile and manufacturing economy. In December 1840, they obtained a city charter from the state of Illinois, which made it possible both to provide essential services to Nauvoo's residents and to protect them from outside difficulties that had plagued the church since its origin.[4]

Building and immigration in Nauvoo seemed to be taking place everywhere. George Miller, later a bishop in the church, captured the city's vitality in the summer of 1840 by commenting that the community "was growing like a mushroom (as it were, by magic)."[5] Near the same time Joseph Smith remarked, "The number of inhabitants is nearly three thousand, and is fast increasing. If we are suffered to remain, there is every prospect of its becoming one of the largest cities on the river, if not the western world. Numbers have moved in from the seaboard, and a few from the islands of the sea."[6] The city continued to grow rapidly thereafter. According to newspaper editor Thomas Gregg of Warsaw, Illinois, during the heyday of Nauvoo, the Saints built about "1,200 hand-hewn log cabins, most of them white-washed inside, 200 to 300 good substantial brick houses and 300 to 500 frame houses."[7]

Nauvoo was, in essence, a boomtown, and no one was a greater booster than Joseph Smith. In December 1841, he wrote to Edward Hunter, a recent convert to Mormonism from Pennsylvania, about business prospects in the city. "There are scarcely any limits which can be imagined to the mills and machinery and manufacturing of all kinds which might be put into profitable operation in this city," he boasted, "and even if others should use a mill before you get here, it need be no discouragement to either you or Brother Buchwalter, for it will be difficult for the mills to keep pace with the growth of the place. . . ."[8]

His enthusiasm seemed justified, for Nauvoo appeared to many Saints the most remarkable place on earth. The city's population doubled every year between 1839 and 1842 and continued to rise until 1846. Most of the inhabitants were Mormons, and they were intent on bringing to fruition the spiritual and secular community that they had long sought. The most important expression of the community's meaning was a majestic temple, symbolizing not only the substantial nature of the church in the 1840s but also a rapidly developing Mormon theology that differed significantly from orthodox American Christianity. Excavation for the foundation began as early as the fall of 1840, but the real impetus to build the temple came on 19 January 1841, when Joseph Smith proclaimed a revelation commanding the building's construction.[9] Thereafter work on that religious centerpiece continued by the Mormons with zest for the next five years. Built of gray limestone, the temple came to dominate Nauvoo from its perch atop the bluffs overlooking the city. It stood 165 feet high, measured 88 by 128 feet, and cost something over a million dollars—an enormous sum at the time.[10]

The demands of temple construction, as well as all the other building taking place in Nauvoo, strained the resources of the Mormons almost to the breaking point, but it also sent an ominous message of what the Mormons could accomplish to other residents of Hancock County. It revealed something of the numerical and economic strength of the community and also symbolized the religious, especially theocratic, tendencies of the Saints. They were willing to sacrifice everything they had to accomplish the work that was defined by the institutional church. When that emphasis on local theocracy was combined with an interest in county and regional politics, the situation soon became explosive.

This section depicts Mormonism's early experience in Hancock County and portrays the church's relations with the non-Mormon population there. It describes the settlement of Hancock County and how and why the various groups came to think as they did. The recollections and documents, dating from the early 1840s, evoke the principles and reflect the ideals that motivated both the Saints and their non-Mormon neighbors.

Notes

1. The best introduction to the Mormon experience in Nauvoo remains Robert B. Flanders, *Nauvoo: Kingdom on the Mississippi* (Urbana: University of Illinois Press, 1965). See also David E. Miller and Della S. Miller, *Nauvoo: The City of Joseph* (Santa Barbara, Calif.: Peregrine Smith, 1974). For perceptive reviews of the literature on Mormon Nauvoo, see Richard D. Poll, "Nauvoo and the New Mormon History: A Bibliographical Survey," *Journal of Mormon History* 5 (1978): 105–23, and Glen M. Leonard, "Recent Writing on Mormon Nauvoo," *Western Illinois Regional Studies* 11 (Fall 1988): 69–93.

2. William V. Pooley, *The Settlement of Illinois from 1830 to 1850* (Madison: University of Wisconsin Extension Service, 1908), 509; Ebenezer Robinson, "Items of Personal History," *The Return* (Davis City, Iowa) 2 (April 1890): 243; Joseph Smith, Jr., *History of the Church of Jesus Christ of Latter-day Saints*, ed. B. H. Roberts, (1902–12; reprint, Salt Lake City: Deseret Book Co., 1976), 3:269–71; and Mrs. Paul Selby, "Recollections of a Little Girl in the Forties," *Journal of the Illinois State Historical Society* 16 (1923–24): 168–69. An intriguing analysis of the development of the Mormon concept of the kingdom of God and its expression in Nauvoo can be found in Klaus J. Hansen, *Quest for Empire: The Kingdom of God and the Council of Fifty in Mormon History* (East Lansing: Michigan State University Press, 1967; reprint, Lincoln: University of Nebraska Press, 1974), 72–89.

3. Flanders, *Nauvoo*, 27–39; Lyndon W. Cook, "Isaac Galland—Mormon Benefactor," *Brigham Young University Studies* 19 (Spring 1979): 261–84; Robert B. Flanders, "Dream and Nightmare: Nauvoo Revisited," in *The Restoration Movement: Essays in Mormon History*, ed. F. Mark McKiernan, Alma R. Blair, and Paul M. Edwards (Lawrence, Kans.: Coronado Press, 1973), 144–45; Ronald K. Esplin, "'Sickness and Faith' Nauvoo Letters," *Brigham Young University Studies* 15 (Summer 1975): 425–34; Joseph Smith III, "The Memoirs of President Joseph Smith (1832–1914)," *Saints' Herald* 81 (13 November 1934, 20 November 1934): 1453–54, 1479; Richard H. Jackson, "The Mormon Village: Genesis and Antecedents of the City of Zion Plat," *Brigham Young University Studies* 17 (Winter 1977): 223–40; and Donald L. Enders, "Platting the City Beautiful: A Historical and Archaeological Glimpse of Nauvoo Streets," *Brigham Young University Studies* 19 (Spring 1979): 409–15.

4. "An Act to Incorporate the City of Nauvoo," *Times and Seasons* (Nauvoo, Ill.) 2 (15 January 1841): 281–89.

5. George Miller to Editor, 22 June 1855, published in *Northern Islander* (Saint James, Mich.) 5 (9 August 1855): 1.

6. *Times and Seasons* 3 (1 April 1842): 750.

7. Thomas Gregg, *The History of Hancock County, Illinois* (Chicago: Charles C. Chapman, 1880), 296–98.

8. Smith, *History of the Church*, 4:482.

9. The revelation was first recorded in "Extracts from a Revelation given to Joseph Smith, Jr., Jan. 19th 1841," *Times and Seasons* 2 (1 June 1841): 424–29. It has been kept in continuous publication, with some alterations, since the Nauvoo era as section 124 of the Doctrine and Covenants of the Church of Jesus Christ of Latter-day Saints (Salt Lake City: Deseret Book Co., 1981) and as section 107 of the Book of Doctrine and Covenants (Independence, Mo.: Herald Publishing House, 1970). On the Nauvoo temple, see Laurel B. Andrew, *The Early Temples of the Mormons: The Architecture of the Millennial Kingdom in the American West* (Albany: State University of New York Press, 1978), chap. 4–5; Stanley B. Kimball, "The Nauvoo Temple," *Improvement Era* 66 (November 1963): 973–84.

10. W. Gerard Huslamp, "The Mormon Colony at Nauvoo, Illinois," *Journal of the West* 2 (October 1963): 470; Henry Lewis, *Making a Motion Picture in 1848* (St. Paul: Minnesota Historical Society, 1936), 51; Flanders, *Nauvoo*, 194–96; Smith, *History of the Church*, 7:434–35.

1

The Lay of the Land

In the winter of 1838–1839 the beleaguered Mormons began to settle in western Illinois, following their expulsion from Missouri. At first many of them moved into Adams County, on the Mississippi River around Quincy, where they were welcomed as an unjustly persecuted people. The Saints, as they called themselves, purchased property in Hancock County, about fifty miles north of Quincy, and settled in an area originally platted as the town of Commerce. They changed the name to Nauvoo and began to build a major river port and religious center for the sect. When the Mormons arrived, Hancock County was a recently settled section of Illinois. The most important town was Warsaw, also located on the Mississippi River about sixteen miles south of Nauvoo. Although only organized in 1834, Warsaw was located where a settlement called Fort Edwards had existed since 1817.

The two articles that follow—"Our Town and County," *Western World* (Warsaw, Ill.), 13 May 1840, p. 2, and "Sketches of Hancock County," *Western World*, 7 April 1841, p. 1—both describe Hancock County and Warsaw. They demonstrate the republican ideology to which the local settlers in western Illinois subscribed. Especially revealing is their sympathy with the freedom fighters of Warsaw, Poland, who had battled invading Russians in 1831, which is clear from their decision to name the new town after that eastern European city.

Our Town and County

Hancock County is bounded on the North by Warren County and the Mississippi river; South by Adams county; East by M'Donough county; and West by the Mississippi river. It contains about 8000 square miles. It was formed from Pike County in 1825, but was not organized as a county for several years afterwards. In 1834, this county gave about 340 votes, and had a population of about 1700 inhabitants; now, its population is supposed to be from 8 to 9000, and it is supposed that from 16 to 1800 votes will be given at the next August election. It is steadily and rapidly filling up with enterprising farmers and industrious mechanics. There are in this county several flourishing towns and villages, viz: Warsaw, Carthage, Commerce, Appanoose, La Harpe, Montebello, Augusta, Pulaski, Plymouth, Chili, St. Marys, &c.

Warsaw, the principal business town in the county, is situated on the fractional Section 9, in Township 4 North, Range 9 West, on a beautiful elevation, on the East bank of the Mississippi. It commands a fine view of the river for several miles in each direction, and has one of the best Steam Boat landings on the river. It is about 3 miles below the foot of the Des Moines rapids, is thriving rapidly, and is destined to attain a high rank among the towns of the west. The advantages of its situation are obvious, being opposite the mouth of the Des Moines river, and the point of termination of the Peoria and Warsaw Rail Road. A company of gentlemen, in February, 1839, obtained a charter from the Legislature of the State for a rail road around the Des Moines rapids, from Commerce to Warsaw, which is believed will be the most profitable Rail Road stock in the United States. The obstructions to Steam Boat navigation on the rapids are so great that the greatest part of the navigable season Steam Boats cannot ascend or descend with their cargoes with safety, and are under the necessity of lighting over the rapids in keel or flat boats drawn by team power. As the settlements on both sides of the river above this town increase, for a distance of some 5 or 600 miles above us, and as the resources of the upper country are brought into action, it is reasonable to suppose that trade and navigation on the Upper Mississippi will increase in the same proportion. If so, the importance of the rail road from Warsaw to Commerce, round the rapids, must be evident to every reflecting mind. It is expected that all the stock will be taken and the road commenced before the end of the present year, which, when completed, will add much to the business and prosperity of the towns of Warsaw and Commerce.

Warsaw is considered to be among the best locations, and one of the strongest points, on the Upper Mississippi. It commands the heavy business of this county; a portion of the business from the north part of Adams, a portion of the business from M'Donough and Warren counties, as also of the settlements on the Des Moines river in Missouri and Iowa.

The 16th or school section in this fractional township sold, in the month of August, 1836, for the sum of $17,014—the principal being kept on interest at 12 percent, payable half yearly in advance, amounts to two thousand and forty-one dollars yearly, which is believed to be the largest township fund in the state, with the exception of Chicago. The interest on this fund, in connection with our proportion of the State fund, will enable the citizens of our town to keep up a sufficient number of schools to educate all the children of a population of at least four times our present number. In addition thereto, we have a university, endowed with a real estate fund to a considerable amount, which will shortly go into operation, the professors being already appointed.

The present population of the town is about eight hundred. It has two steam saw mills, one steam merchant flouring mill of the first order, capable of manufacturing 80 to 100 barrels of superfine flour per day, one newspaper and job printing office, 12 stores, 3 hotels, 2 gunsmiths, 3 blacksmiths, 4 coopers, 2 cabinet makers, 1 tannery, 3 tailors, 1 bakery, 2 boot and shoe makers, 2 plasterers, and 2 wagon makers, all of whom employ more or less journeymen; 1 silver smith; 1 tin, copper, and sheet iron manufactory, besides a great number of other mechanics, such as house carpenters and joiners, brick and stone masons, &c., 3 physicians, and the necessary complement of lawyers. . . .

Sketches of Hancock County

Warsaw—A Town, post office, and precinct some four miles below Des Moines Rapids on the Mississippi river, and the most important location for commerce in the county—was named after the capital of the country and kingdom of Poland, situated on the Vistula river, 300 miles E. of Berlin. The name was chosen in consequence of the strong sympathy entertained by the proprietors at the time of laying off the town, for that oppressed and suffering country, which fell victim to the jealousy of the Colossus of Northern Europe, Russia, in 1831. . . . When this name was proposed, some of the citizens of the county dissented and remonstrated, and were ardent in their advocacy of a purely original designation, asserting that our independence as citizens would be compromised by thus copying names from other places. But so strong was the interest for the downtrodden Poles, who were then (1834) flocking into our country as exiles from despotism, that nothing could prevent its expression in the manner indicated above.

2

Mormon Nauvoo

This short article, "Nauvoo," *Sangamo Journal* (Springfield, Ill.), 9 February 1841, p. 2, is a remarkable non-Mormon description of the establishment of the principal Mormon community in Hancock County. It is a generally sympathetic account, noting that the Saints had been illegitimately expelled from Missouri by force and concluding that they were "generally quiet, industrious and economical." It demonstrates that many people in western Illinois were well disposed toward the Mormons during the first years of their stay in Illinois because they viewed the sect as more quaint than threatening.

This city is in the north-western part of Hancock county, Illinois, and was formerly known by the name of Commerce, but has recently received a city charter by the name of *Nauvoo*, the name given by the Mormons. The town is situated upon a slighty inclined plain, or piece of ground, of from one to two miles in extent, projecting westward into the Mississippi, somewhat in the shape of a man's arm, half bent; presenting a fine appearance for some miles above and below the town. Since the Mormons, or "Latter Day Saints," (as they call themselves) were so wantonly driven from their homes and estates in Missouri, by an *armed mob*, under the excited authorities of that state, these persecuted people have settled in this town, and the adjacent country on both sides of the Mississippi—and added from 72 to 100 buildings, mostly neat and painted, and covering the plain to the bluffs in the rear. These numerous new, bright looking buildings, are scattered about amongst the trees and shrubbery. Under the shade of some beautiful shrubbery near the river's brink, seats are erected for the accommodation of the society, at their religious meetings. The spot selected is favorable to a calm and serene temper, and a devotional frame of mind.

Nauvoo is said to have a population of about 3,000 inhabitants, some 300 buildings, several small Traders, Tavern keepers, Physicians, and various kinds of mechanics and laborers; and some water craft, among which is a small steam boat called Nauvoo. The landing, soil and timber about the town, are favorable to the future growth of this interesting and growing town. It has a fine country in its rear, and if too many drones and rogues do not creep in among these generally quiet, industrious and economical people, we may expect to see a very considerable city built up here—particularly as many of this sect in Europe are now known to be about removing to this country—and indeed some two hundred have already arrived at Nauvoo, and the vicinity. Mr. [Joseph] Smith is reported to have said that it is destined to be the largest city in the world. It is some 18 miles above Warsaw, and 6 or 8 below Fort Madison.

3

The Nauvoo City Charter

Perhaps the most important political act in the early years of the Mormon settlement was the passage of a city charter by the Illinois state legislature in December 1840. The document established the legal bulwark for the erection of the Mormon kingdom at Nauvoo. It might seem surprising, but the Illinois legislature passed this charter rather easily. During the same term, it passed forty-seven other acts of incorporation, seven of which were city charters. The passage of incorporating legislation was routine, but the lawmakers were especially motivated to approve this particular charter for two reasons: (1) the sympathy of fellow Americans for the plight of the Mormons following their expulsion from Missouri, and (2) the awareness by politicians of the potential strength of the Mormons as a voting bloc.

The document that follows—"An Act to Incorporate the City of Nauvoo," *Times and Seasons* (Nauvoo, Ill.) 2 (15 January 1841): 281–89—was relatively innocuous. What the Mormons accomplished under its provisions, however, excited anti-Mormon sentiment in Hancock County. Modeled closely after the Springfield, Illinois, city charter, it was used by the Mormons to create a fairly autonomous government built to the church's unique social and communitarian specifications. Joseph Smith, the Mormon prophet, merged the executive, judicial, and legislative functions of the charter into a single theocratic system and thereby challenged standard American governmental practices. In Nauvoo the mayor eventually became an active member of the city council and the chief justice of the municipal court. Moreover, the city's chief executive was essentially appointed by Smith, since his religious followers elected the first mayor, John C. Bennett, on Smith's recommendation. After Bennett split from the church, he was immediately turned out of the mayor's office and Smith was elected in his place. Additionally, the charter provided for establishment of a powerful state militia, called the Nauvoo Legion, which Smith commanded. That military force later became an important source of contention between the Saints and other residents of Hancock County.

As all of this suggests, in Nauvoo the civil and ecclesiastical governments were essentially identical in the person of Joseph Smith, and the charter was used as his own device, "concocted . . . for the salvation of the church," according to the prophet. For that reason, some of the charter's provisions came under attack during the Mormon conflict of the mid-1840s and led to its revocation in January 1845. The sections included here are those that became most important during the conflict that followed.

Sec. 1. Be it enacted by the people of the State of Illinois, represented in the General Assembly, that . . . the town plats of Commerce and Nauvoo, shall hereafter be called, and known by the name of the "City of Nauvoo," and the inhabitants thereof are hereby constituted a body corporate and politic by the name aforesaid, and shall have perpetual succession, and may have, and use, a common seal, which they may change, and alter, at pleasure. . . .

Sec. 4. There shall be a City Council to consist of a Mayor, four Aldermen, and nine Councillors, who shall have the qualifications of electors of said city, and shall be chosen by the qualified voters thereof, and shall hold their offices for two years, and until their successors shall be elected and qualified. The City Council shall judge the qualifications, elections, and returns, of their own members, and a majority of them shall form a quorum to do business, but a smaller number may adjourn from day to day, and compel the attendance of absent members under such penalties as may be prescribed by ordinance.

Sec. 5. The Mayor, Aldermen, and Councillors, before entering upon the duties of their offices shall take and subscribe an oath or affirmation that they will support the Constitution of the United States, and of this State, and that they will well and truly perform the duties of their offices to the best of their skill and abilities. . . .

Sec. 7. All free white male inhabitants who are of the age of twenty one years, who are entitled to vote for state officers, and who shall have been actual residents of said city sixty days next preceding said election shall be entitled to vote for city officers. . . .

Sec. 11. The City Council shall have power and authority to make, ordain, establish, and execute, all such ordinances, not repugnant to the Constitution of the United States, or of this State, as they may deem necessary for the peace, benefit, good order, regulation, convenience, and cleanliness, of said city; for the protection of property therein from destruction by fire, or otherwise, and for the health, and happiness thereof; they shall have power to fill all vacancies that may happen by death, resignation, or removal, in any of the offices herein made elective; to fix and establish all the fees of the officers of said corporation not herein established; to impose such fines, not exceeding one hundred dollars, for each offence, as they may deem just, for refusing to accept any office in or under the corporation, or for misconduct therein; to divide the city into wards, to add to the number of Aldermen and Councillors, and apportion them among the several wards, as may be most just and conducive to the interests of the city. . . .

Sec. 16. The Mayor and Aldermen shall be conservators of the peace within the limits of said city, and shall have all the powers of Justices of the Peace therein, both in civil and criminal cases arising under the laws of the State: they shall as Justices of the Peace, within the limits of said city, perform the same duties, be governed by the same laws, give the same bonds and security, as other Justices of the Peace in and for said city by the Governor.

Sec. 17. The Mayor shall have exclusive jurisdiction in all cases arising under the ordinances of the corporation, and shall issue such process as may be necessary to carry said ordinances into execution, and effect; appeals may be had from any decision of judgment of said Mayor or Aldermen, arising under the city ordinances, to the Municipal Court, under such regulations as may be presented by ordinance; which court shall be composed of the Mayor as Chief Justice, and the Aldermen as Associate Justices, and from the final judgment of the Municipal Court, to the Circuit Court of Hancock county, in the same manner as appeals are taken from judgments of Justices of the Peace; Provided, that the parties litigant shall have a right to a trial by a Jury of twelve men, in all cases before the Municipal Court. The Municipal Court shall have power to grant writs of habeas corpus in all cases arising under the ordinances of the City Council. . . .

Sec. 25. The City Council may organize the inhabitants of said city, subject to military duty, into a body of independent military men to be called the "Nauvoo Legion," the Court Martial of which shall be composed of the commissioned officers of said Legion, and constitute the law-making department, with full powers and authority to make, ordain, establish, and execute, all such laws and ordinances as may be considered necessary for the benefit, government, and regulation of said Legion; Provided, said Court Martial shall pass no law or act repugnant to, or inconsistent with, the Constitution of the United States or of this State; and; Provided, also, that the officers of the Legion shall be commissioned by the Governor of the State. The said Legion shall perform the same amount of military duty as is now or may be hereafter required of the regular militia of the State, and shall be at the disposal of the Mayor in executing the laws and ordinances of the City Corporation, and the laws of the State, and at the disposal of the Governor for the public defence, and the execution of the laws of the State or of the United States, and shall be entitled to their proportion of the public arms; and Provided, also, that said Legion shall be exempt from all other military duty. . . .

Sec. 28. This act is hereby declared to be a public act, and shall take effect on the first Monday of February next.

Wm. L. D. Ewing,
Speaker of the House of Representatives.
S. H. Anderson,
Speaker of the Senate.
Approved, Dec. 16, 1840.
Tho. Carlin.

4

Mormon Leaders on the Gathering to Nauvoo

In January 1841, fresh from the establishment of Nauvoo as a legally incorporated city, the Latter Day Saint First Presidency issued an important proclamation to followers around the world. It describes the church's rise, phoenixlike, from the ashes of the debacle in Missouri. It also comments favorably on the passage of the Nauvoo Charter as legal protection against persecution. Joseph Smith also recognizes the assistance he and his people had received from several political and business leaders in Illinois in establishing Nauvoo, and contrasts their actions favorably with the hostility and violence the Saints had suffered in Missouri. Most importantly, the document affirms the long-standing Mormon goal of creating a zionic community which will rescue the "righteous" from the "wicked," aim toward human perfection, and lead to the return of Jesus Christ to earth for a millennial reign. Speaking "the word of the Lord," it calls the Saints to gather to Nauvoo to build Zion in the last days before Christ's return. The proclamation is deeply mythic in its perspective, presenting a vision of total righteousness in juxtaposition to extreme evil. It also outlines the Saints' belief in the principles of democracy and the republican ideals upon which the United States was founded.

Signed by Joseph Smith, Sidney Rigdon, and Hyrum Smith as presidents of the church, "A Proclamation, to the Saints Scattered Abroad," *Times and Seasons* 2 (15 January 1841): 273–77, is a critical document in the development of the Mormon conflict in Hancock County. It vividly shows the mind-set of the Saints soon after settling in the region—wanting peace and planning for possible conflict, embracing republicanism and invoking theocracy within the same statement. The authors of the document, however, failed to recognize that their models, "the ancient covenant fathers, and patriarchs," knew nothing of democracy and held values that were incompatible with an open society. Nonetheless, this proclamation is filled with optimism and demonstrates the Saints' commitment to their religious ideas.

Beloved Brethren:—

The relationship which we sustain to the Church of Jesus Christ of Latter Day Saints, renders it necessary that we should make it known from time to time, the circumstances, situation, and prospects of the church, and give such instructions as may be necessary for the well being of the Saints, and for the promotion of those objects, calculated to further their present and everlasting happiness.

We have to congratulate the Saints on the progress of the great work of the "last days"; for not only has it spread through the length and breadth of this vast continent; but on the continent of Europe, and on the Islands of the sea, it is spreading in a manner entirely unprecedented in the annals of time.

This appears the more pleasing when we consider, that but a short time has elapsed, since we were unmercifully driven from the State of Missouri, after suffering cruelties and persecutions in their various, and horrid forms. Then our overthrow, to many, seemed inevitable, while the enemies of truth triumphed over us, and by their cruel reproaches endeavored to aggravate our sufferings. But "the Lord of Hosts was with us, the God of Jacob was our refuge!" and we were delivered from the hands of bloody and deceitful men; and in the State of Illinois we found an asylum, and were kindly welcomed by persons worthy of the characters of FREEMEN. It would be impossible to enumerate all those who in our time of deep distress, nobly came forward to our relief, and like the good Samaritan poured oil into our wounds, and contributed liberally to our necessities, as the citizens of Quincy *en masse* and the people of Illinois, generally, seemed to emulate each other in this labor of love. We would, however, make honorable mention of Governor [Thomas C.] Carlin [and others]. . . who will long be remembered by a grateful community for their philanthropy to a suffering people, and whose kindness on that occasion is indelibly engraven on the tablet of our hearts, in golden letters of love.

We would, likewise, make mention of the Legislature of this State, who, *without respect of parties, without reluctance, freely, openly, boldly, and nobly,* have come forth to our assistance, owned us as citizens and friends, and took us by the hand, and extended to us all the blessings of civil, political, and religious liberty, by granting us, under date of Dec. 16, 1840, one of the most liberal charters, with the most plenary powers, ever conferred by a legislative assembly on free citizens, for the "City of Nauvoo," the "Nauvoo Legion," and the "University of Nauvoo." The first of these charters, (that for the "City of Nauvoo,") secures to us in all time to come, irrevocably, all those great blessings of civil liberty, which of right appertain to all the free citizens of a great civilized republic—'tis all we ever claimed. What a contrast does the proceedings of the legislature of this State present, when compared with that of Missouri, whose bigotry, jealousy, and superstition, prevailed to such an extent, as to deny us our liberty and our sacred rights—Illinois has set a glorious example, to the whole United States and to the world at large, and has nobly carried out the principles of her constitution, and the constitution of these United States, and while she requires of us implicit obedience to the laws, (which we hope ever to see observed) she affords us the protection of law—the security of life, liberty, and the peaceable pursuit of happiness.

The name of our city (Nauvoo,) is of Hebrew origin, and signifies a beautiful situation, or place, carrying with it, also, the idea of *rest;* and is truly descriptive of this most delightful situation. It is situated on the eastern bank of the Mississippi river, at the head of the Des Moines Rapids, in Hancock County; bounded on the east by an extensive prairie of surpassing beauty, and on the north, west, and south, by the Mississippi. This place has been objected to by some, on account of the sickness which has prevailed in the summer months, but it is the opinion of Doctor [John C.] Bennett, a physician of great experience and medical knowledge, that Hancock Co., and all the eastern and southern portions of the City of Nauvoo, are as healthy as any other portions of the western country, (or the world, to acclimated citizens,) whilst the northwestern portion of the city has experienced much affliction from ague and fever, which, however, he thinks can be easily remedied by draining the sloughs on the adjacent islands in the Mississippi.

The population of our city is increasing with unparalleled rapidity, numbering more than three thousand inhabitants. Every facility is afforded in the city and adjacent country, in Hancock County, for the successful prosecution of the mechanical arts, and the pleasing pursuits of agriculture. The waters of the Mississippi can be successfully used for manufacturing purposes, to an almost unlimited extent.

Having been instrumental in the hands of our heavenly Father in laying a foundation for the gathering of Zion, we would say, let all those who appreciate the blessings of the gospel, and realize the importance of obeying the commandments of heaven with the possession of this world's goods, first prepare for the general gathering—let them dispose of their effects as fast as circumstances will possibly admit, without making too great sacrifices, and remove to our city and county—establish and build up manufactories in the city, purchase and cultivate farms in the county—this will secure our permanent inheritance, and prepare the way for the gathering of the poor. *This is agreeable to the order of heaven, and the only principle on which the gathering can be effected*—let the rich, then, and all who can assist in establishing this place, make every preparation to come on without delay, and strengthen our hands, and assist in promoting the happiness of the Saints. This cannot be too forcibly impressed on the minds of all, and the elders are hereby instructed to proclaim this word in all places where the Saints reside, in their public administrations, for this is according to the instructions we have received from the Lord.

The Temple of the Lord is in progress of erection here, where the Saints will come to worship the God of their fathers, according to the order of his house, and the powers of the holy priesthood, and will be so constructed as to enable all the functions of the priesthood to be duly exercised, and where instructions from the Most High will be received, and from this place go forth to distant lands.

Let us then concentrate all our powers, under the provisions of our *magna charta* [*sic*] granted by the Illinois Legislature, at the "City of Nauvoo," and surrounding country, and strive to emulate the actions of the ancient covenant fathers, and patriarchs, in those things, which are of such vast importance to this and every succeeding generation.

The "Nauvoo Legion," embraces all our military power, and will enable us to perform our military duty by ourselves, and thus afford us the power, and privilege, of avoiding one of the most fruitful sources of strife, oppression, and collision with the world. It will enable us to show our attachment to the state and nation as a people, whenever the public service requires our aid—thus proving ourselves obedient to the paramount laws of the land, and ready at all times to sustain and execute them.

The "University of the City of Nauvoo," will enable us to teach our children wisdom—to instruct them in all knowledge, and learning, in the Arts, Sciences and Learned Professions. We hope to make this institution one of the great lights of the world, and by and through it, to diffuse that kind of knowledge which will be of practical utility, and for the public good, and also for private and individual happiness. The Regents of the University will take the general supervision of all matters appertaining to education from common schools up to the highest branches of a most liberal collegiate course. They will establish a regular system of education, and hand over the pupil from teacher to professor, until the regular graduation is consummated, and the education finished. This corporation contains all the powers and prerogatives of any other college or university in this state. The charters for the University and Legion are *addenda* to the city charter, making the whole perfect and complete.

Not only has the Lord given us favor in the eyes of the community, who are happy to see us in the enjoyment of all the rights and privileges of freemen, but we are happy to state that several of the principal men of Illinois, who have listened to the doctrines we promulgate, have become obedient to the faith and are rejoicing in the same; among whom is John C. Bennett, M.D., Quarter Master General of Illinois. . . . He has been one of the principal instruments, in effecting our safety and deliverance from the unjust persecutions and demands of the authorities of Missouri, and also in procuring the city charter—He is a man of enterprise, extensive acquirements, and of independent mind, and is calculated to be a great blessing to our community. . . .

From the kind, uniform, and consistent course pursued by the citizens of Illinois, and the great success which has attended us while here, the natural advantages of this place for every purpose we require, and the necessity of the gathering of the Saints of the Most High, we would say, let the brethren who love the prosperity of Zion, who are anxious that her stakes should be strengthened, and her cords lengthened, and who prefer her prosperity to their chief joy, come, and cast in their lots with us, and cheerfully engage in a work so glorious and sub-lime, and say with Nehemiah, "We, his servants, will arise and build."

It probably would hardly be necessary to enforce this important subject on the attention of the Saints, as its necessity is obvious, and is a subject of paramount importance; but as watchmen to the house of Israel, as Shepherds over the flock which is now scattered over a vast extent of country, and the anxiety we feel for their prosperity and everlasting welfare, and for the carrying out the great and glo-rious purposes of our God, to which we have been called, we feel to urge its neces-sity, and say, let the Saints come *here*—THIS IS THE WORD OF THE LORD, *and in accordance with the great work of the last days.*

It is true the idea of a general gathering has heretofore been associated with most cruel and oppressing scenes, owing to our unrelenting persecutions at the hands of wicked and unjust men; but we hope that those days of darkness and gloom have gone by, and from the liberal policy of our State government, we may expect a scene of peace and prosperity, we have never before witnessed since the rise of our church, and the happiness and prosperity which now awaits us, is, in all human probability, incalculably great. By a concentration of action, and a unity of effort, we can only accomplish the great work of the last days, which we could not do in our remote and scattered condition, while our interests both spiritual and temporal will be greatly enhanced, and the blessings of heaven must flow unto us in an uninterrupted stream; of this, we think there can be no question. The great profusion of temporal and spiritual blessings, which always flow from faithfulness and concerted effort, never attend individual exertion or enterprize. The history of all past ages abundantly attests this fact.

In addition to all temporal blessings, there is no other way for the Saints to be saved in these last days, as the concurrent testimony of all the holy prophets clearly proves, for it is written—"They shall come from the east and be gathered from the west; the north shall give up, and the south shall keep not back"—"the sons of God shall be *gathered* from far, and his daughters from the ends of the earth": it is also the concurrent testimony of all the prophets, that this gathering together of all the Saints, must take place before the Lord comes to "take ven-geance upon the ungodly," and "to be glorified and admired by all those who obey his gospel. . . ."

We would wish the Saints to understand that, when they come here they must not expect to find perfection, or that all will be harmony, peace and love; if they indulge these ideas, they will undoubtedly be deceived, for here there are per-sons, not only from different States, but from different nations, who, although they feel a great attachment to the cause of truth, have their prejudices of education, and consequently it requires some time before these things can be overcome: again, there are many that creep in unawares, and endeavor to sow discord, strife and ani-mosity, in our midst, and by so doing bring evil upon the Saints; these things we have to bear with, and these things will prevail either to a greater or lesser extent until "the floor be thoroughly purged" and "the chaff be burnt up." Therefore let those who come up to this place, be determined to keep the commandments of

God, and not be discouraged by those things we have enumerated, and then they will be prospered, the intelligence of heaven will be communicated to them, and they will eventually see eye to eye, and rejoice in the full fruition of that glory, which is reserved for the righteous.

In order to erect the Temple of the Lord, great exertions will be required on the part of the Saints, so that they may build a house which shall be accepted by the Almighty, and in which his power and glory shall be manifested. Therefore let those who can freely make a sacrifice of their time, their talents, and their property, for the prosperity of the kingdom, and for the love they have to the cause of truth, bid adieu to their homes and pleasant places of abode, and unite with us in the great work of the last days, and share in the tribulation, that they may ultimately share in the glory and triumph.

We wish it, likewise, to be distinctly understood that we claim no privilege but what we feel cheerfully disposed to share with our fellow citizens of every denomination, and every sentiment of religion; and therefore say, that, so far from being restricted to our own faith, let all those who desire to locate themselves in this place, or the vicinity, come, and we will hail them as citizens and friends, and shall feel it not only a duty, but a privilege, to reciprocate the kindness we have received from the benevolent and kind hearted citizens of the State of Illinois.

> Joseph Smith
> Sidney Rigdon
> Hyrum Smith
> Presidents of the Church
> *Nauvoo, January 15, 1841.*

———— •••• 5 •••• ————

A Non-Mormon Reminiscence of Nauvoo

The following reminiscence by Eudocia Baldwin Marsh is a vivid and interesting account of Mormon Nauvoo from the perspective of a non-Mormon girl. Marsh was born in Geneva, New York, in 1829. Her father, Epaphras Baldwin, had been an officer in the army during the War of 1812 and had settled in Illinois in 1833 to claim land in the Military Tract. The Baldwins lived on a farm outside of Carthage, the Hancock County seat, throughout the 1840s. It is clear that they were not sympathetic to the strong Mormon influence in the county, but neither were they anti-Mormons since they hired members of the sect to work on the farm. Marsh expresses her disdain for Joseph Smith, but she was impressed by the faith and persistence of individual church members. Her reminiscence also refers to the frequent depiction of Nauvoo in utopian terms by Mormon missionaries in the British Isles, a practice confirmed by other documents.

Eudocia Marsh lived her entire life in western Illinois—she later married a Warsaw lawyer named John Wellington Marsh—and the incident she describes was but one she witnessed in Hancock County. That she remembered it graphically many years later attests to the impact of the struggle with the Mormons on the minds of regional people. This excerpt is taken from the original account located in the Archives, Knox College Library, Galesburg, Illinois. It was also published in Douglas L. Wilson and Rodney O. Davis, eds., "Mormons in Hancock County: A Reminiscence," *Journal of the Illinois State Historical Society* 64 (Spring 1971): 31–34, 36–38.

<hr />

After the settlement at Nauvoo great numbers came from England, many of them skilled workers in their different crafts, others being mere peasants, scarcely able to take care of themselves in a strange country. Two of this latter class were employed by a friend of ours—the man as laborer on the place, the wife as cook in the family. These people with many others of their kind declared that the Mormon missionaries who at that time swarmed through England, Scotland and Wales, had assured them they could gather tropical fruits of all kinds in the streets of Nauvoo; Oranges, lemons, pineapples, figs—without money and without price, and that they would be furnished with all the gold and silver they needed for the asking. Some of these poor people had verily believed themselves coming to the "New Jerusalem," and expected to see the living waters flowing down golden streets, with the Trees of Life growing upon either side bearing all manner of ripened fruit, which they would be free to pluck. The reality was too great a shock for some of them. Many died of homesickness, privations and diseases of the new country; others went out among the "Gentiles" glad to be employed at low wages, and never again returned to the city, or acknowledged that they had been Mormon dupes. The great mass of emigrants were of course absorbed by the city and sect, and were soon broken in to the weary work of giving tithes both of money and time to build up Smith—his Temple, and other projects. My Father had died before these people became so notorious, and my Mother being left with the care of family and farm, sometimes hired these men for the heavier work— one of them was a dark gloomy looking man of immense size and muscle, employed to split logs into rails for fencing. I remember that for his breakfast he was accustomed to eat, in addition to what most men would consider a bountiful meal, forty buckwheat cakes.—I used to feel sure he could have dispatched many more—for when he rose from the table he still had a gaunt and hungry look; but the young Mormon girl who baked them on a griddle holding eight good sized ones, after the fifth griddle full had been set before him—without any apparent effect upon his appetite, would invariably take the griddle from the crane with a vicious jerk, set it down upon the hearth with a bang, and leave the kitchen muttering "If he wants any more, he may bake them himself."—During the time this man was employed on the farm, a term of the Circuit Court was held in

Carthage, which always brought a large number of people to the town. *His Honor,* The Judge, the lawyers, with clients, witnesses and other interested, made up a much larger number than is attracted by Court week now a days.—There being no railroads, then, these people would be kept there from one to two weeks— with little to do in the long evenings.—So in order to pass the time, or for a little mild recreation, the young lawyers would have impromptu debates, political or forensic speeches, to keep themselves in practice I suppose.—Mutterings too of the coming storm were sometimes heard, and one evening it was understood that some Anti Mormon demonstration was to be made. Butterfield, the big rail split- ter must have heard some rumor as this, for contrary to his usual custom he went into the town that evening and up into the crowded Court room where some gen- tleman was speaking in denunciation of his people. Waiting quietly until the speech was ended, Butterfield arose and striding rapidly to the Judges stand, mounted the steps and began a fanatical tirade in *favor* of Mormonism—rattling off with great volubility their doctrines of "Baptism for the dead"—talking in the unknown tongue—the laying on of hands—anointing for the healing of the Sick—the seeing of visions, and dreaming of dreams; most of which had been copied from the New Testament by Smith & his confederates, and presented to the ignorant as something quite new. The man ended his harangue by declaring that *faith* was the only thing wanting to make of every man and woman a "Latter day Saint," and that he hoped, and expected to live to see all who heard his voice that night believers in the Prophet Joseph Smith and the Book of Mormon. The surprise of the men who had arranged for an Anti Mormon meeting was com- plete,—Butterfield's action had been so sudden, and his talk so unexpected and amazing, that he was listened to for some time in silence; but presently some men and boys went quietly from the room and gathered up a quantity of sticks and small stones and went back and ordering him to "get out," began pelting him— driving him out of the Court room, down the stairs and far on the road to our house, which he reached in rather a dilapidated condition. Nonresistance being one of his tenets, he had taken with patience "these buffetings" making no defense—else I think he could have, (like a modern Sampson) demolished the whole body of his assailants at one blow. His looks after this occurrence were more gloomy and fanatical than before, and my mother felt obliged to dismiss him, which she regretted, as he was a sober, faithful, and efficient worker. No doubt he considered himself a martyr, and was, I believe perfectly sincere in the belief that the Lord, through Joseph Smith, had given to the world a new revela- tion. When these people first came amongst us, fugitives as we afterwards came to believe, from the just and righteous indignation of their Missouri neighbors, Smith was in a Missouri Jail.—Before Spring however he was released, (It was said the authorities had connived at his escape in order to be rid of him) joined his flock and after repeated solicitations from people living on *both* sides of the Mississippi—selected the site of the little village of Commerce on the East side upon which to build his City. Now very soon their condition underwent a great change.—They had been dispersed through the county taking possession of every vacant house or cabin—many having drifted into counties adjoining Hancock, wherever they found toleration or employment. But so soon as Smith and his friends had decided upon a location, they sent out a call to all the faithful to come in and build up the new Zion. The response was general—the "Saints" flocked to Nauvoo taking with them many "Gentile" converts. . . .

During this time of Mormon prosperity, while Nauvoo was growing rapidly and filling up with people from all parts of the world and becoming a place of considerable importance, many excursions and pleasure parties were gotten up to visit the City. Some of the members of our family joined such a party on one occasion, taking me with them.—We dined at the Mansion House, Smith's large Hotel. After dinner we were told that in an adjoining room some Egyptian Mummies were exhibited for a small sum.—Some of the party expressing a wish to see them, we went into the room where we found them presided over by the mother of the Prophet, a trim looking old lady in black silk gown and white cap and kerchief. —— With a long wand she pointed out to us the old King Pharaoh of the Exodus himself, with wife and daughter, and gave us a detailed account of their lives and doings three thousand years before.—— Upon my asking her how she obtained all this information—she replied in a severely virtuous tone and a manner calculated to repress all doubt and further question—"My Son Joseph Smith has recently received a revelation from the Lord in regard to these people and times—and *he* has told all these things to *me*."—— We left the house without faith in these revelations—neither did we believe in the old ladies [sic] faith in them which seemed hard on the mother of the "Prophet. . . ."

———••◦● 6 ●◦••———

A Minister Criticizes Warsaw and Nauvoo

One of the most active missionary organizations in the United States during the 1840s was the American Home Missionary Society, based in New York City. Sponsored by the Presbyterian and Congregational churches, it had twenty ministers working full-time in Illinois by 1840. One of these men was Benjamin F. Morris, who by 1841 was presiding over a mission in Warsaw. From this position in the chief rival community to Mormon Nauvoo, he had a ringside seat for the Mormon conflict in Hancock County. In this quarterly report to the missionary board, he describes his perspectives on Christianity in Hancock County and on the coming of the Mormons and the growth of Nauvoo. He disapproved of Mormon religious ideas, without question, but he was especially opposed to the exercise of secular power in politics and economics by the Mormons at Nauvoo. As a proponent of republican ideology, Morris at a fundamental level resented the merging of church and state in western Illinois. He was likewise critical of the lack of piety he saw in Warsaw.

The original of this letter is located at the Amistead Research Center, New Orleans, Louisiana. It was also published in Roger D. Launius, ed., "American Home Missionary Society Ministers and Mormon Nauvoo: Selected Letters," *Western Illinois Regional Studies* 8 (Spring 1985): 19–22.

Warsaw Ill August 21st 1841

Dear Brethren,

The last quarter of the current year is now about closing, and it becomes my duty to transmit to you, as the agents of benevolence a summary statement of my labors.

I have preached without a single failure, to the church and congregation of Warsaw every alternate Sabbath, and the rest of the time at Keokuk, Iowa T[erritory] at the foot of the rapids, and sometimes in the neighborhood of this place. I have preached the gospel in its simplicity and fullness, and with all plainness, mingled I trust with true Christian love. But it grieves me much, that no immediate positive fruits have been gathered, yet I cannot but believe that some good has been done—some seed sown, to be reaped many days hence, and some impressions made that will lead to salvation.

Warsaw

In one of my former reports I spoke of the importance and natural advantage of this point. So far as nature is concerned, everything desirable has been done. The position is favorable for health, the climate is, in the whole, salubrious and desirable, the country, for fifty or sixty miles in the interior, the produce of which flows to this place, is fertile, almost as on the banks of the Nile, and every feature conspires to render this village—at no distant day—one of the first, above the city of St. Louis. Yet these natural advantages have been wantonly and wickedly abused by the inhabitants. Whilst God has thus signally blessed them, the people, in the mass, have as signally and obviously departed from Him. Almost the entire business policy of the place has been managed on principles not sanctioned by the gospel, the conduct of the leading men and indeed of the majority has practically said,

There is, no God, that rules on high,
or minds the affairs of men.

The minister of the gospel has had to contend with foul mouthed Atheism and rabid infidelity; with selfishness raging at the highest point, with a worldly spirit, in full tide of sweeping energy; with the confederated power of the world the flesh and the Devil; and in addition to the foes without, he had to contend with foes within. The church has not only been asleep, but it really seems as if they designed to keep their spiritual eyes shut forever. Worldly mindedness, sluggishness, indifference, and inconsistency of Christian conduct, have been but too much manifested by those who call and think themselves Christians. Those who could have been the most active and influential in behalf of mortal piety, have been the very ones to hold back the power of the gospel, and to put out the fires of evangelical piety. Yet we have had, some three or four, consistent praying Christians. I cannot, on paper, describe to you the peculiar full and accurate, moral and religious condition of the church and place. It has been such that, seemingly, the whole force of the gospel has been broken, and truth has perished in the streets. The rich gospel privileges so constantly enjoyed have had the apparent effect of hardening instead of softening. In this view of the case you need not be surprised at my discouragement and sorrow. I have been laboring and praying and hoping for better days, but the cloud seems to hang heavier and blacker over the place, and even now scarce a glimmer of moral and spiritual light gleams upon the thick unbroken darkness. The people seem, as intent on being lost now as ever. Oh! that God in the wonder-working power of his grace might appear; pull off this heavy cloud, and pour salvation down upon this people.

Mormons

To give a still gloomier aspect of morals and piety here, this deluded, fanatical and ignorant sect is about to be poured upon us, by the thousands. Measures have been consummated, by which the Mormons will settle on a section of land adjoining Warsaw, and thus, like the locusts of Egypt, consume every green thing in the land, and wither away, so far as they can, every vestige of godliness. Joe Smith, who you know, is the Prophet of this people, has issued a proclamation, for his followers to locate at Lower Warsaw, as it is to be called. His decrees are considered imperative and must be obeyed; so that in a few days, our roads will be lined with the wagons of this deluded people, coming to settle at this new "stake," as they call their places of gathering. I have no doubt before two years elapse, two or three thousand people will be in the midst of us. In view of this prospective state of things nearly all of the old citizens are anxious to sell their property, and many of them I have no doubt will move away. There is not only in this village, but all through the country, a strong disinclination to live near the Mormons.

The Prophet

The power of Smith over his followers is incredible. He has unlimited influence, and his declarations are as the authority and influence of the word of God himself. He is a complete despot, and does as he pleases with his people.

Some people consider him a great man; I do not. He is not possessed of a single element of greatness, unless it be in vice and blasphemy. He is a compound of ignorance, vanity, arrogance, coarseness and stupidity and vulgarity. His present unlimited influence has been gained by the force of circumstances, and not by any intrinsic talents he possesses. He is only the outside agent of a band of as wicked men as ever opposed the gospel. His power and influence are sustained by various high orders of officials such as the "Presidency," the "high priesthood," Elders, Levites, and others whose name is legion. And these men, having no fear of God or man, are artful, vigilant and wicked.

The sect is increasing rapidly. Their recruits are chiefly from New York and England. Their whole number here and in the adjoining counties and in Iowa must amount to from ten to fifteen thousand, the most of whom are in this county. How far they will continue to increase, is known to the Searcher of all hearts. I wish to state before I close here one interesting fact. It is this: The great body of Mormons are from those churches where the great cardinal doctrines of the Bible are kept rather *in the back ground*. Comparatively few have had the privilege of sitting under a thoroughly educated Ministry, & thus of being fully indoctrinated into the prime truths and doctrines of the Bible. If this be true, and the history of Mormonism will prove it so, how infinitely important that just such a ministry as the A.H.M.S. aims to sustain, is the ministry imperiously required by the wants of the West.

B. F. Morris

7

Remarks of the Prophet to Saints Newly Arrived from England 13 April 1843

Beginning in 1840, the Mormon missionaries in England began to send emigrants to settle in Nauvoo. Through 1842 nearly 3,000 had come to America, and in 1843 an additional 769 emigrated. All came in response to Joseph Smith's call for the building up of Nauvoo as a Mormon center, to work on the Nauvoo temple, and to prepare for the advent of Christ's millennial reign. This public speech by Joseph Smith to some immigrants to Nauvoo is a marvelous mixture of American and religious values. It demonstrates something of his mythic vision of mission and destiny. In this document Smith describes to the newcomers the sense of distinctiveness that gave the Mormons a unique identity. The immigrants have come to the place "appointed for the oracles of God to be revealed." Smith also prevented assimilation with non-Mormons, and through this creation of "peopleness," he virtually assured the Mormon conflict in Illinois. Furthermore, Smith demonstrates the common mixture of secular and sacred that was so much a part of early Mormonism by suggesting to the new immigrants that they buy land from him since he will ensure that they receive a fair deal.

This speech was first recorded by Willard Richards in the Joseph Smith Diary for 1843. A microfilm copy of this original diary is located in the Library-Archives,

Reorganized Church of Jesus Christ of Latter Day Saints, Independence, Missouri. The manuscript resides in the Archives, Church of Jesus Christ of Latter-day Saints, Salt Lake City, Utah. The speech is taken for this book from Scott H. Faulring, ed., *An American Prophet's Record: The Diaries and Journals of Joseph Smith* (Salt Lake City: Signature Books in association with Smith Research Associates, 1987), 361–64.

I most heartily congratulate you on your safe arrival at Nauvoo, and on your safe deliverance from all the dangers and difficulties you have had to encounter but you must not think that your tribulations are ended.

I shall not address you on doctrine but concerning your temporal welfare. Inasmuch as you have come here assaying to keep the Commandments of God I pronounce the blessings of heaven and earth upon you, and inasmuch as you will follow counsel and act wisely and do right these blessings shall rest upon you so far as I have power with God to seal them upon you. I am your servant and it is only through the Holy Ghost that I can do you good. God is able to do his own work.

We do not present ourselves before you as anything but your humble servants willing to spend and be spent in your services. We shall dwell upon your temporal welfare on this occasion. In the 1st place, where a crowd is flocking from all parts of the world of different minds, religions, &c., there will be some who do not live up to the commandments. There will be designing characters who would turn you aside and lead you astray. Speculators who would get away your property. Therefore it is necessary that we should have an order here and when emigrants arrive to instruct them concerning these things.

If the heads of the Church have laid the foundation of this place, and have had the trouble of doing what has been done, are they not better qualified to tell you how to lay out your money than those who have had no interest &c?

Some start on the revelation to come here and get turned away and lose all, and then come and enter their complaints to us when it is too late to do any thing for them.

The object of this meeting is to tell you these things and then if you will pursue the same courses you must bear the consequence. There are several objects in your coming here. One object has been to bring you from Sectarian bondage. Another from National bondage, where you can be planted in a fertile soil. We have brought you into a free government. Not that you are to consider yourselves outlaws. By free government, we do not mean that a man has a right to steal, rob, &c., but free from bondage, taxation, oppression. Free in everything if he conduct himself honestly and circumspectly with his neighbor. Free in Spiritual capacity.

This is the place that is appointed for the oracles of God to be revealed. If you have any darkness you have only to ask and the darkness is removed. It is not necessary that the miracles should be wrought to remove darkness. Miracles are the fruits of faith. "How shall we believe on him of whom &c?" God may correct the scripture by me if he choose. Faith comes by hearing the word of God and not faith by hearing and hearing by the word &c. If a man has not faith Enough to do one thing he may do another. If he cannot remove a Mountain he may heal the sick. Where faith is, there will be some of the fruits. All the gifts and power which poured out from heaven were poured out on the heads of those who had faith.

You must have a oneness of heart in all things. You shall be satisfied one way or the other with us before you have done with us! There are a great many old huts here but they are all new. Our city is not 6 or 700 years old as those you came from. It is only a 4 year old—not a 4, but 3 year old. There [are] few old settlers. I got away from my keepers in Missouri and run and come on these shores and found 4 or 500 families. I went to work to get meat and flour. Folks were not afraid to trust me. I went to work and bought all this region of country. I cried Lord what will thou have me do? And the answer was, "build up a city and call my saints to this place!" And our hearts leaped with joy to see you coming here. We have been praying for you all winter, from the bottom of our hearts. We are glad to see you. We are poor and cannot do by you as we would, but will do all we can.

'Tis not to be expected that all can locate in the city. There are some who have money and who will build and hire others. Those who cannot purchase lots can go out in the cou[n]try. The farmers want your labor. No industrious man need suffer in this land.

The claims of the poor on us are such that we have claim on your good feelings for your money to help the poor. The Church debts also have their demands to save the credit of the Church. This credit has been obtained to help the poor and keep them from starvation &c. Those who purchase Church land and pay for it, this shall be their sacrifice.

We have men of 50 and 100,000 dollars who were robbed of every thing in the state of Mo and are laboring in this city for a morsel of bread, and there are those who must have starved but for the providence of God through me. If any man say here is land or there is land, believe it not. We can beat all our competitors in lands, price, and everything. We have the highest prices, best lands, and do the most good with the money we get. Our system is a real smut machine, a bolting machine, and all the shorts, brann and smut runs away and all the flour remains with us.

Suppose I sell you land for $10 per acre and I gave [$] 3.45 per acre, then you are speculating says one. Yes, I will tell you how. I buy other lands and give them to the widow and the fatherless. If the speculators run against me, they run against the buckler of Jehovah. God did not send me up as he did Joshua in former days. God sent his servants to fight, but in the last days he has promised to fight the battle himself. God will deal with you himself and will bless or curse you as you behave yourselves. I speak to you as one having authority that you may know when it comes and that you may have faith and know that God has sent me.

The lower part of the town is most healthy. In the upper part of the town the Merchants will say I am partial &c., but the lower part of the town is much the most healthy. I tell it to you in the name of the Lord I have been out in all parts of the city at all times of night to learn these things.

The Doctors in this region don't know much and the lawyers when I spoke about them began to say, "We will renounce you on the stand," but they don't come up and I take the liberty to say what I have a mind to about them.

Doctors won't tell you where to go to be well. They want to kill or cure you to get your money. Calomel Doctor[s] will give you Calomel to cure a sliver in the big toe and does not stop to know whether the stomach is empty or not, and Calomel on an empty stomach will kill the patient, and the Lobelia doctors will do the same. Point me out a patient and I will tell you whether Calomel or Lobelia will kill him or not. If you give it [for washing], the river Mississippi water is healthy unless they drink it, and it is more healthy than the spring water. Dig wells from 15 to 30 feet and then the water will be healthy.

There are many sloughs on the islands from where Miasma arises in the summer, and is flown over the upper part of the city, but it does not extend over the lower part of the city.

All those persons who are not used to living on a river or lake [or] large pond of water, I do not want you should stay on the banks of the river. Get away to the lower part of the city, back to the hill where you can get good well water. If you feel any inconvenience take some mild physic 2 or 3 times and then some good bitters.

If you can't get anything else take a little salts and cyanne pepper. If you can't get salts take pecoria, or gnaw down a butternut tree, eat some boneset or hoarhound.

Those who have money come to me and I will let you have lands. Those who have no money if they look as well as I do I will give you advice that will do you good. I bless you in the name of Jesus Christ. Amen.

8

A Western Pennsylvanian Reports on Nauvoo

David N. White (1803–88), the editor of the *Pittsburgh Weekly Gazette*, visited Nauvoo in August 1843 and interviewed Joseph Smith at his home. He was attracted to Nauvoo because of the "far-famed kingdom of the 'Latter-day Saints'" and wrote a graphic contemporary description of the city and its inhabitants. Like many other non-Mormons visiting Nauvoo, White was mesmerized by the temple that dominated the city's landscape both physically and culturally. His description is one of the finest contemporary accounts written by a non-Mormon. White sought out Smith and recorded an intriguing interview with the Mormon prophet, one which delineates some of the differences in politics and worldview that affected the Mormon conflict. In the interview Smith reflected on his career and his own sense of being a prophet. He describes for White his "first vision," the call to translate the Book of Mormon, and the establishment of a new religious entity, all of which took place when he was only a teenager. It is clear from these comments that Smith took his role as a prophet very seriously.

White was also impressed with the industriousness of the Mormons. He describes the breadth of activity in the Nauvoo area, from the economics of the region to the social and political repercussions of Mormon settlement. The article, written from Warsaw, appeared as "The Prairies, Nauvoo, Joe Smith, the Temple, the Mormons, &c.," *Pittsburgh Weekly Gazette*, 15 September 1843, p. 3.

———————————•••••◉•••••———————————

You and the readers of the Gazette are doubtless wondering at my long silence, but when I inform you that I have been mostly confined to the house through indisposition, since my arrival in this place, you will take it as a sufficient apology. Having somewhat recovered, however, on last Monday, in company with a friend, I paid a visit to Nauvoo, the far-famed kingdom of the "Latter-day Saints." Nauvoo, as most of your readers probably know, is about 20 miles above this town, on the Mississippi; Warsaw lying at the foot of the Des Moines rapids, and Nauvoo at the head. There are two roads—one by the river bank and one by the prairie. We took the latter, although it is some four or five miles farther. Nauvoo lies about north of this point, but we first took a due east course in order to get on the prairie as the bluff which divides the prairie from the river, all through this region, consists of wooded hills and ravines generally from three to five miles wide. Our road, therefore, for the first four miles was very rough, after which we got out on the open, illimitable prairie, when we altered our course to the north, and stretched away for Nauvoo, over one of the finest roads in the world.

I was much surprised, on arriving at the prairie, to witness the great changes that had taken place within three years. Three years before, on a prairie some fifteen miles across, immediately east of Warsaw, scarcely a house was to be seen; now the whole prairie appeared to be settled, presenting the appearance of an old inhabited country, with the exception that not a tree was to be seen. I was informed that twenty-five farms could be counted from one little hillock on this prairie. But our course north soon took us from this settled country, and we travelled over vast prairies, extending in every direction as far as the eye could reach, except on our right, where lay the bluff which intervened between us and the river. Herds of cattle could occasionally be seen dotting the surface of the earth, and it wanted but a small stretch of the imagination to fancy these the primeval lords of the prairie, the fierce buffalo, that a few years ago roamed in solitude and security over those inland.

As we approached the "kingdom," as Nauvoo is denominated here, the country began to be settled, while the luxuriant herbage of the prairie was cropped quite short by the herds of cattle belonging to the Mormons. Most of the prairie, near Nauvoo, is fenced with turf. A ditch some two feet deep is dug on each side of the fence, and the turf piled up between, making a very good and durable fence. These fences are broad enough on the top for a foot path. Quite a number of the houses or huts in which the inhabitants on the prairies live, are also made of turf, and covered with clapboards. As this turf is black, as is all the soil on the prairies, these huts present a very somber appearance, and as there is not a tree, and scarcely a hillock to ward off the scorching sun of summer, or the cold blast of winter, they present a very bleak and desolate appearance.

As we neared the city, about six o'clock in the evening, we passed an immense herd of cows which were being driven into the city from the prairie, to supply the inhabitants with milk. We also passed a large number of wagons loaded with hay, the produce of the natural grass of the prairie. About three miles from the river, we entered the "kingdom of Nauvoo;" it being about four miles long, up and down the river, and three miles broad. The part near the prairie, about a mile and a half from the river, is quite broken up with ravines; nevertheless, it is all laid out in acre lots, and more or less settled.

We drove down near the river, and put up at a very respectable tavern, kept by one of the elders—a temperance house. After ten we walked out past the house of the prophet, who has a very good garden containing about an acre, with a very fine fence around it, painted white, as is also his house, a moderate sized and humble looking frame dwelling. Near the prophet's house, on the bank of the river, is the site of the "Nauvoo House," building by revelation. The basement is finished. It is built of a good, hard, white stone. The front on the river is about 140 feet, and is entirely above ground of cut stone. It has a wing running back about 100 feet. All this work is of the best and most substantial character. When this building is finished, it will be equal to any hotel in the western country. By special revelation, the prophet and his heirs are to have a suite of rooms in this house forever.

The next morning, after breakfast, we paid a visit to the prophet. We were received in a common sitting room, very plainly furnished, where the prophet and the older members of the family had just been breakfasting, and his numerous children and dependents were then sitting at the table. He received us in quite a good humored, friendly manner, asked us to sit down, and said he hoped for a better acquaintance. On the gentleman who accompanied me asking him how he prospered, he replied, "None can get ahead of me, and few can keep behind me." He seemed to think he had said something very witty, for he laughed very heartily. We spent about an hour conversing on various subjects, the prophet himself, with amazing volubility, occupying the most of the time, and his whole theme was himself. . . . He said he had never asked the Lord anything about politics; if he had done so, the Lord would have told him what to do. "The Lord," said he, "has promised to give us wisdom, and when I lack wisdom I ask the Lord, and he tells me, and if he didn't tell me, I would say he was a liar; that's the way I feel. But I never asked him anything about politics. I am a Whig, and I am a Clay man. I am made of Clay, and I am tending to Clay, and I am going to vote for Henry Clay; that's the way I feel. (A laugh) But I won't interfere with my people, religiously, to affect their votes, though I might to elect Clay, for he ought to be president. . . .

There is five-sixths of my people so led away by the euphonious term 'democrat,' that they will vote the Locofoco ticket. I am a democrat myself. I am a Washington democrat, a Jefferson democrat, a Jackson democrat, and I voted for Harrison, and I am going to vote for Clay. . . ."

In this manner, the prophet ran on, talking incessantly. Speaking of revelations, he stated that when he was in a "quandary," he asked the Lord for a revelation, and when he could not get it, he "followed the dictates of his own judgment, which were as good as a revelation to him, but he never gave anything to his people as revelation, unless it was a revelation, and the Lord did reveal himself to him." Running on in his voluble style, he said, "The world persecutes me, it has always persecuted me. The people at Carthage in a public meeting lately, said, 'As for Joe, he's a fool, but he's got some smart men about him.' I'm glad they give me so much credit. It is not every fool that has sense enough to get smart men about him.

The Lord does reveal himself to me. I know it. He revealed himself to me first when I was about fourteen years old, a mere boy. I will tell you about it. There was a reformation among the different religious denominations in the neighborhood where I lived, and I became serious, and was desirous to know what Church to join. While thinking of this matter, I opened the testament promiscuously on these words, in James, 'Ask of the Lord who giveth to all men liberally and upbraideth not.' I just determined I'd ask him. I immediately went out into the woods where my father had a clearing, and went to the stump where I had stuck my axe when I had quit work, and I kneeled down and prayed, saying, 'O Lord, what Church shall I join?' Directly I saw a light, and then a glorious personage in the light, and then another personage, and the first personage said to the second, 'Behold my beloved Son, hear Him.' I then, addressed this second person, saying, 'O Lord, what Church shall I join?' He replied, 'Don't join any of them, they are all corrupt.'

The vision then vanished, and when I came to myself, I was sprawling on my back and it was some time before my strength returned. When I went home and told the people that I had a revelation, and that all the churches were corrupt, they persecuted me, and they have persecuted me ever since. They thought to put me down, but they haven't succeeded, and they can't do it. When I have proved that I am right, and get all the world subdued under me, I think I shall deserve something.

My revelations have proved to be true, because they have been delivered before they came to pass and they came to pass exactly. I had a revelation in Missouri which was fulfilled to the letter. The Missourians had got us all prisoners and were threatening to kill us. The principal men of us were lying under a log, with a guard standing around us in the night. I fell into a trance. I call it a trance. I heard a voice which said, 'Joseph, fear not, you and all your friends shall be delivered without harm, and shall yet stand upon the hills of Zion.' When I awoke out of the trance, I aroused Elder Rigdon, who was by the side of me, and said, I have a revelation, we shall all escape. Elder Rigdon shouted, and told it to the next one, and in the morning it was told to my family and all our friends, and they all rejoiced. That revelation came to pass, although they were holding a council at the time I had the trance, and had resolved to kill me. They can't harm me. I told my family lately, before I left home for Dixon, that if I was taken up the Lord would deliver me, didn't I, Emma—(appealing to his wife, who was standing behind his chair, playing with his hair, and who answered in the affirmative)—and when they took me I was passive in their hands, and the Lord compelled them to bring me right to Nauvoo. They couldn't help themselves, although they gnashed their teeth with rage."

Speaking of the [Nauvoo] temple, which he is erecting, he said, "I don't know how the world will like it; it suits me; I have no book learning; I'm not capacitated to build according to the world; I know nothing about architecture, and all that, but it pleases me; that's the way I feel."

A good deal of conversation of a similar character took place. . . .

After taking our leave of the prophet, we spent some time in viewing the city and temple. The site of Nauvoo is one of the most beautiful on the Mississippi River. The river at this place makes a large bend, forming a semi-circle, within which lies the lower part of the city, running back to the bluff. This semi-circular piece of ground is perfectly level, and lies above the high water mark, extending at the widest place about three-fourths of a mile back from the river, and is about a mile and a half in length along the bluff. The bluff rises gradually, and is not very high, and presents most beautiful building sites. On the bluff immediately opposite the center of the semi-circle, and a mile from the river, stands the temple. The site is beautifully chosen, as it is in a central and elevated position and can be seen from the river, all around the bend, and from every part of the town.

All over the bluff and bottom, are buildings, either erected, or in progress of erection, but no part of the town is compactly built. The whole space is a conglomeration of houses, fences, gardens, corn fields, stables, huts, etc. One looks in vain for anything like a compactly built street. The object seems to have been to scatter as widely as at all convenient, and to cover as much ground as possible. The ground is sold out in acre lots, and every man builds his house, or shanty or hut, as the case may be, and plants his ground in corn and vegetables for the support of his family. The houses are of all sorts, shapes and sizes. Some, very many, are fine brick dwellings. Others are quite respectable looking frames. Others, again, are mere shanties, some log, some turf, and some mere sheds of boards. There are very few stores, mechanic shops, or business houses, and no trade going on. There is nothing to export, and no ability to import. Everybody seems engaged in putting up houses, taking care of gardens, and getting in hay from the prairies.

As crowds of emigrants are flocking in daily, the whole community is employed in providing shelter, and in procuring the barest necessaries for existence. It is hard to estimate the number of the population, it is scattered over so large a space, and several families are frequently crowded into one house. The prophet stated to me that he estimated their number at 12,000. He said he could muster, in half a day, 3,000 able-bodied men fit to bear arms, who could whip any five thousand Missourians. It is thought there are at least 25,000 Mormons in the county. They have a majority of the voters, and hold nearly all the county offices.

There must be a great deal of suffering in the winter season, from cold and hunger; and there is considerable sickness in the community at this time. One sees many pale faces about the streets. As we approached the city, we met a mournful cavalcade conveying a human being to his last resting place. First came a common wagon driven by horses, in which there was a coffin, a rough looking box, with three men sitting upon it in their shirt sleeves. Behind this came a rough wagon, drawn by oxen, in which was a large family of children of all ages, a young woman about 18 appearing as chief mourner, her cheeks wet with tears, probably burying her father. No prophet, or priest, or elder, or procession of neighbors accompanied the remains to their last resting place.

But I must hasten to some account of the temple and then bring this long, and I fear, dry epistle to a close. This modern structure, which is to revive the departed glories of the temple of Jerusalem, and which is as apparently dear to every Mormon heart, as was that famous and venerated house to the devout Jew, is building, as we stated before on the bluff and is indeed "beautiful for situation." It is about 120 feet long by 90 broad. When finished it is to consist of a basement, and two twenty-five feet stories. The basement and one twenty-five feet story is up, and the remainder in process of completion. The basement story is about 12 feet in the clear, the half of which is under ground. It is divided off into various sized rooms running along each side, with a large hall or room in the center. In this large room stands the consecrated laver, supported by twelve oxen, carved with great fidelity to the living original. Four of the oxen face the north, four the south, and two each, east and west. They, as well as the laver, are composed of wood, and are to be overlaid with gold.

The laver is of oblong shape, some four or five feet deep, and large enough for two priests to officiate in the rite of baptism, for which it is intended, at once. A pump stands by it to supply it with water. Stairs approach it from either side. I walked up and looked in. It contained nothing but a few inches of water. The laver, oxen, and etc., are at present protected from the weather by a temporary roof. What the numerous rooms in this basement are intended for I did not learn. The walls are all exceedingly strong and massy, even the partition walls, generally from two to three feet thick. The basement is lighted by numerous windows, about five feet high, and as many wide; arched over the top between these windows are very heavy pilasters, on the top of which rest the basement stones of the less heavy pilasters between the windows of the upper stories. On each of these basement stones is carved a crescent or figure of the new moon, with the profile of a man's face, as seen in old almanacs. The windows of the upper stories are some fifteen or eighteen feet high, arched over the top in a perfect semicircle. The first story above the basement is divided into two apartments, called the outer and inner courts. The walls between these courts are three feet thick, of solid mason work, with two immense doors for passage between them. The outer court is some twenty-five feet wide by ninety-feet long—the inner court is about ninety-feet square.

These facts about the dimensions of the building I obtained from Joe [Joseph Smith] himself. All the work is of good cut stone, almost white, and it will present a fine appearance when finished. How the second story is to be finished I did not learn. I have been thus particular in my description of this building, as many exaggerated stories are circulated in regard to it.

Having thus visited the prophet, and examined the city, and temple, I left for my temporary home at this place, thankful that I had been preserved from such vain and unhappy delusions, which cannot but work temporal and spiritual woe to all concerned in them, unless speedily repented of. I shall leave tomorrow for Galena, from which point you may hear from me again.

⎯⎯⎯⎯⎯⎯•••• 9 ••••⎯⎯⎯⎯⎯⎯

Josiah Quincy on Joseph Smith

In the spring of 1844 Josiah Quincy (1802–82) visited Nauvoo while on a trip to the West with his cousin, Charles Francis Adams. Both were members of the New England upper class. Adams was the son of former president John Quincy Adams and grandson of Revolutionary War rabble-rouser and second U.S. president John Adams. Charles Francis Adams later was minister to Great Britain and a writer of considerable stature. Quincy's family was only a little less distinguished; his father had been the mayor of Boston and was then the president of Harvard College. In 1845 Quincy was elected mayor of Boston in his own right. When they were introduced to Joseph Smith in Nauvoo, the Mormon prophet recognized their family and went out of his way to welcome them and show them around the city.

Quincy, whose account is from his book, *Figures of the Past* (Boston: Little, Brown, 1883), 377–400 passim, was an astute observer of the Mormons. He recognized the charisma and attraction Joseph Smith had for the Mormons, but he also subtly captured some of the darker aspects of Smith's character. The prophet was in fact depicted as a self-important and dangerously powerful man. Quincy was also impressed with the apparent economic and political strength of the Mormon stronghold at Nauvoo and comments on how these factors were affecting relations with non-Mormons in the region. This portrait is one of the most significant written on Smith and the Mormons in the nineteenth century. It details many of the attitudes that brought on the Mormon conflict in Hancock County.

It is by no means improbable that some future text-book, for the use of generations yet unborn, will contain a question something like this: What historical American of the nineteenth century has exerted the most powerful influence upon the destinies of his countryman? And it is by no means impossible that the answer to that interrogatory may be thus written: *Joseph Smith, the Mormon Prophet.* And the reply, absurd as it doubtless seems to most men now living, may be an obvious commonplace of their descendants. History deals in surprises and paradoxes quite as startling as this. The man who established a religion in this age of free debate, who was and is to-day accepted by hundreds of thousands as a direct emissary from the Most High—such a rare human being is not to be disposed of by pelting his memory with unsavory epithets. Fanatic, imposter, charlatan, he may have been; but these hard names furnish no solution to the problem he presents to us. Fanatics and impostors are living and dying every day, and their memory is buried with them; but the wonderful influence which this founder of a religion exerted and still exerts throws him into relief before us, not as a rogue to be criminated, but as a phenomenon to be explained. . . .

It was on the 25th of April, 1844, that Mr. [Charles Francis] Adams and myself left Boston for the journey West which we had had for some time in contemplation. . . . "We agreed to stop at Nauvoo," says my journal, "provided some conveyance should be found at the landing which would take us up to General Smith's tavern, and prepared our baggage for this contingency. Owing to various delays, we did not reach the landing till nearly midnight [14 May 1844], when our friend, who had jumped on shore the moment the boat stopped, returned with the intelligence that no carriage was to be had, and so we bade him adieu, to go on our way. But, as we still lingered upon the hurricane deck, he shouted that there was a house on the landing, where we could get a good bed. This changed our destiny, and just at the last moment we hurried on shore. Here we found that the 'good bed' our friend had promised us was in an old mill, which had been converted into an Irish shanty. However, we made the best of it, and, having dispossessed a cat and a small army of cockroaches of their quarters on the coverlet, we lay down in our dressing-gowns and were soon asleep."

We left our lowly bed in the gray light of the morning, to find the rain descending in torrents and the roads knee-deep in mud. Intelligence of our arrival had in some mysterious manner reached General Smith, and the prophet's own chariot, a comfortable carryall, drawn by two horses, soon made its appearance. . . . Pre-eminent among the stragglers by the door [at the Smith home] stood a man of commanding appearance, clad in the costume of a journeyman carpenter when about his work. He was a hearty, athletic fellow, with blue eyes standing prominently out upon his light complexion, a long nose, and a retreating forehead. He wore striped pantaloons, a linen jacket, which had not lately seen a washtub, and a beard of some three day's growth. This was the founder of the religion which had been preached in every quarter of the earth. As Dr. [W. G.] Goforth introduced us to the prophet, he mentioned the parentage of my companion. "God bless *you*, to begin with!" said Joseph Smith, raising his hands in the air and letting them descend upon the shoulders of Mr. Adams. The benediction, though evidently sincere, had an odd savor of what may be called official familiarity, such as a crowned head might adopt on receiving the heir presumptive of a friendly court. The greeting to me was cordial—with that sort of cordiality with which the president of a college might welcome a deserving janitor—and a blessing formed no part of it. "And now come, both of you, into the house!" said our host, as, suiting the action to the word, he ushered us across the threshold of his tavern.

A *fine-looking man* is what the passer-by would instinctively have murmured upon meeting the remarkable individual who had fashioned the mould which was to shape the feelings of so many thousands of his fellow-mortals. But Smith was more than this, and one could not resist the impression that capacity and resource were natural to his stalwart person. . . . This is just to say with emphasis; for the reader will find so much that is puerile and even shocking in my report of the prophet's conversation that he might never suspect the impression of rugged power that was given by the man.

On the right hand, as we entered the house, was a small and very comfortless-looking bar-room; all the more comfortless, perchance, from its being a dry bar-room, as no spirituous liquors were permitted at Nauvoo. In apparent search for more private quarters, the prophet opened the door of a room on the left. He instantly shut it again, but not before I perceived that the obstacle to our entrance was its prior occupancy by a woman, in bed. He then ran up-stairs, calling upon us to follow him, and, throwing open a door in the second story, disclosed three Mormons in three beds. This was not satisfactory; neither was the next chamber, which was found, on inspection, to contain two sleeping disciples. The third attempt was somewhat more fortunate, for we had found a room which held but a single bed and a single sleeper. Into this apartment we were invited to enter. Our host immediately proceeded to the bed, and drew the clothes well over the head of its occupant. He then called a man to make a fire, and begged us to sit down. Smith then began to talk about himself and his people, as, of course, we encouraged him to do. He addressed his words to Mr. Adams oftener than to me, evidently thinking that this gentleman had or was likely to have political influence, which it was desirable to conciliate. Whether by subtle tact or happy accident, he introduced us to Mormonism as a secular institution before stating its monstrous claims as a religious system. . . . Its founder told us what he had accomplished and the terrible persecutions through which he had brought his people. He spoke with bitterness of outrages to which they had been subjected in Missouri, and implied that the wanton barbarities of his lawless enemies must one day be atoned for. He spoke of the industrial results of his autocracy in the holy city we were visiting, and of the extraordinary powers of its charter, obtained through his friend, Governor [Thomas] Ford. The past had shown him that a military organization was necessary. He was now at the head of three thousand men, equipped by the State of Illinois and belonging to its militia, and the Saints were prepared to fight as well as to work. "I decided," said Smith, "that the commander of my troops ought to be a lieutenant-general, and I was, of course, chosen to that position. I sent my certificate of election to Governor Ford, and received in return a commission of lieutenant-general of the Nauvoo Legion and of the militia of the State of Illinois. Now, on examining the Constitution of the United States, I find that an officer must be tried by a court-martial composed of his equals in rank; and as I am the only lieutenant-general in the country, I think they will find it pretty hard to try me."

At this point breakfast was announced, and a substantial meal was served in a long back kitchen. We sat down with about thirty persons, some of them being in their shirt-sleeves, as if just come from work. There was no going out, as the rain still fell in torrents; and so, when we had finished breakfast, the prophet (who had exchanged his working dress for a broadcloth suit while we lingered at the table) proposed to return to the chamber we had quitted, where he would give us his views of theology. The bed had been made during our absence and the fire plentifully replenished. Our party was now increased by the presence of the patriarch, Hiram Smith; Dr. [Willard] Richards, of Philadelphia, who seemed to be a very modest and respectable Mormon, Dr. Goforth, and a Methodist minister, whose name I have not preserved. No sooner were we seated than there entered some half-dozen leaders of the sect, among whom, I think, were [Sidney] Rigdon and [Brigham] Young; but of their presence I cannot be positive. These men constituted a sort of silent chorus during the expositions of their chief. They fixed a searching, yet furtive gaze upon Mr. Adams and myself, as if eager to discover how we were impressed by what we heard. Of the wild talk that we listened to I have preserved but a few fragments. Smith was well versed in the letter of the Scriptures, though he had little comprehension of their spirit. He began by denying the doctrine of the Trinity, and supported his views by the glib recitation of a number of texts. From this he passed to his own claims to special inspiration, quoting with great emphasis the eleventh and twelfth verses of the fourth chapter of Ephesians, which, in his eyes, adumbrated the whole Mormon hierarchy. The degrees and orders of ecclesiastical dignitaries he set forth with great precision, being careful to mention the interesting revelation which placed Joseph Smith supreme above them all. This information was plentifully besprinkled with cant phrases or homely proverbs. "There, I have proved that point as straight as a loon's leg." "The curses of my enemies run off from me like water from a duck's back." Such are the specimens which my journal happens to preserve, but the exposition was constantly garnished with forcible vulgarisms of a similar sort. The prophet referred to his miraculous gift of understanding all languages, and took down a Bible in various tongues, for the purpose of exhibiting his accomplishments in this particular. Our position as guests prevented our testing his powers by a rigid examination, and the rendering of a few familiar texts seemed to be accepted by his followers as a triumphant demonstration of his abilities. It may have been an accident, but I observed that the bulk of his translations were from the Hebrew, which, presumably, his visitors did not understand, rather than from the classical languages, in which they might more easily have caught him tripping.

"And now come with me," said the prophet "and I will show you the curiosities." So saying, he led the way to a lower room, where sat a venerable and respectable-looking lady. "This is my mother, gentlemen. The curiosities we shall see belong to her. They were purchased with her own money, at a cost of six thousand dollars"; and then, with deep feeling, were added the words, "And that woman was turned out upon the prairie in dead of night by a mob." There were some pine presses fixed against the wall of the room. These receptacles Smith opened, and disclosed four human bodies, shrunken and black with age. "These are mummies," said the exhibitor. "I want you to look at that little runt of a fellow over there. He was a great man in his day. Why, that was Pharaoh Necho, King of Egypt!" Some parchments inscribed with hieroglyphics were then offered us. They preserved under glass and handled with great respect. "That is the handwriting of Abraham, the Father of the Faithful," said the prophet. "This is the autograph of Moses, and these lines were written by his brother Aaron. Here we have the earliest account of Creation, from which Moses composed the First Book of Genesis." The parchment last referred to showed a rude drawing of a man and woman, and a serpent walking upon a pair of legs. I ventured to doubt the propriety of providing the reptile in question with this unusual means of locomotion. "What, that's as plain as a pikestaff," was the rejoinder. "Before the Fall snakes always went about on legs, just like chickens. They were deprived of them, in punishment for their agency in the ruin of man." We were further assured that the prophet was the only mortal who could translate these mysterious writings, and that his power was given by direct inspiration.

It is well known that Joseph Smith was accustomed to make his revelations point to those sturdy business habits which lead to prosperity in this present life. He had little enough of that inmost spiritual power which flashed out from the spare, neurasthenic body of Andrew Jackson. The prophet's hold upon you seemed to come from the balance and harmony of temperament which reposes upon a large physical basis. No association with the sacred phrases of Scripture could keep the inspirations of this man from getting down upon the hard pan of practical affairs. "Verily I say unto you, let my servant, Sidney Gilbert, plant himself in this place and establish a store." So had run one of the revelations, in which no holier spirit than that of commerce is discernible. This exhibition of these august relics concluded with a similar descent into the hard modern world of fact. Monarchs, patriarchs, and parchments were very well in their way; but this was clearly the nineteenth century, when prophets must get a living and provide for their relations. "*Gentlemen,*" said this *bourgeois* Mohammed, as he closed the cabinets, "*those who see these curiosities generally pay my mother a quarter of a dollar.*"

The clouds had parted when we emerged from the chamber of curiosities, and there was time to see the Temple before dinner. General Smith ordered a capacious carriage, and we drove to that beautiful eminence, bounded on three sides by the Mississippi, which was covered by the holy city of Nauvoo. The curve in the river enclosed a position lovely enough to furnish a site for the Utopian communities of Plato or Sir Thomas More; and here was an orderly city, magnificently laid out, and teeming with activity and enterprise. And all the diligent workers, who had reared these handsome stores and comfortable dwellings, bowed in subjection to a man to whose unexampled absurdities we had listened that morning. . . . Near the entrance to the Temple we passed a workman who was laboring upon a huge sun, which he had chiselled from the solid rock. The countenance was of the negro type, and it was surrounded by the conventional rays.

"General Smith," said the man, looking up from his task, "is this like the face you saw in vision?"

"Very near it," answered the prophet, "except" (this was added with an air of careful connoisseurship that was quite overpowering)—"except that the nose is just a thought too broad."

The Mormon Temple was not fully completed. It was a wonderful structure, altogether indescribable by me. Being, presumably, like something Smith had seen in vision, it certainly cannot be compared to any ecclesiastical building which may be discerned by the natural eyesight. It was built of limestone, and was partially supported by huge monolithic pillars, each costing, said the prophet, three thousand dollars. Then in the basement was the baptistery, which centered in a mighty tank, surrounded by twelve wooden oxen of colossal size. These animals, we were assured, were temporary. They were to be replaced by stone oxen as fast as they could be made. The Temple, odd and striking as it was, produced no effect that was commensurate with its cost. Perhaps it would have required a genius to have designed anything worthy of that noble site. The city of Nauvoo, with its wide streets sloping gracefully to the farms enclosed on the prairie, seemed to be a better temple to Him who prospers the work of industrious hands than the grotesque structure on the hill, with all its queer carvings of moons and suns. This, however, was by no means the opinion of the man whose fiat had reared the building. In a tone half-way between jest and earnest, and which might have been taken for either at the option of the hearer, the prophet put this inquiry: "Is not here one greater than Solomon, who built a Temple with the treasures of his father David and with the assistance of Hiram, King of Tyre? Joseph Smith has built his Temple with no one to aid him in the work."

On returning to the tavern, dinner was served in the kitchen where we had breakfasted. The prophet carved at one end of the board, while some twenty persons, Mormons and travellers (the former mostly coatless), were scattered along its sides. At the close of a substantial meal a message was brought to the effect that the United States marshal had arrived and wished to speak to Mr. Adams. This officer, as it turned out, wanted my companion's advice about the capture of some criminal, for whom he had a warrant. The matter was one of some difficulty, for, the prophet being absolute in Nauvoo, no man could be arrested or held without his permission. I do not remember what was the outcome of this interview, which was so protracted that it caused Mr. Adams to miss one of the most notable exhibitions of the day.

"General Smith," said Dr. Goforth, when we had adjourned to the green in front of the tavern, "I think Mr. Quincy would like to hear you preach." "Then I shall be happy to do so," was the obliging reply; and mounting the broad step which led from the house, the prophet promptly addressed a sermon to the little group about him. Our numbers were constantly increased from the passers in the street, and a most attentive audience of more than a hundred persons soon hung upon every word of the speaker. The text was Mark xvi, 15, and the comments, though rambling and disconnected, were delivered with the fluency and fervor of a camp-meeting orator. The discourse was interrupted several times by the Methodist minister before referred to, who thought it incumbent upon him to question the soundness of certain theological positions maintained by the speaker. One specimen of the sparring which ensued I thought worth setting down. The prophet is asserting that baptism for the remission of sins is essential for salvation. *Minister.* Stop! What do you say to the case of the penitent thief? *Prophet.* What do you mean by that? *Minister.* You know our Saviour said to the thief, "This day shalt thou be with me in Paradise," which shows he could not have been baptized before his admission. *Prophet.* How do you know he wasn't baptized before he became a thief? At this retort the sort of laugh that is provoked by an unexpected hit ran through the audience; but this demonstration of sympathy was rebuked by a severe look from Smith, who went on to say: "But that is not the true answer. In the original Greek, as this gentleman (turning to me) will inform you, the word that has been translated paradise means simply a place of departed spirits. To that place the penitent thief was conveyed, and there, doubtless, he received the baptism necessary for his admission to the heavenly kingdom." The other objections of his antagonist were parried with a similar adroitness, and in about fifteen minutes the prophet concluded a sermon which it was evident that his disciples had heard with the heartiest satisfaction. . . .

I should not say quite all that struck me about Smith if I did not mention that he seemed to have a keen sense of the humorous aspects of his position. "It seems to me, General," I said, as he was driving us to the river, about sunset, "that you have too much power to be safely trusted to one man." "In your hands or that of any other person," was the reply, "so much power would, no doubt, be dangerous. I am the only man in the world whom it would be safe to trust with it. Remember, I am a prophet!" The last five words were spoken in a rich, comical aside, as if in hearty recognition of the ridiculous sound they might have in the ears of a Gentile. I asked him to test his powers by naming the successful candidate in the approaching presidential election. "Well, I will prophesy that John Tyler will not be the next President, for some things are possible and some things are probable; but Tyler's election is neither the one nor the other." We then went on to talk of politics. Smith recognized the curse and iniquity of slavery, though he opposed the methods of the Abolitionists. . . .

Born in the lowest ranks of poverty, without book-learning and with the homeliest of all human names, he had made himself at the age of thirty-nine a power upon earth. Of the multitudinous family of Smith, from Adam down (Adam of the "Wealth of Nations," I mean), none had so won human hearts and shaped human lives as this Joseph. His influence, whether for good or for evil, is potent to-day, and the end is not yet.

I have endeavored to give the details of my visit to the Mormon prophet with absolute accuracy. If the reader does not know just what to make of Joseph Smith, I cannot help him out of the difficulty. I myself stand helpless before the puzzle.

— •••• *10* •••• —

An Iowa Sheriff on the Mormons

In contrast to the elevated, touristlike perspective of Josiah Quincy, Hawkins Taylor (1811-?) presents an everyday view of the Saints in Nauvoo in this recollection written in 1876. He had been born on 15 November 1811 in Kentucky, but within a year or two, his family had moved to southern Indiana, where he grew up. He had only three months of formal schooling but was literate enough to consider studying law for a time. In 1831 he went to Missouri, working in Hannibal, but quickly moved on to the lead-mine country of Galena in the northwestern part of Illinois. In 1834 he married his cousin, Melina Walker, and the next year took her to the hamlet of West Point, near Fort Madison, Iowa Territory. In 1837 Taylor was appointed justice of the peace, and the next year he was elected to the Iowa territorial legislature. In 1839 he was elected sheriff of Lee County, Iowa Territory, and moved to the county seat, Fort Madison.

As the sheriff of Lee County, across the Mississippi River from Nauvoo, he was somewhat less involved in the Mormon conflict, but he was still opposed to the sect. He also had to deal with law-enforcement concerns relative to the Saints, and he thought that Nauvoo, with its powerful city charter and strong military presence, was a haven for outlaws of all types. This problem got bigger as time progressed, for as sides in the conflict crystallized, thieves and other outlaws joined the church and used Mormon noncooperation with outside officials to protect their illegal activities. Whether some of the incidents that Taylor describes in this autobiography represent actual situations or someone's mistaken perception of them, they illustrate the difficult situation beginning to develop between the Mormon and non-Mormon communities in western Illinois. This is the first publication of any part of the autobiography. It is printed by permission from the original in Archives and Special Collections, Western Illinois University Library, Macomb.

In August [1839], I was elected sheriff of the county, by a handsome major-ity, after a hot contest. At that time there was nearly 150 Mormon votes in the county. I got the majority of that vote. By law, I had to live at the county seat. So I moved to Fort Madison. It was a hard office. The county was large, extending along the Mississippi about 40 miles and up the Des Moines River about 30 miles. With Nauvoo the Mormon town across the river (Mississippi) in Illinois, opposite Montrose in Iowa, with Keokuk at the foot of the rapids, then a men wrecker town. There were but a few hundred people in the place [Keokuk], and all engaged in the lighting of freight over the rapids. Amongst the number was the worst class of men that could be found, murderers and gamblers and thieves of every class. Some of them had belonged to Murral's Clan of desperadoes. . . .

Nauvoo was infected at that time with a great number of thieves, who would cross over to Iowa and commit depredations and embark to Nauvoo. I would go over and arrest them and bring them back, the Mormons allowing me to do it. Bill Smith, the brother of Joe the Prophet, acting with me. . . .

One day, late in the fall of 1840, George Miller, an old friend of mine who had lived at McConnel [Macomb], Illinois, and was then an elder in the Presbyterian Church there, but who joined the Mormons and was made a bishop, the next in authority to the Prophet Joe Smith, came in great haste to Fort Madison for an attachment for a flatboat load of onions and potatoes, then lying at the head of the rapids, supposed to belong to a man by the name of [George M.] Hinkle. Hinkle had been one of the Mormon twelve in Missouri, was a learned man and was Joe Smith's scribe. When Smith saw that the Mormons would be obliged to leave Missouri, he sent Hinkle with his carriage and a load of his choice books up to Iowa for safety. The horse carriage and books at that day of low prices were worth twelve or fifteen hundred dollars. Hinkle settled near Muscatine in Iowa and appropriated to his own use the books and carriage and repudiated Joe and his doctrine at the same time and established a church of his own, similar in doctrine to the Mormon. But he, like Tilden and other reformers of the present day, was virtuous. Every dollar that he had was stolen, but that only showed the importance that he should be a reformer. That fall, in company with D. E. Rockafeller, he built a flat boat and loaded it with potatoes and onions to run to St. Louis or New Orleans. He feared the "Danites" of the Mormons, knowing that they would kill if they could catch him. So he figured a plan. In the middle of the boat to hide. The Mississippi was very low. The boat was as deep as could cross the rapids, following the channel. The day they got to the head of the rapids, it was too windy to cross, and while the boat was lying at the bank and no men in sight, Hinkle popped his head out of his hiding place to look around, when he was rec-ognized by a little Mormon girl.

Miller at once went for a writ and the sheriff to attach the property for the debt due the Prophet. I at once went with Miller and attached the boat and served the writ on Hinkle. I have never seen a man worse scared than Hinkle was when I arrested him. The boat had been watched by a lot of Danites. All the time Miller had been gone and he expected to be murdered by them. Rockafeller claimed the boat and load was his own. This put me in a bad situation. It was just at the edge of winter. A freeze would ruin the load. I finally arranged that Rockafeller give a bond to pay the debt if the boat and contents were established to be Hinkle's. When this was done, I released the boat. It was then about 8 o'clock P.M. and full moon and as clear and still as it could be. Hinkle begged me to stay in the boat all night. Said the Mormons would kill him if I did not. He then begged me to remain in town all night. I told him that I had to go to Keokuk that night and laughed at him for his fears. I told him that if any man molested him that I would see that he was properly punished, but that did not quiet him. I got my supper and went on to Keokuk and just as I got there, Hinkle's boat landed. When he found that I would not remain in town, he pulled out and crossed the rapids. He said he knew he would be killed if he stayed, and preferred to be drowned rather than murdered by the Danites. Hinkle and Joe Smith both took the bankruptcy act [and] that ended this suit. I never got my fees. It was a mystery how his boat ever crossed the rapids without sinking, but Hinkle knew the character of the Danites. . . .

During the time I was sheriff, the Mormons built up Nauvoo. The town was situated at the head of the Mississippi rapids, in a great bend of the river. It was an old town called "Commerce," but had but a few hundred people when the Mormons first settled there in 1839. The Mormons bought out the principal settlers and changed the name of the town to Nauvoo and laid out the new town to embrace a territory of some three miles in extent on the river and back from the river from the extreme level of the flat, being in the shape of a half moon. The main street was 200 feet wide and over two miles long, running from a point on the river to the river at a point four miles above, following the river. The ground rose gradually from the river to a point probably 100 feet above the land on the river and then ran back level to the prairie.

It was the most beautiful townsite that I ever saw. The temple was built on the high ground about the middle of the town plat and was a perfect building, built of cut stone 85 by 135 feet and 99 feet high, with a tower, 30 feet by the width of the building, 40 feet high, with a spire running up to 185 feet all told, with stairs to the top of the spire. The basement was 20 feet high, about half underground with one story about 10 and the other 30 feet. In the basement was a baptismal fount, of dressed gray limestone, resting on twelve oxen, but out of stone except the points of the horns, which were natural horns, and the likeness was so perfect in size and shape, legs, ears, and horns, that at first sight you take them to be alive. The next story was the great audience hall, with a pulpit at both ends and changeable seats. The other rooms were never fully finished. On the top of the wall under the cornice, were thirty two faces, cut out of stone. They were about 3 feet broad and 5 feet high, and at a height of 90 feet, they looked perfect likenesses. . . .

The Mormons bought very little of the ground on which they laid out their town. It was what was known as military land and held by Mormons and the title to a very large tract had been long in litigation. The town was laid off in 4 acre blocks minus streets and alleys, and the blocks were divided into four lots. The streets were wide and ran at right angles. The alleys were 20 feet wide, so that each lot contained nearly an acre.

Joe [Smith] selected each lot for the occupants; the best ones on Main street he sold at $300 and the poorest he gave away, but each person felt proud that brother Joseph had selected his home for him.

At that time nearly all of the Mormons were from New England and most of them mechanics of the first quality, so that they had an abundant supply of all kinds of workmen and Joe did not allow them to use either spirits of any kind, tea or coffee, nor tobacco, and all were required to work. Each family was required to farm and cultivate their lots, to keep a cow, and with milk, the poorer class could make a living on their acre of ground.

Joe Smith and other leaders were followed with indictments from Missouri, charged with all classes of crimes. The result was, they had to hide from the officers. The whole country was shocked at the cruel manner in which the Mormons had been driven from Missouri. They were all Democrats. The legislature of Illinois was overwhelmingly Democratic and they, with the full help of the Whigs, gave Nauvoo a city charter with legislative forms such as no other city ever had. They also chartered the Nauvoo Legion, a military organization that was afterwards very troublesome and did much harm.

Joe Smith was elected mayor and the twelve apostles constituted the council. They at once organized a government of their own and set the Missouri writs at defiance. If an arrest was made, he was released by Joe under a writ of Habeas Corpus. The result was that Nauvoo became a refuge for thieves of all kinds.

Nauvoo, within a few years grew to be a city of 20,000, and in everything but their religion and moral practices, was a model city. The homes were all painted, there was no idling, no profanity or drunkenness, but they held that they were the chosen people of the Lord, that all things belonged to the Lord. Under the old Josiah dispensation, each person was required to give one tenth of his substance to the Lord. Each man was required to work every tenth day on the temple or pay for the hire of a substitute. Besides this, several hundred men were hired to work on the temple. These men had to be fed. To do this, they lived on the Smith [stolen] cattle, sheep, and grain of all kinds, all taken to the temple, consecrated and then given to the Lord's workmen on the Lord's temple, as they claimed.

The people had no remedy. The Mormons were the majority in the county and had all the officers of importance. If a writ was taken out, the officer was whittled out of the city. The process of whittling out an officer was as follows: A great tall man by the name of [Hosea] Stout was the captain of the Whittling society, and he had about a dozen assistants. They all had great bowie knives and would get a long piece of pine board and get up close to the officer and pretend to be cutting the pine board, but would cut over it and cut near the officer. In the meantime, small boys would get tin pans, old bells and all sorts of things to make a noise with and surround the officer. No one would touch or say a word to him, but the noise drowned all that he would say. The result would be that he would get out of the city as soon as possible and never come back again. The Mormons would send teams out, load [them] with what they found and take it before the eyes of the owner. Farmers were forced to sell out their farms for whatever they could and went away.

I believe that I was the only officer that ever took a prisoner from Nauvoo without being whittled out, but the Mormons were anxious to keep on good terms with the people of Iowa, while they were at war with Missouri and Illinois. Bill Smith, Joe's brother, always helped me to take off prisoners. I was at Nauvoo a great deal. Few people came to Fort Madison from the east that did not want to go to Nauvoo to see Joe Smith and the temple. I had more business in that section than in any other part of the county, so that I was there every few days during the summer at least. . . .

—•••• 11 ••••—

Celebrating the Power of Mormon Nauvoo

This article, "Celebration of the Anniversary of the Church—Military Parade—Prest. Rigdon's Address—Laying the Corner Stones of the Temple," *Times and Seasons* 2 (15 April 1841): 375–77, is a remarkable description of the secular power of the new Mormon stronghold. The military pomp of the temple cornerstone ceremony described here assured the Saints that they would never again have to suffer the kind of oppression they had experienced in Missouri. With the passage of the Nauvoo Charter and the authority it gave, they felt safe behind the walls of Zion. And the ceremony also symbolized their unity and identity as God's virtuous chosen people, just as surely as the temple itself symbolized the presence of God in their community.

But the very same bulwarks that the Mormons applauded were viewed with consternation by non-Mormons. This anniversary event, witnessed by such non-Mormons as Thomas C. Sharp, crystallized their negative conceptions about the Saints. Sharp, for instance, traced his great animosity toward the Mormons to this event. For him, the ceremonies demonstrated the Mormon Church's political, economic, and military might. Thereafter he viewed the prophet's followers not as mistreated seekers of religious freedom but as threats to the established democratic order of the young American republic.

We should do violence to our feelings, were we to pass by, without comment, the interesting scenes that passed before us during the past week. It being the season for the constituted authorities in the Church of Jesus Christ of Latter Day Saints, to assemble for the purpose of deliberation and action upon the important concerns of the Redeemer's kingdom; to hail and welcome their co-workers in the vineyard; and to instruct and be instructed in things pertaining to their temporal and spiritual salvation; as might be expected, the Saints flocked in from the several stakes, branches, and the surrounding country in multitudes, to witness the interesting operations that were to transpire during the Conference. At an early hour, on the 6th Inst. the several companies constituting the Nauvoo Legion, with two volunteer companies from Iowa T. making sixteen companies in all, assembled at their several places of rendezvous, and were conducted in due order to the ground assigned for general review. The appearance, order, and movements of the Legion, were chaste, grand, and imposing; and reflect great credit upon the taste, skill, and tact of the men comprising said Legion, especially the chief officer of the day, Maj. General [John C.] Bennett. We doubt whether the like can be presented in any city in the western country.

At half past 7 o'clock, A.M., the fire of artillery announced the arrival of Brigadier Generals [Wilson] Law and [Hyrum] Smith, at the front of their respective Cohorts; and at 8 o'clock Major General Bennett was conducted to his post under the discharge of cannon, and took command of the Legion. At half past 9 o'clock A.M. Lieutenant General [Joseph] Smith with his guard, staff and field officers, arrived at the ground, and were presented with a beautiful silk national flag, by the Ladies of Nauvoo, which was respectfully received and hailed by the firing of cannon, and borne off by Colonel Robinson, the Cornet, to the appropriate position in the line; after which, the Lieutenant General with his suit passed the lines in review. At 12 N. the procession arrived upon the Temple ground, inclosing the same in a hollow square, with Lieutenant General Smith, Major General Bennett, Brigadier Generals Law and Smith, their respective staffs, guard, field officers, distinguished visitors, choir, band, &c. in the center, and the ladies and gentlemen citizens surrounding in the interior. The superior officers, together with the banner, architects, principal speaker &c. were duly conducted to the stand at the principal corner stone, and the religious services were commenced by singing from page 65 of the new hymn book.

Pres't. Sidney Rigdon then addressed the assembly. We regret that the address cannot be given to our readers entire instead of a very imperfect outline. He remarked,

"That the circumstances under which he addressed the people were of no ordinary character, but of peculiar and indescribable interest—that it was the third occasion of a similar nature, wherein he had been called upon to address the people, and to assist in laying the corner stones of houses to be erected in honor of the God of the Saints—various scenes had transpired since the first was laid—he, with some who were with him on that occasion, had waded through scenes, that no other people had ever been, not cursed, but blessed with—had seen the blood of the innocent flow, and heard the groans of those dying for the witness of Jesus—in all those scenes of tribulation, his confidence, his courage, and his joy had been increasing instead of diminishing—now the scene had changed; persecution had in a measure subsided; peace and safety, friendship and joy, crowned their assembling; and their endeavors to serve God were respected and viewed with interest—that the Saints had assembled, not to violate law and trample upon equity and good social order; not to devastate and destroy; but to lift up the standard of liberty and law, to stand in defence of civil and religious rights, to protect the innocent, to save mankind, and to obey the will and mandate of the Lord of glory; to call up to remembrance the once crucified, but now exalted and glorified savior—to say that he is again revealed, that he speaks from the heavens, that he reigns; in honor of him to tell the *world* that he lives, and speaks, and reigns, and dictates—that not every people can build a house to him, but those only whom he himself directs—that the present military display is not to usurp; but to command as they are commanded and directed; to honor, not the world, but him that is alive and reigns, the all in all, the invisible, but beholding, and guiding, and directing— that the Saints boast of their King; of his wisdom, his understanding, his power, and his goodness—that they honor a God of unbounded power and glory—that he is the chief corner stone in Zion, also the top stone—that he cannot be conquered—that he is working in the world to guide, to conquer, to subdue—that as formerly, so now he works by revelation—that this is the reason why we are here, and why we are thus—that the Saints have sacrificed all things for the testimony of Jesus Christ, that some from different parts of Europe and from Canada as well as the different parts of the United States are present, and among all a unanimity of purpose and feeling prevails, and why? because the same God over all had spoken from the heavens, and again revealed himself—he remarked, that he defied the devil to collect such an assemblage; none but Jesus would or could accomplish such things as we behold; the devil will not build up, but tear down and destroy; the work of Jesus is like himself in all ages—that as light shines from the east and spreads itself to the west, so is the progress of spiritual light and truth—that Jesus is a God of order, regularity, and uniformity—that he works now by revelation and by messengers as anciently—shows himself—lifts the veil &c. that such things are marvelous, but nevertheless true—that the order of laying the corner stones was expressive of the order of the kingdom—that the minutiae were subject matter of obedience, and understood by the Saints—that the ancient prophets beheld and rejoiced at this scene and are near to witness the fulfillment of their predictions— that we are highly favored of God, and brought near to the spirits of just men made perfect—he then closed by exhortation, first to the surrounding multitude, and lastly to the church. . . ."

The architects then, by the direction of the First Presidency, lowered the first (S.E. corner) stone to its place, and Pres't. Joseph Smith pronounced the benediction as follows, "This principal corner stone, in representation of the First Presidency, is now duly laid in honor of the great God; and may it there remain until the whole fabric is completed; and may the same be accomplished speedily; that the Saints may have a place to worship God, and the Son of Man have where to lay his head." Pres't. Sidney Rigdon then pronounced the following, "May the persons employed in the erection of this house be preserved from all harm while engaged in its construction, till the whole is completed; in the name of the Father, and of the Son, and of the Holy Ghost; even so, *Amen.*"

Adjourned for one hour. Assembled according to adjournment and proceeded to lay the remaining corner stones, according to previous order. . . .

In conclusion we will say, we never witnessed a more imposing spectacle than was presented on this occasion, and during the session of conference. Such an almost countless multitude of people, moving in harmony, in friendship, in dignity, told with a voice not easily misunderstood, that they were a people of intelligence and virtue, and order; in short, that they were *saints;* and that the God of love, purity, and light was their God, their exemplar, and director; and that they were blessed and happy.

12

Life in Nauvoo from a Non-Mormon Perspective

Charlotte Haven, a non-Mormon visitor from Portsmouth, New Hampshire, arrived as a teenager in Nauvoo in December 1842 and stayed for a year with her brother and his wife. There she wrote several letters about life in the Mormon city. A small non-Mormon community existed in Nauvoo, made up of businessmen, their families, and a few nonmember spouses of Mormons. Haven was a part of this community and found that a comfort while living in what she regarded as an alien culture. While there she also joined the Mormons in various social and cultural activities. As a non-Mormon, she was treated with respect and was invited to parties and other gatherings, but she always sensed a distance between her and the Mormons in the city.

Haven observed and recorded the side of Nauvoo that more casual visitors did not see. While individuals like David White and Josiah Quincy remarked on Mormon industriousness, Haven perceived that many people in the city were impoverished. She also believed that there was no sound economic basis on which to build a permanent city and feared for the fate of the Mormon people. Finally, Haven's letters reveal a female perspective on life in Nauvoo that is not duplicated anywhere else. These letters were originally published as "A Girl's Letters from Nauvoo," *Overland Monthly* (San Francisco) 16 (December 1890): 616–38.

City of Nauvoo
Jan. 3., 1843

As I write of Nauvoo I look at the world with perfect amazement and almost doubt my own sense when I find myself an inhabitant of this city of fanatics, for never did I expect to see the place. . . .

At eleven o'clock we came in full sight of the City of the Saints, and were charmed with the view. We were five miles from it, and from our point of vision it seemed to be situated on a high hill, and to have a dense population; but upon our approach and while passing slowly through the principal streets, we thought that our vision had been magnified, or distance lent enchantment, for such a collection of miserable houses and hovels I could not have believed existed in one place. Oh, I thought, how much real poverty must dwell here! Suddenly we missed our traveling companion,—on looking back we beheld her sprawling on the ground, having sprung from the stage as it passed her house.

As we neared our little white cottage with green blinds, we saw, coming very fast across a vacant lot, a strange looking man, making eager gesticulations. He seemed to be covered with snow-flakes, and a woman was following close behind. In a moment we recognized brother, and saw that the snowflakes were feathers. "Oh Henderson!" we both exclaimed; "have the Mormons already treated you with a coat of tar and feathers?"

"No," he laughingly replied. He and the woman, Mrs. Conklin, were having some feather beds filled for us, and seeing the stage, without regard to appearances, hastened to greet us.

The stage left us at the kitchen door. The introduction to this room was discouraging enough—full of smoke from a fire just kindled in the fire-place, no furniture except a red chest and a box of crockery, upon which was extended a half venison, flanked by a basket of vegetables, and sundry parcels of groceries. The only redeeming appendage was a forlorn old bachelor, who stood with his back to the fire and hands crossed before him. Brother introduced him to us as Judge Emmons, adding that he had just engaged to "eat him,"—a Western term used for board without lodging. We glanced into the other rooms,—a large box stove in what is parlor and dining room, a bedstead without bedding in the bed room,— that was all!

Judge Emmons . . . suggested that a search be made in his old quarters to see if some pieces of furniture might remain undisposed of. So we immediately dispatched him and brother for it. They soon returned with a table, three chairs, a coffee-pot and mill, two large tin dippers, and a *spider*. This last our grandmothers might have called a bake-kettle; it has three legs and an iron cover, which is covered with hot coals when anything is baking. . . .

As darkness came on we were reminded that our lamps were at Warsaw, and the stores a mile away. Fortunately we had candles, and H. improvised candlesticks by making holes in the biscuits left from dinner. The next day he got two small blocks of wood, and now we have new shining tin candlesticks. Dr. Weld, another of the stranded bachelors, having gone his round of patients, passed the evening with us, but both gentlemen took their departure before nine o'clock, and we went to bed—on the two feather beds with husk beds beneath. I had mine on the parlor floor and slept comfortably. . . .

Nauvoo, Jan. 22, 1843

My Dear Sister Isa:

. . . Last Sabbath there was preaching at the Prophet's house. Having not a little curiosity to see and hear this strange man, who has attracted so many thousands of people from every quarter of the globe, the Judge and myself sallied forth. We had not proceeded far when a large horse-sled, with a little straw on the bottom upon which were seated men and women, stopped before us; one of the men asked us to get on, and by a little crowding we placed ourselves among them and were borne along with the multitude that were thronging to hear their beloved leader. Such hurrying! one would have thought it was the last opportunity to hear him they would ever have, although we were two hours before the services were to commence. When the house was so full that not another person could stand upright, the windows were opened for the benefit of those without, who were as numerous as those within.

Joseph Smith is a large, stout man, youthful in his appearance, with light complexion and hair, and blue eyes set far back in his head, and expressing great shrewdness, or I should say, cunning. He has a large head and phrenologists would unhesitatingly pronounce it a bad one, for the organs situated in the back part are decidedly the most prominent. He is also very round-shouldered. He has just returned from Springfield, where he has been upon trial for some crime of which he was accused while in Missouri, but he was released on habeas corpus. I, who had expected to be overwhelmed by his eloquence, was never more disappointed than when he commenced his discourse by relating all the incidents of his journey. This he did in a loud voice, and his language and manner were the coarsest possible. His object seemed to be to amuse and excite laughter in his audience. He is evidently a great egotist and boaster, for he frequently remarked that at every place he stopped going to and from Springfield people crowded around him, and expressed surprise that he was so "handsome and good looking." He also exclaimed at the close of almost every sentence, "That's the idea!" I could not but with wonder and pity look upon that motley and eager crowd that surrounded me, as I thought, "Can it be possible that so many of my poor fellow-mortals are satisfied with such food for their immortal souls?" for not one sentence did that man utter calculated to create devotional feelings, to impress upon his people the great object of life, to teach them how they might more faithfully perform their duties and endure their trials with submission, to give them cheering or consoling views of a divine providence, or to fit them for an eternal life beyond the grave; but his whole two hours' discourse had rather a tendency to corrupt the morals and spread vice. . . .

Nauvoo, Feb. 19, 1843

My dear Mother:

A very happy Sunday morning dawned upon us, for about midnight Elizabeth [Haven's sister-in-law] gave birth to a fine, healthy little boy, weighing nine pounds, and all is well. She had two experienced Mormon women with her all day yesterday, and Dr. Weld came towards evening and tarried till after daylight. . . .

We think our visiting society among the Mormons will be very limited, for we understand it is etiquette for new comers to make the first call on old residents, and if the women are like the two that were here yesterday, I can say from the bottom of my heart, "From all such, good Lord, deliver us"; for they kept up one continual stream of talk about their peculiar religion, quoting scripture from Genesis to Revelations. I never heard so much Bible talk in all my life before. . . .

When we consider the short time since the Mormons came here, and their destitution after having had every vestige of property taken from them, and after having undergone great suffering and persecution, their husbands and sons in some instances murdered; when we remember that, driven from their homes in Missouri, with famine before them, five thousand men, women and children, crossed the Mississippi to this State in the winter of 1841 [should be 1838–39], we cannot wonder that they have no fitter dwelling-place and so few of the comforts of life. The hopelessness and despair that must have existed probably led some of them to commit depredations on their more fortunate neighbors,—had they not, we might certainly have considered them morally superior to other communities. Better and more substantial buildings are fast being erected in city and country, and in a few years things will present a very different appearance, and if let alone and persecution ceases, this absurd religious doctrine will surely die a natural death. . . .

We heard that Mrs. Joseph Smith wished to become acquainted with us, and had been expecting us to honor her with a call. As there was no prospect of E[lizabeth]'s going, I proposed to call and represent the family, the Judge volunteering to accompany and introduce me. They live in the Old Town by the river, so it was a mile walk, but we were fortunate to find them home. They seemed pleased to see us and urged us to pass the afternoon, but we politely declined. Sister Emma, for by that name Mrs. S. is known, is very plain in her personal appearance, though we hear she is very intelligent and benevolent, has great influence with her husband, and is generally beloved. She said very little to us, her whole attention being absorbed in what Joseph was saying. He talked incessantly about himself, what he had done and could do more than other mortals, and remarked that he was "a giant, physically and mentally." In fact, he seemed to forget that he was a man. I did not change my opinion about him, but suppose he has good traits. They say he is very kind-hearted, and always ready to give shelter and help to the needy. We may hope so, for a kind heart in this place can always be active. . . .

—•••• *13* ••••—

The Mormon Leadership on Nauvoo

The Mormon community was growing rapidly during the early 1840s. After having been pushed from place to place, and having seen their religious dreams go unfulfilled, the Latter Day Saints regarded Nauvoo as both a refuge for the present and a promise for the future. This report to the church's membership made by the organization's First Presidency, the three-man senior leadership organization, offers thanks for deliverance from Missouri and, like the ceremonial speech of Sidney Rigdon (see Document 11 above) reveals that the myth of religious persecution was essential to the Mormon identity. In other words, interpreting any and all opposition as religious persecution verified the Mormons' innocence, which was the mythic quality that made them the "Saints of God." The report also eloquently expresses the communal dream which the Saints wrapped up in the Nauvoo community. It voices confidence in the ultimate cause of Zion, and it is filled with hope for the future, a future that would turn sour within a matter of months. It was first published as the "Report of the First Presidency," *Times and Seasons* 2 (15 April 1841): 384–86.

—•••••●••••—

The Presidency of the Church of Jesus Christ of Latter Day Saints, feel great pleasure in assembling with the Saints at another general conference, under circumstances so auspicious and cheering; and with grateful hearts to Almighty God for his providential regard, they cordially unite with the Saints, on this occasion, in ascribing honor, and glory, and blessing to his holy name.

It is with unfeigned pleasure that they have to make known, the steady and rapid increase of the church in this State, the United States, and in Europe. The anxiety to become acquainted with the principles of the gospel, on every hand, is intense and the cry of, "come over and help us," is reaching the elders on the wings of every wind, while thousands who have heard the gospel, have become obedient thereto, and are rejoicing in its gifts and blessings.— Prejudice with its attendant train of evils, is giving way before the forces of truth, whose benign rays are penetrating the nations afar off.

The reports of the Twelve in Europe are very satisfactory, and state that the work continues to progress with unparalleled rapidity and that the harvest is truly great.

In the eastern states, the faithful laborers are successful, and many are flocking to the standard of truth. Nor is the south keeping back—churches have been raised up in the southern and western states, and a very pressing invitation has been received from New Orleans for some of the elders to visit that city, which has been complied with.

In our own State and immediate neighborhood, many are avowing their attachment to the principles of our holy religion, and have become obedient to the faith.

Peace and prosperity attend us; and we have favor in the sight of God and virtuous men.

The time was, when we were looked upon as deceivers, and that Mormonism would soon pass away, come to nought, and be forgotten. But the time has gone by when it was looked upon as a transient matter, or a bubble on the wave, and it is now taking a deep hold in the hearts and affections of all those who are noble minded enough to lay aside the prejudice of education, and investigate the subject with candor and honesty.

The truth, like the sturdy oak, had stood unhurt among the contending elements, which had beat upon it with tremendous force. The floods have rolled, wave after wave, in quick succession; and have not swallowed it up. "They have lifted their voice, O Lord, the floods have lifted up their voice; but the Lord of Hosts is mightier than the mighty waves of the sea." Nor, have the flames of persecution, with all the influence of the mobs, been able to destroy it; but like Moses' bush it has stood unconsumed, and now at this moment presents an important spectacle both to men and angels.—Where can we turn our eyes to behold such another? We contemplate a people who have embraced a system of religion unpopular, and the adherence to which has brought upon them repeated persecutions—a people who for their love to God and attachment to his cause, have suffered hunger, nakedness, perils, and almost every privation—a people, who for the sake of their religion, have had to mourn the premature deaths of parents, husbands, wives, and children—a people who have preferred death to slavery and hypocracy, and have honorably maintained their characters, and stood firm and immovable, in times that have tried men's souls.

Stand fast, ye Saints of God, hold on a little while longer, and the storms of life will be past, and you will be rewarded by that God whose servants you are, and who will duly appreciate all your toils and afflictions for Christ's sake and the gospel's. Your names will be handed down to posterity as saints of God, and virtuous men.

But we hope that those scenes of blood and gore will never more occur, but that many, very many such scenes as the present will be witnessed by the saints, and that in the Temple, the foundation of which has been so happily laid, will the saints of the Most High continue to congregate from year to year, in peace and safety.

From the kind and generous feelings manifest, by the citizens of this State, since our sojourn among them, we may continue to expect the enjoyment of all the blessings of civil and religious liberty, guaranteed by the constitution. The citizens of Illinois have done themselves honor in throwing the mantle of the constitution over a persecuted and afflicted people; and have given evident proof, that they are not only in the enjoyment of the privileges of freemen themselves, but, that they willingly and cheerfully extend that invaluable blessing to others, and that they freely award to faithfulness and virtue their due. . . .

In Illinois we've found a safe retreat,
    A home, a shelter from oppressions dire;
Where we can worship God as we think right,
    And mobbers come not to disturb our peace;
Where we can live and hope for better days,
    Enjoy again our liberty, our rights;
That social intercourse which freedom grants,
    And charity requires of man to man.
And long may charity pervade each breath,
    And long may Illinois remain the scene
Of rich prosperity by *peace secured!*

In consequence of the impoverished condition of the saints, the buildings which are in progress of erection do not progress as fast as could be desired; but from the interest which is generally manifested by the saints at large, we hope to accomplish much by a combination of effort, and a concentration of action, and erect the Temple and other buildings, which we so much need for our mutual instruction and the education of our children.

From the reports which have been received, we may expect a large emigration this season. The proclamation which was sent some time ago to the churches abroad, has been responded to, and great numbers are making preparations to come and locate themselves in this city and vicinity.

From what we now witness, we are led to look forward with pleasing anticipation to the future, and soon expect to see the thousands of Israel flocking to this region, in obedience to the heavenly command; numerous habitations of the saints thickly studding the flowery and wide spread prairies of Illinois; temples for the worship of our god erecting in various parts; and great peace resting upon Israel.

We would call the attention of the saints more particularly to the erection of the Temple, for on its speedy creation great blessings depend. The zeal which is manifested by the saints in this city is indeed praise worthy, and we hope will be imitated by the saints in the various stakes and branches of the church, and that those who cannot contribute labor, will bring their gold and their silver, their brass, and their iron, with the pine tree and box tree, to beautify the same.

We are glad to hear of the organization of the different quorums in this city, and hope that the organization will be attended to in every stake and branch of the church, for the Almighty is a lover of order and good government.

From the faith and enterprise of the saints generally, we feel greatly encouraged, and cheerfully attend to the important duties devolving upon us, knowing that we not only have the approval of Heaven, but that our efforts for the establishing of Zion and the spread of truth, are cheerfully seconded by the thousands of Israel.

In conclusion we would say, brethren, be faithful; let your love and moderation be known unto all men; be patient; be mindful to observe all the commandments of your heavenly Father; and the God of all grace shall bless you, even so, Amen.

Part II

The Origins of the Conflict

Thomas Sharp. Courtesy of Archives and Special Collections, Western Illinois University Library, Macomb.

---●●●● PART II ●●●●---

INTRODUCTION

M any non-Mormons in Hancock County probably disliked the Mormons from the first, in the same way that most Americans have generally disliked what they have viewed as religious fanaticism, but they were initially disposed toward tolerance because they sympathized with the Saints as refugees from oppression in Missouri. That view, however, soon began to change. Some of the Mormons, embittered against Gentiles because of their recent experience and impoverished because of their forced abandonment of homes in Missouri, stole food, livestock, and other things from farms in the Nauvoo area. And non-Mormons soon learned that trips to Nauvoo in search of stolen goods, or to seek payment for items sold to the Mormons, were fruitless—and could even be frightening. The highly unified, separatist community did not cooperate with outsiders, and some of the Saints resorted to intimidation. Two of the memoirs in this section refer to the "whistling and whittling brigade," which made unwelcome visitors fear for their lives.[1] Nauvoo quickly developed a reputation among Hancock County residents as a place where lawbreakers friendly to the church were shielded from arrest.

The amount of Mormon theft is impossible to determine, since some stealing by others was undoubtedly blamed on the Saints, nor can Joseph Smith's involvement be established with any certainty, despite what some of the memoirs in this section imply. Certain Mormon raiders may have felt they had Smith's approval when in fact they did not. In any case, the evidence of Mormon theft is substantial, and that activity caused some non-Mormons in townships near Nauvoo to oppose the Saints.

But of far greater importance to the development of non-Mormon animosity and the eventual eruption of mobocratic violence was the perceived threat to democratic government posed by Smith and his theocratic community. That view was expressed as far away as Macomb, Quincy, Alton, and other Illinois communities, but it was centered in Hancock County, where the Mormons dominated local politics by 1842. Warsaw, a town of about five hundred people in the early 1840s, spearheaded the opposition to Smith and political Mormonism. Founded in 1834 as a place for shipping and commerce, Warsaw was something of a microcosm of pluralistic America, an open, ambitious, progressive community where residents did not hold the religious preconceptions that made Nauvoo's theocracy possible. Instead local residents firmly subscribed to republicanism, the ill-defined civil religion of the Jacksonian era.[2] Common democratic ideals bound the people together, and the rituals of self-government affirmed the community's ideological bond. To the people of Warsaw, the nation had transcendent value, and republicanism was the operative faith of their town.[3] So it is not surprising that residents there objected to Smith's theocratic domination of government at Nauvoo, his encouragement of bloc voting for candidates he supported, his use of the Nauvoo Charter to avoid prosecution, and, eventually, his violation of the civil rights of his critics. That he also headed a huge militia, the Nauvoo Legion, made the threat of despotism seem all the more real. When a united political effort, the Anti-Mormon Party of 1841–42, failed to curb Smith's secular power, non-Mormons became increasingly frustrated, and there was talk of mobocratic measures to stop the threat of political Mormonism.

At the same time, after two arrests by Missouri officials, the prophet became increasingly fearful of the authorities in that state, whom he regarded as thoroughly evil. He drew his supporters more closely around him by depicting the Saints as innocent chosen people and himself as their champion fighting the enemies of God. Critics and opponents in Illinois were associated with those enemies, and thus fear and intolerance increased among the Mormons, and governmental authority at Nauvoo became centered in Smith. Apparently unaware of the contradiction between real democratic government and his theocratic control of Nauvoo, the prophet placed the church on a collision course with the non-Mormons in Hancock County—and ultimately with America.

Notes

1. A study of this band by Thurmon D. Moody, "Nauvoo's Whistling and Whittling Brigade," *Brigham Young University Studies* 15 (Summer 1975): 480–90, concluded that it was organized in 1845 in response to the repeal of the Nauvoo Charter, as a means of guarding the city. However, he fails to take into consideration any non-Mormon accounts of the band, such as that of Eudocia Baldwin Marsh included here, which depicts whistlers and whittlers when Joseph Smith was still alive. Likewise, Mosiah Lyman Hancock, a Mormon who belonged to the band, refers in his memoir to guarding the house of the prophet—and riding men on a sharp, three-cornered rail and making them "cross the great river," whatever that might mean (Hancock "Autobiography," pp. 26–27, Special Collections, Harold B. Lee Library, Brigham Young University, Provo, Utah). Perhaps the prophet had a group who guarded his house and took care of unwelcome visitors distinct from the organization formed in 1845. In any case, Hawkins Taylor, the sheriff of Lee County, Iowa Territory, who made frequent trips to Nauvoo, asserted that the band, under the leadership of Hosea Stout, sometimes whittled law officers out of town (see Part I, Document 10).

2. On the nature of civil religion in America, see Russell E. Richey and Donald G. Jones, eds., *American Civil Religion* (New York: Harper and Row, 1974), especially pp. 3–18.

3. Republicanism at Warsaw is discussed in "Our Anniversary," *Warsaw Message*, 26 July 1843, p. 1; Cleon, "The Science and Progress of Government: An Essay in Three Parts," *Warsaw Message*, 7 January 1843, p. 4; 21 January 1843, p. 4; 28 January 1843, p. 4; "Sketches of Hancock County," *Western World* (Warsaw, Ill.), 7 April 1841, p. 1; John E. Hallwas, "Mormon Nauvoo from a Non-Mormon Perspective," *Journal of Mormon History* 16 (1990): 53–69; John E. Hallwas, "Warsaw: An Old Mississippi River Village," *Illinois Magazine* 18 (December 1979): 8–15; John E. Hallwas, *Thomas Gregg: Early Illinois Journalist and Author,*

Western Illinois Monograph Series, no. 2 (Macomb: Western Illinois University, 1983), 37–48; and Kenneth H. Winn, *Exiles in a Land of Liberty: Mormons in America, 1830–1846* (Chapel Hill: University of North Carolina Press, 1989), 152–81.

---·••••· *1* ·••••·---

A Non-Mormon Report of Mormon Theft

Shortly after the Mormons arrived in Hancock County and before much political antagonism had developed, residents in some townships noted a significant increase in theft. Livestock, food, clothes, and other items were taken, and the Mormons were immediately blamed. As early as 15 July 1840, for example, the *Warsaw Message* reported that Hancock County residents were griping about "petty depredations . . . such as the loss of various small instruments of agriculture." After the killing of Joseph and Hyrum Smith in 1844, some non-Mormons responded to public criticism of the mob violence at Carthage jail by forming a Central Committee to document Mormon theft. Reports from a few townships were published in the *Warsaw Signal*, and individual accounts of Mormon theft appeared in several Illinois and Iowa newspapers.

The item excerpted here appeared in the *Warsaw Signal* on 22 January 1845, p. 2. Entitled "Mormon Stealing," it includes reports to the Central Committee documenting losses in Montebello and Nauvoo townships, as well as the village of Golden's Point. The report is introduced by Thomas C. Sharp, editor of the *Warsaw Signal*, whose comments are intended to convince the public of Mormon infamy. He opens by quoting from an 1831 revelation that Joseph Smith received in Kirtland, Ohio, which was printed in the Doctrine and Covenants of the Church of the Latter Day Saints (Kirtland, Ohio: F. G. Williams and Co., 1835), section 61:6. In more complete form than Sharp quotes, it does seem to condone theft by the Saints as "agents" of God: "Behold it is said in my laws, or forbidden to get in debt to thine enemies; but behold it is not said at any time, that the Lord should not take when he please, and pay as seemeth him good: wherefore, as ye are agents, and ye are on the Lord's errand . . . and he hath sent you to provide for his Saints in these last days . . . they shall obtain it." Sharp closes the article by itemizing thefts from non-Mormon store owners in Nauvoo, which portion is printed here.

Of course, some of the stealing may not have been done by Mormons. However, reports to the Central Committee, such as this one, together with individual recollections, such as items two and three in this section, are significant evidence that non-Mormons in Hancock County believed they had a problem with the Mormons in this regard. This concern about theft, and the belief that it was officially sanctioned by the church, created a perception about the Mormons that helped lead to the conflict in western Illinois.

———•••◦◉◦•••———

Report of C. Keegan of Nauvoo Precinct

To the Central Committee:—Being requested to give some statements of the amount of articles stolen from the old settlers in this district, to the committee appointed in Montebello, I proceed to lay before the Central Committee such facts as, on investigation, have come to my knowledge.

CHRISTOPHER KEEGAN had stolen sundries of clothes, wearing apparel, furniture, leather, &c. &c., in the city of Nauvoo, to the amount of $150.00; also a 4 gal. jar of preserves; also 1 very large fat cow; also two cords of wood; also orchard stealing and numerous acts of Trespass.

THOMAS MOFFITT, near Nauvoo, had 30 hogs stolen; also milk pans, shirts, socks, bee stands, and continued wood stealing, and he was threatened in the most violent manner, when endeavoring to prevent these aggressions.

JOHN MOFFITT, near Nauvoo, had stolen, 1st., one veal calf—2nd., stand bees—3d., corn and pumpkins—4th., two stand bees—5th., two stands bees—6th., two 2 year old heifers—7th., between 2 and 3 acres of corn—8th., a quantity wearing apparel—9th., a log chain, ring bolt, hammer and pitch fork—10th., 30 cords of chopped wood; besides continued trespassing on orchard, standing wood, &c. &c.

CHRISTOPHER TALLANT, near Nauvoo, had 2 horses shot; also, one bee stand and four hogs stolen.

DAVIDSON HIBBARD, in Nauvoo, had stolen, 1st., three bushels of corn from crib; 2nd., a bee stand; 3d., a washing of cloths; 4th., twelve yards of domestic; 5th., a bee stand; 6th., a fat cow, taken from his premises, which did not belong to him; but on notice being given by the owner, that the cow was his only dependence, ½ of a beef was returned to him in the night, with a letter, stating, that they thought it was Gentile beef that had been taken; 7th., a 3 year old colt; 8th., some 10 or 12 bushels of corn, besides many other similar acts.

JAMES MOFFITT in Nauvoo, had stolen, 50 cords chopped wood, one steer, one cow, one 2 year old hog, 5 bushels wheat, 6 bush. corn, with numerous acts of trespass.

JOHN WILLIAMS, near Nauvoo, had stolen 6 hogs.

Note. There is a numerous body of men in this district large losers by theft, (which can be attributed to no other cause, than their proximity to the Mormons) who are deterred from exposing their losses, from the fear of incurring vengeance of the rabble as well as the LAW ABIDING AUTHORITIES of this place!

In addition to the above, an item has been handed us, of $160.00, in cash stolen from William White in Nauvoo, in 1839. Messrs. Kilbourn's store in Nauvoo was robbed in 1839, of about $100.00 in goods. Messrs. Robinson & Finch's store in Nauvoo, was robbed of $800.00 worth of goods. Mr. Bryant in Nauvoo, we learn, was lately robbed of about $200.00 worth of goods. There are a host of other items which we have taken measures to collect from Nauvoo, and as soon as received, will lay them before our readers.

——— •••● 2 ●••• ———

Oral History Accounts of Mormon Theft

Recollections of Mormon theft remained vivid in the minds of some non-Mormons until late in their lives and were often passed along to family members. In the later nineteenth century Foster Walker of Pontoosuc, located ten miles north of Nauvoo, began conducting interviews with pioneers who recalled the Mormon era and with relatives of others who had already died. He had been born in Ohio in 1836 and had come to the Pontoosuc area with his family during the 1850s. His father was a farmer, and Walker himself farmed for many years. At the turn of the century he was president of the Pontoosuc Village Board.

During 1902 and 1903 Walker wrote a long series of articles entitled "The Mormons in Hancock County" for the *Dallas City Review*, published about twelve miles north of Nauvoo on the Mississippi River, and he included many reminiscences and family stories, either taken down verbatim or written in paraphrase, that he had gathered from dozens of informants over many years. Among them are the three accounts of Mormon theft reprinted here. Of course, the dialogue in them is an approximation of what was said, condensed and shaped by the memories of those who told these stories. Unlike the Mormons, who had a sense of historical importance, the non-Mormons kept few written records of their experiences, so the oral accounts collected by Walker are particularly helpful. Of course, they must be read with the understanding that there are limitations on memory after the passage of years, and they reflect—as do the Mormon documents—the bias of those who produced them. These accounts appeared in Walker's "The Mormons in Hancock County," on page two of the *Dallas City Review*, May 1, 8, 29, 1902, and are reprinted from photocopies at the Illinois State Historical Library.

——— •••●◆●••• ———

John M'Auly Also Pays Tribute

Major John McAuly came to the county in the spring of 1833. He settled on land lying on the western side of Pontoosuc town, in the edge of the prairie; was in easy circumstances; had a large family of children, and has left a number of grand children who still live in the county. His son William is an honored resident of Carthage, and he gave me a history of some of his father's troubles with the new neighbors:

"My father had two fine young horses taken off of the prairie west of our house (as everybody turned their stock out to graze in those days), and we hunted for them in the timber and in the bottom lands, but could not hear of them. They were gone for good. Father was inclined to sympathize—as nearly everybody, at that time, did,—with the Mormons; as they told some tough tales of how they had been run out of the slave state by the people who lived over in Missouri. My father was always an old line Whig of the Henry Clay school. When the 'Saints' first came to this county they were in a sorry plight, and father helped them in several ways, until after the laying of the cornerstone of the temple. After that incident, he was always suspicious of them. At the time his two horses were missed, he would not lay the taking of them to the Saints. At another time—perhaps a year afterward—he had a fine young horse stolen, and the thief, in making for Nauvoo, kept well into the timber, and getting down well into Appanoose township, he ran into some Anti-Mormons. Among them was Alexander Martin, who knew the horse and wanted to know why he was riding Mr. McAuly's horse. 'I got him up in Pontoosuc, and am taking him to Nauvoo.' 'Well, that is not yours, and you must get down and let me have him, and I will take him back home.' 'I guess you'll not get the horse: I've got it now and propose to keep it. The Lord told me where it was, and sent me after it. I received orders from the church to go and get him.' Mr. Martin was an old man, but he signaled to one of the neighbors to catch the bridle rein, which he did, and he ordered the man, for the second time to dismount, as he had known the fellow for some time to be a Mormon. But he again refused, when Martin hit him a welt with a club, that he had armed himself with. This sent him to the ground in a dazed and bewildered condition, and he was then told to get up and get out, which he did. The horse was sent home and had not been missed out of the pasture. We were always satisfied after that that the Mormons got the other two horses."

From that hour, the war goes on and John McAuly, with his son William, gave much of their time and aid toward getting rid of their troublesome neighbors. John McAuly acted as Major of one of the Hancock battalions until the closing scenes.

Robert Atherton's Grievance

Mr. Atherton came from Hamilton County in the year 1834 and settled on bottom lands in section 6, below Pontoosuc, and had quite a lot of lands in cultivation and passed among his neighbors as a number one man, and on many occasions did lend a helping hand to the fresh emigrants that came to settle in and about him, giving with a liberal hand during their arrival from Missouri, believing their terrible tale of persecution and woe. He gave them employment and extra amounts of provisions. He was at one time quite a favorite in Nauvoo. In common with others he heard stories about stealing going on in Appanoose and elsewhere and many of Atherton's neighbors laid it to the new sect, as they had constantly been traveling over the county in all directions for several years with no apparent aim or object.

Some of Atherton's nearest neighbors and among them J. R. Tull, Squire John McAuly and others had lost property and insisted that our new neighbors were the guilty parties. Mr. Atherton thought otherwise. In the spring of 1842 our Mormon sympathizer (so-called) missed a fat heifer and, taking the track, he followed close up on the heels of two footmen and the heifer, to within a block of the place where she was supposed to be secreted on one of the leading thoroughfares of the sacred city. A man who knew Atherton wanted to know why he was in town so early in the morning. On being informed of the reason, he took from a side pocket a whistle and blew several shrill short notes, and as if by magic, a dozen of men came running with knives and pine sticks and surrounded the man, whittling their sticks pointed towards him, exclaiming to each other and Atherton, in particular, "If you don't want to cut yourself always whittle from you"—cutting the outer garments into shreds. Backing off to where his horse was, he mounted it and they told him "not to come back and accuse our people of robbery; if he did he might be cut to pieces." He rode home a sad but wiser man, to be laughed at by his neighbors. The Mormons lost a faithful, honest friend, but gained an implacable, relentless, dangerous foe, who lived long enough that by his aid they were driven out of their stronghold and out of the state—[he] being then nearly 35 years old. He was one of the leading leaders and was never satisfied until the end was attained. We were personally acquainted with Mr. Atherton for ten years. He died in December 1860.

Uncle Nelson Lofton Receives a Revelation

John Lofton, a nephew [of Nelson Lofton], is sponsor for this story. He says: "I have heard Uncle Nels say when the country was new (being unmarried) he took up claims, improved them to sell, and kept oxen to do [sod] breaking with. He had a claim over on Camp creek where he had built a cabin, stable and yards, and was breaking prairie. He would keep all stock close to his shanty at night, as thieves were annoying the settlers, robbing henroosts and smokehouses, driving off hogs, sheep, young cattle, and now and then getting away with a horse. Uncle had fared overly well, as what he had lost was of minor importance. When breaking he always got up by daylight and turned the cattle out to graze. It was in the year of '42 when one morning he discovered his oxen were out and gone, the gap in the fence being closed. On taking a survey, he discovered human footprints among the cattle tracks. Feeding and saddling his best horse and eating a bite, uncle was on the road and after the freebooters, who could be easily followed. He overtook the outfit on the road to Nauvoo, to find four men afoot going leisurely over the prairie. Taking through the brush, my uncle headed them off and, riding slowly up, stopped both the cattle and men, when the following colloquy took place: N.— "Well boys, where are you driving the stock?" B.—"Oh, taking them to Nauvoo." N.—"What for?" B.—"Taking them to the butchers to supply the destitute Saints, who, you know, must be fed." N.—"Where did the cattle come from?" B.—"Out there on the prairie." N.—"That so? Who told you to take them?" B.—"Our prophet and seer, Joseph Smith, had a revelation from the Lord, and he told us where to go and find some fat cattle that were needed for meat for the poor brethren and we are going to take them and turn them over to Brother Joseph, and as it is getting leate [*sic*], we must go on, for he is waiting to receive us." N.—"Is that so?" (Being armed with a rifle and two pistols and having a horse he had trained to hunt deer.) "You men hold up! Let me explain to you that I am a sort of seer and prophet myself, and I have received a later revelation from God Almighty that says 'Joseph Smith is mistaken, and that you men are required by me to return the cattle to the pen whence they came; and that I must accompany you all the way.' So, step around lively, and start on as I am in a hurry to return." Slinging the rifle strap over his shoulder and pulling out his two pistols from the holsters and cocking them, they took their way back—Uncle Nels bringing up the rear. Coming to his home he said: "Now men, let me tell you of a second revelation I have received from Almighty God while coming along the road; God tells me 'you fellows are a set of thieves, as well as your Joe Smith'; and God also tells me to 'kill all thieves if they come on my land'; and if you are seen in these parts by me or anyone else, you can make up your mind that daylight will be let through your worthless carcasses. Now get! And make yourselves scarce."

It was the writer's lot to know Mr. Lofton for many years and we knew him to be of easy balance, slow to anger, faithful to friends, lenient to enemies, and strictly honest. By stealing his cattle—to be caught in the act—the Mormons "caught a tartar" and added a dangerous opponent to their already increasing number of foes. Nelson Lofton was ever after with the Antis.

— ●●●● *3* ●●●● —

A Farmer's Wife on Mormon Theft

The memoir of Eudocia Baldwin Marsh (located in the Archives, Knox College Library, Galesburg, Illinois; see the headnote for Part I, Document 5) includes the following account of how Joseph Smith avoided paying a debt to a non-Mormon farmer. Although she does not name the farmer, he was apparently John W. Marsh, who later married her, according to a footnote by Douglas L. Wilson and Rodney O. Davis, who edited this reminiscence as "Mormons in Hancock County: A Reminiscence," *Journal of the Illinois State Historical Society* 64 (Spring 1971): 42–45. As Marsh's introductory comments reveal, she regarded Smith's failure to pay the debt as a kind of theft—a part of the Mormon effort to plunder non-Mormon farms in Hancock County. It is impossible to determine whether the prophet encouraged Mormon raiding of area farms, but he apparently instructed Nauvoo's "whistling and whittling" brigade to run farmer John W. Marsh out of town. There is no evidence, contrary to Marsh's comments, that the whittlers were part of the Danites, a secret Mormon group formed in Missouri that was committed to violent reprisals against enemies of the church.

There is some other evidence that suggests that Mormon leaders may have used deliberate nonpayment as a means of getting back from Gentiles the supplies that violent Missourians had taken from them. William Law, a member of the First Presidency under Joseph Smith, recalled a meeting at Nauvoo with the prophet, Hyrum Smith, and others at which the idea was floated that Mormons should intentionally run up bad debts. Law asserted, in an interview that appeared in the *Salt Lake Tribune* on 31 July 1887, that Hyrum Smith made the case:

> "The Missourians have robbed, plundered and murdered our people. We should take our revenge on them as thoroughly as possible, and regain what we have lost in Missouri. The simplest way would be if our people would go to Missouri and buy their horses and cattle on credit, and *then not pay for them;* and our merchants would go to St. Louis and take their large quantities of goods on credit and then, when the notes became due, simply not pay them. . . ." Some of those present applauded the proposition, and said that would be *only fair.*

When Law objected that such a plan would "punish the innocent to hurt the guilty," the meeting broke up in disagreement. In any case, to many Mormons, Gentiles, especially Missourians, were enemies—part of the wicked world that God's chosen people had to contend with—so unscrupulous dealing with them may have seemed justified.

——————•••●◉●•••——————

All the world knows who and what manner of people the Mormons are at this date—at least in some degree—and my object has not been to give a detailed account of them as a sect—but merely to relate a few incidents which I remember as having occurred in connection with the death of the Smiths, and subsequent events resulting in their expulsion from our state.—— Very soon after their settlement at Nauvoo the citizens of the County became convinced that a great mistake had been made in giving them aid and comfort, and encouragement to settle among them—for driven by thier [*sic*] own needs and the mandates of their leaders, they were obliged to produce the means to keep many people and projects alive and moving.—Raids into the surrounding county for the purpose of "lifting" cattle, horses and produce of evry [*sic*] kind became frequent—and there was little or no redress, because of the City Charter which gave Smith as Mayor the right to resort to the Habeas Corpus act on all occasions—no matter how many arrests of criminals were made by County officers—a resort to this act set them at liberty, and before any further steps could be taken they were out of reach.——I was told some years after the occurrences by a gentleman who had suffered severely from their depredations, that Smith had been in the habit of sending men to him with orders for cattle, hay, grain and other articles of farm produce which he had for sale—promising to pay from time to time, as they should be furnished. He received payment at intervals, but finally the bills had become a large sum which he demanded without result. Becoming impatient, and the orders continuing to arrive, he mounted his horse one morning and rode to Nauvoo to see Smith and to get the money due him. The latter received him with great show of courtesy and hospitality—promised immediate payment and charged him a round sum for his entertainment. After waiting some time, the money not being forthcoming and Smith having disappeared, temporarily as the gentleman supposed, he walked out upon the street for a short stroll through the town (which was being rapidly built up and which presented a very lively appearance—) intending to return in a few moments [to] receive his money and leave for his home. Before he had walked a block he was surrounded by half a dozen rough looking fellows each one of whome [sic] had a large pine stick in his hand which he was vigorously whittling with a bowie knife. They gradually pressed nearer and nearer to him until the points of their knives almost touched him as they cut viciously at the pine. Surprised and indignant, the gentleman inquired what they meant by such conduct, giving some of these nearest him a vigorous kick or two to emphasize his words—but taking no notice whatever either of his words or actions they merely closed up a little nearer and whittled faster.—A crowd was gathered around them and seeing no way of ridding himself of these men, and feeling sure there must be some sinister motive in this demonstration—he turned and walked toward the Hotel which he soon reached—the men all leaving him and disappearing as he went up the steps. He inquired for Smith and was told *he had left town*. He ordered his horse, went out and mounted him, and was immediately surrounded again by the whittlers who accompanied him outside the city limits—still cutting at the pine sticks and occasionally giving his horse a prick with the points of their knives to hasten his movements. Not one of these men uttered a word from beginning to end of this affair, which made it all the more uncannie [sic].—It is needless to say the gentleman who was unarmed was too thankful to get away with his life and limb to make much ado about his money. He had heard of this practice of getting rid of objectionable creditors, but had given little or no credence to the tales of murder and disappearance which were rife in the County—above all he would not have believed that he himself would ever be subjected to such treatment—as he had always been on the best of terms with Smith who had ever treated him with great attention and courtesy.—He never received a penny of the money due him but bore his loss with resignation when he thought of "what might have been."——These Whittlers were a part of the "Danite Band" whome [sic] Smith termed his "Destroying Angels" and who were ready to do his bidding in all things, and had no doubt done it in this case.—In the course of a fortnight another demand for supplies was made upon this same gentleman which was promptly refused—the consequence being that within a month an orchard of several hundred beautiful young fruit trees was girdled in the night and totally destroyed.

4

An 1840 Assessment of Smith's Political Power

Located almost fifty miles south of Nauvoo was Quincy, an important Mississippi River town where the Mormons had found temporary refuge in 1839. The editor of the *Quincy Whig* from 1838 until his death in 1851 was Sylvester M. Bartlett, a native of Massachusetts who had edited newspapers in St. Louis and Galena, Illinois, before moving to Quincy. During the 1840s he took an interest in Mormon affairs and was present, for example, at the laying of the temple cornerstone at Nauvoo in 1841. Perhaps his most interesting article is focused on Joseph Smith a few months after his return from Washington, D.C. Early in 1840 the prophet had approached President Martin Van Buren about reparations to the Mormons for being violently expelled from Missouri, but the president was not responsive to the Mormon plea. Neither was the Senate, which was petitioned by other Mormon leaders. The article by Bartlett gives Smith's views on the president. A similar position is expressed in numerous other Mormon accounts about the redress of their Missouri grievances.

Of greater interest is Smith's contention that he intends to wield political influence, a course that led to conflict with non-Mormons in Hancock County. Bartlett was concerned about the potential for despotism in Smith because of his "claims of divine inspiration" and his unusual control of his followers, so the article ends with a warning of danger to democracy. Soon the non-Mormons in Hancock County would become alarmed by the same possibility.

Smith's assertion that the membership in his church was about a "hundred thousand souls" is greatly exaggerated. Twenty to thirty thousand would be a more accurate figure. He may not have known the real membership of the Latter Day Saints, but even if he did, Smith was talking to a newspaperman and wanted to create an impression among the public that his church was a political force to be reckoned with. This article appeared in the *Quincy Whig*, 17 October 1840, p. 1, and it reveals very early in the tenure of the Mormons in Illinois fundamental disagreements over how best to ensure the welfare of Hancock County citizens.

He [the Prophet] gave us distinctly to understand that his political views had undergone an entire change; and his description of the reception given him at the executive mansion was any thing but flattering to the distinguished individual who presides over its hospitalities.

Before he had heard the story of our wrongs, said the indignant Prophet, Mr. Van Buren gave us to understand that he could do nothing for the redress of our grievances lest it should interfere with his political prospects in Missouri. *He is not as fit,* said he, *as my dog, for the chair of state;* for my dog will make an effort to protect his abused and insulted master, while the present chief magistrate will not so much as lift his finger to relieve an oppressed and persecuted community of freemen, whose glory it has been that they were citizens of the United States.

You hold in your hands, I observed, a large amount of political power, and your society must exert a tremendous influence, for weal or woe, in the coming elections.

Yes, said he, I know it; and our influence, as far as it goes, we intend to use. There are probably not far short of an hundred thousand souls in our society, and the votes to which they are entitled throughout the Union must doubtless be extensively lost to Mr. Van Buren.

Not being myself disposed in any way to intermeddle in party politics I made no definite reply; but immediately taking leave we returned to Montrose, abundantly satisfied that the Society over which he presides has assumed a moral and political importance which is but very imperfectly understood. Associated on the religious principle, under a prophet and leader whose mysteries and awful claims of divine inspiration make his voice to believers like the voice of God; trained to sacrifice their individuality; to utter one cry; and to think and act in crowds, with subjection, and left to wander, like lost stars, amid the dark mazes and winding way of religious error; these remarkable sectaries must necessarily hold in their hands a fearful balance of political power. In the midst of contending parties, a single hand might turn their influence, with tremendous effect, to whichever side presented the most potent attraction, and should they ever become disposed to exert their influence for evil, which may Heaven prevent, they would surround our institutions with an element of danger, more to be dreaded than an armed and hundred-eyed police.

5

"Our Position—Again":
An Editorial by Thomas Sharp

Thomas C. Sharp (1813–94), editor of the *Warsaw Signal*, became one of the most vocal opponents of the Mormons in Illinois and did much to incite the murders of Joseph and Hyrum Smith in 1844. Born in Mount Holly, New Jersey, he studied at Dickinson College in Carlisle, Pennsylvania, and was admitted to the bar in 1840. Later that year he came west to Quincy, where he briefly practiced law before moving to Warsaw. In November 1840, he and printer James Gamble bought the local newspaper, which Sharp soon renamed the *Warsaw Signal*. Except for later 1842 and 1843, when he tried farming, Sharp edited the newspaper until the Mormons were forced to leave Illinois.

Although some non-Mormons regretted Sharp's eventual turn to mob-ocratic means for ridding the county of Smith and the Latter Day Saints, in the minds of many he was a much-admired champion of republican virtue and law. After the Mormon era, he was chosen as a delegate to the convention that drafted the 1848 Illinois Constitution, and he was elected justice of the peace and, later, county judge. He also practiced law in Carthage and edited newspapers there and in Warsaw.

Raised as a Jacksonian Democrat but supportive of the Whigs in 1840, Sharp was devoted to individualism and democratic values, which he felt were threatened by the theocratic, militaristic community headed by Joseph Smith. Like many other editors of his era, he was outspoken in support of Jacksonian-era political views and did not hesitate to denounce or ridicule a leader that he opposed. To Sharp, Mormonism mythically represented despotism, which haunted the American mind in the decades prior to the Civil War. The editorial printed here, entitled "Our Position—Again," appeared in the *Warsaw Signal* on 16 June 1841, p. 2. In it Sharp voices his opposition to "religious despotism in a land of freedom and laws" and champions individual rights "in opposition to the dictates of a political and military Church." He also criticizes those politicians who were beginning to court Smith for the sake of Mormon votes, thus giving inordinate influence to the prophet and corrupting the operation of popular government.

We have several times been asked whether we profess to represent the *Whig party* in the controversy in which we have engaged, relative to the Mormon ascendancy in this county. If by the Whig party is meant certain individuals calling themselves leaders, who make Party their God, and sacrifice everything at her shrine—or if is meant those *kind-hearted* and *sympathetic* gentlemen whose feelings are so deeply touched at the idea of "*persecution*," as our poor action of *self-defense* is perversely termed—or if is meant that class of *high-minded* politicians whose highest glory is to fawn upon and flatter Joe Smith, and who are ready to toss coppers for the honor of escorting him from place to place—or if is meant that class of persons who yet think the Mormons may be some *political* utility in future elections—we answer, that we do not profess to represent *any of these*. On the contrary, we profess to represent in this controversy those high-minded and independent citizens of Hancock who *dare to think*, and *fear not to speak* their thoughts. We profess to represent those of *both* political parties, who are not shackled by self-interest, and who have the manliness to stand up for their rights in opposition to the dictates of a political and military Church. We profess to represent that class of our fellow citizens who would save the county and state from the disgrace of being ruled by an ignorant and unprincipled aspirant for power—from the degradation of submitting to religious despotism in a land of freedom and laws. We profess to represent those, too, who are not willing to wait until they are trodden under foot before they make resistance.

In this controversy, therefore, we act not as politicians—nor do we believe that those who have proper views of the question will suffer political feeling in the least to sway their conduct. In this neighborhood, party feeling is almost entirely absorbed in the determination to oppose the further progress of political Mormonism. Members of both parties unite cordially in battling with a power which threatens to deprive us of our dearest rights. Let but the independent and unbought citizens throughout the county act with the same determination, and political leaders will soon learn to treat him as he deserves—namely, as an arrant knave and imposter, who has duped hundreds to follow his foul standard through rebellion and blood, and who now takes advantage of the misery and suffering which he himself has occasioned them, in order to arouse public sympathy in his behalf.—This is our position.

6

A Brief Historical Sketch of the Anti-Mormon Party

No resident of early Hancock County was more interested in history than Thomas Gregg (1808–92), a newspaperman who eventually wrote an extensive county history and a biography of Joseph Smith. Born in Belmont, Ohio, Gregg was raised in a Quaker family. In 1822 he became a printer's devil, an apprentice, in nearby St. Clairsville. He was already writing poetry and essays when he moved to Cincinnati in 1835. Later that year he came west, to Carthage, Illinois, where he founded the town's first newspaper and a short-lived magazine. In the decades that followed, Gregg edited several other newspapers and magazines—in Montrose and Keokuk, Iowa, and in Warsaw, Plymouth, and Hamilton, Illinois. Among them was the *Warsaw Message* (formerly the *Warsaw Signal),* which he edited in 1842 and 1843. Although opposed to the Mormons as a nondemocratic force in the region, Gregg was committed to nonviolent measures in opposing them. Unfortunately, Thomas Sharp reassumed control of that newspaper (renamed the *Warsaw Signal)* early in 1844 and did not share his convictions.

Gregg's most important historical works are his 1,000-page *The History of Hancock County, Illinois* (Chicago: Charles C. Chapman, 1880), which includes a 136-page chapter on "The Mormon Period," and his biography of Joseph Smith, *The Prophet of Palmyra* (New York: John B. Alden, 1890). Both view the Mormons critically but not unfairly. Gregg also wrote many historical articles for his newspapers, and in 1846 produced a 10,000-word broadside entitled "A Descriptive, Statistical, and Historical Chart of the County of Hancock." It provides an overview of the recently concluded Mormon conflict and includes the following account of the Anti-Mormon Party. As the party's convention resolutions reveal, by 1841 many non-Mormons in Hancock County viewed Smith's community as a threat to democratic values. Although the party itself was short lived, it contributed to the emerging political polarization of the county.

———————————•••◉◉◉••◉•◉•————————————

In the summer of 1841, the old citizens of the county, becoming alarmed at the increasing power and tyranny of Smith, began to enquire as to the best mode of counteracting them. A large county convention was held on the 28th of June, composed of citizens of all classes and both political parties, for the purpose of taking the subject into consideration. It was decided to nominate candidates to office, equally from both parties, to be run as Anti-Mormon candidates, and who were pledged to use their influence against the political corruption which had become so prevalent. Accordingly, Robert Miller, Whig, and Richard Wilton, Democrat, were nominated for county commissioner and school commissioner, and in August [1841], were elected by a small majority.

From that convention may be dated the rise of the Anti-Mormon party; and as the first organized attempt to oppose the encroachments of Mormonism, one or two of the resolutions of the convention will not be out of place here. It was

"Resolved, That with the peculiar religious opinions of the people calling themselves Mormons, or Latter-Day Saints, we have nothing to do—being at all times perfectly willing that they shall remain in the full possession of all the rights and privileges which our constitution and laws guarantee and other citizens enjoy.

"Resolved, That in standing up as we do to oppose the influence which these people have obtained, and are likely to obtain, in a political capacity, over our fellow citizens and their liberties, we are guided only by a desire to defend ourselves against a despotism, the extent and consequences of which we have no means of ascertaining."

In the succeeding year another convention was held and candidates nominated; but the Mormon strength had so much increased, that these nominees were defeated by Mormons and those in their interest. Wm. Smith, a brother to the prophet, was elected to the Legislature.

————————————•••◉ 7 ◉•••————————————

The Prophet on the Local Political Campaign

The Illinois gubernatorial election of 1842 pitted Democrat Adam W. Snyder against Whig Joseph Duncan, who had been governor from 1834 to 1838. Joseph Smith became an outspoken supporter of Snyder, urging his followers to

vote for him and for John Moore, the Democratic candidate for lieutenant governor. That immediately brought criticism from non-Mormons, especially Whigs, who felt that Smith was using his religious position to subvert popular government. One such critic was Sylvester M. Bartlett, editor of the *Quincy Whig*, whose article from the 22 January 1842 *Whig*, p. 2, is reprinted here. (See the headnote for Part II, Document 4 for biographical information.) He includes an endorsement of the Democrats by the prophet, whose apparent reason for throwing Mormon support to Snyder and Moore was that the Nauvoo city charter had been passed by a Democratic legislature. And Bartlett warns that such political Mormonism will cause hatred and hostility.

As the campaign continued, Joseph Duncan began to express Whig fears about Mormon political power and called for repeal of the Nauvoo Charter. Unfortunately for Smith, Snyder died in May of 1842, and he was replaced on the Democratic ticket by Judge Thomas Ford, who also called for repeal or revision of the Nauvoo Charter. Hence Smith ended up with no friend in either party. Ford carried Hancock County by a large margin, perhaps—as Robert Flanders suggested in *Nauvoo: Kingdom on the Mississippi* (Urbana: University of Illinois Press, 1965)— because Smith and the Mormons did not take his criticism seriously. In any case, the Illinois election of 1842 brought nothing for the Mormons but resentment by the Whigs and increasing concern in both parties about Mormon political behavior.

<hr />

JOSEPH SMITH, Lieutenant General of the Nauvoo Legion, has a proclamation in the last "Times and Seasons," directing the Mormons in this State to vote for the locofoco [Democratic] candidates for Governor and Lieut. Governor next August. This is, indeed, a highminded attempt to usurp power and to tyrannize over the minds of men. We are sorry to see this move on the part of President Smith—not so much on account of the influence which his people voting in body will have in the election—but because, it will have a tendency to widen the breach which already exists between this people and those who are not of their faith, and as a consequence create difficulties and disturbances growing out of an unsettled state of feeling in the community. We should suppose that prudence would have dictated a different course to Mr. Smith. Why not let his people enjoy all the privileges guaranteed to them by the Constitution of the country unbiased by their *religious* teachers? Why not allow them the exercise of their own best judgments in the choice of civil rulers? Have the whigs as a party so far departed from the principles of liberal[i]ty which have always governed them, as to call forth this public demonstration of opposition? We have seen no evidence of it. Many of the Mormons—in fact a great number of them—are men of intelligence and patriotism, who will not be swayed to and fro in their support of men or party, by the *dictum* of their leader in the church, and to these we look for aid and assistance in carrying the principles of reform into our State Government. The Mormons have

a right to vote for SNYDER and MOORE, if they choose, as a matter of course,—but this clannish principle of voting in a mass, at the dictation of one man, and this a man who has acquired an influence over the minds of his people through a peculiar religious creed which he promulgates, is so repugnant to the principles of our Republican form of Government, that its consequences and future effects will be disagreeable to think of—bitter hatred and unrelenting hostility will spring up, where before peace and good will had an abiding place.

The following is the Proclamation alluded to. It is truly a curiosity in its way. We give it *verbatim*, with all its capitals and italics staring through it like pepper and salt in a dish of hotch-potch:

> "From the Times and Seasons.
> State Gubernatorial Convention.
> City of Nauvoo, Illinois,
> December 20th, A.D. 1841.

TO MY FRIENDS IN ILLINOIS;—

The Gubernatorial Convention of the State of Illinois has nominated Colonel ADAM W. SNYDER for GOVERNOR, and Col. JOHN MOORE, for LIEUTENANT-GOVERNOR of the *State of Illinois*—election to take place in August next.—COLONEL MOORE, like JUDGE DOUGLAS, and ESQ. WARREN, was an intimate friend, and General Bennett informs us that no men were more efficient in assisting him to procure our *great charter privileges* than were *Colonel Snyder* and *Col. Moore.* They are sterling men, and friends of equal rights—opposed to the oppressor's grasp, and the tyrant's rod. With such men at the head of our State Government we have nothing to fear. In the next canvass we shall be influenced by no *party* consideration—and no Carthagenian coalescence or collusion, with our party, will be suffered to affect or operate against *General Bennett or any other of our tried friends already semi-officially in the field;* * so the partisans in this county who expect to divide the friends of humanity and equal rights will find themselves mistaken—we care not a fig for *Whig* or *Democrat;* they are both alike to us; but we shall go for our *friends*, our TRIED FRIENDS, and the cause of *human liberty* which is the cause of God. We are aware that *"divide and conquer"* is the watchword with man, but with us it cannot be done.—We have suffered too much to be easily duped—we have no cat's paws amongst us. We voted for Gen. Harrison because we *loved* him—he was a *gallant officer* and a *tried statesman;* but this is no reason why we should always be governed by his friends—he is now DEAD, and *all* of *his* friends are not *ours.* We claim the privileges of freemen, and shall act accordingly. DOUGLAS is a *Master Spirit* and *his* friends—they are *ours.* These men are free from the prejudices and superstitions of the age, and such men we *love*, and such men will ever receive our support, be their *political predilections* what they may. Snyder and Moore, are known to be our friends; their friendships are *vouched* for by those whom we have tried. We will never be justly charged with the sin of ingratitude—they *have* served us, and we *will* serve them.

> JOSEPH SMITH,
> Lieutenant General of the Nauvoo Legion."

*It is understood from this that Gen. Bennett is in the field for Senator for Hancock.—This gentleman at present is General of the Nauvoo Legion, Mayor of Nauvoo, and Master in Chancery for Hancock county, and in addition, we believe is a practicing Physician. It seems to us, that he must also be a "Master Spirit," if he can fulfill all these duties and that of Senator to boot!

———————●●●● *8* ●●●●———————

The Prophet and the 1843 Congressional Race

Smith's delivery of Mormon votes for a congressional candidate also led to criticism. In 1843 he had at first promised his support to Cyrus Walker, a Whig from nearby McDonough County. Walker was a brilliant lawyer who had defended Smith against charges brought from Missouri at Dixon, Illinois, a few months earlier—probably in exchange for Smith's political support. But there was a change in plans, evidently because Democratic leaders had agreed to provide Smith with protection from his Missouri pursuers. At a meeting in Nauvoo on 6 August 1843, Smith told his followers to listen to the counsel of his brother on the upcoming election. "Brother Hyrum tells me this morning that he has had a testimony [revelation] to the effect that it would be better for the people to vote for [Joseph P.] Hoge," Walker's opponent in the election, Smith told the Nauvoo congregation, "and I never knew Hyrum to say he ever had a revelation and it failed. Let God speak and all men hold their peace" (Joseph Smith, Jr., *History of the Church of Jesus Christ of Latter-day Saints*, ed. B. H. Roberts [Salt Lake City: Deseret Book Co., 1902–12], 5:526). The Mormon bloc surely decided the election, for Hoge was elected by only 574 votes but enjoyed a plurality of 1,355 in Hancock County.

The following account was written by a non-Mormon who was at that meeting, and who had witnessed messengers riding between Springfield and Nauvoo, apparently to warn Smith of pursuit by Missouri officials—the payoff for Mormon votes. As the writer points out, he was a close friend of Walker's cousin, Hawkins Taylor, who also wrote about Smith's political bargain with the Democrats in "The Late Cyrus Walker," *Carthage Gazette*, 1 January 1876, p. 1. This memoir appeared as "Politics and Mormons," *Macomb Journal*, 25 January 1877, p. 2. In the obituary of Cyrus Walker, one of the most admired settlers of McDonough County, a version of it appeared as "Death of Cyrus Walker," *Carthage Gazette*, 8 December 1875, p. 2.

Messrs Editors:

Having perused the reminiscences of the late Cyrus Walker, as prepared by my old friend Hawkins Taylor, I offer some remarks on the same subject, from my standpoint, commencing with Mr. Walker's becoming a candidate for Congress. Previous to this time Mr. Walker had been the attorney for Joe Smith, and had been the means of delivering him from arrest, to the great joy of the Mormons, and the displeasure of many of the anti-Mormon old settlers of both political parties. When the canvas for the election of members of Congress arrived, new points were presented. The anti-Mormon Whigs of Hancock county discovered that their former old friend, Walker, was being monopolized by their enemies, the Mormons. This created a distrust not easily reconciled with them. He found it expedient to address the Whigs at a meeting at Carthage, called expressly, at which he endeavored to quiet their fears, and at the close used a quotation from an ancient author, requesting that he "might be delivered from his *friends*." Suspicion being aroused, this address did not restore perfect confidence. In consequence, some Whig votes were probably lost by his acceptance of the Mormon assistance. The Democratic leaders foresaw that with the apparent great immigration of the Mormons, and if the vote of this multitude could be controlled by the beck of one man, the balance of power in the state might suddenly be changed from the Democrats to the Whigs. As Walker was popular with the Mormons, the crisis appeared to the Democrats as imminent. There is satisfactory evidence to me that Mr. Taylor's conclusion was correct,—that there was a bargain either with Gov. Ford or the leading Democrats at Springfield, and the Mormons, that the Mormons at this election should vote for Hoge and not for Walker, and for this favor the Mormons were guaranteed due notice before service of any requisitions from Missouri against any of the Mormon leaders. For instance: At this date the only available accommodations between Springfield and Nauvoo, were by a tri-weekly stage. On a morning, twelve hours before the arrival of the stage, a horse-man would arrive at Hamilton's Hotel, in Carthage, from Springfield, the horse covered with sweat and frost. Here, after breakfast, the rider would take a fresh horse and go to Nauvoo, and return the same day. At evening the stage would bring an officer from Springfield to make the arrests. On enquiring for Joseph Smith he would be told, "the last seen of him he was on a white horse going to Heaven." Similar events occurred twice, and perhaps three times, within the writer's observation. These notices, it may be supposed, were the payments for the bribe to Joe Smith for the Democratic vote. In may be supposed that Smith was in earnest in his request for Walker to become the candidate, but the offer made him for his own and his friends' safety, changed his political sentiments. The writer was present at the meeting in Nauvoo on the Saturday preceding the Monday election, to promulgate to [Mormons in] Hancock and the adjacent counties for whom they should vote. Hyrum Smith addressed the meeting purely Democratic, with no admixture of Mormonism. He was followed by William Law (not Wilson Law) for Walker and Whig principles. After each party had spoken twice, Mr. Law committed himself beyond recovery. Near his conclusion he added, "I am as obedient to revelation as any man; Bro. Hyrum does not say he had a revelation." The Hancock county election ticket had been printed on yellow post office wrapping paper, and a portion of the impression was present in Nauvoo on Saturday procedidg [*sic*] the election. Hyrum Smith arose, elevated both arms, and holding one of the tickets up said, "Thus saith the Lord, those that vote this ticket, this flesh colored ticket, this Democratic ticket, shall be blessed; those who do not shall be accursed." A general whoop was given by the audience. The runners from the adjacent counties said, "Now we'll go home." The writer was present on Sunday when Joe Smith gave his address. He spoke highly of Mr. Walker as a lawyer, and the part he had performed for him. He added, "My old mother come to me with tears in her eyes saying, 'The church ought to vote for Mr. Walker.' Mr. Walker done well for me and I have paid him. I am not indebted to Mr. Walker. I have not enquired of God about the election; I suppose he would have told me if I had enquired. Bro. Hyrum says he has. He is as good a man as God ever made, and I never knew him to tell a lie. God told him the church must vote the Democratic ticket." On election day the Mormons commenced their voting agreeable to Hyrum's revelation. Perhaps Joe Smith considered it would be some palliation to Walker and the Whig party for his pledge of the vote of the church for Walker should he individually vote for Walker. However, he did. The report of some of the citizens of Carthage who attended the election at Nauvoo, say that some of the brethren, observing how their Prophet had voted, supposed it would be correct for them to vote as he did. Smith, fearing the contract with the Democrats might be impaired, said: "What a strange people these Mormons are. They are like a flock of sheep; if I should jump into hell, I believe they would follow me!" The Mormons, after this remark, voted almost wholly in conformity with Hyrum's revelation.

B.

Macomb, Jan. 22, 1877

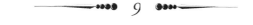

9

A Mormon Account of Smith's Missouri Troubles

Lyman O. Littlefield (1819–88), a long-standing adherent to Mormonism, had been expelled from Missouri in 1839 with the other Latter Day Saints and came to Quincy, eventually settling in Nauvoo in 1841. When the Mormons started leaving the city in 1846, he remained behind for a time to edit the *Hancock Eagle*, but that newspaper failed in the fall. He subsequently took his family to the

Great Basin and was one of the founders of the Mormon community of Logan, Utah, where he edited a newspaper, the *Utah Journal*. He also published a memoir of his experience in the church, *Reminiscences of Latter-day Saints* (Logan: The Utah Journal Co., 1888), from which these excerpts are taken, pp. 121–23, 127–29.

Littlefield gives brief accounts of the "Missouri troubles" of Joseph Smith that occurred in 1842 and 1843. The first depicts the prophet's arrest on charges of conspiring to murder Governor Lilburn W. Boggs. Boggs had issued in October 1838 an order to his militia demanding that the Mormons be expelled from the state or "exterminated," so he was the focus of intense Mormon hatred. Orrin Porter Rockwell, a violence-prone former Danite intensely loyal to Joseph Smith, was in Missouri when Boggs was shot and nearly killed at his Independence home in May 1842 and was immediately arrested for the crime. Although charged with the attempted murder, he was acquitted.

The second excerpt deals with Smith's arrest at Dixon, Illinois, on charges of escaping from Missouri authorities while under arrest for treason (violence against the state) in 1839. Both episodes reveal how Smith used the Nauvoo court—of which he was the chief justice—to obtain writs of habeas corpus and thus free himself from arrest. That practice led to charges by non-Mormons that Smith was above the law and to criticism of the Nauvoo city charter and court structure. In fact, the city charter only granted the court "power to grant writs of habeas corpus in all cases arising under the ordinances of the City Council," and not in regard to state charges such as those from Missouri. The Mormons were abusing their charter to defy the law, but Littlefield saw only the triumph of God's prophet.

On the 6th of May, 1842, an attempt was made to assassinate ex-governor L. W. Boggs, by some party unknown at his residence in Independence, Jackson County, Missouri. His injuries, however, did not prove fatal. Boggs made affidavit that he had reason to believe that the assault upon him was made by O. P. Rockwell as principal and Joseph Smith as accessory before the fact. He applied to Thomas Reynolds, governor of Missouri, to make a demand on the governor of Illinois to deliver Joseph Smith up to an authorized agent of Missouri to be dealt with according to the laws of that state for the crime charged. Governor [Thomas] Carlin, of Illinois, accordingly issued a warrant for the arrest of O. P. Rockwell as principal and Joseph Smith as accessory to the shooting of Boggs. The papers for their arrest were placed in the hands of the deputy sheriff of Adams County, who at once came to Nauvoo, and, on August 8, 1842, made the arrests. A writ of habeas corpus was applied for and granted by the municipal court of Nauvoo. But the sheriff refused to comply, claiming that that tribunal had no legal jurisdiction in the case. Leaving the prisoners in the care of the city marshal—but failing to leave the original writ without which they could not be held—the sheriff returned to Quincy and the brethren were, under the circumstances, allowed their liberty to go where they pleased. When the sheriff returned on the 10th, he was unable to find the whereabouts of the prisoners, relative to which the following extract contains interesting particulars:

> Joseph crossed the river and stayed at his Uncle John's house for a few days in the settlement called Zarahemla; but on the night of the eleventh of August, he met by appointment, his brother Hyrum, Rockwell, his wife Emma, and several other friends at the south point of the island, that we have already described as being midway between Montrose and Nauvoo.
>
> It has been rumored that the governor of Iowa had also issued a warrant for the arrest of Joseph and Rockwell, whereupon it was decided that it would be better for them to remain on the Illinois side of the river. Subsequent events, however, proved that this rumor was a false one. Joseph was rowed up the river by a Brother Dunham to a point near the home of a Brother Derby. Rockwell had been set ashore and he proceeded to the same point on foot, where he built a fire on the bank of the river that Dunham might know where to land. At Derby's the Prophet remained in hiding for some time, and Rockwell went east, remaining for several months in Pennsylvania and New Jersey.
>
> From his place of concealment, Joseph directed the movements of the people at Nauvoo, and managed his own business through faithful agents, who met with him occasionally. Emma spent considerable of her time with him, and beguiled the loneliness of those weary hours of inactivity, that he whose very life is the synonym for intense activity, had to endure. . . .

Still another demand was made for Joseph Smith by the governor of Missouri and his arrest took place near Dixon, Lee County, Iowa, June 23, 1843. The officers making the arrest were Joseph H. Reynolds, sheriff of Jackson County, Missouri, and the other was constable Harmon T. Wilson of Carthage, Illinois. He was most shamefully treated by them. They attempted to run him into Missouri without giving him any chance to obtain legal or other aid. But they failed in this as Joseph found an opportunity to procure assistance from two lawyers at Dixon through whose aid a writ of habeas corpus was obtained and made returnable before the nearest tribunal in the Fifth Judicial district authorized to hear and determine such writs. Joseph informed the lawyers that the nearest tribunal possessing such jurisdiction was the municipal court of the city of Nauvoo. This was found to be correct. A writ was sued out against Reynolds and Wilson, Joseph claiming $10,000 damages. The sheriff in charge took Reynolds and Wilson also into custody, and the company began to travel in the direction of Nauvoo.

Immediately after Joseph's arrest, William Clayton had been dispatched to Nauvoo, and Hyrum Smith, upon learning the condition of his brother, forthwith obtained over three hundred volunteers who immediately started in various directions through the state, they not knowing what direction Joseph might be compelled to travel. Also the steamboat Maid of Iowa, with Elder John Taylor and others on board, steamed down the Mississippi and up the Illinois River to Peru, then back to Nauvoo, to have an eye on steamboats and detect, if possible, any move that might be made to take Joseph to Missouri by such conveyance.

Joseph started from Dixon on the 26th of June. When about forty-five miles from that place, he began to meet the advance of the company from Nauvoo, when he said: "I am not going to Missouri this time. These are my boys." The joy that was felt by Joseph and his accompanying friends at this meeting was beyond description; but his brutal captors were seized with trembling and declared they would "never go to Nauvoo alive." The sheriff demanded their arms. They remonstrated, but finally delivered them to the sheriff.

On the 30th day of June, 1843, Joseph was met by the Nauvoo brass and martial bands, his wife, brother Hyrum and hundreds of citizens, who escorted him in triumph through the streets to his residence, while "Hail Columbia" was being played. His grounds were thrown open to receive the multitude that assembled to welcome their great leader, who, through God's interposing mercy, had once more triumphed and been permitted to reach his home and the protection of friends.

Joseph's table was sumptuously spread with every luxury, and Reynolds and Wilson were seated at the head of it and served with the utmost kindness by Mrs. Smith in person.

Once more the Prophet was free, and he, as well as the entire Church over which he presided, felt to thank the God of Israel for his deliverance. As he stepped inside of his enclosure, before washing or brushing away the dust with which his clothing was covered, he sprang quickly upon the fence and obtained a firm footing upon one of the gate posts which had quite a broad top. Then, taking off and swinging his hat, he exclaimed in a loud voice so that all might hear: "Hosannah! Hosannah! Hosannah! to God and the Lamb! I am once more delivered from the hands of the Missourians!"

A shout went up from the assembled thousands of his friends, and springing from the fence, he passed into his house to exchange happy greetings with the members of his family.

A full hearing of the case was had before the municipal court of Nauvoo, and Joseph was discharged.

—••••• *10* •••••—

The Prophet's Speech on His Arrest and Habeas Corpus

After Joseph Smith returned to Nauvoo, following his arrest by a Missouri official at Dixon, Illinois, in June 1843, he delivered a speech to the Mormon people who had welcomed him back in triumph. It reveals his resentment of the Missouri authorities and his determination to oppose them with military force if necessary. The speech also expressed his view of Nauvoo as a kind of city-state, loosely federated with Illinois, where Mormon power was absolute. "All the power there was in Illinois she gave to Nauvoo," he announced. Of course, no legislator in Illinois would have supported that view, nor was the habeas corpus provision in the Nauvoo Charter intended to allow the municipal court to free anyone arrested on state or federal charges. But Smith portrayed himself as the defender of the city's rights, and his listeners were enthralled.

This speech illustrates the importance of one characteristic feature of Smith's community—the mass meeting. Nauvoo was composed of old and new converts from many places, but by periodically listening to the prophet as part of a mass audience that represented his town and his church, his followers became unified members of a distinctive cultural group. They developed a Mormon consciousness, the key to which was their subjection to divine authority in the person of Joseph Smith. And he carefully directed that psychological transformation. The prophet encouraged his followers to view him in theocratic terms, as God's chosen leader of their separatist city-state, whose control of temporal affairs was appropriate and unquestionable because he spoke for God—"like Moses to the Children of Israel." And in this particular speech, when he called for a show of hands as an expression of support for his God-taught use of habeas corpus to escape from law officers and his listeners responded universally with "a sea of hands," he achieved the kind of mass surrender of the will upon which his theocratic government was actually based. Nauvoo was indeed "the City of Joseph," and as non-Mormons so readily believed, it was a clear threat to American democracy because it supplanted civil with theocratic authority.

And like so many of Smith's Nauvoo speeches, this one resonates with deeper meaning. It clearly embodies the Mormon myth of persecuted innocence ("innocent men" were being oppressed by "ungodly men"; the chosen people of "Israel" were beset by "hellish" and "unhallowed" enemies). That dichotomous vision was later employed to portray non-Mormon critics in the county and dissidents within the church as enemies of the righteous, and no concept promulgated by Smith at Nauvoo has had a more pervasive impact on the Mormon mind. This speech also reveals Smith's conception of himself as God's anointed champion, a strong "giant" who draws his strength from "God Almighty" and stands ready to lead his follow-ers in a holy battle and to die, if necessary.

Hence, the speech helped to forge the Mormons' sacred sense of identity, elevated Smith to heroic stature, and taught his followers to regard critics as the enemies of God. The speech is reprinted from Joseph Smith, Jr., *History of the Church of Jesus Christ of Latter-day Saints*, ed. B. H. Roberts (Salt Lake City: Deseret Book Co., 1909), 5:465–73. An unedited version is available in the journal of Wilford Woodruff as published in Andrew F. Ehat and Lyndon W. Cook, eds., *The Words of Joseph Smith: The Contemporary Accounts of the Nauvoo Discourses of the Prophet Joseph* (Provo, Utah: BYU Religious Studies Center, 1980), 216–22.

••••◉••••

The congregation is large. I shall require attention. I discovered what the emotions of the people were on my arrival at this city, and I have come here to say, "How do you do?" to all parties; and I do now at this time say to all "How do you do?" I meet you with a heart full of gratitude to Almighty God, and I presume you all feel the same. I am well—I am hearty. I hardly know how to express my feel-ings. I feel as strong as a giant. I pulled sticks with the men coming along, and I pulled up with one hand the strongest man that could be found. Then two men tried, but they could not pull me up, and I continued to pull, mentally, until I pulled Missouri to Nauvoo. But I will pass from that subject.

There has been great excitement in the country since Joseph H. Reynolds and Harmon T. Wilson took me; but I have been cool and dispassionate through the whole. Thank God, I am now a prisoner in the hands of the municipal court of Nauvoo, and not in the hands of Missourians.

It is not so much my object to tell of my afflictions, trials and troubles as to speak of the writ of habeas corpus, so that the minds of all may be corrected. It has been asserted by the great and wise men, lawyers and others, that our munici-pal powers and legal tribunals are not to be sanctioned by the authorities of the state; and accordingly they want to make it lawful to drag away innocent men from their families and friends, and have them put to death by ungodly men for their religion!

Relative to our city charter, courts, right of habeas corpus, etc., I wish you to know and publish that we have all power; and if any man from this time forth says any thing to the contrary, cast it into his teeth.

There is a secret in this. If there is not power in our charter and courts, then there is not power in the state of Illinois, nor in the congress or constitution of the United States; for the United States gave unto Illinois her constitution or charter, and Illinois gave unto Nauvoo her charters, ceding unto us our vested rights, which she has no right or power to take them from us. All the power there was in Illinois she gave to Nauvoo; and any man that says to the contrary is a fool.

The municipal court has all the power to issue and determine writs of habeas corpus within the limits of this city that the legislature can confer. This city has all the power that the state courts have, and was given by the same authority—the legislature.

I want you to hear and learn, O Israel, this day, what is for the happiness and peace of this city and people. If our enemies are determined to oppress us and deprive us of our constitutional rights and privileges as they have done, and if the authorities that are on the earth will not sustain us in our rights, nor give us that protection which the laws and constitution of the United States and of this state guarantee unto us, then we will claim them from a higher power—from heaven—yea, from God Almighty.

I have dragged these men here by my hand, and I will do it again; but I swear I will not deal so mildly with them again, for the time has come when forbearance is no longer a virtue; and if you or I are again taken unlawfully, you are at liberty to give loose to blood and thunder. But be cool, be deliberate, be wise, act with almighty power; and when you pull, do it effectively—make a sweep-stakes for once!

My lot has always been cast among the warmest hearted people. In every time of trouble, friends, even among strangers, have been raised up unto me and assisted me.

The time has come when the veil is torn off from the state of Illinois, and its citizens have delivered me from the state of Missouri. Friends that were raised up unto me would have spilt their life's blood to have torn me from the hands of Reynolds and Wilson, if I had asked them; but I told them no. I would be delivered by the power of God and generalship; and I have brought these men to Nauvoo, and committed them to her from whom I was torn, not as prisoners in chains, but as prisoners of kindness. I have treated them kindly. I have had the privilege of rewarding them good for evil. They took me unlawfully, treated me rigorously, strove to deprive me of my rights, and would have run with me into Missouri to have been murdered, if Providence had not interposed. But now they are in my hands; and I have taken them into my house, set them at the head of my table, and placed before them the best which my house afforded; and they were waited upon by my wife, whom they deprived of seeing me when I was taken.

I have no doubt but I shall be discharged by the municipal court. Were I before any good tribunal, I should be discharged, as the Missouri writs are illegal and good for nothing—they are "without form and void."

But before I will bear this unhallowed persecution any longer—before I will be dragged away again among my enemies for trial, I will spill the last drop of blood in my veins, and will see all my enemies in hell! To bear it any longer would be a sin, and I will not bear it any longer. Shall we bear it any longer? [One universal "No!" ran through all the vast assembly, like a loud peal of thunder.]

I wish the lawyer who says we have no powers in Nauvoo may be choked to death with his own words. Don't employ lawyers, or pay them money for their knowledge, for I have learned that they don't know anything. I know more than they all.

Go ye into all the world and preach the gospel. He that believeth in our chartered rights may come here and be saved; and he that does not shall remain in ignorance. If any lawyer shall say there is more power in other places and charters with respect to habeas corpus than in Nauvoo, believe it not. I have converted this candidate for congress [pointing to Cyrus Walker, Esq.] that the right of habeas corpus is included in our charter. If he continues converted, I will vote for him.

I have been with these lawyers and they have treated me well; but I am here in Nauvoo, and the Missourians too. I got here by a lawful writ of habeas corpus issued by the master in chancery of Lee County. . . . However indignant you may feel about the high handed oppression which has been raised against me by these men, use not the hand of violence against them, for they could not be prevailed upon to come here till I pledged them my honor and my life that a hair of their heads should not be hurt. Will you all support my pledge, and thus preserve my honor? [One universal "Yes!" burst from the assembled thousands.] This is another proof of your attachment to me. I know how ready you are to do right. You have done great things, and manifested your love toward me in flying to my assistance on this occasion. I bless you, in the name of the Lord, with all the blessings of heaven and earth you are capable of enjoying.

I have learned that we have no need to suffer as we have heretofore: we can call others to our aid. I know the Almighty will bless all good men: he will bless you; and the time has come when there shall be such a flocking to the standard of liberty as never has been or shall be hereafter. What an era has commenced! Our enemies have prophesied that we would establish our religion by sword. It is true? No. But if Missouri will not stay her cruel hand in her unhallowed persecutions against us, I restrain you not any longer. I say in the name of Jesus Christ, by the authority of the holy priesthood, I this day turn the key that opens the heavens to restrain you no longer from this time forth. I will lead you to the battle; and if you are not afraid to die, and feel disposed to spill your blood in your own defense, you will not offend me. Be not the aggressor: bear until they strike you on the one cheek; then offer the other, and they will be sure to strike that; then defend yourselves, and God shall bear you off, and you shall stand forth clear before his tribunal.

If any citizens of Illinois say we shall not have our rights, treat them as strangers and not as friends, and let them go to hell and be damned! Some say they will mob us. Let them mob and be damned! If we have to give up our chartered rights, privileges, freedom, which our fathers fought, bled, and died for, and which the constitution of the United States and of this state guarantee unto us, I will do it only at the point of the sword and bayonet.

Many lawyers contend for those things which are against the rights of men, and I can only excuse them because of their ignorance. Go forth and advocate the laws and rights of the people, ye lawyers. If not, don't get into my hands, or under the lash of my tongue.

Lawyers say the powers of the Nauvoo charter are dangerous; but I ask, is the constitution of the United States or of this state dangerous? No. Neither are the charters granted to Nauvoo by the legislature of Illinois dangerous, and those that say they are are fools. We have not enjoyed unmolested those rights which the constitution of the United States of America and our charters grant.

Missouri and all wicked men raise the hue-and-cry against us, and are not satisfied. Some political aspirants of this state also are raising the hue-and-cry that the powers in the charters granted unto the city of Nauvoo are dangerous; and although the general assembly have conferred them upon our city, yet the whine is raised—"Repeal them—take them away." Like the boy who swapped off his jack-knife, and then cried, "Daddy, daddy, I have sold my jack-knife and got sick of my bargain, and I want to get it back again."

But how are they going to help themselves? Raise mobs? And what can mobocrats do in the midst of Kirkpatrickites? No better than a hunter in the claws of a bear. If mobs come upon you any more here, dung your gardens with them. We don't want any excitement; but after we have done all, we will rise up, Washington-like, and break off the hellish yoke that oppresses us, and we will not be mobbed.

The day before I was taken at Inlet Grove, I rode with my wife through Dixon to visit some friends, and I said to her, "here is a good people." I felt this by the Spirit of God. The next day I was in their midst, in the hands of Reynolds, of Missouri, and Wilson, of Carthage. As the latter drove up, he exclaimed, "ha, ha, ha! By G——, we have got the Prophet now." He gloried much in it, but he is now our prisoner. When they came to take me, they held two cocked pistols to my head, and saluted me with—"G——d—— you, I'll shoot you! I'll shoot you, G——d—— you," repeating these threats nearly fifty times, from first to last. I asked them what they wanted to shoot me for. They said they would do it, if I made any resistance.

"Oh, very well," I replied; "I have no resistance to make." They then dragged me away, and I asked them by what authority they did these things. They said, "By a writ from the governors of Missouri and Illinois." I then told them I wanted a writ of habeas corpus. Their reply was, "G——d—— you, you shan't have it." I told a man to go to Dixon, and get me a writ of habeas corpus. Wilson then repeated, "G——d—— you, you shan't have it: I'll shoot you."

When we arrived at Dixon, I sent for a lawyer, who came; and Reynolds shut the door in his face, and would not let me speak to him, repeating, "G——d—— you, I'll shoot you." I turned to him, opened my bosom, and told him to "shoot away. I have endured so much persecution and oppression that I am sick of life. Why, then, don't you shoot and have done with it, instead of talking so much about it?"

This somewhat checked his insolence. I then told him that I would have counsel to consult, and eventually obtained my wish. The lawyers came to me, and I got a writ of habeas corpus for myself, and also a writ for Reynolds and Wilson for unlawful proceedings and cruel treatment towards me. Thanks to the good citizens of Dixon, who nobly took their stand against such unwarrantable and unlawful oppression, my persecutors could not get out of town that night, although, when they first arrived, they swore they should not remain in Dixon five minutes. . . .

The charter says that "the city council shall have power and authority to make, ordain, establish, and execute such ordinances not repugnant to the constitution of the United States, or of this state, as they may deem necessary, for the peace, benefit, and safety of the inhabitants of said city." And also that "the municipal court shall have power to grant writs of habeas corpus arising under the ordinances of the city council."

The city council have passed an ordinance "that no citizens of this city shall be taken out of this city by any writ, without the privilege of a writ of habeas corpus." There is nothing but what we have power over, except where restricted by the constitution of the United States. . . .

If these powers are dangerous, then the constitution of the United States and of this state are dangerous, but they are not dangerous to good men: they are only so to bad men who are breakers of the laws. So with the laws of the country, and so with the ordinances of Nauvoo: they are dangerous to mobs, but not to good men who wish to keep the laws.

We do not go out of Nauvoo to disturb anybody, or any city, town, or place. Why, then, need they be troubled about us? Let them not meddle with our affairs, but let us alone. After we have been deprived of our rights and privileges of citizenship, driven from town to town, place to place, state to state, with the sacrifice of our homes and lands, our blood has been shed, many having been murdered, and all this because of our religion—because we worship Almighty God according to the dictates of our own conscience, shall we longer bear these cruelties which have been heaped upon us for the last ten years in the face of heaven, and in open violation of the constitution and laws of these United States and of this state? God forbid! I will not bear it. If they take away my rights, I will fight for them manfully and righteously until I am used up. We have done nothing against the rights of others.

You speak of lawyers. I am a lawyer too; but the Almighty God has taught me the principle of law; and the true meaning and intent of the writ of habeas corpus is to defend the innocent and investigate the subject. Go behind the writ and if the form of one that is issued against an innocent man is right, he should [nevertheless] not be dragged to another state, and there be put to death, or be in jeopardy of life and limb, because of prejudice, when he is innocent. The benefits of the constitution and laws are alike for all; and the great Eloheim has given me the privilege of having the benefits of the constitution and the writ of habeas corpus; and I am bold to ask for that privilege this day, and I ask in the name of Jesus Christ, and all that is sacred, that I may have your lives and all your energies to carry out the freedom which is chartered to us. Will you all help me? If so, make it manifest by raising the right hand (There was a unanimous response, a perfect sea of hands being elevated). Here is truly a committee of the whole. . . .

If the legislature have granted Nauvoo the right of determining cases of habeas corpus, it is no more than they ought to have done, or more than our fathers fought for. Furthermore, if Missouri continues her warfare, and to issue her writs against me and this people unlawfully and unjustly, as she has done, and to take away and to trample upon our rights, I swear, in the name of Almighty God, and with uplifted hands to heaven, I will spill my heart's blood in our defense. They shall not take away our rights; and if they don't stop leading me by the nose, I will lead them by the nose; and if they don't let me alone, I will turn up the world—I will make war. When we shake our own bushes, we want to catch our own berries. The lawyers themselves acknowledge that we have all power granted us in our charters that we could ask for—that we had more power than any other court in the state; for all other courts were restricted, while ours was not; and I thank God Almighty for it. I will not be rode down to hell by the Missourians any longer; and it is my privilege to speak in my own defense; and I appeal to your integrity and honor that you will stand by and help me, according to the covenant you have this day made.

———— •••• 11 •••• ————

The State of Warsaw: A Lyceum Speech

In the fall of 1843 some residents of Warsaw formed a civic group called the Warsaw Legislature, which was devoted to formulating and espousing their political ideology. It was a lyceum in which people of the community, pretending that Warsaw was a separate state, acted as a democratic assembly to discuss current issues and propose possible legislation. Without question the organization was a response to Mormon influence in the county. By the fall of 1843 Smith's control of his followers had been repeatedly criticized, and most Hancock County offices were in the hands of church members or Mormon sympathizers. The lyceum was an attempt to reaffirm the republican values that Warsaw residents felt were threatened by the growth of political Mormonism.

William N. Grover was named "governor" of the organization. Born in New York in 1817, he had come to Warsaw in 1837, just a few years after the town had been founded, and he was noted for his patriotism and his speaking ability. Grover was admitted to the bar shortly after his arrival in Hancock County and was a successful lawyer for half a century thereafter. During the early 1850s he was a federal judge in St. Louis, but he later returned to Warsaw, where he served for many years as a justice of the peace. A leader in the Warsaw militia during the mid-1840s, he was at the Carthage jail when the Smith brothers were killed in June 1844.

On 17 November 1843, Grover gave a speech that he called his "inaugural" and laid out many of the democratic principles of the community. In a deeply mythic discussion of republicanism, he celebrated the rights of the individual and the democratic nature of American society and suggested that freedom was a sacred cause. He believed that personal liberty was essential and that strict limits must be set on governmental power. Grover subscribed to the Lockean precept that all authority rested with the people and was then delegated to the government in a compact. He also referred to the Mormons condescendingly as "Nephites" and showed the contempt that many in Hancock County were beginning to feel toward the sect because Smith and his followers did not accept that democratic precept and instead subscribed to a theocratic kingdom. The speech was first published in the *Warsaw Message*, 29 November 1843, pp. 1–2. A candid exposition of the myths of republican virtue and national destiny, in reponse to Mormonism's myths of persecuted innocence and zionic separatism, this speech helped set the stage for the contention between the two groups in the county.

———————•••●◉●●••———————

INAUGURAL of GOV. GROVER: At the First Session of the Warsaw Legislature, Held November 17, 1843.

Fellow citizens of the Senate and House of Representatives. . . .

Fortunately, we live in an age, when liberal principles have so far encroached upon the unhallowed assumptions of despotism, that it is no longer treason for the humblest citizen to express, freely and fully, his views of government, or sacrilege to aspire to the most dignified offices of the state. The capacity of the people for self-government is no longer a debatable proposition:—their RIGHT is one of the inalienable gifts of Deity.

In the exercise of this right, a noble race, children of far distant climes, impelled by an honorable spirit of enterprising adventure, have sought liberty and happiness in this fair prairie land, where but a few short years gone by, all was an uncultivated waste, & silence reigned unbroken, save by the fierce howl of the wolf, or the savage whoop of the red man, who roamed undisputed lord of the soil.—But the wilderness has been made to blossom—the howl of the wild bea[s]t, and the savage war cry, no longer echo on the stillness of night;— the untamable spirit of the wild hunter has found a more congenial home in the far-off regions of the Great West; and in this place we behold an enlightened people, peaceably and successfully prosecuting all the various pursuits of civilized life.

Gathered from nearly every state in the Union, and from many of the nations of the Old World;—born under different laws, and educated in different schools,—it would be strange, if we did not find great varieties of character. Without indulging in any invidious comparisons, it may be fairly presumed that all have their virtues and their faults: but in the assimilation which a few years must effect, it is not unreasonable to hope, that while their virtues will receive new luster from the conflict of opposing opinions, their vices will be lost with the identity of their origin.

With that indomitable love of civil and religious liberty, which acknowledges no restraints inconsistent with laws of conscience and moral right,—a perseverance that laughs at common difficulties, and yields to none,—exalted patriotism, untiring energies, and a peculiar independence of thought and action, combined with deep penetration and great natural shrewdness of character,—our people may be said to possess, in their highest degree, all the elements of true greatness.

And what country can be better adopted than our own, to the full development and efficient exercise of the capacities of such a people?

Unsurpassed in the fertility of her soil and the salubrity of her climate,—abounding in rich mineral resources,—unequalled in her natural facilities for easy and cheap intercommunications with other States,—she offers to the agriculturist, the artisan and the manufacturer, the surest rewards of well-disposed industry.

Her central position in the North American Republic,—about midway between the Atlantic and Pacific Oceans,—the mighty Father of Waters dividing in nearly equal divisions the great East from the great West, with his numerous tributaries flowing almost from the extremes of either section,— must eventually make the Mississippi Valley the grand depot of commerce and manufacturers—the center of science and of art—of learning and government. And our own fair State of Warsaw is the center of this great Valley!

Westward the Star of Empire has borne for centuries;—westward it still bears, and must, until it concentrates its glorious effulgence upon the State of Warsaw; and, unless in the long lapse of ages, the destroying hand of Time shall sweep every vestige of civilization from the land, here it will shine, and shine forever; and from Warsaw shall go forth the bright rays of moral and intellectual light, that shall guide the world to the fulfillment of her destiny!

Occupying this important position among the great Nations of the Earth,—bound, inevitably, to exercise a powerful control over their civil policy, their morals, and their learning; it becomes us as patriots and statesmen, to look well to it, that our institutions be based upon the most liberal and comprehensive principles, consistent with permanent justice and the natural rights and privileges of the people.

In conformity with the enlightened and independent spirit of the age, and the example of the older States, the people of Warsaw have expressed their preference for a representative government. Claiming all political power as inherent in themselves, they have delegated to you their authority to carry out the details of their policy. They have made you their servants, not their rulers:—from them you derive all your power and authority,—they will hold you responsible for the judicious use of the trust.

As the object of all legislation should be to secure the greatest good of the greatest number, in enacting such laws as you may deem necessary to promote the peace and prosperity of our young state, it should be your aim to employ the least possible coercion upon the will and action of the people.

The rights of conscience should be placed above all human laws; and such acts only as are wrong in themselves, impairing the natural rights of individuals or of society, should justify any restraints upon personal liberty. . . .

With regard to most of the general political questions that now agitate the country, it would perhaps be premature for me to recommend any particular course of action; it may not be improper, however, to suggest what seem to me, to be the great cardinal principles, that should govern our policy.

I deem it important to the interests of all classes—the agriculturalist, the mechanic, the merchant and the manufacturer, that we should have a well regulated paper currency, of fixed and uniform value throughout our whole territory; and controvertible into gold and silver, at the pleasure of the holder. To prevent sudden, and disastrous fluctuations in the prices of property, and the general operations of trade, it should be, as nearly as possible, uniform in amount as well as value. . . .

A railroad, or canal, around the rapids of the Mississippi River, to the Capital of His most Sublime Excellency, the President of the Nephites, is essentially important to the interests of that people, as well as ourselves! and I am extremely happy, to have it in my power to inform you, that His most Sublime Excellency the aforesaid President, is understood to have expressed his most gracious determination to put the work under construction as soon as the new palace for his Excellency, and his Excellency's most excellent family, and the temple for his Excellency's most excellent oxen, are fully complete; upon both of which some progress has already been made.

Our neighbors, the Nephites, furnish an example of military organization and discipline, worthy our imitation. As long as it remains the disposition of the strong to oppress the weak, the art of war should be cultivated, as well as the arts of peace. The only sure guaranty of our rights, is the power to resist wrong. At this time, we are without arms, and without any effective organization, totally unprepared to repel any invasion that might be made upon our property and liberties. I would recommend an early and thorough organization of our militia, under such regulations as you may deem proper,—as one of the most necessary and efficient means of preserving peace and good order at home, and with maintaining our present amicable relations with surrounding nations.

There are many matters of deep public interest, of which I have not thought it necessary to speak; as they will naturally suggest themselves, in the course of your deliberations, and I doubt not, receive their due share of your attention.

In conclusion I would beg leave, most respectfully, to urge upon each and all of you, whatever your politics, whether Whig, Democrat, or Tylerite, to lay aside all mere party considerations. It is a commendable—it is a holy ambition, that prompts the patriot to identify himself with his country's service, and the history of her glory! but that man, who, for the paltry honors of office, of the "loaves and fishes" of the state, will either yield a blind faith to the spotless purity of party leaders, and willing obedience to their dictates, or suffer himself to be bound down by the craven fear of party proscription, for presuming to think and act for himself—that man—if any such there be—is unworthy a seat within these walls. Governments are made for the governed. . . .

●●●● *12* ●●●●

A Neighboring County Becomes Alarmed

The emergence of the Mormons as the dominant political force in Hancock County and the stories about Joseph Smith bargaining for political favors by controlling Mormon votes had an impact on non-Mormons elsewhere in western Illinois. In the adjacent county to the east, McDonough, a resolution was adopted that reflected the growing alarm about the Mormon threat to democratic government. Although it may not have been published in 1842 or 1843 when it was first drafted—for McDonough County had no newspaper until 1851—the resolution was probably posted as a broadside. A copy of it was later found and printed in the *Macomb Journal*, 28 July 1870, p. 2.

The resolution was apparently passed at a special meeting of the McDonough County citizens, convened to discuss the Mormon issue in western Illinois. It expresses concern that a religious group, voting as its leaders direct, has gained political control of the adjoining county and predicts that the continued influx of Mormons into McDonough County "would inevitably lead to outrage and bloodshed, and their forcible expulsion." However, no violence occurred there, and when armed conflict finally did take place in Hancock County, McDonough County militia were not involved. Some five hundred volunteers did go to Carthage for a few days in June of 1844 to join the militia group that brought the Smith brothers in for trial and that reveals much about McDonough County's perspective. In any case, this document shows that by late 1842 or 1843 fear about Mormon subversion of democracy had spread beyond the limits of Hancock County.

●●●●●●●●●

In looking over some old papers, a short time since, we found a manuscript, of which the following is a copy. It bears no date, but carries evident marks of age. It was nicely folded up and marked on the back "Adopted." If any of our old settlers know anything about, or claim the manuscript, we should like to hear from them, but here is the document:

"The attention of the people of McDonough county, having been called to the fact that a large number of the people called Mormons, have recently settled in the county, and it being understood and believed that many others are preparing to come, we, who are now assembled, deem it proper to warn all such, that there exists a strong and deep rooted dislike, an antipathy amounting to detestation, which is constantly spreading and increasing on the part of our citizens, towards that mis-guided, most troublesome, and ambitious people. We have been attentive observers, for some years, of their conduct; we have seen them come into our State, not as peaceable individuals, not as good citizens disposed to yield a cheerful and ready obedience to the laws, but as a *sect* affecting to hold themselves aloof from, and superior to others, and to act as a *sect*, or a politico-religious body. We are well assured that there are amongst them, a large proportion of dishonest, unprincipled, desperate characters, and though we would not hold a whole people responsible for the misdeeds of a few, yet it is notorious and within the personal knowledge of some of us, that the authorities and leaders as well as the mass of their people have, in numerous instances, gone to unwarrantable heights in shielding and protecting individuals accused of crimes, and fugitives from justice. From their first coming amongst us, they have shown a disposition to violate and set at defiance the laws and authority of the State, and their audacity in this and all other respects had kept pace with the increase of their number, and the impunity, which unfortunately even for themselves, attended their outrages. True to their clannish, sectarian and ambitious spirit, we have seen them turn the elective franchise into mockery, and that for the avowed purpose of making their power in numbers, and, as a body, felt and feared—to be dreaded or courted in the future, as the case might be; thus setting the pernicious, demoralizing example—the first instance in America of a body professedly religious, acting as a band of mercenary troops, in throwing their power and weight, without regard to the merits of the contest, to that side which will pay the best. All other sects allow their members to vote as to each seems right; but here is a body of some thousands, so lost to their sacred duties as American citizens, as to prostitute themselves, in voting as their leaders direct.

"There is another trait in this people's character, most alarming to us. They have shown, in Hancock county, most unequivocally, their determination, not only to keep themselves distinct as a body, but, also, to avail themselves of the superior numerical strength they possess, to monopolize the county offices, thus betraying their lust for civil and political power. It is well known that the offices in Hancock are now in their hands, or under their influence. Our citizens enquire, shall we sit still and see the same calamity overtake us, or shall we prevent it while it may yet be done? They believe that such an ascendancy would be intolerable, that it would be subversive of our industry and prosperity, and destructive of all peace and harmony. Earnestly deprecating such a state of things, we, as a portion of the citizens, convened in public meeting, feel not only authorized, but bound to say and proclaim on the behalf of the good people of this county, that so hostile already are the sentiments and feelings of the people to the Mormons, that the coming of any considerable more, would inevitably lead to outrage and bloodshed, and their forcible expulsion. And we would recommend, more especially, those recently settled here, to leave as soon as they possibly can, for should the catastrophe happen, which we deem certain should Mormons continue to come, all of the sect, whether recent or old settlers, would be involved in the general calamity."

―――――●●● *13* ●●●――――

Concerns about Mormon Despotism: An 1844 Historical Account

Perhaps the earliest historical account of the conflict between Mormons and non-Mormons in Hancock County was published shortly after the death of Joseph Smith and his brother at the hands of an anti-Mormon mob in Carthage. Written by George T. M. Davis (1810–?) of Alton, Illinois, just north of St. Louis on the Mississippi River, it was entitled *An Authentic Account of the Massacre of Joseph Smith, the Mormon Prophet, and Hyrum Smith, His Brother, Together with a Brief History of the Rise and Progress of Mormonism, and All the Circumstances Which Led to Their Death* (St. Louis: Chambers and Knapp, 1844). Davis was born in Valletta, Malta, where his father was U.S. consul-general to the Regency of Tripoli. He later studied law at Syracuse, New York, and then in 1832 moved to Alton. Davis was a well-known lawyer and was also coeditor of the *Alton Telegraph and Democratic Review* during the Mormon era in Hancock County. Moreover, he was mayor of Alton from 1844 to 1846, when it was among the leading communities in the state. He later served in the Mexican War, worked in Washington for the War Department, and became a railroad executive.

Davis studied the Mormon conflict while it was developing. He even traveled to Hancock County, where he spent much of June 1844, obtaining documents and conducting interviews. He sent some reports to the Alton newspaper, but he may have had plans for a separately published historical account even before the killings in Carthage. Although convinced that Smith was a charlatan, Davis was not primarily concerned with countering his religious influence. Rather, he portrays the prophet as a power-hungry leader whose governance of the Mormons was despotic. As the following excerpt reveals, he had even heard about the secret Council of Fifty, which had started planning for the creation of a political kingdom of God in America and had ordained Smith king in a coronation ceremony.

However one-sided his historical account may be, Davis was not motivated by religious bigotry but by political anxiety. As such, he reveals much about the non-Mormon mind in the period leading to the violence at Carthage. The section printed here comes from *An Authentic Account*, 5–9.

―――――●●●●●●――――

Shortly after the settlement of the Mormons at Nauvoo, in consequence of the principle inculcated by the Prophet, that they were to *be one* in all things, in the disposition of all their suffrages, as well as every thing else, their numbers daily augmenting, and holding the balance of power in Hancock county, they became the *special favorites* of politicians of both sides in their vicinity. Joe seeing the advantage of his position, and correctly judging that great importance was attached by political aspirants of both parties, to the favor or prejudice with which he regarded the one side or the other, applied to the Legislature of Illinois, for various incorporations. Among them, was a charter incorporating Nauvoo into a city, with the privilege of organizing its inhabitant into a military corps, to be designated the Nauvoo Legion, who were to be exclusively under the control of the authorities of the city of Nauvoo, and in no way subject to the Militia Laws of the State, save in the case of war or rebellion. They also had the power of establishing a court of record, to be denominated the Municipal Court of the City of Nauvoo, the presiding officers of which, were to be the Mayor and Aldermen of said city. This court had also the power given to it, to issue the writ of habeas corpus, and to determine, under its exercise, all cases that might arise under the ordinances of the city. There were many other powers granted by this charter, which were extraordinary in their character, oppressive in their operations, and in direct conflict with the spirit and letter of the Constitution. But such was the desire of both parties in the Legislature to secure the political co-operation of this unprincipled despot and knave, as well as his followers, that all their charters were passed *sub silentio*, and without undergoing even the form of reading before either House. It is true, the charters were regularly referred to the appropriate standing committees, and that those committees reported favorably to their passage. Yet that furnishes *no excuse* for the action of the two Houses, in granting to a religious sect, powers and privileges, which no other denomination of christians would dare to ask, and which, if they did ask, would most assuredly have had their application neglected. The capability of those bestowing these charters is rendered more inexcusable, from the fact that during that session, other religious denominations could scarcely procure a single charter, at the hands of the majority, merely incorporating them into a body capable of holding the real estate upon which their buildings were erected, through the *morbid sensibility* that it favored too much, at this *democratic* period, of a union of Church and State; but Joe Smith, as the founder and Prophet of the Latter Day Saints, could ask and receive any legislative boon he pleased. From the hour that the inhabitants of Nauvoo organized under their charter, established their court, marshalled their Legion into a separate and distinct military corps, from the residue of the militia of the State, and commenced promulgating through the public press at that place, the ordinances which their Common Council passed, under the real or *assumed* powers contained in their charter, the jealousy and well founded fears of the citizens, or at least many of them, were aroused. They feared that, sooner or later, disasters the most lamentable would result from the importance that had been attached to Joe Smith, and the exercise, as well as abuse, of the powers which the Legislature had clothed him with. The late fatal termination of his, as well as his brother's life, and the consequences leading to it, show, that those fears were not without reasonable foundation.

The contemplated limits of this work will not admit of my going into detail, and exposing as minutely as I deem the importance of the subject demands, the unheard of character of the ordinances passed by the Common Council of Nauvoo, the powers exercised by the Prophet under them, and the length to which he went in obtaining unlimited control over the actions, and I may say *the minds* of his followers. The greatest difficulty I apprehend is, that even in what I shall develop, and which I have obtained from the most reputable and intelligent of those heretofore connected with the "*Saints*," as well as others who know, the reflecting and intelligent portion of the world will look upon these developments with distrust. And when I reflect that it is in the nineteenth century, that the revolting and extraordinary scenes have been enacted, which have marked the progress of Joe Smith since his settlement in Illinois, I ought not to wonder that the *statement of the truth* would be received by those unacquainted with the facts, and beyond the limits of personal observation, with distrust, if not entire disbelief.

The great aim of Joseph Smith was evidently to cloth himself with the most unlimited power, civil, military and ecclesiastical, over all who became members of his society. And to that end his whole efforts were put in requisitions from the day of their organization under their charters, down to the hour of his death. The first step taken by him, was to satisfy his people that he had received a revelation from God, disclosing his origin as well as that of his wife, and detailing the events that were to occur, as well as the part he and his descendants were to take, in their consummation. This he succeeded in, and gave the following as the substance of his revelation. He stated that Emma his wife, was of Indian descent, in a line from one of the tribes of Israel. That he (Joseph) was a descendant from Joseph of old through the blood of Ephraim. And that God had appointed and ordained that he, with his descendants, should rule over all Israel, meaning the Latter Day Saints or Mormons, the Indian tribes and ultimately the Jews and Gentiles. That the authority with which God had clothed him, being "*Jure Divino*," extended over all mankind, and was paramount and superior to any Human authority. Joe further stated, that God had revealed to him, that the Indians and Latter Day Saints, under Joe as their King and Ruler, were to conquer the Gentiles, and that their subjection to this authority was to be obtained *by the sword!* From this revelation, he enforced upon them that it was necessary he should be crowned King, and they, believing in the gross imposition, yielded to his edict. Joe was accordingly crowned KING under God, over the immediate house of Israel. This ceremony was performed in 1842, by a council of fifty in number, denominated the "ANCIENT OF DAYS." And thenceforward his authority as such was recognized and obeyed by the church and its authority in all respects and under all circumstances. The peculiar attributes of his power, Joe insisted, were—that he could direct the actions of the entire House of Israel—that they were bound to obey his commands, *whatever they might be*—and that finally the whole earth was to become under subjection to him. He further impressed upon the council crowning him, that God's desire was, as revealed to him, (Joe,) that, for the time being, this was to remain a *perfect secret* until God should reveal to the contrary. And accordingly Joe swore them all to present secrecy, *under the penalty of death!* It is also a fact, ascertained beyond controversy, that the Indian tribes of Sacs and Foxes, Siouxs and Potowattamies, were consulted, and their assent obtained previous to the *mock* crowning of this unmitigated Impostor, and that delegations were sent to Nauvoo from each of the above tribes about the time of the ceremony being performed, by the council of fifty. These delegations of Indians were seen by hundreds and hundreds at Nauvoo, but the object of their visitation never was ascertained without the pale of the church, until secessions commenced taking place from the Mormons.

The reader may naturally inquire, how these facts have been ascertained. I state, from the only *sources possible* to derive information; that is, from those who aided in the ceremony, but who have since returned to their reason and come out from among this den of wicked and perverse men. It is stated upon the authority of one who was a member of the High Council of the Church, and first council to the Presidency of the Church, a man in whom all (in no way connected with Mormonism,) who have conversed with him, have much confidence. I state unhesitatingly, upon the best authority, that the above facts in regard to the crowning of Joe, the revelation he professed to have received, and his swearing those entrusted with taking part, to secrecy, *under penalty of death*, would all have been proved upon their trial for treason, by at least two witnesses, unless—as I do not believe—they had sworn entirely contrary to what their statements had been, not only to the Council but to the Governor of the State.

All will concede that the power and influence which Joe wielded over the minds, and actions of his followers, must have been unlimited in the extreme, if, as had been shown, he was able to secure his coronation as King, in this land of liberty and equal rights, whose citizens acknowledge no other King than He in whose hands are the destinies of all nations. Neither can it be denied, such must have been the confidence reposed in him, that no matter what the requisition made of them, if done under his *kingly authority*, and as the Prophet of the Lord, that requisition would be faithfully obeyed. All his actions and conduct since, prove such to be the case. In addition to the power conferred upon him by this coronation, he occupied the highest military station, that of Lieutenant General of the Nauvoo Legion. He was also Mayor of the city, (with the exception of one year that H[on]. [John C.] Bennett filled that office,) from its organization to the day of his death. He and his Common Council composed the bench that presided in their Municipal Court, and as Mayor he became the chief presiding officer of that court. He was the trustee of the Church of Latter Day Saints, and held in his name the title to their real estate, and was the depository of the funds belonging to the church. In addition to all this, he held the funds of many of his followers, (especially the foreigners,) who came to Nauvoo with money. This fact I ascertained from a source that admits of no cavil or doubt. Under our revenue laws, every person, in surrendering to the assessor a list of his or her property, has to state under oath, if required by the assessor, the amount of cash on hand or the sums loaned out by them. The assessor, for a previous year, informed me that between thirty and forty thousands were listed by different persons in Nauvoo, as being by them deposited with Joseph Smith; and that the sums thus reported, were assessed and taxes collected upon the same. He further stated as his opinion, that not *one half* the sums put in the hands of Joe Smith, by the inhabitants of Nauvoo, were ever reported by them to him. Thus it will be seen, that the church, the military, and the judiciary, as well as the Common Council of Nauvoo, were solely and entirely under his unlimited control. And the first great step towards making him a DES-POT, had been acquired by him, the union of the purse and the sword, and the mingling of the civil and ecclesiastical governments. Nauvoo was, to all intents and purposes, a separate and distinct Government, acknowledging no superior power to their own, and assuming to themselves the power to make their own laws and administer them in their own way. The character of their ordinances show this beyond controversy.

They have defined *by ordinance* what shall constitute slander and what shall be the mode of redress and extent of the punishment. They have abridged the freedom of speech, by declaring by ordinance, that if any person *shall speak disrespectfully* of any of the Latter Day Saints, that person shall be liable to prosecution, and upon conviction, shall be fined a sum not exceeding five hundred dollars, and *imprisoned* for a time not to exceed six months. They have provided by ordinance, that no man should be taken without the limits of the City of Nauvoo, upon any charge or process issuing from any court, either State or Federal, until that person had first been brought before the Municipal Court, by writ of Habeas Corpus, and his guilt or innocence determined there; and that if the judgment of the court was in favor of the accused, he should *be discharged.* Under this ordinance Joe Smith, when arrested upon process issuing from the Courts of this State, as also upon requisitions from the Governor of Missouri, has caused himself to be taken before the Municipal Court of which *he was the presiding officer,* and DISCHARGED FROM ARREST! . . . Other ordinances, equally as obnoxious, and repugnant to the genius and spirit of our republican institutions, have been passed and put in force by the Prophet and his hirelings; but the limits prescribed for this publication will not admit of my going further into detail. I regret my inability to procure a copy of those ordinances, to attach them to this publication. But they cannot be procured, and for reasons best known to the Mormons themselves. I was informed by Gov. Ford, that he had *twice* made application to the Common Council of the City of Nauvoo, as the Executive of the State of Illinois, for true copies of all their ordinances, but that his applications had proven unsuccessful, and his request was not complied with. That they (the Mormons,) grossly violated the constitution of the State and trampled upon the rights of those who differed from them, whose persons or property were within the limits of Nauvoo, can admit of no doubt.

Joseph Smith's home in Nauvoo, known as the Nauvoo Mansion House. It was built in 1843 at the corner of Water and Main streets, in the southern part of town and near the Mississippi. Before moving to the Mansion, Smith and his family had lived in a log cabin across the street. Photograph of the modern restoration by Roger D. Launius.

PART III

THE TROUBLE IN NAUVOO

John C. Bennett in the uniform of the Nauvoo Legion in 1842. Frontispiece from John C. Bennett, *History of the Saints* (Boston: Leland and Whiting, 1842). Courtesy of the Library-Archives, Reorganized Church of Jesus Christ of Latter Day Saints, the Auditorium, Independence, Missouri.

———— •••• PART III •••• ————

INTRODUCTION

No aspect of the Mormon conflict has been less thoroughly and critically examined than the developments within Nauvoo in 1843 and 1844 that led to dissent, repression, and violence.[1] For too long the trouble in Nauvoo has been understated rather than understood. The vast majority of scholars interested in Mormon history have been believing Latter-day Saints for whom the Mormon past is a sacred drama, and a thoroughgoing scholarly examination of the assertions, conflicts, and events that culminated in the *Expositor* affair inevitably challenges cherished Mormon conceptions of the past. These scholars, honest in intent and sound in methodology, have seldom explored beyond the safe boundaries of the Latter-day Saint faith story to analyze the *Expositor* affair for what it was, an ethical protest by some Nauvoo church members against what they believed was oppression from an ecclesiastical institution gone awry. Such an interpretation undermines the Mormon myth of innocence, the image of virtuous Saints being persecuted by an immoral mob.

While a thorough discussion of Mormon myth is beyond the scope of this introduction, some commentary is essential to understanding the development of the trouble in Nauvoo. In particular, the myth of innocence, which is ubiquitous in the Mormon documents of this period, reveals that the retreat from American religious pluralism to the theocratic separatist community of Nauvoo represented an escape from moral ambiguity, the fear of making the wrong choices.[2] As a religious city-state under tight control, Nauvoo was a haven where the followers of Joseph Smith had their most important choices—what they should do to serve God—made for them. They went on missions, worked on the temple, and served in various church offices at the prophet's direction. Also, their devotion to the Mormon millennium was defined by Smith, and their identity as God's chosen people was assured through him. Their innocence was thus guaranteed, and their potential for evil was minimized.

As is common in such situations, the threat of evil was projected onto others—in this case the Gentiles, who were regarded as ungodly enemies.[3] Another way of saying the same thing is that a chosen people always defines itself against an unchosen opposite, and through that mythic dichotomy, differences in human culture (beliefs, values) are transmuted into differences in human nature (the good versus the evil). Hence, at Nauvoo the innocent children of God realized their identity through their struggle against the evil followers of Satan, who dominated American society everywhere except in the city of the Saints.

The problem, of course, with this kind of dichotomous myth is that, for the people who hold it, guilt and innocence become matters of belief, not evidence.[4] Thus, at Nauvoo Joseph Smith could engage in secret polygamy, lie to his followers about it, and when accusations were made against him, he could go into a public meeting, denounce his accusers, and be regarded by the Mormons as a persecuted innocent. He could repress the civil rights of his critics, denying them due process of law, freedom of the press, and the right to promote their own church unmolested, and then be celebrated by his followers as a champion of righteousness, protecting the innocent community of believers. And the identity of the Mormons as the inherently innocent, and of Smith as the archetype of Mormon innocence, was verified in the process.[5]

Conversely, men of integrity who criticized the prophet, such as William and Wilson Law, could be defamed as enemies of the people and instantly regarded—to quote Willard Richards—as "thieves, counterfeiters, bogus-makers, gamblers, debauchers, murderers, and all that is vile" (Part III, Document 14). The dissenters, by their very act of disagreeing, were cast out of the ranks of the inherently innocent and transmuted in the Mormon mind into the inherently evil. Dissidents were always characterized as misbegotten, woeful malcontents whose arguments were without foundation. The problem had to be with their own characters, not with the church or its leadership. Often dissenters were accused of personal sins and their private lives laid open to the public. If no sins were apparent, they might be trumped up. Crimes real and imagined were described in a depth not seen except in the most vicious political campaigns.

The dissenters, because of supposed flaws in their characters, were threats to the integrity of the gospel and deserved expulsion. The institution was always judged to be sound and the dissidents defective. Commenting on this practice, one historian has concluded:

> Defectors became a kind of bogey to haunt all inhabitants of the Mormon kingdom. Without vigilance and strength of character they [other members], like the defectors, could become overwhelmed by the baseness of their character and, thus, open to Satan's enticements. In this way blame was shifted from the kingdom to the individual defector. More importantly, dissent was portrayed as the outward sign of personal weakness and sin. Dissent, therefore, could no more be tolerated than sin itself. This attitude within the kingdom militated against any legitimate expression of doubt. There was no loyal opposition within the kingdom of God. As no dissent from orthodox opinion was allowed, either the inhabitant accepted it or he was compelled to withdraw.[6]

This process served as a defense mechanism for Mormonism in the 1840s and greatly contributed to the trouble in Nauvoo.

This mythic shift, the transmutation of the dissenters from innocent to evil, justified any and all acts of aggression on the part of the church against them, including destroying the Nauvoo *Expositor* press and building, setting fire to other dissidents' buildings, threatening their lives, and forcing them to flee from their homes into Iowa Territory.[7] Of course, the tragic irony in all this is that the myth of innocence prevented the Mormons from learning anything about the need to respect the rights of others from their own violent expulsion from Missouri. So they reenacted it, with themselves in the role of the aggressors.

At the same time, non-Mormons and dissenters developed their own myth of innocence and rectitude. Because they were reacting against an oppressive, anti-democratic force in the county, they believed they were totally innocent of any wrongdoing. Instead they were acting in defense of the cherished principles of the American Revolution. Using rhetorical arguments that went back to that time, some Hancock Countians justified their actions against the Mormons, even violent ones, as necessary to avoid subjugation to the theocracy of Mormon Nauvoo. Local residents put forward a coherent, if ill-informed, conspiracy theory that the Mormons intended to rob Americans of their democratic rights. Ultimately, they argued that a grand plot was under way to enslave Americans and that they had to stand together to defend their liberties and defeat a determined oppressor.[8]

The fascinating array of Mormon and non-Mormon documents in Part III reveals various facets of this unfortunate process. At the same time, they show how deeply the prophet's sense of innate authority and narrow focus on his own religious/political purposes brought him into conflict with a larger American democratic ideal, where conformity of belief was not the proof of innocence, and criticism of authority was not the sign of evil. And the documents reveal much about the power of myth to unify the members of a cultural group, give meaning to their lives, and control their perception of reality.

Notes

1. As an example of the inattention given to this matter in church histories, Leonard J. Arrington and Davis Bitton, in *The Mormon Experience: A History of the Latter-day Saints* (New York: Alfred A. Knopf, 1979), 77–78, devote only one short paragraph to the whole topic of dissent at Nauvoo and the destruction of the *Expositor*. None of Smith's critics are named, nor are their purposes, views, or rights considered. Even article-length studies frequently ignore such key matters as the formation of the Reformed Mormon Church, the wide-ranging critique of Smith and the Mormon theocracy in the *Expositor*, and the forcing of the dissenters from the community. See, for example, George R. Gaylor, "The 'Expositor' Affair: Prelude to the Downfall of Joseph Smith," *Northwest Missouri State College Studies* 25 (February 1961): 3–15, and Dallin H. Oaks, "The Suppression of the Nauvoo *Expositor*," *Utah Law Review* 9 (Winter 1965): 862–903. For more recent studies that relate the dissent at Nauvoo to the overall ideological clash between Mormons and non-Mormons, see John E. Hallwas, "Mormon Nauvoo from a Non-Mormon Perspective," *Journal of Mormon History* 16 (1990): 53–69; Kenneth H. Winn, *Exiles in a Land of Liberty: Mormons in America, 1830–1846* (Chapel Hill: University of North Carolina Press, 1989); and Lyndon W. Cook, *William Law: Biographical Essay, Nauvoo Diary, Correspondence, Interview* (Orem, Utah: Grandin Book Co., 1994).

2. For a discussion of this psychological process, see Rollo May, *Freedom and Destiny* (New York: W. W. Norton and Co., 1981), especially 121–22, 227–28. Also relevant is Erich Fromm's classic study, *Escape from Freedom* (New York: Holt, Rinehart, and Winston, 1941). This escape from pluralism is the theme of Marvin S. Hill, *Quest for Refuge: The Mormon Flight from American Pluralism* (Salt Lake City: Signature Books, 1989).

3. This psychosocial process was common under similar circumstances during the Middle Ages. See Norman Cohn, *The Pursuit of the Millennium* (Fairlawn, N.J.: Essential Books, 1957), 69–74. For discussions that focus on repression, pseudoinnocence, scapegoating, and similar matters from a Jungian perspective, see Connie Zweig and Jeremiah Abrams, eds., *Meeting the Shadow: The Hidden Power of the Dark Side of Human Nature* (Los Angeles: Jeremy P. Tarcher, 1991), especially the essays in pt. 7, "Devils, Demons, and Scapegoats: A Psychology of Evil."

4. The persistence of this mythic perspective in Mormon culture has been noted by at least one scholar, who has discussed the challenges to freedom among modern church members in Utah. Without referring explicitly to myth, Waldemer P. Read has commented, "The local culture penalizes the reluctant believer by holding him suspect as to character. Too frequently, it is assumed that an attitude of skepticism or of unbelief is a sign of moral turpitude and of spiritual rebellion. For too many, the idea that an unbeliever may be a good man is quite unthinkable." From "What Freedom Is Found in Local Culture?" *Great Issues Concerning Freedom*, ed. Waldemer P. Read (Salt Lake City: University of Utah Press, 1962), 126.

5. On this issue, see Richard S. Van Wagoner, "Mormon Polyandry in Nauvoo," *Dialogue: A Journal of Mormon Thought* 18 (Fall 1985): 67–83; Richard S. Van Wagoner, "Sarah M. Pratt: The Shaping of a Mormon Apostate," *Dialogue: A Journal of Mormon Thought* 19 (Summer 1986): 69–99; "Epistle of Wm. Marks," *Zion's Harbinger and Baneemy's Organ* (St. Louis), July 1853, p. 53; William Marks to Isaac Sheen, 23 October 1859, in *True Latter Day Saints Herald* (Cincinnati) 1 (January 1860): 22–23.

6. Gordon D. Pollock, "In Search for Security: The Mormons and the Kingdom of God on Earth, 1830–1844" (Ph.D. diss., Queen's University, 1977), 292–93.

7. A similar process took place in Europe during the fifteenth, sixteenth, and seventeenth centuries as heretics were transmuted into enemies of the Christian public and therefore of God, who were then purged from their communities as witches. See Norman Cohn, *Europe's Inner Demons* (New York: Basic Books, 1975), and Alan McFarlane, *Witchcraft in Tudor and Stuart England* (New York: Harper and Row, 1970), especially 158–64, 192–206. Certainly the most well-known example of repression and projection, leading to purgation, in American history is the infamous witchcraft persecution in Salem, Massachusetts, which occurred in a similar theocratic, authoritarian, anxiety-ridden context. See Paul Boyer and Stephen Nissenbaum, *Salem Possessed: The Social Origins of Witchcraft* (Cambridge, Mass.: Harvard University Press, 1974), especially 212–16.

8. On the theme of slavery, see William J. Cooper, Jr., *Liberty and Slavery: Southern Politics to 1860* (New York: Alfred A. Knopf, 1983), 28–46.

—••• *1* •••—

John C. Bennett's Exposé

The most explosive issue within Nauvoo was polygamy, and the man who brought it to public attention was John Cook Bennett (1804–67). Born in Fairhaven, Massachusetts, he received a license to practice medicine in Ohio in 1825. Although he claimed to have degrees from the University of Ohio at Athens and a medical college in Montreal, existing records do not support his assertions. After attempting to start colleges in Ohio, Virginia, Indiana, and Pennsylvania, Bennett moved to Illinois, leaving behind a wife and two children in Ohio. He later received a divorce. Bennett settled at Fairfield in southern Illinois, where he incorporated a volunteer military company and had himself appointed brigadier general. By 1840 he was directing the state medical association and had been appointed quartermaster general of the state militia.

Always opportunistic, Bennett saw a chance to get ahead by helping the Mormons who were coming as refugees into Illinois. In 1840 he moved to Nauvoo and ingratiated himself with Joseph Smith, who was impressed with his persona and powerful connections in the state. Bennett demonstrated his considerable organizational ability and leadership on behalf of the Mormons in the fall of 1840 by spearheading the effort to guide the Nauvoo city charter through the state legislature. He then helped to organize the Nauvoo Legion and secured arms from the state arsenal. After these successes, Joseph Smith was even more impressed with the sophisticated physician/politician/businessman/army officer, and he rewarded him with great power and influence in Nauvoo, something that Bennett apparently craved more than anything else. Smith made Bennett a major general in the Nauvoo Legion and helped him win the election as mayor of the city early in 1841. Soon afterward, Stephen A. Douglas appointed him master in chancery for Hancock County. No one else in Nauvoo had risen so quickly.

But Bennett's fall was just as rapid. He and Smith soon quarreled over a variety of issues. They became rivals in several arenas—church business, city issues, political activities, sexual escapades—and the clashes soon became overpowering. By May 1842, a public break had taken place, both Bennett and Smith charging each other with all types of crimes. There can be no doubt that sexual politics played a key role, as each accused the other of indiscretions. Smith's powerful position as prophet ensured that he won the battle for the allegiance of the citizens of Nauvoo, however, and Bennett fled the town. He then set about to expose Smith in speeches across the state and letters to Illinois newspapers.

Bennett, of course, knew about Joseph Smith's most volatile theological innovation, the concept of plural marriage. Gossip about the practice had swirled about Mormonism since the mid-1830s—an 1835 General Conference had even adopted a resolution explicitly denying the charge—but the practice emerged full blown in Nauvoo during the early 1840s. By the time of Bennett's disaffection,

Smith had married no fewer than eight women, and because of his close association with Smith, Bennett knew about some of these liaisons. He was especially
aware of the marriage of Joseph Smith to Louisa Beaman on 5 April 1841, and
even mentioned it in his 1842 book-length exposé of the church.

Smith wanted desperately to keep plural marriage a secret, however, and took
steps to ensure that no one would violate the confidence. If he was not sure of
some followers' loyalty, and therefore silence, the prophet apparently attempted to
coerce them or to destroy their credibility. Bennett, whose reputation was not
exactly clean anyway, became the target of a smear campaign in Nauvoo. He was
charged with everything from rape to attempted murder, and his character has
been sullied ever since. While there is certainly some truth to the charges made by
Joseph Smith against John Bennett in 1842, some of them were mere fabrications.
He became a scapegoat for secret polygamy—seduction, deception, and hypocrisy.

Even though some of them were probably untrue, especially those concerning sexual improprieties, Bennett countered with his own set of charges against
Joseph Smith. Many of his descriptions of the evolution of Mormon theocracy,
temple endowments, and plural marriage have proved to be pretty much on the
mark. Within days of leaving Nauvoo, Bennett launched into an exposé of
Mormonism on the lecture circuit and in newspapers and magazines. His series of
four letters to an Illinois newspaper, the *Sangamo Journal*, were soon expanded
into a book, *The History of the Saints; or, An Exposé of Joe Smith and Mormonism*
(Boston: Leland and Whitney, 1842). The core of the book was a discussion of
plural marriage, or "spiritual wifery," and its frankness scandalized non-Mormon
readers and convinced many that Smith was involved in secret sexual activity with
various women. Bennett boldly named people who could attest to the truth of his
assertions, and he included some documents, including a letter Smith had sent to
Nancy Rigdon, urging her to put aside her objections and engage in polygamous
relations with him. The prophet flatly denied any wrongdoing, however, and most
Mormons believed him.

The document that follows is one of the letters by Bennett, written from
Carthage to Simeon Francis, editor of the Springfield *Sangamo Journal*, where it
appeared on 5 July 1842, p. 3. The entire series had an enormous influence on the
non-Mormons surrounding Nauvoo and made them question the moral fabric of
Mormonism.

July 2, A.D. 1842

To the Editor of the Journal,

I am now in this place, in order to attend to some of my official duties, as
Master in Chancery; and having some leisure time, I shall proceed with my history
of Joe Smith and his Saints.—It is my determination to state *facts*, and such facts
as will arous[e] the public indignation, if there is yet virtue and courage left in

man—for we are exhorted to be enterprising and courageous—but the *beast* and *false prophet* (Joe Smith) shall tremble in the days of his captivity like an aspen leaf in the wilderness. The "Lord's anointed," as Joe is called, must be washed in the *laver of the law* until his polluted carcass, and corrupt soul, shall be purified by fire. And to begin:

1st. THE DURESSE.—On the 17th day of May, A.D. 1842, Joe Smith requested to see me alone in the preparation room of the Nauvoo Lodge, U.D., on some important business. We entered, and he locked the door, put the key in his pocket, and drew a pistol on me and said— "The peace of my family requires that you should sign an affidavit, and make a statement before the next City Council, on the 19th, exonerating me from all participation whatever, either directly or indirectly, in word or deed, in the *spiritual wife* doctrine, or private intercourse with females in general; and if you do not do it with apparent cheerfulness, I will make *catfish bait* of you, or deliver you to the Danites for execution tonight—for my dignity and purity must and shall be maintained before the public, even at the expense of life,—will you do it or die?" I replied that he had better procure some other person or persons to do so, as there were a plenty who could do it in *truth*. "No," said he, "that will not do—for it is known that you are well acquainted with all my private acts, better than any other man, and it is in your power to save me or damn me; and as you have now withdrawn from the church in an honorable manner, over my own signature, a priv-ilege never granted to any other person, you must and shall, place it out of your power to injur[e] me or the church,—do it or the Mississippi is your portion—will you do it?" I remarked that it was a hard case, and that I would leave peaceably, and without any public exposition, if he would excuse me. He replied, "I tell you as I was once told, 'your die is cast—your fate is fixed—your doom is sealed,' if you refuse. Will you do it, or die?" I remarked that I would, under the circumstances, but that it was hard to take the advantage of an unarmed man. "If you tell *that* publicly," said he, "death is your portion—*remember the Danites!*" He then unlocked the door—we went into the room below, and I gave the affidavit as subscribed before Alderman Wells, (who was then doing business in the lower room) and made the statement required before the City Council on the 19th. . . .

My affidavit, and statement, under DURESSE, were published in the Nauvoo Wasp on the 25th of June, 1842. It is now high time that this band of murderers should be made to feel the just penalty of the law. It is certainly a most alarming state of society when men are above the reach of law, and free to perpetuate the blackest crimes of cruelty and oppression. All this in the land of boasted freedom! Great God! where is the arm of power? Where is liberty, and the rights of man? Arise, ye officers of justice, and assert the majesty of your insulted laws. Let the sound of the clarion give the alarm! and horsemen and chariots will tell the story, until one stone shall not be left upon another, or a vestige of iniquity and crime to pollute the goodly land.

2nd. THE FULFILLMENT OF PROPHECY.—In 1841, Joe Smith predicted or prophesied in a public congregation in Nauvoo, that Lilburn W. Boggs, ex-Gover-nor of Missouri, should die by violent hands within one year. From one to two months prior to the attempted assassination of Gov. Boggs, Mr. O. P. Rockwell left Nauvoo for parts unknown to the citizens at large. I was then on terms of close intimacy with Joe Smith, and asked him where Rockwell had gone. "Gone," said he, "GONE TO FULFILL PROPHECY!" Rockwell returned to Nauvoo the day before the report of the assassination reached there, and the Nauvoo Wasp remarked, "it yet remains to be known who did the noble deed!" Rockwell remarked to a person now in Nauvoo, and whose name I forbear to mention *for the present*, from motives of prudence and safety to the person, but which shall be forthcoming in due time, that he had "been all over Upper Missouri, and all about where Boggs lives," and this was communicated to me by that person before I withdrew from the church, and we had considerable conversation upon that daring act. Rockwell is a Danite. Joe's *public* memory is very treacherous on this subject, I presume; but his *private* memory is so good that he had a guard around his house every night, with the State cannon and a full supply of small arms, for the protection of his person against any attempted arrest.—He, likewise, requested me to write to Gov. Carlin for his protection, which I agreed to do, and accordingly did, asking the Governor whether he would be protected from any *illegal* act of violence,—to which the Governor replied that ALL citizens should receive equal protection, but that he knew of no privileged man or order of men, and that the dignity of the State should be preserved according to the strict letter of the constitution and the laws. This letter I refused to show to Joe, as open hostilities had come between us, and he accordingly detailed a Court Martial to try me for treason against the citizens of the State of Illinois!!! This Court I regarded as illegal and treated with the utter contempt which such an assemblage of *inferior officers* will always receive at my hands. Now I call upon Colonel Francis M. Higbee to come out and tell what he told General Robinson and myself in relation to the MURDER of a certain prisoner in Missouri. Col. Higbee, do not fear to tell the dreadful story—tell exactly how Joe had the murder done up, and what part he ORDERED you to take in the affair, but which you did NOT take. Tell it as Robinson knows it, and as you told me, and DO NOT FEAR. Gov. Reynolds will make another demand, and Joe shall be delivered over. I will visit Missouri and tell the dreadful story. Let the call be made, and the laws shall be executed.

3d. My late visit to Springfield. On my arrival in Carthage I found, as all the citizens well know, that I was followed by Mr. O. P. Rockwell, a Danite, who on his arrival late in the night, made strict enquiries as to where I was—his ostensible business was to *put a letter in the post office!!* but judge ye the real desing [sic]. I was prepared for the gentleman and he approached me not; but another swift rider, Captain John D. Parker, another Danite, followed me to Springfield, to *carry a letter to Dr. Helm;* but he had *another object*, and *you* may well suppose what it was. I told Captain Parker that I was aware of his object, but I feared him not. . . .

4th. Mrs. Sarah M. Pratt, wife of Professor Orson Pratt, of the University of the city of Nauvoo. Joe Smith stated to me at an early day in the history of that city, that he intended to make that amiable and accomplished lady one of his *spiritual wives,* for the Lord had given her to him, and he requested me to assist him in consummating his hellish purposes, but I told him that I would not do it—that she had been much neglected and abused by the church during the absence of her husband in Europe, and that if the Lord had given her to him he must attend to it himself. I will do it, said he, for there is no harm in it if her husband should never find it out. I called upon Mrs. Pratt and told that Joe contemplated an attack on her virtue, *in the name of the Lord*, and that she must prepare to repulse him in so infamous an assault. She replied that "Joseph cannot be such a man. I cannot believe it until I know it for myself or have it from his own lips; he cannot be so corrupt." Well, I replied, you will see unless he changes his mind; accordingly in a few days Joe proposed to me to go to Ramus with him. I consented to go, and we started from his house about 4 o'clock P.M., rode into the prairie a few miles, and returned to the house of Captain John T. Barnett, in Nauvoo, about dusk, where we put up the horse with Barnett's permission. He, Joe, pretended we were looking for thieves. We then proceeded to the house where Mrs. Pratt resided, and Joe commenced discourse as follows: "Sister Pratt, the Lord has given you to me as one of my spiritual wives. I have the blessings of Jacob granted me, as he granted holy men of old, and I have long looked upon you with favor, and hope you will not deny me." She replied: "I care not for the blessings of Jacob, and I believe in no such revelations, neither will I consent under any circumstances. I have one good husband, and that is enough for me." Joe could not come it! He then went off to see Miss—— at the house of Mrs. Sherman. He remained with her an hour or two and then returned to Barnett's, harnessed our horse, started for Ramus, and arrived at Carthage at early breakfast. We then went to Ramus, and returned to Carthage that night, and put up at the house of Esq. Comer. Next day we returned to Nauvoo. I called upon Mrs. Pratt and asked her what she thought of Joseph? She replied, "He is a bad man beyond a doubt." Mrs. Pratt in a conversation with Mrs. Goddard, wife of Stephen H. Goddard, said, "Sister Goddard, Joseph is a corrupt man; I know it, for he made an attempt upon me." Three times afterwards he tried to convince Mrs. Pratt of the propriety of his doctrine, and she at last told him: "Joseph, if you ever attempt any thing of the kind with me again, I will tell Mr. Pratt on his return home. I will certainly do it." Joe replied, "Sister Pratt, I hope you will not expose me; if I am to suffer, all suffer; so do not expose me. Will you agree not to do so?" "If," said she, "you will never insult me again, I will not expose you unless strong circumstances require it." "Well, sister Pratt," says Joe, "as you have refused me; it becomes sin, unless sacrifice is offered"; and turning to me he said, "General, if you are my friend I wish you to procure a lamb, and have it slain, and sprinkle the door posts and the gate with its blood, and take the kidneys and entrails and offer them upon an altar of twelve stones that have not been touched with a hammer, as a burnt offering, and it will save me and my priesthood. Will you do it?" I will, I replied. So I procured the lamb from Captain John T. Barnett, and it was slain by Lieutenant Stephen H. Goddard, and I offered the kidneys and entrails in sacrifice for Joe as he desired; and Joe said, "all is now safe—the destroy-ing angel will pass over, without harming any of us." Time passed on in apparent friendship until Joe grossly insulted Mrs. Pratt again, after her husband had returned home, by approaching and kissing her. This highly offended her, and she told Mr. Pratt, who was much enraged and went and told Joe never to offer an insult of the like again.—Joe replied, "I did not desire to kiss her, Bennett made me do it!" Joe, you can't come it! Mrs. Pratt is far above your foul and polluted breath, your calumny and detraction. I now appeal to Mrs. Pratt if this is not true to the very letter. Just speak out boldly.

5th. Miss Nancy Rigdon, daughter of Sidney Rigdon, Esq. Joe Smith said to me last summer, "If you will assist me in procuring Nancy as one of my spiritual wives, I will give you five hundred dollars, or the best lot on Main Street." I replied, "I cannot agree to it. Elder Rigdon is one of my best friends, and his family are now pure and spotless, and it would be a great pity to approach the truly virtuous." "But," says Joe, "the Lord has given her to me to wife. I have the blessings of Jacob, and there is no wickedness in it. It would be wicked to approach her unless I had permission of the Lord, but as it is, it is as correct as to have a legal wife in a *moral* point of view." It may be so, said I, but you must see her yourself; I *cannot* approach her on a subject of the kind. Then I supposed the matter had ended; but at the funeral of Mr. Ephraim R. Marks, Mrs. Hyde told Miss Rigdon, that Joseph desired to see her at the printing office, where Mrs. Hyde resides, on special business. She said she would go, and accordingly did, but Joe was busily engaged at his store; Dr. Willard Richards, however, one of the holy twelve Mormon apostles, came in and said, "Miss Nancy, Joseph cannot be in today, please call again on Thursday." This she agreed to do; but she communicated the matter to Colonel Francis M. Higbee, who was addressing her, and asked his advice as to the second visit. I then came to a knowledge of the facts, and went immediately to Joe, and said to him, "Joseph, you are a Master Mason, and Nancy is a Master Mason's daughter, so stay your hand, or you will get into trouble." Joe said, "you are my enemy, and wish to oppose me."—"No," said I, "I am not your enemy, but you had better stop where you are."

I then went to Col. Higbee and told him Joe's designs, and requested him to go immediately and see Miss Rigdon and tell her the infernal plot—that Joe would approach her in the name of the Lord, by revelation, &c., and to put her on her guard, but advise her to go and see for herself what Joe would do. He did so, and she went down. Joe was there, and took her into a private room, LOCKED THE DOOR, and commenced by telling her that he had long loved her, and had asked the Lord for her, and that it was his holy will that he should have her—he told her that it would not prevent her from marrying any other person—that he had the blessings of Jacob granted to him—and all that was right; he desired to kiss her, and wished her to kiss him, but Joe couldn't come it. She said she would alarm the neighbors if he did not open the door, and let her out—he did so, and requested Mrs. Hyde to explain matters to her. Joe swore her to eternal secrecy. Mrs. Hyde told her that these things looked strange to her at first, but she would become more reconciled on mature reflection. Miss Rigdon replied, "I never shall." Joe agreed to write her, and did so in a few days thro' Dr. Richards. That letter is now safe in the hands of her friends. I have seen it, so has her father, and various other persons.—One Tuesday last, Joe came up to Mr. Rigdon's, accompanied by his High Priest, Geo. Miller, of sable notoriety, for a witness, and by boisterous words and violent gestures tried to deny the attempted seduction and alarm the girl; but she told him he was a cursed liar, and that he could not face her to it. Joe then made a full acknowledgment of the whole affair. All the family, and many other persons were present. The holy George observed, "You must not harm the Lord's anointed—the Lord will not suffer his anointed to fall!!!" Now call upon Miss Rigdon for the truth of the foregoing. Joe, did you offer another lamb in sacrifice as a burnt-sin offering on an altar of twelve stones? If not, look out for the destroying angel, for he will surely get you. . . .

—•••• 2 ••••—

A Young Woman Rejects
a Polygamous Relationship

M artha Brotherton, an immigrant from England, also came forward with an account of her attempted seduction at Nauvoo. At the request of John C. Bennett (see Part III, Document 1), she wrote him a long letter, which was a formal affidavit, and gave him permission to use it. He sent it to various newspapers and later printed it in his book, *The History of the Saints; or, An Exposé of Joe Smith and Mormonism* (Boston: Leland and Whitney, 1842), 236–40.

The letter is a detailed description of being pressured by Brigham Young to become one of his plural wives. Even allowing for some exaggeration by the scandalized young woman, the affidavit reveals psychological stress with which most other women could sympathize, and it excited non-Mormon emotions against church leaders engaged in the secret practice. Especially when approached by Smith himself, many women surely must have felt that they were in no position to refuse. Martha Brotherton apparently realized that she either had to acquiesce or leave Nauvoo, so she left.

In his exposé, Bennett satirizes Young and his two helpers, Joseph Smith and Heber C. Kimball, as "celestial gladiators, armed with the 'sword of the Spirit,' leaguing themselves in a Holy Alliance for the destruction of a defenceless and innocent woman" (236). Readers across the country must have agreed, for some even wrote letters to Bennett or their local newspapers, expressing their outrage.

—••○●◐●○••—

St. Louis, Missouri, *July* 13, A.D. 1842.

General John C. Bennett:

Dear Sir.—

I left Warsaw a short time since for this city, and having been called upon by you, through the "Sangamo Journal," to come out and disclose to the world the facts of the case in relation to certain propositions made to me at Nauvoo, by some of the Mormon leaders, I now proceed to respond to the call, and discharge what I consider to be a duty devolving upon me as an innocent, but insulted and abused female. I had been at Nauvoo near three weeks, during which time my father's family received frequent visits from Elders Brigham Young and Heber C. Kimball, two of the Mormon Apostles; when, early one morning, they both came to my brother-in-law's (John McIlwrick's) house, at which place I then was on a visit, and particularly requested me to go and spend a few days with them. I told them I could not at that time, as my brother-in-law was not at home; however, they urged me to go the next day, and spend one day with them. The day being fine, I accordingly went. When I arrived at the foot of the hill, Young and Kimball were standing conversing together. They both came to me, and, after several flattering compliments, Kimball wished me to go to his house first. I said it was immaterial to me, and accordingly went. We had not, however, gone many steps when Young suddenly stopped, and said he would go to that brother's, (pointing to a little log hut but a few yards distant,) and tell him that you (speaking to Kimball) and brother Glover, or Grover, (I do not remember which,) will value his land. When he had gone, Kimball turned to me and said, "Martha, I want you to say to my wife, when you go to my house, that you want to buy some things at Joseph's store, (Joseph Smith's,) and I will say I am going with you, to show you the way. You know you want to see the Prophet, and you will then have an opportunity." I made no reply. Young again made his appearance, and the subject was dropped. We soon reached Kimball's house, where Young took his leave, saying, "I shall see you again, Martha." I remained at Kimball's near an hour, when Kimball, seeing that I would not tell the lies he wished me to, told them to his wife himself. He then went and whispered in her ear, and asked if that would please her. "Yes," said she, "or I can go along with you and Martha." "No," said he, "I have some business to do, and I will call for you afterwards to go with me to the debate," meaning the debate between yourself and Joseph. To this she consented. So Kimball and I went to the store together. As we were going along, he said, "Sister Martha, are you willing to do all that the Prophet requires you to do?" I said I believed I was, thinking of course *he* would require nothing wrong. "Then," said he, "are you ready to take counsel?" I answered in the affirmative, thinking of the great and glorious blessings that had been pronounced upon my head, if I adhered to the counsel of those placed over me in the Lord. "Well," said he, "there are many things revealed in these last days that the world would laugh and scoff at; but unto us is given to know the mysteries of the kingdom." He further observed, "Martha, you must learn to hold your tongue, and it will be well with you. You will see Joseph, and very likely have some conversation with him, and he will tell you what you shall do." When we reached the building, he led me up some stairs to a small room, the door of which was locked, and on it the following inscription: "Positively no admittance." He observed, "Ah! brother Joseph must be sick, for, strange to say, he is not here. Come down into the tithing-office, Martha." He then left me in the tithing-office, and went out, I know not where. In this office were two men writing, one of whom, William Clayton, I had seen in England; the other I did not know. Young came in, and seated himself before me, and asked where Kimball was. I said he had gone out. He said it was all right. Soon after, Joseph came in, and spoke to one of the clerks, and then went up stairs, followed by Young. Immediately after, Kimball came in. "Now, Martha," said he, "the Prophet has come; come up stairs." I went, and we found Young and the Prophet alone. I was introduced to the Prophet by Young. Joseph offered me his seat, and, to my astonishment, the moment I was seated, Joseph and Kimball walked out of the room, and left me with Young, who arose, locked the door, closed the window, and drew the curtain. He then came and sat before me, and said, "This is our private room, Martha." "Indeed, sir," said I, "I must be highly honored to be permitted to enter it." He smiled and then proceeded—"Sister Martha, I want to ask you a few questions; will you answer them?" "Yes, sir," said I. "And will you promise not to mention them to any one?" "If that is your desire, sir," said I, "I will not." "And you will not think any the worse of me for it, will you, Martha?" said he. "No, sir," I replied. "Well," said he, "what are your feelings toward me?" I replied, "My feelings are just the same towards you that they ever were, sir." "But, to come to the point more closely," said he, "have not you an affection for me, that, were it lawful and right, you could accept of me for your husband and companion?" My feelings at that minute were indescribable. God only knows them. What, thought I, are these men, that I thought almost perfection itself, *deceivers?* and is all my fancied happiness but a dream? 'Twas even so; but my next thought was, which is the best way for me to act at this time? If I say *no*, they may do as they think proper; and to say *yes*, I never would. So I considered it best to ask for time to think and pray about it. I therefore said, "If it was lawful and right, perhaps I might; but you know, sir, it is not." "Well, but," said he, "brother Joseph has had a revelation from God that it is lawful and right for a man to have two wives; for, as it was in the days of Abraham, so it shall be in the last days, and whoever is the first that is willing to take up the cross will receive the greatest blessings; and if you will accept of me, I will take you straight to the celestial kingdom; and if you will have me in this world, I will have you in that which is to come, and brother Joseph will marry us here to-day, and you can go home this evening, and your parents will not know any thing about it." "Sir," said I, "I should not like to do any thing of the kind without the permission of my parents." "Well, but," said he, "you are of age, are you not?" "No, sir," said I, "I shall not be until the 24th of May." "Well," said he, "that does not make any difference. You will be of age before they know, and you need not fear. If you will take my counsel, it will be well with you, for I know it to be right before God, and if there is any sin in it, I will answer for it. But brother Joseph wishes to have some talk with you on the subject—he will explain things—will you hear him?" "I do not mind," said I. "Well, but I want you to say something," said he. "I want time to think about it," said I. "Well," said he, "I will have a kiss, anyhow," and then rose, and said he would bring Joseph. He then unlocked the door, and took the key, and locked me up alone. He was absent about ten minutes, and then returned with Joseph. "Well," said Young, "sister Martha would be willing if she knew it was lawful and right before God." "Well, Martha," said Joseph, "it is lawful and right before God—I *know* it is. Look here, sis; don't you believe in me?" I did not answer. "Well, Martha," said Joseph, "just go ahead, and do as Brigham wants you to—he is the best man in the world, except me." "O," said Brigham, "then you are as good." "Yes," said Joseph. "Well," said Young, "we believe Joseph to be a Prophet. I have known him near eight years, and always found him the same." "Yes," said Joseph, "and I know that this is lawful and right before God, and if there is any sin in it, I will answer for it before God; and I have the keys of the kingdom, and whatever I bind on earth is bound in heaven, and whatever I loose on earth is loosed in heaven, and if you will accept Brigham, you shall be blessed—God shall bless you, and my blessing shall rest upon you; and if you will be led by him, you will do well; for I know Brigham will take care of you, and if he don't do his duty to you, come to me, and I will make him; and if you do not like it in a month or two, come to me, and I will make you free again; and if he turns you off, I will take you on." "Sir," said I, rather warmly, "it will be too late to think in a month or two after. I want time to think first." "Well, but," said he, "the old proverb is, 'Nothing ventured, nothing gained'; and it would be the greatest blessing that was ever bestowed upon you." "Yes," said Young, "and you will never have reason to repent of it—that is, if I do not turn from righteousness, and that I trust I never shall; for I believe God, who had kept me so long, will continue to keep me faithful. Did you ever see me act in any way wrong in England, Martha?" "No, sir," said I. "No," said he; "neither can any one else lay any thing to my charge." "Well, then" said Joseph, "what are you afraid of, sis? Come, let me do the business for you." "Sir," said I, "do let me have a little time to think about it, and I will promise not to mention it to any one." "Well, but look here," said he, "you know a fellow will never be damned for doing the best he knows how." "Well, then," said I, "the best way I know of, is to go home and think and pray about it." "Well," said Young, "I shall leave it with brother Joseph, whether it would be best for you to have time or not." "Well," said Joseph, "I see no harm in her having time to think, if she will not fall into temptation." "O, sir," said I, "there is no fear of my falling into temptation." "Well, but," said Brigham, "you must promise me you will never mention it to any one." "I do promise it," said I. "Well," said Joseph, "you must promise me the same." I promised him the same. "Upon your honor," said he, "you will not tell." "No, sir, I will lose my life first," said I. "Well, that will do," said he, "that is the principle we go upon. I think I can trust you, Martha," said he. "Yes," said I, "I think you ought." Joseph said, "she looks as if she could keep a secret." I then rose to go, when Joseph commenced to beg of me again. He said it was the best opportunity they might have for months, for the room was often engaged. I, however, had determined what to do. "Well," said Young, "I will see you to-morrow. I am going to preach at the school-house, opposite your house. I have never preached there yet; you will be there, I suppose." "Yes," said I.—The next day being Sunday, I sat down, instead of going to meeting, and wrote the conversation, and gave it to my sister, who was not a little surprised; but she said it would be best to go to the meeting in the afternoon. We went, and Young administered the sacrament. After it was over, I was passing out, and Young stopped me, saying, "Wait, Martha, I am coming." I said, "I cannot; my sister is waiting for me." He then threw his coat over his shoulders, and followed me out, and whispered, "Have you made up your mind, Martha?" "Not, exactly, sir," said I; and we parted. I shall proceed to a justice of the peace, and make oath to the truth of these statements, and you are at liberty to make what use of them you may think best.

Yours, respectfully,
Martha H. Brotherton

Sworn and Subscribed before me, this 13th day of July, A.D. 1842.
De Bouffeay Fremon,
Justice of the Peace for St. Louis County.

———•••••• *3* ••••••———

An Apostle's Wife Recalls Smith, Bennett, and Polygamy

Corroboration for part of John C. Bennett's exposé came from Sarah Pratt, the wife of Mormon apostle Orson Pratt. In 1842 she had been approached by Smith about becoming his "spiritual wife" while her husband was on a mission to England and Scotland. Brigham Young told her to say nothing but "do as Joseph wished." She refused him and apparently declined to keep the matter quiet, so she was slandered as a loose woman who was having an affair with Bennett in order to discredit her comments about Smith.

When her husband returned to Nauvoo, he found a sordid situation with charges and countercharges. Ultimately Pratt sided with his wife and on 22 July 1842 refused to endorse a resolution affirming Joseph Smith's moral character. Wilford Woodruff, another apostle, noted that several colleagues tried to get Pratt to "recall his sayings against Joseph and the twelve, but he persisted in his wicked course and did not recall any of his sayings which were unjust and untrue" ("John C. Bennett," *Times and Seasons* 3 [1 August 1842]: 868–69). On 20 August 1842, both Pratts were excommunicated, he for "insubordination" and Sarah for "adultery." They were also accused of planning to expose Mormonism.

However, Pratt had no intention of abandoning the church, and within three months he had publicly "confessed his error and his sin in criticizing Joseph." The Pratts were rebaptized in January 1843, and Orson was returned to the Quorum of Twelve Apostles. Two years later Orson Pratt embraced polygamy and married several more women.

A few years later, the Pratts left with the main body of Mormons who were driven from Illinois. There Orson remained a leader in the church, but Sarah Pratt did not forget the attempt by Smith to damage her reputation. She halfheartedly went along with Mormon polygamy in Utah for a quarter century, according to her son, "from an earnest, conscientious desire to do what was right as a Mormon, and to please a husband whom she loved with all the strength of her nature" (Arthur Pratt, "Statement," *Anti-Polygamy Standard*, February 1882, p. 81). Finally, in 1868 she could stand this relationship no longer and turned her back on her husband and the Mormon Church. Forty years after the exodus, after her husband had died, she discussed the Nauvoo episode and the Smith/Bennett relationship in a revealing interview with William Wyl. The latter was gathering information for a book, entitled *Joseph Smith, the Prophet, His Family and His Friends* (Salt Lake City: Tribune Printing, 1886), from which this interview is reprinted (pp. 60–63).

Sarah Pratt's account is important not only because it provides details about early Mormon marriage practices but also because it reveals the sexual aspect of such activities. While parts of this recollection may have been overstated after the fact, Sarah Pratt's recollection provides an important first-person view of the prophet's relationships with women from a Mormon insider, and it illustrates the deception and coercion associated with his secret polygamy.

———————•••◦●◦•••———————

May 21, 1886, I had a fresh interview with Mrs. Sarah M. Pratt, who had the kindness to give me the following testimony additional to the information given by her in our interviews in the spring of 1885. "I want you to have all my statements correct in your book," said the noble lady, "and put my name to them; I want the truth, the full truth, to be known, and to bear the responsibility of it."

"I have told you that the prophet Joseph used to frequent houses of ill-fame. Mrs. White, a very pretty and attractive woman, once confessed to me that she made a business of it to be hospitable to the captains of the Mississippi steamboats. She told me that Joseph had made her acquaintance very soon after his arrival in Nauvoo, and that he had visited her dozens of times. My husband (Orson Pratt) could not be induced to believe such things of his prophet. Seeing his obstinate incredulity, Mrs. White proposed to Mr. Pratt and myself to put us in a position where we could observe what was going on between herself and Joseph the prophet. We, however, declined this proposition. You have made a mistake in the table of contents of your book in calling this woman 'Mrs. Harris.' Mrs. Harris was a married lady, a very great friend of mine. When Joseph had made his dastardly attempt on me, I went to Mrs. Harris to unbosom my grief to her. To my utter astonishment, she said, laughing heartily: 'How foolish you are! I don't see anything so horrible in it. Why, I AM HIS MISTRESS SINCE FOUR YEARS!'"

"Next door to my house was a house of bad reputation. One single woman lived there, not very attractive. She used to be visited by people from Carthage whenever they came to Nauvoo. Joseph used to come on horseback, ride up to the house and tie his horse to a tree, many of which stood before the house. Then he would enter the house of the woman from the back. I have seen him do this repeatedly."

"Joseph Smith, the son of the prophet, and president of the re-organized Mormon church, paid me a visit, and I had a long talk with him. I saw that he was not inclined to believe the truth about his father, so I said to him: 'You pretend to have revelations from the Lord. Why don't you ask the Lord to tell you *what kind of man your father really was?*' He answered: 'If my father had so many connections with women, where is the progeny?' I said to him: 'Your father had mostly intercourse with married women, and as to single ones, Dr. Bennett was always on hand, when anything happened.'"

"It was in this way that I became acquainted with Dr. John C. Bennett. When my husband went to England as a missionary, he got the promise from Joseph that I should receive provisions from the tithing-house. Shortly afterward Joseph made his propositions to me and they enraged me so that I refused to accept any help from the tithing house or from the bishop. Having been always very clever and very busy with my needle, I began to take in sewing for the support of myself and children, and succeeded soon in making myself independent. When Bennett came to Nauvoo Joseph brought him to my house, stating that Bennett wanted some sewing done, and that I should do it for the doctor. I assented and Bennett gave me a great deal of work to do. He knew that Joseph had his plans set on me; Joseph made no secret of them before Bennett, and went so far in his impudence as to make propositions to me in the presence of Bennett, his bosom friend. Bennett, who had a sarcastic turn of mind, used to come and tell me about Joseph to tease and irritate me. One day they came both, Joseph and Bennett, on horseback to my house. Bennett dismounted, Joseph remained outside. Bennett wanted me to return to him a book I had borrowed from him. It was a so-called doctor book. I had a rapidly growing little family and wanted to inform myself about certain matters in regard to babies, etc.,—this explains my having borrowed that book. While giving Bennett his book, I observed that he held something in the left sleeve of his coat. Bennett smiled and said: *'Oh, a little job for Joseph, one of his women is in trouble.'* Saying this, he took the thing out of his left sleeve. It was a pretty long instrument of a kind I had never seen before. It seemed to be of steel and was crooked at one end. I heard afterwards that the operation had been performed; that the *woman* was very sick, and that Joseph was very much afraid that she might die, but she recovered."

"Bennett was the most intimate friend of Joseph for a time. He boarded with the prophet. He told me once that Joseph had been talking with him about his troubles with Emma, his wife. 'He asked me,' said Bennett, smilingly, 'what he should do to get out of the trouble?' I said, 'this is very simple. GET A REVELATION that polygamy is right, and all your troubles will be at an end.'"

"The only 'wives' of Joseph that lived in the Mansion House were the Partridge girls. This is explained by the fact that they were the servants in the hotel kept by the prophet. But when Emma found that Joseph went to their room, they had to leave the house. . . ."

"You should bear in mind that Joseph did not think of a marriage or sealing ceremony for many years. He used to state to his intended victims, as he did to me: '*God does not care if we have a good time, if only other people do not know it.*' He only introduced a marriage ceremony when he had found out that he could not get certain women without it. I think Louisa Beaman was the first case of this kind. If any woman, like me, opposed his wishes, he used to say: 'Be silent, or I shall ruin your character. My character must be sustained in the interest of the church.' When he had assailed me and saw that he could not seal my lips, he sent word to me that he would *work my salvation,* if I kept silent. I sent back that I would talk as much as I pleased and as much as I knew the truth, and as to my salvation, I would try and take care of that myself."

"In his endeavors to ruin my character Joseph went so far as to publish an extra-sheet containing affidavits against my reputation. When this sheet was brought to me I discovered to my astonishment the names of two people on it, man and wife, with whom I had boarded for a certain time [Stephen H. Goddard and his wife]. I never thought much of the man, but the woman was an honest person and I knew that she must have been *forced* to do such a thing against me. So I went to their house; the man left the house hurriedly when he saw me coming. I found the wife and said to her rather excitedly: 'What does it all mean.' She began to sob. 'It is not my fault,' said she. 'Hyrum Smith came to our house, with the affidavits all written out, and forced us to sign them. "*Joseph and the church must be saved,*" said he. We saw that resistance was useless, they would have ruined us; so we signed the papers.'"

——————— •••• 4 •••• ———————

Polygamy and Politics:
A Non-Mormon Response

Charlotte Haven, a non-Mormon whose letters about life in Nauvoo appear in Part I, wrote briefly about the most controversial aspects of the community—polygamy and politics—in a letter dated 8 September 1843. With respect to

Mormon political activity, Haven commented that Smith used his brother Hyrum to switch Mormon support from one party to another. (For a discussion of that matter, see the headnote to Part II, Document 8). Her remarks show that at least some of the non-Mormons in the area recognized that "political ruse" for what it was—an attempt to deliver votes to the Democrats without seeming to break the promise that Smith had made to the Whigs.

Haven's letter also reveals that rumors about the existence of a revelation sanctioning plural wives were widespread by the late summer of 1843, and she refers to one Mormon apostle who was openly living with two wives. Most Nauvoo residents did not know at that time that Smith had dictated a "Revelation on the Eternity of the Marriage Covenant, including the Plurality of Wives" on 12 July 1843 or that it had been presented to the High Council a month later. The document became the legal bulwark upon which nearly half a century of Mormon polygamous relations were based. This revelation remained unpublished during Joseph Smith's lifetime and was only publicly acknowledged in 1852, but it has appeared in the Doctrine and Covenants of the Church of Jesus Christ of Latter-day Saints, section 132, since it was first canonized in 1876. Haven mistakenly thinks that Hyrum Smith was responsible for this clandestine revelation, and she predicts the end of a unified Mormon society if Joseph Smith sanctions it. Her comment is prophetic, for Nauvoo experienced serious internal strife by the following spring.

This letter was originally published in "A Girl's Letters from Nauvoo," *Overland Monthly* (San Francisco) 16 (December 1890): 635–36.

••••●◆●••••

Nauvoo, Sept. 8. [1843]

My Dear friends at home:

The last letter we received from you bears the remote date of June 9th. I have been expecting another this long, long time, have taken the mile walk to the post-office every mail day three times a week, buoyed up with hope and lively expectation, but have turned back disappointed and crestfallen, and have almost envied the pigs I have met on the way, so contented and happy as they roam the streets. . . .

A few Sabbaths ago Joseph announced to his people that the gift of prophecy was taken away from him until the Temple and Nauvoo House should be finished, but that his mantle had fallen on his brother Hyrum, to whom it belonged by birthright, and he charged his people to obey implicitly all the commands revealed to Hyrum. We hear that he has already had some wonderful revelations not yet made public, but that a few of the elders put their heads together and whisper what they dare not speak aloud. What it is we can only surmise by faint rumors. A month ago or more one of the Apostles, [George J.] Adams [actually a member of the Quorum of the Seventies] by name, returned from a two years' mission in

England, bringing with him a wife and child, although he had left a wife and family here when he went away, and I am told that his first wife is reconciled to this certainly at first unwelcome guest to her home, for her husband and some others have reasoned with her that plurality of wives is taught in the Bible, that Abraham, Jacob, Solomon, David, and indeed all the old prophets and good men, had several wives, and if right for them, it is right for the Latter Day Saints. Furthermore, the first wife will always be first in her husband's affection and the head of the household, where she will have a larger influence. Poor, weak woman!

I cannot believe that Joseph will ever sanction such a doctrine, and should the Mormons in any way engraft such an article on their religion, the sect would surely fall to pieces, for what community or State could harbor such outrageous immorality? I cannot think so meanly of my sex as that they could submit to any such degradation.

Our Gentile friends say that this falling of the prophetic mantle on to Hyrum is a political ruse. Last winter when Joseph was in the meshes of the law, he was assisted by some politicians of the Whig party, to whom he pledged himself in the coming elections. Now, he wanted the Democratic party to win, so Hyrum is of that party, and as it is revealed for him to vote, so go over all the Mormons like sheep following the bell sheep over a wall. Nauvoo, with its 15,000 inhabitants, has a vote that tells in the State elections, and all summer politicians, able men of both parties, have been here making speeches, caressing and flattering.

Yesterday being parade day, to show a little attention to our guest, brother engaged a team and carried us out on the prairie to view the troops. There were over 2,000 men, it was said, divided into four divisions, and when marching in line with two bands of music they made quite an imposing appearance. Their costumes, for I can't say uniforms, were more fantastic than artistic. They were quite picturesque, certainly, for every officer and private consulted his individual taste; no two were alike. Nearly all had some badge, stripe, or scarf, or bright color. Some wore the breeches and knee-buckles of a hundred years ago. I thought if some Eastern military company would send out discarded uniforms, they might make a good speculation. However, they went through their drill, marching, countermarching, and forming squares and other military combinations, very nicely.

This is probably the last letter I shall write to you in our little cottage, for we move in two or three weeks to our new brick house, a block beyond the Temple. Business is coming up that way. Love to all.

Your affectionate sister,

Charlotte.

——— ••• 5 ••• ———

The Reformed Mormon Church

In April 1844, a group of Mormon dissidents who opposed polygamy and objected to the decline of civil rights in Nauvoo broke with the prophet and established the Reformed Mormon Church. Under the leadership of William Law (1809–92), who was chosen as president, the dissenters began to hold meetings at which the prophet was publicly criticized and to visit local families to see who would join with them. Law had come from the Toronto area late in 1839. A leading businessman, he became a counselor to Joseph Smith in the church presidency. (For more on Law, see the headnote to Part III, Document 13.) In establishing the new church, he was joined by his brother Wilson, Dr. Robert D. Foster and his brother Charles A. Foster, Francis M. Higbee and his brother Chauncey L. Higbee, James A. Blakeslee, Charles Ivins, Austin Cowles, and several others. Together they represented well-informed, respectable dissent in Nauvoo.

This was a hopeful note for non-Mormons, who reported the early activities of the new church in the pages of the *Warsaw Signal*, the newspaper published by Thomas C. Sharp. As the short articles reprinted here demonstrate, they hoped that vocal opposition within the Mormon community would curb Smith's power and bring an end to the theocratic control of Nauvoo. The first of these appeared in the *Warsaw Signal* on 8 May 1844, p. 2, under the title, "Matters and Things at Nauvoo," and the other three appeared as untitled articles on 15 May 1844, p. 2.

——— ••• ———

Well at last, the Mormons are at it amongst themselves in good earnest. A new church has been organized and we understand that a press will soon be procured, and a paper started which will be devoted to the building up of the cause of the seceders, and to an exposition of Joe Smith's enormities and mal-practices. The creed of the new church differs but little from the old—they acknowledge the authority of the Book of Mormon, Doctrine and Covenants, &c.; the only essential difference being in relation to the inspiration of Joe Smith. The seceders believe that Joe *was* a prophet, but that he is now fallen from grace. They have a new prophet, therefore, who is William Law.

The members of the new church are among the most intelligent and respectable of the Mormon body, and it is said that their number is already quite respectable.

On Saturday last, Law preached in Nauvoo, and in the severest terms denounced Smith, for his arbitrary and immoral conduct. Some think that this breach will soon be healed, but we are inclined to believe that the disaffected have gone so far as to preclude the possibility of retreat—sure it is, they cannot retreat honorably. . . .

We stated last week that William Law was the Prophet of the New Church at Nauvoo. This was denied, we hear, by Mr. Law, who says no man can assume the Spirit of Prophecy. He is President of the New Church, but will not venture to publish any revelations.

The New Church appears to be going ahead. On last Sunday, there were about three hundred assembled at Mr. Law's house in Nauvoo, and listened with much seeming pleasure to a sermon from Elder Blakely [James A. Blakeslee], who denounced Smith as a fallen Prophet. He treated the Spiritual wife doctrine without gloves, and repudiated Smith's plan of uniting Church and State.

After Blakely had concluded, William Law gave his reasons in strong language for leaving the false prophet.

Francis M. Higbee, then read a series of resolutions which set forth the reasons for withdrawing from Joe. After this a number of Affidavits were read testifying to Joe's villainy, and showing the evils under which a huge portion of the citizens are obliged to labor.

The new church and those opposed to Mormonism in Nauvoo, are said to be strongly in favor of repealing their Charter, it having been made an instrument of oppression rather than a benefit.

The Nauvoo Expositor is the title of a new paper about to be started at Nauvoo, by the opponents of Joe. The Prospectus has been issued, in which the proposed character of the paper is set forth. It will have nothing to do with religion, but goes in for the repeal of the Nauvoo City Charter, against political revelations and unconstitutional ordinances. As the conductors of this paper are well acquainted with Joe, it will in all probability make some disclosures which will render Nauvoo too hot either for Joe or his enemies. We will endeavor to keep our readers well apprised of everything of interest to them. In the mean time we say, success to the new undertaking, for "a kingdom divided against itself cannot stand."

—————— 6 ——————

An Exposé Poem on Smith's Polygamy

In 1844 two lyrics appeared in the Warsaw newspaper under the pseudonym Buckey. Both criticized Smith's polygamy. They were obviously written by a very well-informed person who had become disenchanted with him. Mormon historians have traditionally assigned the authorship to Wilson Law, the brother of dissident leader William Law. The Laws had come to Nauvoo late in 1839. Wilson became a well-respected leader, serving one term as president of the city council. He was also appointed brigadier general of the Nauvoo Legion, a position that he held until his association with the dissenting Mormons caused him to be dismissed in May 1844.

The first poem, not reproduced here, was "Buckey's Lamentation for Want of More Wives," which appeared in the *Warsaw Message* on 7 February 1844, p. 2. It asserted that Smith and the Quorum of Twelve Apostles do "slyly practice" the "secret doctrine," although "in public they deny." And the poet used bird images to reveal the identity of some of the prophet's plural wives:

> He sets his snares around for all—
>   And very seldom fails
> To catch some thoughtless PARTRIDGES
>   SNOW-birds or KNIGHT-ingales!

The references are to the daughters of Edward Partridge, Emily Dow and Eliza M., who were married to Smith in 1843; Eliza R. Snow, married to Smith in 1842; and Lydia Knight, the wife of Vinson Knight. The poet clearly knew a great deal about the inner workings of Nauvoo, and he viewed polygamy as a corrupt practice—the seduction of women by men in positions of religious authority.

The second poem, which is reprinted here, is entitled "The Buckey's First Epistle to Jo," and it appeared in the *Warsaw Signal* on 25 April 1844, p. 1. A more effective lyric, it is a verse epistle—a poetic form that had been popular with eighteenth-century satirists like Alexander Pope. The poet views Smith as a fallen prophet, who has betrayed his "mighty and sublime" calling by engaging in "dark deeds." As an example, the poet describes the prophet's attempt to induce Nancy Rigdon, daughter of Mormon leader Sidney Rigdon, to enter into a polygamous relationship. The detailed nature of his account, in stanzas six through fourteen, suggests that the poet knew what he was talking about. Moreover, he accuses the rejected prophet of resorting to his "usual plan," that is, "circulating lies" about the young woman to cover himself in case she spoke out against him. When confronted by the influential Sidney Rigdon—who may have been the source of this detailed account—Smith asserted instead that he was just testing her virtue. In short, the poem depicts Smith as not only a seducer but a man who spread lies to cover his tracks. This was an important and timely denunciation of Mormonism's leader and helped to solidify opposition to him in Hancock County.

Of equal significance is the poet's view of himself. As the closing stanzas reveal, Law—or whoever was the author—had begun to see himself as a champion of freedom, standing opposed to a tyrant. The events of recent months—including the increasing conflict with Smith, the formation of a new Reformed Mormon Church, and the subsequent excommunication of the dissidents—had given the poet a new sense of authority. He was a man with a cause, and perhaps his most powerful weapon was his insider's knowledge of Smith's "dark deeds" in both Nauvoo and Missouri, as outlined in stanza twenty. Clearly, by April of 1844, Smith had formidable critics within the community.

1

Friend Jo, I have been told of late,
That you had got it in your pate
A certain chief, to vent his hate,
   Had learned to sing;
And had turn'd out a poet great,
   Or some such thing.

2

Because the "Warsaw Message" came
With tidings from the *state* of fame,
Like some great herald to proclaim
   Your wicked ways,
Your *tyranny*, your *sin* and *shame*,
   In these last days.

3

With Buckey's trumpet sounding clear,
That Democrat and Whig might hear,
And *Priest-rid* Mormons, who in fear,
   Bow down to thee;
That there is still one child who dare[s]
   And will be free.

4

That Buckeye child lives in Nauvoo,
And some there are, who know how true
A friend, he ever was to you,
   In days that's past,
Till *slanders base* around you threw,
   Fair fame to blast.

5

Till for himself he's fairly seen
That you were not what you had been,
But that iniquity you'd screen
   In every way;
And from fair virtue's path did lean
   Vile plans to lay.

6

Have you forgot the snare you laid
For NANCY, (lovely Buckeye maid?)
With all your priestly arts array'd
    Her to seduce;
Assisted by that wretched bawd
    Who kept the house.

7

But she, in virtues armour steel'd,
Was proof against what you *reveal'd*,
And to *your doctrines* would not yield
    The least belief;
Although the scriptures you did wield
    In your relief.

8

And when you saw, she would detest
Such doctrines, in her noble breast,
And did despise the man, 'tho priest,
    who taught them too,
A sallow, yellow, lustful beast,
    Poor Jo, like you.

9

'Twas then you chang'd your *lovers sighs*
And vengeful hate flash'd in your eyes
When you found out she did despise
    You as a man;
You took to circulating lies,
    Your usual plan.

10

Just that you might destroy her fame,
And give to her a ruin'd name,
So that if she should ever proclaim
    What you had tried;
Your friends might turn on her the shame
    And say she lied.

11

But Joe, in this you fairly tail'd,
Though you her father's house assail'd
She met you face to face; you quail'd
    Before her frown,
And like a counterfeit she nail'd
    You tightly down—

12

Although you tried, by priestly power
To make this gentle creature cower
And eat her words, that you might tower
    In priestly pride;
But strong in truth, she in that hour
    Told you you lied.

13

And when you found it would not do,
Then like a coward paltroon [*sic*], you
Acknowledg'd what she had said was true
    Unto her sire;
But then you'd nothing more in view
    Than just to try her—

14

And put her on her guard, that she
Might keep her[self] pure and free
From base seducers like to me,
    And *Joab* vile—
For that it was *reveal'd* to thee
    We would beguile.

15

O Jo! Jo!! thy slanderous tongue
Some burning tears from me have wrung,
And I had thought t' have held my tongue
    And nothing said—
If thou had'st but repentance shown
    And shut thy head.

16

But thy repeated slanders vile
Shall not be long borne by this child;
Although by nature he is mild,
   And well disposed;
Thy sins from continent to isle
   Shall be exposed.

17

Missouri's deeds shall come to light
Though perpetrated in the night,
By hirelings who thought it right
   To do thy will—
By cabin conflagration bright
   To *scalp* and kill.

18

Repent, repent, there still is time—
And add no more dark crime to crime,
But think, how mighty and sublime
   Thy calling first—
And in black sackcloth bow thee down
   Low in the dust—

19

And put away far from thy heart,
Each wicked, *sensual* sinful art;
And from the truth no more depart
   Long as you live—
But stop and make another start,
   And I'll forgive.

20

If not, your dark deeds in Nauvoo,
As well as in Missouri too—
Like *Hamlet's* ghost shall rise to view,
   With *old white hat*—
Then tremble tyrant, for but few
   Will sanction that.

21

But I must stop this long epistle,
"My pen is worn down to the gristle,"
And 'tis the poet's only missill [*sic*]
   In truth's relief—
For, be it known to all, this child
   Ain't yet a chief—

22

'Tho he his lineage can trace
Back to the *Bruce* and *Wallace* days,
When they for Liberty did raise
   The sword, and broke
(As I intend in these last days)
   A tyrant's yoke.

--------•••• 7 ••••--------

The Prophet Denies "Spiritual Wifeism"

The public accusations of polygamy leveled against Smith by the dissidents forced him to respond. He did so in a speech to the community on 26 May 1844, reprinted here from Joseph Smith, Jr., *History of the Church of Jesus Christ of Latter-day Saints*, ed. B. H. Roberts (Salt Lake City: Deseret Book Co., 1912), 6:408–12. Despite his long practice of taking plural wives and his issuance of a revelation—to close associates only—that justified polygamy, Smith continued publicly to deny all such charges. Moreover, those who accused him—including William and Wilson Law, who are named in the speech—were defamed as "false swearers" and "wolves," whose charges were "of the devil." Two months earlier, in another speech, he had accused the Laws and other dissenters of conspiring to murder him, and he repeated that charge here. As this document reveals, Joseph Smith employed public denunciation as an important means of counteracting his critics.

Like many other speeches that Smith delivered at Nauvoo, this one is deeply mythic. He depicts himself as the innocent leader of "a virtuous and good people," who are surrounded by the wicked. Of course, once the myth of persecuted innocence was accepted by the Mormons, they were incapable of criticizing Smith's behavior or of detecting his deceptions. Moreover, Smith encouraged them to verify his guiltlessness experientially by appealing to their deeply held belief in his inherent innocence. As he said, "I am innocent of all these charges, and you can bear witness of my innocence, for you know me yourselves." This is an example of equivocation because the words "innocent" and "innocence" have two different meanings here. What Smith was saying was this: because you know I am inherently innocent (as all Mormons are, as God's chosen people), you therefore know—and can bear witness—that I am innocent of the polygamy charges. Of course they actually knew no such thing, and he was in fact guilty, but he made his followers feel they were somehow witnesses to his innocence. Such is the power of myth.

This speech also reveals the prophet's deep anxiety about William Law and the Reformed Mormon Church. As the *Expositor* made clear, the dissenters were criticizing Smith, not the Mormon people, but the prophet continually told his followers that *they* were under attack and he was their selfless defender. That strategy developed precisely because he feared that Law and his new church might succeed in separating more Mormons from his leadership. As Smith said toward the close of his speech, "When I shrink not from your defense will you throw me away for a new man who slanders you?" Of course, neither Law nor any other dissenter had slandered the Mormon people, nor did the people need any defense, but convinced by such remarks that the wicked were at the gates ready to destroy them, the Mormons rallied around their champion. And Smith soon orchestrated the community's attack on the new religious group.

———————————•••◗◗◉◖◖•••———————————

President Joseph Smith read the 11th Chapter II Corinthians. My object is to let you know that I am right here on the spot where I intend to stay. I, like Paul, have been in perils, and oftener than anyone in this generation. As Paul boasted, I have suffered more than Paul did. I should be like a fish out of water, if I were out of persecutions. Perhaps my brethren think it requires all this to keep me humble. The Lord has constituted me so curiously that I glory in persecution. I am not nearly so humble as if I were not persecuted. If oppression will make a wise man mad, much more the fool. If they want a beardless boy to whip all the world, I will get on the top of a mountain and crow like a rooster: I shall always beat them. When facts are proved, truth and innocence will prevail at last. My enemies are no philosophers: they think that when they have my spoke under, they will keep me down; but for the fools, I will hold on and fly over them.

God is in the still small voice. In all these affidavits, indictments, it is all of the devil—all corruption. Come on! ye prosecutors! ye false swearers! All hell, boil over! Ye burning mountains, roll down your lava! for I will come out on the top at last. I have more to boast of than ever any man had. I am the only man that has ever been able to keep a whole church together since the days of Adam. A large majority of the whole have stood by me. Neither Paul, John, Peter, nor Jesus ever did it. I boast that no man ever did such a work as I. The followers of Jesus ran away from Him; but the Latter-day Saints never ran away from me yet. You know my daily walk and conversation. I am in the bosom of a virtuous and good people. How I do love to hear the wolves howl! When they can get rid of me, the devil will also go. For the last three years I have a record of all my acts and proceedings, for I have several good, faithful, and efficient clerks in constant employ: they have accompanied me everywhere, and carefully kept my history, and they have written down what I have done, where I have been, and what I have said; therefore my enemies cannot charge me with any day, time, or place, but what I have written testimony to prove my actions; and my enemies cannot prove anything against me. They have got wonderful things in the land of Ham. I think the grand jury have strained at a gnat and swallowed the camel. . . .

Another indictment has been got up against me. It appears a holy prophet has arisen up [William Law], and he has testified against me: the reason is, he is so holy. The Lord knows I do not care how many churches are in the world. As many as believe me, may. If the doctrine that I preach is true, the tree must be good. I have prophesied things that have come to pass, and can still.

Inasmuch as there is a new church, this must be old, and of course we ought to be set down as orthodox. From henceforth let all the churches now no longer persecute orthodoxy. I never built upon any other man's ground. I never told the old Catholic that he was a fallen true prophet. God knows, then, that the charges against me are false.

I had not been married scarcely five minutes, and made one proclamation of the Gospel, before it was reported that I had seven wives. I mean to live and proclaim the truth as long as I can.

This new holy prophet [William Law] has gone to Carthage and swore that I had told him that I was guilty of adultery. This spiritual wifeism! Why, a man dares not speak or wink, for fear of being accused of this.

William Law testified before forty policemen, and the assembly room full of witnesses, that he testified under oath that he never had heard or seen or knew anything immoral or criminal against me. He testified under oath that he was my friend, and not the "Brutus." There was a cogitation who was the "Brutus." I had not prophesied against William Law. He swore under oath that he was satisfied that he was ready to lay down his life for me, and he swears that I have committed adultery.

I wish the grand jury would tell me who they are—whether it will be a curse or blessing to me. I am quite tired of the fools asking me.

A man asked me whether the commandment was given that a man may have seven wives; and now the new prophet has charged me with adultery. I never had any fuss with these men until that Female Relief Society brought out the paper against adulterers and adulteresses.

Dr. [W. G.] Goforth was invited into the Laws' clique, and Dr. [Robert D.] Foster and the clique were dissatisfied with that document, and they rush away and leave the Church, and conspire to take away my life; and because I will not countenance such wickedness, they proclaim that I have been a true prophet, but that I am now a fallen prophet.

[Joseph H.] Jackson has committed murder, robbery, and perjury; and I can prove it by half-a-dozen witnesses. Jackson got up and said—"By God, he is innocent," and now swears that I am guilty. He threatened my life.

There is another Law, not the prophet, who was cashiered for dishonesty and robbing the government. Wilson Law also swears that I told him I was guilty of adultery. Brother Jonathan Dunham can swear to the contrary. I have been chained. I have rattled chains before in the dungeon for the truth's sake. I am innocent of all these charges, and you can bear witness of my innocence, for you know me yourselves.

When I love the poor, I ask no favors of the rich. I can go to the cross—I can lay down my life; but don't forsake me. I want the friendship of the brethren.—Let us teach the things of Jesus Christ. Pride goes before destruction, and a haughty spirit before a downfall.

Be meek and lowly, upright and pure; render good for evil. If you bring on yourselves your own destruction, I will complain. It is not right for a man to bear down his neck to the oppressor always. Be humble and patient in all circumstances of life; we shall then triumph more gloriously. What a thing it is for a man to be accused of committing adultery, and having seven wives, when I can only find one.

I am the same man, and as innocent as I was fourteen years ago; and I can prove them all perjurers. I labored with these apostates myself until I was out of all manner of patience; and then I sent my brother Hyrum, whom they virtually kicked out of doors.

I then sent Mr. [Jacob B.] Backenstos, when they declared that they were my enemies. I told Mr. Backenstos that he might tell the Laws, if they had any cause against me I would go before the Church, and confess it to the world. He [Wm. Law] was summoned time and again, but refused to come. Dr. Bernhisel and Elder Rigdon know that I speak the truth. I cite you to Captain Dunham, Esquires Johnson and Wells, Brother Hatfield and others, for the truth of what I have said. I have said this to let my friends know that I am right.

As I grow older, my heart grows tenderer for you. I am at all times willing to give up everything that is wrong, for I wish this people to have a virtuous leader. I have set your minds at liberty by letting you know the things of Christ Jesus. When I shrink not from your defense will you throw me away for a new man who slanders you? I love you for your reception of me. Have I asked you for your money? No; you know better. I appeal to the poor. I say, Cursed be that man or woman who says that I have taken of your money unjustly. Brother [Almon W.] Babbitt will address you. I have nothing in my heart but good feelings.

8

The Nauvoo Expositor

In May 1844, leaders of the Reformed Mormon Church, aided by non-Mormon Sylvester Emmons, launched a newspaper that was independent of the control of the Latter Day Saint hierarchy. The *Expositor* was a means to express dissent— perhaps the ultimate form of adherence to an ideal, for the dissenters felt their cause was so important that they were willing to endure censure for it—and through it the publishers hoped to arouse the community against the secret practice of polygamy, raise concern about other doctrines, and curb Joseph Smith's theocratic control.

The first—and only—issue appeared on 7 June 1844. It condemned the taking of plural wives and exposed the villainy of the practice by depicting the psychological pressure that was brought to bear on the selected women. It also deplored Smith's attempts to gain and wield political power and called for the separation of church and state at Nauvoo. The publishers listed a whole series of resolutions designed to bring religious, moral, and political reform to the community. Among other things, they opposed Smith's efforts to hold himself above the law (no. 5) and the practice of stealing from non-Mormons ("spoiling of the gentiles," no. 14).

The *Expositor* not only opposed Smith's control of Nauvoo but also held his behavior up to precisely the kind of critical examination that he had managed to avoid within the church. And the publishers were very well informed. They addressed their fellow Mormons with authority—as men "thoroughly acquainted with [the church's] rise, its organization, and its history." Moreover, the *Expositor* challenged the myth of persecuted innocence upon which the gathering of the Saints at Nauvoo had been based. If the zionic community had serious shortcomings, as the publishers asserted, Nauvoo was part of an imperfect America after all—not a bastion of virtue in a corrupt nation, but a place where moral, social, and political problems existed and public pressure could bring change. Hence, the opposition newspaper offered a view of the community which the prophet could not tolerate. His conception of Nauvoo as a God-led, separatist theocracy was at stake.

The *Expositor* is available on microfilm at the Illinois State Historical Library; Archives, Church of Jesus Christ of Latter-day Saints; Library-Archives, Reorganized Church of Jesus Christ of Latter Day Saints; Chicago Historical Society; and other locations.

———•••◉◉◉•••———

We give place this week to the following Preamble, Resolutions and Affidavits, of the seceders from the Church at Nauvoo.—The request is complied with on account of their deeming it very important that the public should know the true cause of their dissenting, as all manner of falsehood is spread abroad in relation to the schism in the Church. In our subsequent numbers several affidavits will be published, to substantiate the facts alleged. Hereafter, no further Church proceedings will appear in our columns, except in the form of brief communications.—ED.

Preamble

It is with the greatest solicitude for the salvation of the Human Family, and of our own souls, that we have this day assembled. Fain would we have slumbered, and, "like the Dove that [?] and conceals the arrow that is preying upon its vitals," for the sake of avoiding the furious and turbulent storm of persecution that will gather, soon to burst upon our heads, have covered and concealed that which, for a season, has been brooding among the ruins of our peace: but we rely upon the arm of Jehovah, the Supreme Arbiter of the world, to whom we this day, and upon this occasion, appeal for the rectitude of our intentions.

. . . .

As for our acquaintance with the Church of Jesus Christ of Latter Day Saints, we know no man or set of men can be more thoroughly acquainted with its rise, its organization, and its history, than we have every reason to believe we are. We all verily believe, and many of us know of a surety, that the religion of the Latter Day Saints, as originally taught by Joseph Smith, which is contained in the Old and New Testaments, Book of Covenants, and Book of Mormon, is verily true, and that the pure principles set forth in those Books, are the immutable and eternal principles of Heaven, and speaks a language which, when spoken in truth and virtue, sinks deep into the heart of every honest man. . . .

We are earnestly seeking to explode the vicious principles of Joseph Smith, and those who practice the same abominations. . . .

Many of us have sought a reformation in the church, without a public exposition of the enormities of crimes practiced by its leaders, thinking that if they would hearken to council, and show fruit meet for repentance, it would be as acceptable with God, as though they were exposed to public gaze. . . . But our petitions were treated with contempt, and in many cases the petitioner spurned from their presence, and particularly by Joseph, who would state that if he had sinned, and was guilty of any charges we would charge him with, he would not make acknowledgment, but would rather be damned; for it would detract from his dignity, and would consequently prove the ruin and overthrow of the Church.

We would ask him on the other hand, if the overthrow of the Church was not inevitable, to which he often replied, that we would all go to Hell together, and convert it into a Heaven, by casting the Devil out; and says he, Hell is by no means the place this world of fools suppose it to be, but on the contrary it is quite an agreeable place, to which we would now reply he can enjoy it if he is determined not to desist from his evil ways, but as for us, and ours, we *will* serve the Lord our God!

It is a notorious fact that many females in foreign climes, and in countries to us unknown, even in the most distant regions of the Eastern Hemisphere, have been induced, by the sound of the gospel, to forsake friends, and to embark upon a voyage across waters that lie stretched over the greater portion of the globe, as they supposed, to glorify God, that they might thereby stand acquitted in the great day of God Almighty. But what is taught them upon their arrival in this place? They are visited by some of the Strikers, for we know not what else to call them, and are requested to hold on and be faithful, for there are great blessings awaiting the righteous; and that God has great mysteries in store for those who love the Lord, and cling to brother Joseph. They are also notified that brother Joseph will see them soon, and reveal the mysteries of Heaven to their full understanding, which confidence in the Prophet, as well as a great anxiety to know what God has laid up in store for them, in return for the great sacrifice of father and mother, of gold and silver, which they gladly left far behind, that they might be gathered into the fold, and numbered among the chosen of God.—They are visited again, and what is the result? They are requested to meet brother Joseph, or some of the Twelve, at some insulated point, or at some particularly described place on the bank of the Mississippi, or at some room which wears upon its front—*Positively* NO *Admittance*. The harmless, inoffensive, and unsuspecting creatures are so devoted to the Prophet, and the cause of Jesus Christ, that they do not dream of the deep-laid and fatal scheme which prostrates happiness and renders death itself desirable; but they meet him, expecting to receive through him a blessing, and learn the will of the Lord concerning them, and what awaits the faithful followers of Joseph, the Apostle and Prophet of God, when in the stead thereof, they are told, after having been sworn in one of the most solemn manners, to never divulge what is revealed to them, with a penalty of death attached, that God Almighty has revealed it to him, that she should be his (Joseph's) spiritual wife; for it was right anciently, and God will tolerate it again; but we must keep those pleasures and blessings from the world, for until there is a change in the government, we will endanger ourselves by practicing it—but we can enjoy the blessings of Jacob, David, and others, as well as to be deprived of them, if we do not expose ourselves to the law of the land. She is thunderstruck, faints, recovers, and refuses. The Prophet damns her if she rejects. She thinks of the great sacrifice, and of the many thousand miles she had traveled over sea and land, that she might save her soul from pending ruin, and replies, God's will be done, and not mine. The Prophet and his devotees in this way are gratified. The next step to avoid public exposition from the common course of things, they are sent away for a time, until all is well; after which they return, as from a long visit. Those whom no power or influence could seduce, except that which is wielded by some individual feigning to be a God, must realize the remarks of an able writer, when he says, "if woman's feelings are turned to ministers of sorrow, where shall she look for consolation? . . ."

Our hearts have mourned and bled over the wretched and miserable condition of females in this place; many orphans have been the victims of misery and wretchedness, through the influence that has been exerted over them, under the cloak of religion and afterwards, in consequence of that *jealous disposition* which predominates over the minds of *some*, have been turned upon a wide world, fatherless and motherless; destitute of friends and fortune; and *robbed of that which nothing but death can restore.*

It is difficult—perhaps impossible—to describe the wretchedness of females in this place, without wounding the feelings of the benevolent, or shocking the delicacy of the refined; but the truth shall come to the world.

. . . .

The next important item which presents itself for our consideration, is the attempt at political power and influence, which we verily believe to be preposterous and absurd. We believe it is inconsistent, and not in accordance with the christian religion. We do not believe that God ever raised up a Prophet to christianize a world by political schemes and intrigue. It is not the way God captivates the heart of the unbeliever; but on the contrary, by preaching truth in its own native simplicity, and in its own original purity, unadorned with anything except its own indigenous beauties. Joseph may plead he has been injured, abused, and his petitions treated with contempt by the general government, and that he only desires an influence of a political character that will warrant him redress of grievances; but we care not; the faithful follower of Jesus must bear in this age as well as Christ and the Apostles did anciently; although a frowning world may have crushed him to the dust; although unpitying friends may have passed him by; although hope, the great comforter in affliction, may have burst forth and fled from his troubled bosom; yet, in Jesus there is a balsam for every wound, and a cordial to assuage an agonized mind.

Among the many items of false doctrine that are taught the Church, is the doctrine of *many* Gods, one of the most direful in its effects that has characterized the world for many centuries. We know not what to call it other than blasphemy, for it is most unquestionably speaking of God in an impious and irreverent manner.—It is contended that there are innumerable Gods as much above the God that presides over this universe, as he is above us; and if he varies from the law unto which he is subjected, he, with all his creatures, will be cast down as was Lucifer; thus holding forth a doctrine which is effectually calculated to sap the very foundation of our faith: and now, O Lord, shall we sit still and be silent, while thy name is thus blasphemed, and thine honor, power, and glory, brought into disrepute? . . .

. . . .

On Thursday evening, the 18th of April [1844], there was a council called, unknown to the Church, which tried, condemned, and cut off Wm. Law, Wilson Law, and sister Law, (Wm.'s wife,) brother R. D. Foster, and one brother Smith, with whom we are unacquainted; which we contend is contrary to the book of Doctrine and Covenants, for our law condemnest no man until he is heard. We abhor and protest against any council or tribunal in this Church, which will not suffer the accused to stand in its midst and please their own cause. If an Agrippa would suffer a Paul, whose eloquence surpassed, as it were, the eloquence of men, to stand before him, and plead his own cause, why should Joseph, with others, refuse to hear individuals in their own defence?—We answer, it is because the court fears the atrocity of its crimes will be exposed to public gaze. We wish the public to thoroughly understand the nature of this court, and judge of the legality of its acts as seems to them good.

On Monday, the 15th of April, brother R. D. Foster had a notice served on him to appear before the High Council on Saturday following, the 20th, and answer to charges preferred against him by Joseph Smith. On Saturday, while Mr. Foster was preparing to take his witnesses, 41 in number, to the council-room, that he might make good his charges against Joseph, president Marks notified him that the trial had been on Thursday evening, before the 15th, and that he was cut off from the Church, and that the same council cut off the brother Laws', sister Law, and brother Smith, and all without their knowledge. They were not notified, neither did they dream of any such thing being done, for William Law had sent Joseph and some of the Twelve, special word that he desired an investigation before the Church in General Conference, on the 6th of Ap'l. The court, however, was a tribunal possessing no power to try Wm. Law, who was called by special Revelation, to stand as counsellor to the President of the Church, (Joseph), which was twice ratified by General Conferences, assembled at Nauvoo, for Brigham Young, one of the Twelve, presided, whose duty it was not, but the President of the High Council.—See Book of Doctrine and Covenants, page 87.

Resolutions

Resolved 1st, That we will not encourage the acts of any court in this church, for the trial of any of its members, which will not [allow] the members to be present and plead their own cause; we therefore declare our decided disapprobation to the course pursued last Thursday evening, (the 18th inst.) in the case of William and Wilson Law, and Mrs. William Law, and R. D. Foster, as being unjust and unauthorized by the laws of the Church, and consequently null and void; for our law judgeth no man unless he be heard; and to all those who approbate a course so unwarranted, unprecedented, and so unjust, we would say beware lest the unjust measure you meet to your brethren, be again meeted out to you.

Resolved 2nd, Inasmuch as we have for years borne with the individual follies, and iniquities of Joseph Smith, Hyrum Smith, and many other official characters in the Church of Jesus Christ, (conceiving it as a duty incumbent upon us so to bear,) and having labored with them repeatedly with all Christian love, meekness and humility, yet to no effect, feel as if forbearance has ceased to be a virtue, and hope of reformation vain; and inasmuch as they have introduced false and damnable doctrines into the Church, such as a plurality of Gods above the God of this universe, and his liability to fall with all of his creations; the plurality of wives, for time and eternity; the doctrine of unconditional sealing up to eternal life, against all crimes except that of shedding innocent blood, by a perversion of their priestly authority, and thereby forfeiting the holy priesthood, according to the word of Jesus: "If a man abide not in me, he is cast forth as a branch and is withered, and men gather them and cast them into the fire, and they are burned," St. John, xv, 6. "Whosoever transgresseth and abideth not in the doctrine of Christ, hath not God, he that abideth in the doctrine of Christ, hath both the Father and the Son; if there come any unto you and bring not this doctrine, receive him not into your house, neither bid him God speed, for he that biddeth him God speed is a partaker of his evil deeds," we therefore are constrained to denounce them as apostates from the pure and holy doctrines of Jesus Christ.

Resolved 3rd, That we disapprobate and discountenance every attempt to unite church and state; and that we further believe the effort now being made by Joseph Smith for political power and influence, is not commendable in the sight of God.

Resolved 4th, That the hostile *spirit* and *conduct* manifested by Joseph Smith, and many of his associates towards Missouri, and others inimical to his purposes, are decidedly at variance with the true spirit of Christianity, and should not be encouraged by any people, much less by those professing to be ministers of the gospel of peace.

Resolved 5th, That while we disapprobate malicious persecutions and prosecutions, we hold that all [persons should be] alike amenable to the laws of the land; and that we further discountenance any chicanery to screen them from the just demands of the same.

Resolved 6th, That we consider the religious influence exercised in financial concerns by Joseph Smith, as unjust as it is unwarranted, for the Book of Doctrine and Covenants makes it the duty of the Bishop to take charge of the financial affairs of the Church, and of all temporal matters pertaining to the same.

Resolved 7th, That we discountenance and disapprobate the attendance at houses of revelling and dancing; dramshops and theatres; verily believing they have a tendency to lead from paths of virtue and holiness, to those of vice and debauchery.

Resolved 8th, That we look upon the pure and holy doctrines set forth in the Scriptures of Divine truth, as being the immutable doctrines of salvation; and he who abideth in them shall be saved, and he who abideth not in them can not inherit the Kingdom of Heaven.

Resolved 9th, That we consider the gathering in haste, and by sacrifice, to be contrary to the will of God; and that it has been taught by Joseph Smith and others for the purpose of enabling them to sell property at most exorbitant prices, not regarding the welfare of the Church, but through their covetousness reducing those who had the means to give employment to the poor, to the necessity of seeking labor for themselves; and thus the wealth which is brought into the place is swallowed up by the one great throat, from whence there is no return, which if it had been economically disbursed among the whole would have rendered all comfortable.

Resolved 10th, That notwithstanding our extensive acquaintance with the financial affairs of the Church we do not know of any property which in reality belongs to the Church, (except the Temple) and we therefore consider the injunction laid upon the saints compelling them to purchase property of the trustee in trust for the Church is a deception practiced upon them, and that we look upon the sending of special agents abroad to collect funds for the Temple and other purposes as a humbug practiced upon the saints by Joseph and others, to aggrandize themselves, as we do not believe that the monies and property so collected have been applied as the donors expected, but have been used for speculative purposes, by Joseph, to gull the saints the better on their arrival at Nauvoo, by buying the lands in the vicinity and selling again to them at ten-fold advance; and further that we verily believe the appropriations said to have been subscribed by shares for the building of the Nauvoo House to have been used by J. Smith and Lyman Wight for other purposes, as out of the mass of stock already taken the building is far from being finished even to the base.

Resolved 11th, That we consider all secret societies, and combinations under oaths and obligations, (professing to be organized for religious purposes,) to be anti-Christian, hypocritical, and corrupt.

Resolved 12th, That we will *not* acknowledge any man as king or law-giver to the church; for Christ is our only king and law-giver.

Resolved 13th, That we call upon the honest in heart, in the Church, and throughout the world, to vindicate the pure doctrines of Jesus Christ, whether set forth in the Bible, Book of Mormon, or Book of Covenants, and we hereby withdraw the hand of fellowship from all those who practice or teach doctrines contrary to the above, until they crave so to do, and show works meet for repentance.

Resolved 14th, That we hereby notify all those holding licenses to preach the gospel, who know they are guilty of teaching the doctrine of other Gods above the God of this creation; the plurality of wives; the unconditional sealing up against all crimes, save that of shedding innocent blood; the spoiling of the gentiles, and all other doctrines, (so called) which are contrary to the laws of God, or to the laws of our country, to cease preaching and to come and make satisfaction, and have their licenses renewed.

Resolved 15th, That in all our controversies in defense of truth and righteousness, the weapons of our warfare are not carnal but mighty through God, to the pulling down of the strong holds of Satan; that our strifes are not against flesh, blood, nor bones; but against principalities and power[s], against spiritual wickedness in high places, and therefore we will not use carnal weapons save in our own defence.

——————— •••• *9* •••• ———————

The Nauvoo City Council Acts against the "Expositor"

Perhaps no document shows more clearly how Joseph Smith dominated the government of his community than the account of the 8 June 1844 city council meeting (continued on 10 June), at which the *Expositor* was declared a nuisance that must be destroyed. Reprinted here are the council minutes as they appeared in the *Nauvoo Neighbor*, 19 June 1844, pp. 2–3. They show that Smith called the newspaper a "treasonable" threat to the city's "chartered rights," asserted that the dissenters wanted to incite violence against Nauvoo, and called for the paper's destruction no less than four times during the meeting. And when a council member had the audacity not to follow his lead, Smith showed his disapproval, remarking that "he was sorry to have one dissenting voice in declaring the *Expositor* a nuisance." He expected total compliance with his plan for removing the threat to his control of the community, just as he wanted compliance in all things from the leaders of the Reformed Mormon Church.

These proceedings violated the constitutional rights of the dissenters, for there was no due process of law. The city council was not a court, nor were the accused charged with anything, notified of the proceedings against them, or allowed to defend themselves. Furthermore, there was no existing nuisance law with respect to newspapers. An ordinance to cover the action was passed after the *Expositor* started publishing, and it was used as a pretext to destroy the press and intimidate the publishers. Clearly, the purpose of the city council meeting was not to seek the truth or administer justice, but to eliminate critics and purge from the community an influence that was heretical, because the dissenters' reform proposals challenged the central Mormon myths of inherent innocence and leadership by revelation. No other Mormon action revealed so convincingly to non-Mormons around Nauvoo the threat that Smith's theocratic government posed to democracy.

More importantly, during the proceedings all sorts of slanderous remarks were made about the publishers which were unrelated to the contents of the Expositor and unsupported by evidence. That reveals much about the Mormon mythic consciousness, in which guilt and innocence were matters of belief, not evidence. Moreover, the entire council meeting was deeply influenced by psychological projection. Aspects of the self—and of the community, approved by the conscious self—that were disturbing to the Mormon mind (multiple sexual relationships, false swearing, etc.) were attributed to the dissenters, thereby relieving the inner tensions of the accusers. When council member Orson Spencer said, "We have found these men covenant breakers with God, with their wives!! &c.," he unconsciously put his finger on the repressed anxieties that haunted the Mormon mind. The council meeting was, in fact, an act of scapegoating, a psychological purgation or a casting out of "iniquity" by attributing it to others. When council member Levi Richards exclaimed about the press, "Let it be thrown out of this city," he was expressing symbolically what everyone really wanted: the casting out of the dissenters for whom the press had spoken. Within two days of the council meeting, that had been accomplished.

Mr. Editor:

In your last week's paper I proposed giving your readers an account of the proceedings of the City Council but time forbids any thing more than a brief SYNOPSIS of the PROCEEDINGS of the MUNICIPALITY of the City of Nauvoo, relative to the destruction of the press and fixtures of the "Nauvoo Expositor."

> *City Council, Regular Session*
> *June 8th, 1844.*

In connection with other business as stated in last week's paper, the Mayor remarked that he believed it generally the case, that when a man goes to law, he has an unjust cause, and wants to go before some one who wants business, and that he had very few cases on his docket, and referring to Councilor Emmons, editor of the Nauvoo Expositor, suggested the propriety of first purging the City Council; and, referring to the character of the paper and proprietors, called upon Theodore Turley, a mechanic, who being sworn, said that the Laws, (Wm. and Wilson,) had brought *Bogus Dies* to him to fix.

Councillor Hyrum Smith inquired what good Foster, and his brother, and the Higbee's [sic], and Laws had ever done; while his brother Joseph was under arrest, from the Missouri persecution, the Laws and Robert D. Foster would have been rode on a rail, if he had not stepped forward to prevent it, on account of their oppressing the poor.

Mayor said, while he was under arrest by writ from Gov. [Thomas] Carlin, Wm. Law pursued him for $40.00 he was owing Law, and it took the last expense money he had to pay it.

Councillor H. Smith referred to J. H. Jackson's coming to this city, &c. Mayor said, Wm. Law, had offered Jackson, $500.00 to kill him.

Councillor H. Smith continued—Jackson told him he (Jackson) meant to have his daughter; and threatened him if he made any resistance. Jackson related to him a dream; that Joseph and Hyrum were opposed to him, but that he would execute his purposes; that Jackson, had laid a plan with four or five persons to kidnap his daughter, and threatened to shoot any one that should come near after he had got her in the skiff; that Jackson, was engaged in trying to make Bogus, which was his principal business—referred to the revelation, read to the High Council of the Church, which has caused so much talk about a multiplicity of wives; that said Revelation was in answer to a question concerning things which transpired in former days, and had no reference to the present time. That when sick, Wm. Law confessed to him that he had been "guilty of adultery," and "was not fit to live," and had "sinned against his own soul," &c. and enquired, who was Judge Emmons? When he came here he had scarce two shirts to his back, but he had been dandled by the authorities of the city, &c. and was now editor of the "Nauvoo Expositor," and his right hand man [was] Francis M. Higbee, who had confessed to him that he had had the P * * [pox, syphilis]. . . .

Mayor suggested that the Council pass an ordinance to prevent misrepresentation and libelous publications, and conspiracies against the peace of the city; and referring to the reports that Dr. Foster had set afloat, said he had never made any proposals to Foster to come back to the church. Foster proposed to come back; came to Mayor's house and wanted a private interview; had some conversation with Foster in the hall, in presence of several gentlemen, on the 7th inst.; offered to meet him and have an interview in presence of friends, three or four to be selected by each party—which Foster agreed to; and went to bring his friends for the interview, and the next notice he had of him was the following letter:

June 7th 1844

To General J. Smith,

Sir, I have consulted my friends in relation to your proposals of settlement, and they as well as myself are of opinion that your conduct, and that of your unworthy, unprincipled, clan is so base that it would be morally wrong & detract from the dignity of Gentlemen to hold any conference with you. The repeated insults and abuses, I as well as my friends have suffered from your unlawful course towards us demands honorable resentment. We are resolved to make this our motto; nothing on our part has been done to provoke your anger but have done all things as become men; you have trampled upon everything we hold dear and sacred, you have set all law at defiance and profaned the name of the most high to carry out your damnable purposes—and I have nothing more to fear from you than you have already threatened, & I as well as my friends will stay here and maintain and magnify the law as long as we stay—and we are resolved never to leave until we sell or exchange our property that we have here, the proposals made by your agent, Dimick Huntington as well as the threats you sent to intimidate me, I disdain and despise as I do their unhallowed author; the right of my family and my friends demands by my hand a refusal of all your offers; we are united in virtue and truth, and we set hell at defiance and all her agents adieu.

R. D. Foster.

Mayor continued:—And when Foster left his house, he went to a shoe shop on the hill and reported, that Joseph said to him, if he would come back he would give him Law's place in the Church, and a hat full of specie. . . .

Mayor said if he had a City Council who felt as he did, the establishment (referring to the Nauvoo Expositor) would be declared a nuisance before night—and then he read an editorial from the Nauvoo Expositor. He then asked who ever said a word against Judge Emmons until he attacked this council—or even against Joseph H. Jackson or the Laws, until they came out against the city? Here is a paper (Nauvoo Expositor) that is exciting our enemies abroad. Joseph H. Jackson has been proved a murderer before this council, and declared the paper a nuisance, a greater nuisance than a dead carcass—they make it a criminality, for a man to have a wife on the earth, while he has one in heaven, according to the keys of the Holy Priesthood—and he then read a statement of William Law's from the Expositor, where the truth of God was transformed into a lie concerning this thing.—He then read several statements of Austin Cowles in the Expositor concerning a private interview, and said he never had any private conversation with Austin Cowles on these subjects—that he preached on the stand from the bible, shewing the order in ancient days, having nothing to do with the present times. What the opposition party wants is to raise a mob on us and take the spoil from us, as they did in Missouri—he said it was as much as he could do to keep his clerk, Thompson, from publishing the proceedings of the Laws and causing the people to rise up against them—said he would rather die to-morrow and have the thing smashed, than live and have it go on, for it was exciting the spirit of mobocracy among the people and bringing death and destruction upon us.

Peter Hawes, recalled a circumstance which he had forgot to mention concerning a Mr. Smith who came from England and soon after died—the children had no one to protect them; there was one girl 16 or 17 years old and a younger sister—witness took these girls into his family out of pity. Wilson Law, then Major General of the Nauvoo Legion, was familiar with the oldest daughter.—Witness cautioned the girl.—Wilson was soon there again and went out in the evening with the girl, who when charged by the witness's wife confessed that Wilson Law had seduced her. Witness told her he could not keep her—the girl wept, made much ado, and many promises—witness told her if she would do right, she might stay, but she did not keep her promise.—Wilson came again and she went with him—witness then required her to leave his house.

Mayor said certain women came to complain to his wife—that they had caught Wilson Law with the girl on the floor at Mr. Hawes' in the night.

Councillor H. Smith proceeded to shew the falsehood of Austin Cowles in the "Expositor," in relation to the revelation referred to, that it was in reference to *former* days, and not the present time as related by Cowles.

Mayor said he had never preached the revelation in private, as he had in public—had not taught to the anointed in the church in private, which statement many present confirmed, that on enquiring concerning the passage on the resurrection concerning "they neither marry nor are given in marriage," &c., he received for answer, men in this life must marry in view of eternity, otherwise they must remain as angels, or be single in heaven, which was the doctrine of the revelation referred to, and the Mayor spoke at considerable length in explanation of this principle and was willing for one to subscribe his name, to declare the "Expositor" and whole establishment a nuisance.

2 o'clock P.M.

The clerk of the Council [Willard Richards], bore testimony of the good character and high standing of Mr. Smith and his family, whose daughter was seduced by Wilson Law, as stated by the last witness before the morning council— that Mrs. Smith died near the mouth of the Mississippi, and the father and eldest daughter died soon after their arrival in this place and that the seduction of such a youthful, fatherless, and innocent creature by such a man in high standing as the Major General of the Nauvoo Legion, was one of the darkest, damnedest and foulest deeds on record.

Councillor Hyrum Smith concurred in the remarks made by the clerk concerning the excellent character of Mr. Smith and his family.

Mayor said the constitution did not authorize the press to publish libels and proposed that the Council make some provision for putting down the "Nauvoo Expositor."

Councillor Hyrum Smith called for a prospectus of the "Expositor."

Councillor Phelps read article 8, section 1, Constitution of Illinois.

Mayor called for the charter.

The clerk read the prospectus of the "Nauvoo Expositor."

Mayor read the statements of Francis M. Higbee from the "Expositor" and asked, "is it not treasonable against all chartered rights and privileges, and against the peace and happiness of the city?"

Councillor H. Smith was in favor of declaring the "Expositor" a nuisance.

Councillor Taylor—said no city on earth would bear such slander, and he would not bear it, and was decidedly in favor of active measures.

Mayor made a statement of what Wm. Law said before the City Council under oath, that he was a friend of the Mayor &c. &c., and asked if there were any present who recollected his statement, when scores responded, yes!

Councillor Hunter "was one of the grand jury," said Wm. Law stated before the grand jury that he did not say to the Council that he was Joseph's friend.

Councillor Taylor continued—Wilson Law was president of this Council during the passage of many ordinances, and referred to the Records; Wm. Law and Emmons were members of the Council, and Emmons has never objected to any ordinance while in the Council; but has been more like a cypher, and is now become Editor of a libellous paper, and is trying to destroy our charter and ordinances; he then read from the constitution of the United States on the freedom of the press, and said, "we are willing they should publish the truth"; but it is unlawful to publish libels; the Expositor "is a nuisance, and stinks in the nose of every honest man."

Mayor read from Illinois Constitution, Article 8, Section 12, touching the responsibility of the press for its constitutional liberty.

Councillor Stiles said a nuisance was any thing that dtsturbs [*sic*] the peace of a community and read Blackstone on private wrongs, Vol. 2, page 4, and "the whole community has to rest under the stigma of these falsehoods"; referring to the "Expositor," and if we can prevent the issuing of any more slanderous communications, he would go for it; it is right for this community to show a proper resentment, and he would go in for suppressing all further communications of the kind.

Councillor H. Smith believed the best way was to smash the preess [*sic*] and "pi" the type.

Councillor Johnson concurred with the councillors who had spoken.

Alderman Bennett referred to the statement of the "Expositor" concerning the Municipal Court in the case of Jeremiah Smith as a libel, and considered the paper a public nuisance.

Councillor Warrington considered his peculiar situation, as he did not belong to any church or any party; thought it might be considered rather harsh for the council to declare the paper a nuisance, and proposed giving a few days limitation and assessing a fine of $3,000 for every libel and if they would not cease publishing libels to declare it a nuisance and said the statutes made provisions for a fine of $500.

Mayor replied that they threatened to shoot him when at Carthage and the women and others dare not go to Carthage to prosecute, and read a libel from the "Expositor" concerning the imprisonment of Jeremiah Smith.

Councillor H. Smith spoke of the Warsaw Signal and disapprobated its libelous course.

Mayor remarked he was sorry to have one dissenting voice in declaring the "Expositor" a nuisance.

Councillor Warrington did not mean to be understood to go against the proposition; but it would not be in haste in declaring a nuisance.

Councillor H. Smith referred to the mortgages and property of the proprietors of the "Expositor" and thought there would be little chance of collecting damages for libels.

Alderman E.[lias] Smith considered there was but one course to pursue, that the proprietors were out of the reach of the law; that our course was to put an end to the thing at once; believed by what he had heard that if the city did not do it, others would.

Councillor Hunter believed it to be a nuisance; referred to the opinion of Judge Pope on habeas corpus and spoke in favor of the charter &c.; asked Francis M. Higbee, before the grand jury, if he was not the man he saw at Joseph's house making professions of friendship; Higbee said he was not; (Hundreds know this statement to be false;) he also asked R. D. Foster if he did not state before hundreds of people that he believed Joseph to be a prophet; "no" said Foster. They were all under oath when they said it. (Many hundreds of people are witness to this perjury).

Alderman Orson Spencer accorded with the views expressed, that the "Nauvoo Expositor," is a nuisance, did not consider it wise to give them time to trumpet a thousand lies, their property could not pay for it; if we pass only a fine or imprisonment, have we any confidence that they will desist? none at all! we have found these men covenant breakers with God! with their wives!! &c., have we any hope of their doing better? Their characters have gone before them, shall they be suffered to go on, and bring a mob upon us; and murder our women and children, and burn our beautiful city! No! I had rather my blood would be spilled at once, and would like to have the press removed as soon as the ordinance would allow— and wish the matter might be put into the hands of the mayor, and every body stand by him, in the execution of his duties—and hush every murmur.

Councillor Levi Richards, said he felt deeply on this subject, and concurred fully in the view General Smith had expressed of it this day, thought it unnecessary to repeat what the council perfectly understood; considered private interest as nothing in comparison with the public good:—every time a line was formed in Far West, he was there, for what? to defend it against just such scoundrels, and influence as the Nauvoo Expositor and its supporters were directly calculated to bring against us again.— Considered the doings of the counci[l] this day of immense moment, not to this city alone, but to the whole world,—would go in to put a stop to the thing at once, let it be thrown out of this city, and the responsibility of countenancing such a press, be taken off our shoulders, and fall on the state, if corrupt enough to sustain it.

Councillor Phineas Richards said that he had not forgotten the transaction at Haun's mills, and that he recollected that his son George Spencer, then lay in the well referred to, on the day previous, without a winding-sheet, shroud, or coffin; he said he could not sit still when he saw the same spirit raging in this place; he considered the publication of the Expositor as much murderous at heart as David was before the death of Uriah; was prepared to take his stand by the Mayor and whatever he proposes, would stand by him to the last. The quicker it is stopt [*sic*] the better.

Councillor Phelps had investigated the constitution, charter, and laws: the power to declare that office a nuisance is granted to us, in the Springfield charter, and a resolution declaring it a nuisance is all that is required.

John Birney sworn—said Francis M. Higbee, and Wm. Law, declared they had commenced their operations, and would carry them out, *law or no law*.

Stephen Markham, sworn, said that Francis M. Higbee said the interest of this city is done, the moment a hand is laid on their press.

Councillor Phelps continued, and referred to Wilson Law in destroying the character of a child, an orphan child, who had the charge of another child.

Warren Smith sworn, said F. M. Higbee came to him, and proposed to have him go in as a partner in making bogus money. Higbee said he would not work for a living; that witness might go in with him, if he would advance fifty dollars and showed him (witness) a half dollar which he said was made in his dies.

Councillor Phelps continued and said, he felt deeper this day than ever he felt before, and wanted to know, by yes, if there was any present who wanted to avenge the blood of the innocent female, who had been seduced by the then Major General of the Nauvoo Legion, Wilson Law; when yes!! resounded from every quarter of the house; he then referred to the tea plot, at Boston, and asked if anybody's rights were taken away with that transaction, and are we offering, or have we offered to take away the rights of any one these two days? (*No!!!* resounded from every quarter.) He then referred also to Law's grinding the poor during the scarcity of grain, while the poor had nothing but themselves to grind; and spoke at great length in support of active measures to put down iniquity, and suppress the spirit of mobocracy.

Alderman Harris spoke from the chair, and expressed his feelings that the press ought to be demolished.

The following resolution was then read and passed unanimously, with the exception of Councillor Warrington:

Resolved, by the City Council of the City of Nauvoo, that the printing office from whence issues the "Nauvoo Expositor" is a public nuisance, and also all of said Nauvoo Expositors, which may be, or exist in said establishment, and the Mayor is instructed to cause said printing establishment and papers to be removed without delay, in such manner as he shall direct. Passed June 10th, 1844.

GEO. W. HARRIS,
Prest. pro tem.

━━━━━●●●● 10 ●●●●━━━━━

A Dissenter Reports the Destruction of the "Expositor"

Joseph Smith moved very quickly against the *Expositor*. After the city council agreed on what should be done about the press, Smith acted as mayor to order the city police to destroy it, and then he acted as lieutenant general of the Nauvoo Legion to provide military support for the institutionalized violence. The press was destroyed without prior notice on the evening of 10 June 1844, before the dissenters could get out their second issue. (Smith's haste was no doubt prompted by the editors' statement that subsequent issues of the *Expositor* would publish "Affadavits . . . to substantiate the facts alleged.") Afterward the men involved returned to the prophet's home, where, as recorded in his journal, "I gave them a short address and told them they had done right," and assured them "that I would never submit to have another libelous publication . . . established in this city" (Scott H. Faulring, ed., *An American Prophet's Record: The Diaries and Journals of Joseph Smith* [Salt Lake City: Signature Books, 1987], 489). The men cheered him and went home.

The earliest published accounts of the violence by an eyewitness came from Charles A. Foster, one of the owners of the newspaper. He and copublisher Francis Higbee were at the *Expositor* office when Smith's forces invaded the building, destroyed the press, and burned newspapers, furniture, and press fragments in the street. As Higbee and Foster so clearly recognized, the event was a mob action. It had simply been licensed by Smith, who controlled the government as well as the Nauvoo Legion, which carried out the destruction under the direction of the marshal.

Higbee took the matter to court, charging Smith and others with riot, but since the Nauvoo court was under Smith's control, he was "honorably discharged," and Higbee was accused by the court of "malicious prosecution" and assessed the court costs. Moreover, Smith then acted in his judicial capacity to exonerate the others who were accused with him, including Hyrum Smith and John Taylor. In short, the prophet's activities in the *Expositor* affair were clear evidence to those outside Nauvoo that *he* was the repository of governmental authority and that local institutions—the city council, the police, the military, the court—served the people only insofar as they served his purposes. This, of course, infuriated others watching these events from the villages about Nauvoo.

Realizing that justice was impossible at Nauvoo, Foster took the matter to the public. He fled to Warsaw, where on 11 June 1844 he wrote a brief account of the violence for the *Warsaw Signal*, edited by Mormon hater Thomas C. Sharp, expressing his outrage at the "Mormon MOBOCRATS." He then took the steamboat *Osprey* to St. Louis. While on board, he wrote a longer, more detailed account, which appeared as "Tremendous Excitement—Unparalleled Outrage. On Board Steamer 'Osprey'" in the *St. Louis Evening Gazette*, 12 June 1844, p. 2. It is reprinted here.

Foster's letters and reports by others did alert people to what had occurred, and as a result, public opinion of Smith and the Mormon leaders reached its lowest point. Many western Illinois residents became alarmed and wondered what the Mormons would do next. In Hancock County various meetings were held to express concern, and men began to organize into military companies.

———————•••◦◉◦•••———————

Mr. Editor: —In behalf of the publishers of the "Nauvoo Expositor," and for the purpose of informing the public, I hasten to lay before your readers and the community generally, the particulars of one of the most unparalleled outrages ever perpetrated in the country.

On Monday evening, last, a company consisting of some two or three hundred of the Nauvoo Legion, assisted by as many volunteers, armed with Muskets, Swords, Pistols, Bowie Knives, &c., marched up in front of the office of the "Expositor"—entered the building by breaking open the door with a sledge-hammer, and destroyed the Press and all the materials, by throwing them into the street and setting the whole on fire.

This took place between the hours of 7 and 10 P.M. The particulars are as follows. A large and respectable portion of the citizens having become fully convinced by the most conclusive testimony, and their own observation, that the character of Jo Smith, in connection with many of the Mormon leaders, had become so base and corrupt that longer countenance would be crime. They early in April last, resolved themselves into a new Society, styled the "Reformed Mormon Church," and appointed William Law their President. The old church party felt very uneasy about the establishment of this new party, and commenced a tirade of abuse and slander, against the characters and persons of those who had heretofore stood in high estimation, simply because they dared to think for themselves and express their honest opinions.

The new party, having no organ through which to speak, being denied the privilege of publishing any thing *against* Joe (however true it might be), had the only alternative left, to establish a Press of their own, or else, quietly submit to the foul and false assertions which were heaped upon them by wholesale, as often as the "Nauvoo Neighbor" made its appearance.

For the purpose then, of establishing a free and independent press in Nauvoo, thro' which we might advocate equal rights to every citizen, and whereby all might speak for themselves, a company of several gentlemen (some of whom were members of the new church, and some of no church) formed themselves into a Committee to publish the "Nauvoo Expositor," the first number of which appeared on the 7th inst. as proposed in the Prospectus. The next day an extra session of the City Council was called for the purpose of adopting means and measures to bring our youthful paper to an immediate and untimely fate.—The Expositor was eagerly sought on all hands—some had the audacity to read it in the public street, while others,—poor, pitiable creatures,—would conceal it in their pockets and repair to some private corner, and there peruse it! In the council various opinions were expressed, as to the *modus operandi* of suppressing our odious paper, whose only offence was, telling the truth and exposing to public gaze the iniquities of those who were governing us with a heart of steel and a rod of iron. Some suggested the propriety of passing an *ordinance* in relation to libels, but Joe and Hiram (Joe's brother) raved and swore away with a vengeance, declaring it a *nuisance*, which should be demolished on the spot, together with the property of all concerned in its publication, if they made any resistance or defence. One liberal councilman thought they should notify, but this was objected to, the ordinance was passed, the orders given, and the troops presented themselves, as full of fight as old Joe is of folly.

The excitement here became tremendous. Surrounded on all sides by a ruthless and merciless gang of ruffians, and being few in number, ourselves, we knew not what to do: our feelings were too deeply wounded for utterance—already insulted beyond endurance, we must now submit to the forfeiture of our rights to the mercy of a mob, and that under sanction of law. We concluded to make no resistance. When they had marshalled their troops before the office, F. M. Higbee and myself, in behalf of the Publishers, forbade their entering the premises or laying hands on the press; they paid no regard to our commands, but marched upstairs, broke open the door—entered the office, and demolished the Press: threw out the tables, stands, desks, &c., and scattered the type in all directions. After clearing out the office, they piled up the combustible materials and set them on fire, and burnt them to ashes, while the multitude made the air ring with their hideous yells.

This constitutes the history of this disgraceful and most outrageous affair. We have given a simple statement of the facts as they took place, without the aid of fancy or fiction and shall conclude this sketch by stating to the Public that this is but a specimen of the injustice that is meted out to those whose ambition soars higher than to obey the *dictum* of such a tyrannical wretch as Jo Smith. . . .

In this our situation—robbed of our property—stripped of our rights, and outraged on every hand, we present our case before a free and enlightened public, leaving it with them to say how long we shall be subjected to a sacrifice of our nearest and dearest rights at the shrine of unhallowed ambition.

Respectfully, &c.,

CHARLES A. FOSTER

◦••● *11* ●••◦

John Taylor Defends the Destruction of the "Expositor"

The actions of Joseph Smith and the Nauvoo City Council in destroying the *Expositor* were defended by John Taylor (1808–87), the editor of the *Nauvoo Neighbor*. Born and raised in Milnthorpe, England, he immigrated to Canada in 1830 and was baptized in Toronto in 1836. After joining the Mormon Church and making an important missionary trip to England, he moved to Kirtland, Ohio, then to Missouri, and finally to the Nauvoo area in 1839. He edited *The Millennial Star*, assisted Joseph Smith in publishing the *Times and Seasons*, and later founded and edited the *Nauvoo Neighbor*. All were sanctioned by the church hierarchy, and indeed Taylor was a key member of the Quorum of Twelve Apostles. Taylor shared Smith's intolerance of the Law brothers' dissent and was anxious to eliminate the rival newspaper. He was a member of the Nauvoo City Council and vigorously supported Smith's effort to have the *Expositor* destroyed. In 1846 Taylor left Nauvoo with the main body of Saints who went to the Great Salt Lake valley, and in subsequent years he was a very active missionary and church leader. He served in the Great Basin as the third Mormon church president from 1880 to 1887.

Taylor wrote an article entitled "Retributive Justice," which appeared in the *Nauvoo Neighbor* on 12 June 1844, p. 2. As it reveals, he used his newspaper to defame the prophet's critics and portray them as enemies of the people. He called the dissenters "blacklegs and bogus makers," and the *Expositor* itself was labeled as a "murderous paper," suggesting that the publishers were threatening people's lives. All of this is highly ironic: Taylor condemned the *Expositor* for printing "libels and slanderous articles," but those were, in fact, his own tactics, as this article demonstrates.

He employed the Mormon myth of persecuted innocence to arouse the fears of his readers and justify the destruction of the press. The newspaper, he wrote,

was intended to "raise another mob" to assault and plunder "the innocent inhabitants of this city," an irrational comment, considering that the dissenters and their
families were also members of the community. There is no evidence, furthermore,
that the dissidents wanted anything but the reforms they mentioned in their
newspaper.

The closing paragraph had a deeper, more unfortunate irony. Taylor called
for freedom of religion while praising an attack on religious dissenters by a theocratic government that did not achieve the separation of church and state upon
which religious freedom rests. However effective he may have been in supporting
the Mormon cause, John Taylor did not comprehend "the rights of Americans."

As his comments show, Mormon leaders continued to voice the rhetoric of
freedom, not realizing that their own actions had put an end to freedom in theocratic Nauvoo. They failed to acknowledge their persecution of the dissidents
because to do so would have subverted their identity as the innocent chosen people.

———————————•••••◉◉•••••———————————

A knot of base men, to further their wicked and malicious designs towards
the church of Jesus Christ of Latter Day Saints, and to bolster up the intents of
blacklegs and bogus makers, and advocate the characters of murderers, established a
press in this city last week, and issued a paper entitled the "Nauvoo Expositor."
The prospectus showed an intention to destroy the charter, and the paper was
filled with libels and slanderous articles upon the citizens and city council from
one end to the other.

"A Burnt child dreads the fire"; the church as a body and individually has
suffered till "forbearance has ceased to be a virtue": the cries and pleadings of men,
women and children, with the authorities, were, will you suffer that servile mur-
derous-intended paper to go on and vilify and slander the innocent inhabitants of
this city, and raise another *mob* to drive and plunder us again as they did in
Missouri? Under these pressing cries and supplications of afflicted innocence, and
in the character, dignity, and honor of the corporate powers of the charter, as
granted to the city of Springfield, and made and provided as part of our charter for
legislative purposes: viz, *"to declare what shall be a nuisance, and to prevent and
remove the same,"* the city council of Nauvoo on Monday the 10th, inst. declared
the establishment and Expositor a *nuisance;* and the city Marshall at the head of
the police in the evening took the *press*, materials and paper into the street and
burnt them.

And in the name of freemen, and in the name of God, we beseech all men,
who have the spirit of honor in them, to cease from persecuting us collectively or
individually. Let us enjoy our religion, rights, and peace, like the rest of mankind:
why start presses to destroy rights and privileges, and bring upon us mobs to plunder and murder? We ask no more than what belongs to us—the *rights of Americans.*

———•••• *12* ••••———

The Dissenters Flee to Burlington

D avid Wells Kilbourne (1803–76) was a well-to-do farmer who had immi-grated to Iowa Territory from England. He had nothing to do with the events in Hancock County, but he was a resident of Fort Madison on 12 June 1844, when word came that Joseph Smith had destroyed the Reformed Church newspaper at Nauvoo and that the Mormon dissenters had been threatened and feared for their lives. The people of Fort Madison responded with a riverboat of volunteers to assist in their evacuation. The dissident families were taken to Burlington.

Kilbourne was apparently one of the volunteers, and during the miniature exodus from the hostile city, he spoke with Reformed Church leader William Law. His 15 June 1844 letter to Reverend T. Dent, a minister in England, is well informed, although he mistakenly places the destruction of the *Expositor* on 11 June, rather than the evening of 10 June. The original letter is available in the David W. Kilbourne Papers, State Historical Society of Iowa, Des Moines. It is published here for the first time.

———•••◉••◉•——

Fort Madison
Upper Mississippi River
June 15 1844

Revd. T. Dent
Billington near Whalley
Lancashire England

My dear Sir

Your kind & interesting letter of April 16th was rec^d on the 24th Ultimo. I can say in all sincerity that your correspondence has been a source of great pleasure as well as profit to me & I shall always be very happy in my [?] way to keep you advised of events of any interest as they transpire at the famous City of Nauvoo.

Since I last wrote you the troubles at Nauvoo have continued to increase among the Mormons themselves. The eyes of some among the most honest of the leaders have been opened to see Jos. true character. In the case of a Mr Law, a man who had stood high among them & who has considerable property—has a steam flouring mill at Nauvoo—& several dwelling houses—the one in which he has resided being a fine two story brick home—this man was sent out some time last fall on a mission to preach & during his absence Joe made proposals to his wife which she rejected & on her husbands return communicated the fact to him—this led to an outbreak between Law & Joe which has continued to the present time, and has resulted in creating great excitement there. Some few weeks since Law & his friends withdrew from the Church & formed a new one which had been daily increasing in numbers. This new Society also commenced the publication of a News Paper called the Nauvoo Expositor—the first no. of which I shall send to you with this letter. This will give you a full history of the new Society.

After this *no* was issued Joe (as Mayor) call^d a meeting of the City Council— at which meeting resolutions were pass^d declaring this new paper to be a public nuisance & finally pass^d an ordinance to destroy it; this meeting of [the] council took place on the 10th Inst, & on the 11th about sunset Joe ordered the Marshall & all the City officers with Volunteers to commence the work of destruction. About three hundred marched in a body to the printing office—took the press out & broke it into ten thousand peices [*sic*]—they then took the tables & made a pile in front of the house & burnt them—they then proceeded to Joe^s residence & gave him three cheers. They then went to the resident [*sic*] of Law & also his brother & several others who had dissented & gave them notice that they must not be found in Nauvoo the next day at 4 O clock P.M. at the risk of their lives.

The next morning the 12th Inst a messenger came up here to get a steam boat to go & bring them off—accordingly a boat started from here with some 50 of our citizens to assist removing those families whose lives were threatened.—

About dark the boat return^d here laden with men, women & children. With horses, waggons, furniture &c.—The boat proceeded to Burlington about 20 miles above this where Mr. Law told me they intended to secure quarters for the women & children & return to Nauvoo to fight if necessary.

Law told me that he would just as soon live in h——l as in Nauvoo—that Joe would have no scruples to cause any man's life to be taken to carry out his plans.

There is a great excitement throughout the state of Ill. especially in the Counties contiguous to Nauvoo.

Joe & his men were arrested the day after the press was destroyed—but he immediately cleared himself & the others by the exercise of his writ of Habeas Corpus authority—[?] the city charter.

Another writ is out for him & an [unknown line] in the surrounding counties to raise sufficient force to arrest him & take him out of the City.

I anticipate [two unknown words] then soon[er] or later bloodshed must take place. Nauvoo has become the receptacle of outlaws & robbers for the whole country, & the people it seems to me will be oblige[d] to resolve themselves into the original elements of society & rise in their majesty & disperse the banditti.

The night after Law left two attempts were made to fire his mill & house. . . .

—•••• *13* ••••—

William Law Recalls the "Expositor" Affair

The destruction of the *Expositor* was a tragedy for William Law (1809–92), the president of the new Reformed Mormon Church and a copublisher of the newspaper. A native of Ireland, Law had immigrated to America as a child and later settled in Churchville, Ontario. Converted to the Mormon Church in 1836, he led a caravan of Canadian Saints to Nauvoo three years later. He became a leading businessman and in 1841 was selected as a counselor in the First Presidency to advise Joseph Smith. However, in 1843 he objected to the new doctrine of polygamy and to the concentration of political and economic power in the prophet's hands, so early in 1844 Smith dismissed him. Two months later Smith publicly denounced Law and other critics as enemies of the people—conspirators who were planning a mass murder of all the heads of the church—thus opening the floodgates of slander and intimidation which he hoped would force them from the community.

Instead of leaving, Law and others established the Reformed Mormon Church and began holding meetings and recruiting members. Smith had several of them—including Law—excommunicated in April, but the dissenters continued their work. In May they established their opposition newspaper, the *Expositor*, which was soon destroyed. At the same time, their lives were threatened by Mormons who had been inflamed by the prophet's denunciations. Law fled with his family to Burlington, Iowa Territory, leaving behind his home, flour mill, and other property. He first went to Hampton, then Galena, and finally to Apple River, Illinois, where he practiced medicine, as he had done in Canada. He moved to Shullsburg, Wisconsin, in 1866, where he remained until his death.

Regarding his activities as a dissenter, Law wrote a letter to the editors of the *Rock Island Upper Mississippian*, which appeared on 7 September 1844, p. 1. At that time he and other former dissenters were living in Hampton, several miles northeast of Rock Island. His letter is reprinted here. It is a defense of the values and purposes of the dissenters, and Law wrote it because all Mormons at that time were viewed with suspicion by other Illinois residents. As the letter reveals, he viewed himself and the other dissenters as victims of tyranny whose civil rights had been violated and who had been driven from their homes for daring to speak against the prophet. The Mormons had, in fact, done to them what the Missourians had earlier done to the Mormons.

Equally interesting are the religious and moral values of the dissenters, for whom Law was speaking. Trying to reconcile their earlier commitment to Smith's church with more recent developments, Law asserted that "modern Mormonism is a complete apostasy from the original doctrines"—which is precisely the view that Smith had developed about Christianity in general. In short, the dissenters were Mormon Puritans, driven by a desire to cleanse the church of perceived evils. As

Law's closing comments reveal, the group stood for apostolic purity of religion and constitutional adherence in government, which have often been deeply related in the American mind. Through his revelation on polygamy and his suppression of civil rights, Smith had become an enemy of both, and that prompted Law to oppose him.

———————————•••••◉◉•••———————————

Hampton, Ill. Aug. 1844

To the Editors of the Upper Mississippian.

Gentlemen— Having seen, in your paper of the 3rd Ult., some remarks concerning myself and others, with whom I have the pleasure of being associated, in relation to our settlement at this place, &c., I take the liberty of offering a few reflections on the subject; believing that the people of this county, as well as those of the State in general, are liberal in their sentiments, and consequently willing to extend to all *law abiding* citizens that toleration and protection which they themselves expect at the hands of their fellow men. We profess to be law-abiding and industrious. We love our country and respect her institutions; and although we have been illegally and cruelly exiled from our homes and pleasant places, by the hands of Tyrants, even under the shadow of the *Eagle's wing;* yet we will not murmur, inasmuch as we have found so pleasant a resting place as this. We are sorry to learn that some of the citizens, of your county, are fearful lest we disturb their peace. They have nothing to fear from us;—why should they, even for a moment, suspect that we, who have jeopardized our lives and sacrificed some fifty thousand dollars worth of property in endeavoring to break the *yoke of tyranny* from off the necks of our fellow beings? Why think we would infringe upon the rights of any? No! Our object is altogether different from that: we desire the good, the safety, and the peace of *all*. We believe in that order of government, whether in a family, in a village, in a city, or in a nation, which distributes justice to all. We believe in that kind of religion which strengthens the cords of love between man and man—fills the mind with intelligence, and gives God glory.

It is not intended from the beginning that one should trample upon the rights of another; but that *love*, and *kindness*, and *honor*, should be manifest in all our acts. When we contemplate the *heavenly bodies*, and behold the *harmony* of the planets, as they move in the magnificence of their power, we are led to exclaim, Why is it that man does not dwell in peace with his fellow man?

You say in your paper that you are not informed whether we intend to build up another Mormon Church, with or without the peculiar odious traits of the one which we have left. To this, we say that *modern Mormonism* is a complete apostasy from the original doctrines of the Church of Jesus Christ of Latter-day Saints; and the odious traits you speak of, are as odious and disgusting to us as to any other people. The Gospel of Jesus Christ, as we find it recorded in the Scriptures of the Old and New Testament, in which we most firmly believe and upon which we base our hopes of eternal salvation, does not admit of murder, false swearing, lying, stealing, robbing, defrauding, polygamy, adultery, fornication, blasphemy. And yet those evils have been introduced into the Church at Nauvoo, by Joseph Smith and others, for the purpose of accomplishing their base designs. We have always disapproved of such things, and opposed them both privately and publicly; and *for our opposition to them*, we were driven from our homes in Nauvoo. Our lives are yet threatened by a *band of desperate men*, who have sworn with a solemn oath, *to shed our blood, even to the third generation.*—Our homes here in your peaceful county are to be given to the burning flame, and our wives to be left widows in your midst. But we trust in the arm of Almighty God to protect us. He has hitherto been our shield and strong buckler, and is still mighty to save those who put their trust in him, and *he* knows the purity of our intentions in all we have done. It may be asked, why did you stay so long in Nauvoo? To this we would answer that, until within the last year, we had no conception of the *depths of iniquity* that existed there. We knew there were some evils, but thought they might be remedied. Our homes were there, and our friends too, and many good people. We had hoped that, through the columns of the *Nauvoo Expositor*, we would have been able to place Joseph Smith and his base accomplices in crime, before the world in their true character; but the destruction of the press hindered. We next thought that a full and impartial investigation would have been had before the courts of justice, where an exposition of crimes most gross, dark, loathsome, and cruel, would have been made; but the sudden and unexpected death of the Smiths frustrated our designs. We regret exceedingly the turn things have taken. . . .

We desire to live in peace with our fellow men—we only ask the rights and privileges guarantied to us by the glorious Constitution of our country. We intend to worship God according to the dictates of our conscience, and making the Scriptures of the Old and New Testament the standard of our faith, being organized according to the Apostolic order, as near as may be, considering the manners and customs of the present age; adding to our faith, virtue; and to virtue, knowledge; and to knowledge, temperance; and to temperance, patience; and to patience, godliness; and to godliness, brotherly kindness; and to brotherly kindness, charity. Surely none can object to this!

Most Respectfully
Your Ob't serv't,
Wm. Law.

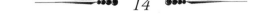

14

Willard Richards Pleads for Help

One of Joseph Smith's most trusted associates was Willard Richards (1804–54). He had been born and raised in Massachusetts and was a physician living in Boston in 1835 when he first read the Book of Mormon. He decided to move to Kirtland, Ohio, where he joined the church the following year. He was one of the first missionaries to England in 1837, and while on the mission in 1840, he was called to fill a vacancy in the Quorum of Twelve Apostles and was ordained in England by his cousin, Brigham Young. In the closing years of the prophet's life, Richards was his private secretary. He traveled west in 1846, entered the Mormon First Presidency with Brigham Young in 1847, and edited the church's newspaper in Salt Lake City, the *Deseret News*, from 1849 until his death in 1854.

The letter reprinted here was written at Smith's request but not dictated by him, so the words reflect Richards's view of the Mormon situation shortly after the destruction of the *Expositor*. It is an appeal for assistance to James Arlington Bennet, a wealthy New York businessman who had been a friend of the church for several years. But more importantly, it reflects the mindset of a true believer whose view of men and events was shaped by Mormon myth. Richards regarded the dissenters as totally evil "demons" with "hellish plans" to overthrow righteousness and destroy the innocent. Hence, they were automatically guilty of all possible wickedness. For that reason, he later even placed the names of William Law, Wilson Law, Francis M. Higbee, and other dissenters on a list of those who were in the mob that killed the Smiths, even though there is no evidence that any of them were involved and some were not even in Illinois at the time.

It apparently never occurred to Richards that Smith and the Mormon leaders had been guilty of gross civil rights violations and that their destruction of the *Expositor* and expulsion of the dissenters had understandably alarmed the surrounding public, unfortunately raising the possibility of mobocratic response. Instead he viewed the authoritarian Mormon leader as America's last, best hope, whose election to the presidency would be the "only method of saving our free institutions" in an otherwise corrupt society. As that statement demonstrates, Mormon leaders claimed to be serving the universal American good when in fact they were striving to maintain their theocracy against rising democratic pressures within the community. Richards's comments are a reminder that the suppression of freedom is often perpetrated under the guise of preserving liberty.

This letter is in the Joseph Smith, Jr., Papers. A microfilm copy is located in the Library-Archives, Reorganized Church of Jesus Christ of Latter Day Saints, Independence, Missouri. The manuscript is housed in the Archives, Church of Jesus Christ of Latter-day Saints, Salt Lake City, Utah. It is also printed in Joseph Smith, Jr., *History of the Church of Jesus Christ of Latter-day Saints*, ed. B. H. Roberts (Salt Lake City: Deseret Book Co., 1912), 6:516–18, from which the following text is taken.

Mayor's Office, Nauvoo, June 20th, 1844.

Dear General.—Yours of the 14th of April was received at a late date. A multiplicity of business on account of the peculiar state of affairs, has prevented a reply till now. Your views about the nomination of General Smith for the Presidency are correct. We will gain popularity and external influence. But this is not all: we mean to elect him, and nothing shall be wanting on our part to accomplish it; and why? Because we are satisfied, fully satisfied, that this the best or only method of saving our free institutions from a total overthrow.

You will discover by this day's extra *Nauvoo Neighbor*, and previous papers which I shall forward with this, that we are already being surrounded by an armed mob; and, if we can believe a hundredth part of their statements we have no alternative but to fight or die. All the horrors of Missouri's murders are crowding thick upon us, and the citizens of this country declare in mass-meetings, "No peace till the Mormons are utterly exterminated from the earth." And for what?

A band of thieves, counterfeiters, bogus-makers, gamblers, debauchers, murderers, and all that is vile, established a printing-press in this city for the purpose of carrying on all their hellish plans and overthrowing every principle of righteousness; and after publishing one number, called the *Nauvoo Expositor*, filled in every column with lies and libel the most dark and damnable it was possible for men or demons on the earth or in the shades of Gehenna, calculated to destroy every chartered right to our peaceful city, and constitutional principles to our nation, being destitute of every vestige of truth, and without one redeeming quality, either in the paper or the characters of its publishers.

The City Council, on the 10th instant, ordered the press and fixtures to be abated as a nuisance which order was executed by the proper authorities without delay, without noise, tumult or confusion.

The proprietors immediately evacuated their houses and the city, and the night following fired one or more of their buildings, just as they did in Missouri, thinking to raise a hue-and-cry that the Mormons had done it, and by that means bring a mob on us without a moment's delay; but our vigilant police discovered the fire and abated that also.

Chagrined at their disappointment, and drunk with madness, they next went to Carthage, the county seat and headquarters of mobocracy, and swore that Joseph and about seventeen others had committed a riot, and sent a warrant for their apprehension. They offered to go before any magistrate in the vicinity and answer to the charge. The officer would not consent, but would take them to Carthage. They had threatened their lives at Carthage and did not consider it safe to go thither, and prayed out a writ of *habeas corpus* from the Municipal Court, and were set free.

This only enraged the mob the more, and another writ was issued by a county magistrate in the vicinity, not a Mormon, before whom they were brought, and every exertion made to convict them, but the magistrate discharged them.

This does not satisfy them. They are determined to have "Joe Smith," brought before themselves for trial at the headquarters of mobocracy swearing that all they want is to get him out of the city; and they will shoot the "damned rascal."

Cannon, ammunition and men are passing over the Mississippi from Missouri to Illinois, and the mob is collected by hundreds at different points in the county swearing vengeance; and when their oaths and writs will end, God knows.

We have sent messengers to the Governor, but had no returns, and shall dispatch messages to the President of the United States next boat.

If the virtuous part of the community, the state, the nation, will come to the rescue of innocence and the rights our fathers bled to purchase, that our peace and happiness may be secured to us in common with others, it is all we ask; but if they will not, and the mob goes on, we say a dishonorable life is worse than an honorable death, and we are ready for the onset; and we call upon all patriots, far and near, to lend a helping hand to put down the mob and restore peace.

If this is not done immediately, and the mob attempt to execute their threats, you may soon have the opportunity of beholding that glorious "vision in the west" you have sublimely contemplated in your letter.

I write you at this time at the request of the Prophet, and I invite you to come to our assistance with as many volunteers as you can bring. And if the mob cannot be dispersed, and the Government will not espouse our righteous cause, you may soon, very soon, behold the second birth of our nation's freedom; for live without the free exercise of thought, and the privilege of worshiping God according to the dictates of our conscience, we will not! We will die rather, and go where the wicked cease to trouble. But we firmly believe there are virtuous men and patriots enough yet left to sustain those principles which alone are worth living for. Will you come?

Here is Oregon. Here is California. Where is your ambition? Patriotism? Your "separate and independent empire," if you sit calmly still and see the most virtuous and noble people that ever trod upon the footstool of Jehovah ground to powder by a miscreant mob and not stretch forth your potent arm for their defense in all the majesty of a God? If you do not, your turn may come next; and where will it cease?

Let the first blow be struck upon us from this hour, and this field is open for every honest patriot from the east to the west sea, and from the river Mississippi to the ends of the earth.

General, will you stand neutral? Come, and you will know for yourself.

I close in haste, with good wishes to yourself and family.

W. Richards.

—————— •••• *15* •••• ——————

Isaac and Sarah Scott Comment on the Trouble in Nauvoo

Joseph Smith's more controversial doctrines and his suppression of the dissenters caused some members of the church to become disenchanted. Isaac and Sarah Scott were two of them. Isaac was born in Ireland and immigrated to the United States with his parents in 1819. Sarah was born in 1823 and raised in Sutton, Massachusetts. In 1843 they were married in Sutton and then moved to Nauvoo, where Isaac farmed and Sarah taught school. By that time they had been members of the Latter Day Saints Church for several years.

Their letter of 16 June 1844 is reprinted from a collection by George F. Partridge, ed., called "The Death of a Mormon Dictator: Letters of Massachusetts Mormons, 1843–1848," *New England Quarterly* 9 (December 1936): 583–617; this letter appears on pp. 593–97. Isaac wrote most of it at the urging of his wife, and she added the last two paragraphs.

The Scotts object specifically to three doctrines taught in Nauvoo: "plurality of gods," polygamy, and the sealing up of the Saints against all sins but murder. These doctrines were also criticized by the dissenters in the *Expositor*. Clearly the Scotts are impressed by what the leaders of the Reformed Church have brought to light, and they are indignant about the suppression of civil rights and threats of violence that have forced the dissidents to flee the city.

They write as Mormons who are disillusioned and recognize that much deception has occurred because Smith, who was held above criticism by most Mormons, and other leaders have publicly denied what they knew to be true. This letter reveals the inner state of people who have rejected the core myths of their church—innocence and leadership by revelation—and thus no longer view Nauvoo as the "Sanctum-Sanctorum of all the Earth." In other words, after the suppression of the dissenters, the Scotts felt alienated. They still lived in Nauvoo but were no longer part of it. Ironically, the spread of that change of consciousness was precisely what Smith wanted to prevent when he destroyed the *Expositor*.

—————— ••••●•••• ——————

Vicinity of Nauvoo,
June 16, 1844.

My Dear Father and Mother:

For such I suppose I may call you, on account of the relationship that now exists between us. Altho far distant, and having never had the privilege of beholding your faces, yet I rejoice exceedingly in the pleasure which I this day enjoy of sitting down to write a few lines to *two so near and dear to me as you are*. I have greatly desired to see you since I became acquainted with your daughter, and adopted into your family. But I have had to do with only hearing from you thus far. By a letter that Mrs. Haven received from you a few days since, we have the pleasing intelligence that you are all well, which blessing we also enjoy. I am glad that I ever became united to your family, for by this step I have gotten what Solomon says is a good thing. He says he that hath gotten a wife from the Lord, hath gotten a good thing. So say I. And were it not for troubles that exist in the land, we would rejoice continually.

But because of the things that *are* and *have been* taught in the Church of Latter Day Saints for two years past which now assume a *portentous aspect*, I say because of these things we are in trouble. And were it not that we wish to give you a fair unbiased statement of facts as they really exist, we perhaps would not have written you so soon. But we feel it to be our duty to let you know how things are going on in *this land of boasted liberty*, this Sanctum-Sanctorum of all the Earth, the City of Nauvoo. The elders will likely tell you a different tale from what I shall as they are positively instructed to deny these things abroad. But it matters not to us what they say; our object is to state to you the *truth*, for we do not want to be guilty of *deceiving any one*. We will now give you a correct statement of the doctrines that are taught and practiced in the Church according to our own knowledge. We will mention three in particular.

A plurality of Gods. A plurality of *living* wives. And unconditional sealing up to eternal life against *all sins* save the shedding of innocent blood or consenting thereunto. These with many other things are taught by Joseph, which we consider are *odious* and doctrines of devils.

Joseph says there are Gods above the God of this universe as far as he is above us, and if He should transgress the laws given to Him by those above Him, He would be hurled from his Throne to hell, as was Lucifer and all his creations with him. But God says there is no other God but himself. Moses says he knows of no other God. The Apostles and Prophets almost all testify the same thing.

Joseph had a revelation last summer purporting to be from the Lord, allowing the saints the privilege of having ten living wives at one time, I mean certain conspicuous characters among them. They do not content themselves with young women, but have seduced married women. I believe hundreds have been deceived. Now should I yield up your daughter to such wretches?

Mr. Haven knows these statements are correct, for they have been in the quorum to which he belongs by the highest authority in the Church. He has told me that he does not believe in these teachings but he does not come out and oppose them; he thinks that it will all come out right. But we think God never has nor ever will sanction such proceedings, for we believe he has not changed; he says *"I am God I change not."* These things we can not believe, and it is by Sarah's repeated request that I write this letter.

Those who can not swallow down these things and came out and opposed the doctrine publicly, have been cut off from the Church without any lawful process whatever. They were not notified to trial, neither were they allowed the privilege of being present to defend themselves, neither was any one permitted to speak on their behalf. They did not know who was their judge or jury until it was all over and they delivered over to all the buffetings of Satan; although they lived only a few rods from the council room. These are some of their names: William Law, one of the first Presidency; Wilson Law, brigadier general; Austin Cowles, president of the High Council; and Elder Blakesly, who has been the means of bringing upwards of one thousand members into the Church. He has been through nearly all the states in the Union, the Canadas, and England preaching the Gospel. Now look at the great sins they have committed: the Laws, un-Christian-like conduct—Blakesly and others, *Apostasy*. If it is apostasy to oppose such doctrines and proceedings as I have just mentioned (which are only a few of the enormities taught and practiced here), then we hope and pray that *all* the Church may apostasize.

After they had been thus shamefully treated and published to the world they went and bought a printing press determined to defend themselves against such unhallowed abuse. It cost them six hundred dollars. [They] commenced their paper, but Joseph and his clan could not bear the truth to come out; so after the first number came out Joseph called his Sanhedrin together; tried the press; condemned it as a nuisance and ordered the city marshal to take three hundred armed men and go and burn the press, and if any offered resistance, to *rip them from the guts to the gizzard*. These are his own words. They went and burnt the press, papers, and household furniture. The Laws, Fosters, Coles, Hickbies [*sic*], and others have had to leave the place to save their lives. Those who have been thus unlawfully cut off have called a conference; protested against these things; and reorganized the Church. William Law is chosen president; Charles Ivans, bishop, with the other necessary officers. The Reformed Church believe that Joseph has transgressed in his priestly capacity and has given himself over to serve the devil, and his own lusts. We will endeavor to send you a paper and you can judge for yourselves. They had only commenced publishing the dark deeds of Nauvoo. A hundredth part has not been told yet. [Written by Isaac Scott to this point; the rest is in Sarah Scott's hand.]

The people of the state will not suffer such things any longer. But I am sorry that the innocent must suffer with the guilty. I believe there are hundreds of honest hearted souls in Nauvoo, but some of them I think have forgotten what they were once taught: that cursed is he that putteth his trust in man. It would offend some of them more to speak irreverently of Joseph, than it would of God himself. Joseph says that he is a God to this generation, and I suppose they believe it. Any one needs a throat like an open sepulchre to *swallow down* all that is taught here. There was an elder once wrote in confidence to a friend in England; told him the state of the Church here, and they showed it to some of the elders there, and they wrote back to the heads of the Church, and it caused him a great deal of trouble. I think if you would once come here, you would not put so much confidence in all who go by the name of Mormons.

I am very much obliged for the pin ball; I think it is very pretty, and it comes from Mother so far, from old Massachusetts. I shall appreciate it highly. My health has been very good since I came to the West notwithstanding it is a sickly part of the country. I enjoy myself *well* this summer. My husband is every thing I could wish, and I hope we may live all the days of our appointed time together. Joseph had two balls last winter and a dancing-school through the winter. There was a theatre established in the spring; some of the twelve took a part—Erastus Snow and many of the leading members of the Church. Dear Mother, I hope the time is not far distant when we can enjoy each other's society, but when and where I suppose time only will determine. There is a report that a mob is coming to Nauvoo.

Sarah Scott

PART IV

THE MURDERS IN CARTHAGE

The last public address of Joseph Smith on June 18, 1844. In 1888 John Hafen painted this romantic work depicting Smith, as the Nauvoo Legion looks on, raising his sword to Heaven and declaring that the Saints would be free. Smith spoke from the unfinished frame of a house across the street from his home, the Mansion House (shown in the background). Hyrum Smith is standing behind Joseph, and significantly the temple can be seen on the left (something that was not possible given Nauvoo geography). Courtesy of the Library-Archives, Reorganized Church of Jesus Christ of Latter Day Saints, the Auditorium, Independence, Missouri.

INTRODUCTION

Perhaps the greatest mistake of Joseph Smith's life—certainly it was the most costly—was the destruction of the *Expositor*, published by Mormon dissidents in June 1844. In another time, another circumstance, Smith might have gotten away with this action. Not this time. The individuals Smith sought to destroy were part of Mormonism's middle class, persons who enjoyed both power and prestige—as well as professional acceptance and understanding—outside the church. Paul M. Edwards suggests that within the church this class is often at odds with authorities and "feel[s] excluded from power because they are neither rich enough (in terms of holding authority) nor poor enough (willing to trade obedience for protection)."[1] Led by William Law, a successful businessman and a counselor to Joseph Smith in the First Presidency during the early 1840s, some of the most solid and dignified men of the community were involved.[2]

William Law had friends and influence elsewhere. He immediately went to Carthage, the seat of Hancock County, to swear out a complaint against Smith for inciting a riot and unlawfully destroying property. He claimed that losses incurred from this act amounted to about thirty thousand dollars, including the dissenters' homes, farms, city lots, a large steam flour- and sawmill, and a store.[3] The local magistrate issued a warrant for the arrest of Joseph Smith, his brother Hyrum, and several other Nauvoo officials. Robert C. Foster, one of Law's colleagues in publishing the *Expositor*, sent a blustery missive to Thomas C. Sharp, the anti-Mormon editor of the *Warsaw Signal*, which asked that the public "avenge this climax of insult & injury."[4]

Meantime, the public reacted against the Mormon silencing of the *Expositor*. Sharp's own caustic comments appeared in the 12 June 1844 *Warsaw Signal*. He wrote: "War and extermination is inevitable! CITIZENS ARISE, ONE AND ALL!!! Can you *stand* by, and suffer such INFERNAL DEVILS! to ROB men of their property rights, without avenging them? We have no time for comment! Every man will make his own. LET IT BE WITH POWDER AND BALL!"[5] Citizen's committees formed to bring Smith to justice. A series of meetings also took place throughout the county, which demonstrated the people's outrage over the *Expositor* affair.[6]

David Bettisworth, a local constable, visited Nauvoo on 12 June and arrested Smith and seventeen other leading Mormons, charging them with committing "riot" by destroying the *Expositor*. Smith explained that he had no confidence in the county's judicial system and would not submit to the constable's writ for appearance in the county seat. Instead he agreed to go before a Nauvoo justice, citing the warrant indicating that the arrested could see "some other justice of the peace of said county." Bettisworth refused, suggesting that Smith would be perfunctorily released by a Mormon judge. The most interesting aspect of this exchange is that it established early in the controversy that neither the Mormons nor their neighbors had confidence in the legal system in Hancock County. While a presumably equitable judicial system was fully functional, opposition between the two cultural groups had become so extreme that neither side would trust it. Both feared that judges in their rival's strongholds were mere pawns and would accede to the wishes of factional leaders.[7]

Smith pulled a fast one on Bettisworth by having his legal counsel ask Aaron Johnson, a Nauvoo justice of the peace, for a writ of habeas corpus requiring the constable to bring the prisoner before him. When Bettisworth did so on the afternoon of 12 June, a remarkable trial ensued that fully justified the constable's concerns. The court ruled, after testimony and oratory,

> that Joseph Smith had acted under proper authority in destroying the establishment of the Nauvoo Expositor on the 10th Inst; that his orders were executed in an orderly and judicious manner, without noise or tumult; that this was a malicious prosecution on the part of Frank M. Higbee; and that said Higbee pay costs of suit, and that Joseph Smith be honorably discharged from the acquisition of the writ, and go hence without delay.[8]

The next day Smith, as a member of the Nauvoo Municipal Court, sat in judgment on the cases of the seventeen others arrested by Bettisworth. Each was acquitted.

When Bettisworth returned to Carthage without his prisoners, the non-Mormons in Hancock County went into an uproar. One remarked, "Joe has tried the game too often."[9] The anti-Mormons sent out messengers in all directions to drum up support for action against the Saints. A consensus was building, even among those far removed from the situation, that Smith's group was opposing legally constituted authority and concerted action was required to force subjugation. George Rockwell, a Warsaw druggist and active anti-Mormon, on 22 June 1844 reported "lending my humble aid to expel a band of citizens from the State, the leaders of whom, are deserving a thousand deaths. I have been constantly engaged for the last two weeks trying to accomplish it, and now take pleasure in saying that I have no doubt as to our ultimate success."[10]

Both sides appealed to Governor Thomas Ford to resolve a situation that was fast becoming explosive. The Mormons wrote Ford explaining why they had taken action against the *Expositor* and asking him to intervene to prevent bloodshed.[11] A non-Mormon delegation visited him and asked that Ford send troops to help arrest Smith and bring him to trial. An honest man without much personal charisma, Ford had nothing in his background that prepared him to deal with the Mormon war in 1844. His legal training and respect for the judicial system served as an impediment to his action; he never understood why legal methods could not effectively redress everyone's grievances. He also never fathomed the deep rift between the Mormons and non-Mormons in Hancock County.[12]

Meantime, Bettisworth made a second attempt to arrest Joseph Smith. It ended the same way, but this time Nauvoo's sympathetic non-Mormon justice of the peace, Daniel H. Wells—who later joined the church and was a significant force in Utah territorial government—freed Smith on a writ of habeas corpus. Bettisworth again returned to Carthage empty handed, and this time some seven hundred non-Mormons came out for a rally to oppose the Mormons. Samuel Williams, an officer in the Carthage Greys militia unit, summarized the atmosphere: "Such excitement I never witnessed in my life." He added that "we all felt that the time had come where either the Mormons or old citizens had to leave."[13] Citizen's groups throughout the county rallied to demand the arrest of Smith and his accomplices. Communities in other counties, even in Iowa and Missouri, also promised help. All agreed, according to the *Warsaw Signal*, that "compromise is out of the question" and violence would probably result.[14]

In response to this threat, on 18 June 1844, Smith declared martial law in Nauvoo and called out the Nauvoo Legion to protect the city. In his last public address, dressed in full military regalia, Smith told the legion and a large number of others that the tense situation required extreme measures. Next, in a fit of high drama, he drew his sword and pointed it skyward: "I call God and angels to witness that I have unsheathed my sword with a firm and unalterable determination that this people shall have their legal rights, and be protected from mob violence, or my blood shall be spilt upon the ground like water, and my body consigned to the silent tomb." He then told his followers to stand firm and not to flinch from violence in standing up for their liberty.[15] Following this speech, the legion deployed troops to defend Nauvoo.

As this was taking place, Governor Ford traveled to Hancock County, arriving at the county seat on 21 June. When he got there, he reported finding "an armed force assembled, and hourly increasing, under the summons and direction of the constables of the county, to serve as a posse comitatus" to arrest Smith and his associates. He placed this force under his direct command and sent a messenger to Nauvoo to ask that representatives of the Saints visit him in Carthage "to lay their side of the question before me." Smith's representatives met with Ford on 22 June and learned that he believed the destruction of the *Expositor* had been "illegal, and not to be endured in a free country."[16] Ford demanded that Smith and his accomplices submit to arrest and stand trial in Carthage. If they did not do so, he told the Saints, "I have great fears that your city will be destroyed, and your people many of them exterminated."[17]

Smith did not receive Ford's summons until late at night, but when he replied early the next morning, he refused to surrender unless the governor could guarantee his safety. Instead he asked the governor to come to Nauvoo and meet him.[18] When this request failed, Smith tried to escape from Ford, by crossing the Mississippi into Iowa the following night with his brother.[19] Others prevailed on him to return, however, Reynolds Cahoon even shaming him into it. "You always said if the church would stick with you," he told Smith, "you would stick with the church; now trouble comes and you are the first to run!"[20] Smith responded, "If my life is of no value to my friends it is of none to myself."[21]

At 6:30 A.M. on Monday, 24 June 1844, Joseph Smith, Hyrum Smith, John Taylor, W. W. Phelps, and thirteen other members of the Nauvoo City Council set out for Carthage, accompanied by several others not wanted for the *Expositor's* destruction. It was a somber group. Smith supposedly told his comrades, "If my death will atone for any faults I have committed during my life time I am willing to die."[22] When Smith and his companions arrived in Carthage, militia, towns-people, and thrill seekers from outside gathered in the center of the town to see them. It was a cross between a carnival and a riot as fourteen hundred people crowded the Mormons. Some shouted abuses, others merely watched; all were impressed. At one point an impromptu "Hurrah for Tom Ford" rose from the crowd. As the locals began to disperse, the Mormons found lodging in Hamilton's tavern near the courthouse, with formal proceedings against them set to begin the next morning.[23]

For most of the next three days the Smiths underwent a series of legal actions and public displays before they were assassinated on 27 June 1844.[24] For instance, there was great curiosity about the Mormon prisoners, and the governor agreed on the morning of 25 June to parade them next to the militia. While it was probably Ford's intent merely to keep his troops as happy as possible, the exhibition of the Smith brothers ensured that those who later attacked the Carthage jail and mur-dered them would recognize them.

The Smiths were released from the riot charge on the afternoon of 25 June by voluntarily posting bail to guarantee their appearance at the circuit court. Immediately thereafter, the two brothers were arrested for treason against the State of Illinois, supposedly for unlawfully declaring martial law in Nauvoo. They were incarcerated in the local jail, but allowed to occupy the debtor's quarters rather than standard cells. In an irony of the foremost magnitude, whether one believes all the charges levied against the Smiths or not, they were vulnerable to the mob because they had been arrested for exercising the same kind of undemocratic power which the Nauvoo dissenters were protesting.

As legal maneuvering took place, Ford decided to take the militia and go to Nauvoo on 27 June to impress upon the Saints that illegal action would not be tol-erated. He left one company in Carthage to guard the prisoners, but because he feared that the troops accompanying him might riot in the Mormon stronghold, he disbanded all but one company en route. Prompted by rabble-rousers who played to the fear that the Smiths might escape one more time, a group returned to Carthage and murdered the brothers.[25]

The bodies of Joseph and Hyrum Smith were returned to Nauvoo the next day and buried on 29 June. An eerie quiet then settled over the county. This sec-tion presents, through contemporary letters, diaries, and publications, as well as later recollections, a detailed account of the murders in Carthage.

Notes

1. Paul M. Edwards, "Ethics and Dissent in Mormonism: A Personal Essay," in *Let Contention Cease: The Dynamics of Dissent in the Reorganized Church of Jesus Christ of Latter Day Saints*, ed. Roger D. Launius and W. B. Spillman (Independence, Mo: Graceland/Park Press, 1991), 249–50.

2. On these men see Lyndon W. Cook, "William Law, Nauvoo Dissenter," *Brigham Young University Studies* 22 (Winter 1982): 47–62; Robert B. Flanders, *Nauvoo: Kingdom on the Mississippi* (Urbana: University of Illinois Press, 1965), 305–10; John F. Glaser, "The Disaffection of William Law," in *Restoration Studies Vol. 3*, ed. Maurice L. Draper and Debra Combs (Independence, Mo: Herald Publishing House, 1986), 163–75. Marvin S. Hill's *Quest for Refuge: The Mormon Flight from American Pluralism* (Salt Lake City: Signature Books, 1989), chap. 2, describes the early Saints as generally destitute and the social and economic policies of the church they embraced as radical, in part because there was little for the Saints to lose in a complete restructuring of their lives and their religion.

3. "Dr. Wyl and Dr. Wm. Law, A Deeply Interesting Talk on Old Nauvoo Days," *Salt Lake Tribune*, 30 March 1887, p. 2.

4. *Warsaw Signal* (Warsaw, Ill.), 12 June 1844, p. 1.

5. Ibid.

6. Joseph Smith, Jr., *History of the Church of Jesus Christ of Latter-day Saints* (1902–12; reprint, Salt Lake City: Deseret Book Co., 1976), 6:463–67.

7. Despite its simplistic interpretation on certain key points relative to the destruction of the *Expositor*, on this situation see Edwin B. Firmage and Richard C. Mangrum, *Zion in the Courts: A Legal History of the Church of Jesus Christ of Latter-day Saints, 1830–1900* (Urbana: University of Illinois Press, 1988), 106–13.

8. Edward Stevenson, *The Autobiography of Edward Stevenson, 1820–1897*, ed. Joseph G. Stevenson (Provo, Utah: Stevenson's Genealogical Center, 1986), 100.

9. Letter to the *Missouri Republican* (St. Louis), 21 June 1844.

10. George Rockwell to Thomas H. Rockwell, 22 June 1844, in "The Mormon War in Hancock County," *Warsaw Bulletin*, 13 March 1925.

11. See Joseph Smith, Jr., to Thomas Ford, 14 June 1844, 16 June 1844, and 22 June 1844, *The Personal Writings of Joseph Smith*, ed. Dean C. Jessee (Salt Lake City: Deseret Book Co., 1984), 586–95; the originals are in the Joseph Smith, Jr., Papers, Church of Jesus Christ of Latter-day Saints Archives, Salt Lake City, Utah.

12. On Ford, see Rodney O. Davis, "Judge Ford and the Regulators, 1841–1842," in *Selected Papers in Illinois History 1981*, ed. Bruce D. Cody (Springfield: Illinois State Historical Society, 1982), 25–36; Keith Huntress, "Governor Thomas Ford and the Murderers of Joseph Smith," *Dialogue: A Journal of Mormon Thought* 4 (Summer 1969): 41–52; Thomas Ford, *A History of Illinois, from its Commencement as a State in 1818 to 1847* (Chicago: S. C. Griggs and Co., 1854).

13. Samuel Otho Williams to John Prickett, 10 July 1844, Mormon Collection, Chicago Historical Society.

14. "The Preparation," *Warsaw Signal*, 19 June 1844, p. 2.

15. Smith, *History of the Church*, 6:498–500.

16. Thomas Ford, *Message from the Governor, in Relation to the Disturbances in Hancock County* (Springfield, Ill.: Walters & Weber, Public Printers, 1844), 3–4.

17. Smith, *History of the Church*, 6:533–37.

18. Joseph Smith, Jr., to Thomas Ford, 22 June 1844 *The Personal Writings of Joseph Smith*, 592–95.

19. Joseph Smith, Jr., to Emma Smith, 23 June 1844, *The Personal Writings of Joseph Smith*, 597–98.

20. Wandle Mace, "Journal," p. 144, Utah State Historical Society, Salt Lake City, Utah.

21. Smith, *History of the Church*, 6:550–52.

22. This was a Smith family recollection. See Mary B. Smith Norman to Ina Smith Coolbrith, 27 March 1908, Smith Family Collection, Reorganized Church of Jesus Christ of Latter Day Saints Library-Archives, Independence, Mo.

23. Smith, *History of the Church*, 6:559–600.

24. Dean C. Jessee, "Return to Carthage: Writing the History of Joseph Smith's Martyrdom," *Journal of Mormon History* 8 (1981): 3–21.

25. "Awful Assassination of Joseph and Hyrum Smith!—The Pledged Faith of the State of Illinois Stained with Innocent Blood by a Mob!" *Times and Seasons* 5 (1 July 1844): 560–65.

———— ••◗ *1* ◖•• ————

Fanning Flames

Close on the heels of the Nauvoo City Council's action to silence the *Expositor* on 10 June 1844, anti-Mormon groups began to organize opposition designed to get rid of the problem of Joseph Smith permanently. The *Expositor* incident provided the type of flagrant violation of law that diehard anti-Mormons required to take action against Smith. They saw it as the final act in a long list of abuses of legal secular authority by Nauvoo officials and felt it demanded a prompt response. They quickly found support even among those non-Mormons without strong antipathies because of the Nauvoo authorities' violation of due process and use of a legal mandate to carry out what amounted to a mob action. Accordingly, many non-Mormons in Hancock County met during the second week of June 1844 to formally protest against Smith and determine ways to bring him to trial for riot.

Thomas C. Sharp (see Part II, Document 5 for biographical information) contributed significantly to the anti-Mormon sentiment in the area. In fact, if there was a nucleus to the effort, it was Sharp. He published the following report of mass meetings and demonstrations in Hancock County as a "Broadside Extra," *Warsaw Signal*, 14 June 1844, p. 1. It reflects the outrage of non-Mormons in the county after the *Expositor* episode and foreshadows the final events of Joseph Smith's life. It also demonstrates that the anti-Mormons did not view themselves as a mob but as a group which intended to uphold the supremacy of the law against what they saw as dictatorial power in Nauvoo. The article espouses the republican ideology so common in the nation. It celebrates "Virtue and Liberty," extolls the constitution, and ironically complains of "mob violence" as it justifies mob action against the Mormons.

———— ••◗●◖•• ————

At a meeting of the citizens of Warsaw, convened the 14th June, the following address, reported by Thos. C. Sharp, Esq. was unanimously adopted, and ordered to be published in connexion [*sic*] with the Resolutions adopted by the mass meeting at Carthage yesterday.

The following resolutions were adopted by a meeting of the citizens of Warsaw, on Wednesday last, and the same, as will be perceived by the proceedings that followed, were also adopted by the mass meeting assembled at Carthage yesterday. These Resolutions are of the strongest character, and indicate a depth of feeling which can find vent only in revenge for the repeated insults and injuries which the citizens of this vicinity have endured; as well as for the recent outrage, in destroying by mob violence, the press of the Nauvoo Expositor, a paper opposed to the interest of Joe Smith, and his miscreant band.

In presenting these Resolutions to the world, it seems necessary, least [sic] our motives and conduct should be censured, to submit to a candid, public, plain and unvarnished statement, of the situation in which we are placed, but a combination of circumstances, against which no prudence could guard us, and from which no thing but desperate means can rescue us.

The City Council of Nauvoo have, within the last two years, passed a series of ordinances, contrary to the spirit and intent of their Charter, which were intended as they avowed, to screen the adherents of the Prophet, as also the Prophet himself, from arrest, by the state authorities, and to liberate them from custody whenever they should be so arrested. Repeated attempts have been made to arrest Smith, but he has been uniformly screened from the officers of Justice, by the aid of the Municipal Court, which is the tool and echo of himself. Our state authorities have not seen proper heretofore, to call out force sufficient to put the law in execution. Having repeatedly set all law at defiance, both in his own case, as well as that of his favorites, with impunity, he has grown more daring, and recently, we behold him giving shelter and protection to a criminal who had offended against the laws of the State, rescuing him from the custody of its officers, and refusing to surrender him, until the Executive had given the minister of the Law plenary power, to call in the aid of the military.

The high-handed measures of this self-constituted despot had raised, even within his own dominion, a powerful opposition. The honest and respectable of his followers became alarmed at the usurpation and tyranny, daily practiced in the city. They protested against his high-handed measures; but they were only heard to be insulted, and spurned with contempt. Finding reformation impossible they manfully came out, and avowed their determination to resist, and subvert his power. To that end they procured a press and printing materials, that they might have an organ through which to speak.

The *Prophet* finding that his villainies and usurpations were about to be exposed in their naked deformity, and seeing the impossibility of sustaining himself with so powerful an engine as the Press located in the midst of his followers, leveled at his villainies and usurpations, determined on its destruction. He called together the City Council, and without shadow of authority and in the teeth of the Constitution of this State, and of the U. States, ordered the destruction of the press. . . .

This community will throw itself for protection on its reserved rights, if the safety of our lives and property cannot be ensured to us by legal means; and we hope to be sustained by those generous communities that surround us, who, we are sure will not stand by and suffer with impunity the virtuous to be trampled . . . [for] the Law is again put at defiance, and the only recourse left us is to take up arms. It we fail in this, (which God forbid) we must bow the knee and submit to the yoke of a tyrant, who is the masterpiece of Hell's workmanship. . . .

To the communities that surround us we appeal! Will you come to the rescue? Will you aid us to rid the Earth of a pest such as has never before poluted [sic] its surface since it was redeemed from Chaos? Come on then Ye men of generous souls! Lay aside sectional prejudices and former grudges, and unite with us in the cause of Virtue and Liberty! We are no mob setting ourselves up above the law, but we seek to establish by every means in our power the supremacy of the law over villains that have long defied it. . . .

At a mass meeting of the citizens of Hancock County, convened at Carthage on the 13th day of June, 1844, Mr. Knox was appointed President, John Day and Lewis F. Evans, Vice Presidents, and Wm. Y. Head, Secretary.

Henry Stephens, Esq. presented the following resolutions, passed at a meeting of the Citizens of Warsaw, and urged the adoption of them as the sense of the meeting:

Preamble and Resolutions

WHEREAS, information has reached us, about which there can be no question, that the authorities of Nauvoo, did recently pass an Ordinance, declaring a Printing Press and Newspaper published by the opponents of the Prophet, a nuisance, and in pursuance thereof, did direct the Marshal of the city and his adherents to enter by force, the building from whence the paper was issued, and violently, (if necessary,) to take possession of the press and printing material, and thereafter to burn and destroy the same.

And WHEREAS, in pursuance of said ordinance, the Marshall [*sic*] and his adherents together with a mob of Mormons, did after sunset on the evening of the 10th inst., violently enter said building in a tumultuous manner, burn and destroy the press and other materials found on the premises.

And WHEREAS, Hyrum Smith did in the presence of the City Council, and the citizens of Nauvoo, offer a reward for the destruction of the printing press and materials of the Warsaw Signal,—a newspaper also opposed to his interest.

And WHEREAS, the liberty of the press is one of the cardinal principles of our Government, firmly guaranteed by the several Constitutions of the States, as well as the United States.

And WHEREAS, Hyrum Smith has within the last week publicly threatened the life of one of our valued citizens—Thos. C. Sharp, the editor of the Signal.

Therefore, be it solemnly *Resolved*, By the citizens of Warsaw in Public Meeting, assembled,

That, we view the recent ordinance of the City of Nauvoo, and the proceedings thereunder, as an outrage, of an alarming character, revolutionary and tyrannical in its tendency, and being under colour of law, as calculated to subvert and destroy in the minds of the community, all reliance on the Law.

Resolved. That as a Community, we feel anxious, when possible, to redress our greviences [*sic*] by legal remedies; but the time has now arrived, when the Law has ceased to be a protection to our lives and property; a mob at Nauvoo under a city ordinance, has violated the highest privilege in our Government, and to seek redress in the ordinary mode, would be utterly ineffectual.

Resolved, That the public threat made in the Council of the City, not only to destroy our Printing Press, but to take the life of its Editor, is sufficient, in

connection with the recent outrage, to command the efforts and the services of
every good citizen, to put an immediate stop to the career of the mad Prophet and
his demoniac coadjutors. We must not only defend ourselves from danger, but we
must resolutely carry the War into the enemy's Camp. We do therefore declare,
that we will sustain our Press and the Editor, at all hazards. That we will take full
vengeance,—terrible vengeance, should the lives of any of our citizens be lost in
the effort. That we hold ourselves at all times in readiness to co-operate with our
fellow citizens in this State, Missouri and Iowa, to exterminate, utterly exterminate, the wicked and abominable Mormon Leaders, the authors of our troubles.

Resolved, That a Committee of five be appointed forthwith to notify all persons in our Township suspected of being the tools of the Prophet, to leave immediately on pain of instant vengeance. And we do recommend the inhabitants of the
adjacent Townships to do the same, hereby pledging ourselves to render all the
assistance they may require.

Resolved, That the time, in our opinion, has arrived, when the adherents of
Smith, as a Body, should be driven from the surrounding settlements, into Nauvoo.
That the Prophet and his miscreant adherents, should then be demanded at their
hands, and if not surrendered, a war of extermination should be conducted. . . .

Resolved, That every citizen arm himself, to be prepared to sustain the resolutions herein contained.

Mr. Roosevelt rose, and made a brief, but eloquent speech; and called upon
the citizens throughout the country to render efficient aid in carrying our the spirit
of the resolutions. Mr. Roosevelt then moved a Committee of seven be appointed
by the Chair to draft resolutions expressive of our action in [the] future. . . .

The Committee appointed to draft resolutions, brought in the following
report, which after some considerable discussion was unanimously adopted:

Whereas, the officer charged with the execution of a writ, against Joseph
Smith and others, for riot in the county of Hancock, which said writ said officer
has served upon said Smith and others—and whereas, said Smith and others refuse
to obey the mandate of said writ—and whereas, in the opinion of this meeting, it
is impossible for said officer, to raise a posse of sufficient strength to execute said
writ—and whereas, it is the opinion of this meeting that the riot is still progress-
ing, and that violence is meditated, and determined on. It is the opinion of this
meeting that the circumstances of the case require the interposition of Executive
power: Therefore,

Resolved, That a deputation of two discreet men, be sent to Springfield to
solicit such interposition.

2nd, *Resolved*, That said deputation be furnished with a certified copy of
this resolution—and be authorized to obtain evidence by affidavit and otherwise
in regard to the violence, which has already been committed, and is still further
meditated.

Dr. Evans here rose and expressed his wish that the above resolutions would
not retard our operations—but that we would each one arm and equip ourselves
forthwith.

The resolutions passed at Warsaw were again read by Dr. [Thomas L.] Barnes, and passed by acclamation. . . .

—————•••• *2* ••••—————

Mormon Justifications

When it became clear to Smith that the non-Mormons of Hancock County had united in opposing the destruction of the *Expositor* and were committed, like never before, to arresting and penalizing the Mormons responsible for the action, he tried to explain his position to Governor Thomas Ford of Illinois and implore his intercession. In the midst of the crisis, on Wednesday, 12 June 1844, the first attempt was made to arrest the Mormon leaders. David Bettisworth, a constable from Carthage, visited Nauvoo with a warrant for Joseph and Hyrum Smith, W. W. Phelps, John Taylor, and several others on the charge of riot. "After the officer got through reading the writ," according to the journal of William Clayton, a close associate of Smith's, "Joseph referred him to this clause in the writ 'before me or some other justice of the peace of said County' saying we are ready to go to trial before Esqr [Aaron] Johnson [of the Nauvoo Municipal Court], for that was their privilege allowed by the Statute," (William Clayton journal in *Clayton's Secret Writings Uncovered* [Salt Lake City: Modern Microfilm Co., 1982], p 56). Bettisworth at first objected, but when presented with a Nauvoo writ of habeas corpus he decided to bring the prisoners before a local justice of the peace. After a lengthy court appearance, the justice dismissed the case against the Mormons and assessed the costs to the complainant.

This development incensed the non-Mormons of the county, further crystallizing sides in the issue. Thomas Ford demanded that Smith appear to answer charges in the Hancock County seat. Ford called the proceedings surrounding the destruction of the *Expositor* illegal and the actions of the city council and the municipal court unprecedented in the state. Both to dissuade him from his position and to explain the city council's actions, Smith wrote a series of letters to Ford. Among other things they reveal Smith's inability to find shortcomings within himself or those loyal to him. Rather, as he says, "our troubles are invariably brought upon us by falsehood & misrepresentations by designing men." And he vilifies the dissenters who published the *Expositor*. To Smith, those who opposed him were always guilty of wrongdoing, not he and his supporters. So he must have been shocked when Governor Ford replied, on 22 June 1844, and told him flatly that "your conduct in the destruction of the press was a very gross outrage on the laws and liberties of the people" (Joseph Smith, Jr., *History of the Church of Jesus Christ of Latter-day Saints*, ed. B. H. Roberts [Salt Lake City: Deseret Book Co., 1902–12], 6:534). Ford also enumerated Smith's constitutional violations.

The prophet's letters printed here are taken from the microfilm copy in the Library-Archives, Reorganized Church of Jesus Christ of Latter Day Saints, Independence, Missouri. The originals are in the Joseph Smith, Jr., Papers, Church of Jesus Christ of Latter-day Saints Archives, Salt Lake City, Utah. They have also been published in *The Personal Writings of Joseph Smith*, ed. Dean C. Jessee (Salt Lake City: Deseret Book Co., 1984), 586–95.

———————————•••●•●•••———————————

Nauvoo June 14, 1844

His Excellency Thomas Ford

Sir—I write you this morning, briefly to inform you of the facts relative to the removal of the Press and fixtures of the "Nauvoo Expositor" as a nuisance.

The 8th and 10th instant were spent by the city council of Nauvoo, in receiving testimony concerning the character of the Expositor, and the character and designs of the proprietors.

In the investigation it appeared evident to the council that the proprietors were a set of unprincipled, lawless, debauchees, counterfeiters, Bogus Makers, gamblers, peace disturbers, and that the grand object of said proprietors was to destroy our constitutional rights and chartered privileges; to overthrow all good and wholesome regulations in society; to strengthen themselves against the municipality; to fortify themselves against the church of which I am a member, and destroy all our religious rights and privileges, by libels, slanders, falsehoods, perjury & sticking at no corruption to accomplish their hellish purposes, and that said paper was libelous of the deepest dye, and very injurious as a vehicle of defamation,—tending to corrupt the morals, and disturb the peace, tranquillity and happiness of the whole community, and especially that of Nauvoo.

After a long and patient investigation of the character of the Expositor, and the characters and designs of its proprietors—the constitution, the charter (See addenda to Nauvoo charter from the Springfield charter, Sec. 7) and all the best authorities on the subject (See Blackstone III, 5. and n. &c&c); The city council decided that it was necessary for the "peace, benefit, good order, and regulations" of said city, "and for the protection of property" and for "the happiness and prosperity of the citizens of Nauvoo": that said Expositor should be removed; and declaring said Expositor a nuisance, ordered the Mayor—to cause them to be removed without delay, which order was committed to the Marshall, by due process, and by him executed the same day. By removing the paper, press, and fixtures into the street, and burning the same, all which was done without riot, noise, tumult, or confusion, as has already be[en] proved before the municipality of the city, and the particulars of the whole transaction may be expected in our next "Nauvoo Neighbor."

I send you this hasty sketch that your Excellency may be aware of the lying reports that are now being circulated by our enemies,—that there has been a "*mob at Nauvoo,*" "*and blood and thunder*" and "*swearing that two men were killed*" &c&c

as we hear from abroad,—are false,—false as Satan himself could invent, and that nothing has been transacted here but what has been in perfect accordance with the strictest principles of law and good order, on the part of the authorities of this city,—and if your Excellency is not satisfied, and shall not be satisfied, after reading the whole proceedings which will be forth coming soon, and shall demand an investigation of our municipality before Judge Pope or any legal tribunal at the Capital, you have only to write your wishes—and we will be forth coming: we will not trouble you to fill a writ or send an officer for us.

I remain as ever a friend to truth, good order and your Ex.'s humble Sert.

Joseph Smith

Nauvoo Ill: June 16, 1844

His Excellency
Thomas Ford

Sir I am informed from credible sources as well as from the proceedings of a public meeting at Carthage &c as published in the "Warsaw Signal" extra, that an energetic attempt is being made by some of the citizens of this and the surrounding counties to drive and exterminate "the Saints" by force of arms. And I send this information to your Excellency by a Special Messenger Hugh McFall—Adjutant General—Nauvoo Legion—who will give all particulars, and I ask at your hands, immediate council and protection.

Judge [Jesse B.] Thomas has been here and given his advice in the Case which I shall strictly follow until I hear from your Excellency—and in all cases shall adhere to the Constitution and Laws.

The Nauvoo Legion is at your service to quell all insurrections and support the dignity of the common weal.

I wish, urgently wish your Excellency to come down in person with your Staff, and investigate the whole matter, without delay and cause peace to be restored to the Country—and I know not but this will be the means of stopping an effusion of blood.

The information referred to above is before me, by affidavit. I remain Sir the friend of peace, and your Excellency's humble servant.

Joseph Smith

Nauvoo Saturday Morning
June 22nd 1844

To His Excellency
Thomas Ford Governor

Dear Sir:—I this morning forward you the remainder of the affidavits which are ready to present to you by the hands of a gentleman who is fully competent to give you information on the whole subject which have been the cause of the origin of our present difficulties. I would respectfully recommend the bearers, Col [Lucius] Woodworth as one of my aids & [his] men, whose testimonies can be relied upon.

I presume you are already convinced that it would be altogether unsafe for me or any of the city council to come to Carthage on account of the vast excitement which has been got up by false report and libellous publications. Nothing would afford me a greater pleasure than a privilege of investigating the whole subject before your Excellency in person, for I have ever held myself in readiness to comply with your orders and answer for my proceedings before any legal tribunal in the state.

I would thereby respectfully pray your Excellency to come to Nauvoo, if congenial with your feelings and give us a privilege of laying the whole matter before you in its true colors, and where abundance of testimony can be forthcoming to prove every point by disinterested persons; men of character and of worth and notoriety, strangers, who were here all the time, but I am satisfied your Excellency does not wish men to expose the lives of the citizens of this place by requiring them to put themselves into the power of an infuriated, blood thirsty mob, a part of whom have already several times fired upon our people without the least shadow of cause or provocation.

I am informed this morning that some gentleman has made affidavit that he had a private conversation with me in which I stated that I had secret correspondence with you &c. If any person has been wicked enough to do this he is a perjured villain, for in the first place I do not suffer myself to hold private conversation with any stranger, and in the second place I have never even intimated any thing of the kind as having secret correspondence with your excellency.

Our troubles are invariably brought upon us by falsehood & misrepresentations by designing men; we have ever held ourselves amenable to the law, and for myself Sir, I am ever ready to conform to and support the laws and constitution even at the expense of my life. I have never in the least offered any resistance to law, or lawful process which is a fact well known to the public, all of which circumstances made us the more anxious to have you come to Nauvoo and investigate the whole matter.

Now Sir is it not an easy matter to distinguish between those who have pledged themselves to exterminate innocent men, women and children, and those who have only stood in their own defence and in defence of their innocent families and that too in accordance with the constitution & laws of the country as required by their oaths and as good and law abiding citizens.

In regard to the destruction of the press the truth only needs to be presented before your Excellency to satisfy you of the Justice of the proceedings. The press was established by a set of men who had already set themselves at defiance of the laws and authorities of the city and had threatened the lives of some of its principle [*sic*] officers, and who also made it no private matter that the press was established for the express purpose of destroying the city as will be shown by the affidavit of Joseph Jackson and as they stated to me in their threats.

Mr [Almon W.] Babbitt informs me that reports are in circulation that we have taken property which belongs to the Mr Laws and others.

There has been no property meddled with to my knowledge belonging to any person, except property to a Mr Hicks to pay a debt. This I purchased of Mr Hicks and I am responsible to him for the amount. We have been especially careful to preserve the property of those who are exciting the public against us, inasmuch as we knew that every means would be used which could be invented to raise excitement, and we have appointed the police to watch this property and see that no harm was done to it by any person as they had tried to fire their own building and was detected in the act; the fire was extinguished by the policemen and no property damaged.

There has been no prisoners taken in this city neither any persons held as hostage, only some who are residents of this place who had broke the laws; no stranger has been interfered with, nor detained in the city, under any circumstances.

In haste I have the honor too [*sic*] remain Dr Sir your most obedt. Sevt.

Joseph Smith
L Genl NL

Bank of the River Mississippi
June 23d 1844

His Excellency
Thomas Ford

Sir: I wrote you a long communication at 12 last night, expressive of my views of your Excellency's communication of yesterday. I thought your letter rather severe, but one of my friends has just come to me with an explanation from the captain of your possie [*sic*] which softened the subject matter of your communication, and gives us greater assurance of protection, and that your excellency has succeeded in bringing in subjection the spirits, which surround your Excellency, to some extent. And I declare again the only objection I ever had or ever made to trial by my country at any time was what I have made in my last letter—on account of assassins, & [the] reason I have to fear deathly consequences from their hands. But from the Explanation I now offer to come to you at Carthage on the morrow as early as shall be convenient for your possie to escort us in to Head Quarters, provided we can have a fair trial, not be abused, not have my witnesses abused, and have all things done in due form of law, without partiality, and you may depend on my honour without the show of a great armed force to produce excitement in the minds of the timid.

We will meet your possie if this letter is satisfactory; if not inform me at or near the Mound at or about two oclock tomorrow afternoon, which will be as soon as we can get our witnesses & prepare for trial. We shall expect to take our witnesses with us and not have to wait a subpoena, or a part at least, so as not to detain the procedings [*sic*], although we may want time for counsel.

We remain most Respectfully your Excellencys Humble servants

Joseph Smith
Hyrum Smith

————•••• 3 ••••——

The Last Speech of Joseph Smith

As pressure on Joseph Smith grew stronger in the two weeks following the destruction of the *Expositor* press, he responded with increasingly tough comments. He wrote to his uncle, John Smith, in another Mormon settlement outside Nauvoo on 17 June 1844, "that we feel determined in this place not to be dismayed if hell boils over all at once." He told him to "defend yourselves to the very last, and if they fall upon you with a superior force, and if you think you are not able to compete with them, retreat to Nauvoo. But we hope for better things, but remember if your enemies do fall upon you be sure and take the best and most efficient measures the emergency of the case may require." He also told him to "never give up your arms, but die first" (Joseph Smith, Jr., Papers, Church of Jesus Christ of Latter-day Saints Archives, Salt Lake City, Utah).

His unwillingness to surrender to state authority also prompted Joseph Smith to proclaim, on 18 June 1844, in the midst of the governor's attempts to arrest him, martial law in the city of Nauvoo. Smith's proclamation gave his reasons:

> From the newspapers around us, and the current reports as brought in from the surrounding country, I have good reason to fear that a mob is organizing to come upon this city and plunder and destroy said city, as well as murder the citizens; and by virtue of the authority vested in me as mayor, and to preserve the city and lives of the citizens, I do hereby declare the said city, within the limits of its corporation, under martial law. The officers, therefore, of the Nauvoo legion, the police, as well as all others, will strictly see that no persons or property pass in or out of the city without due orders. (Joseph Smith, Jr., *History of the Church of Jesus Christ of Latter-day Saints*, ed. B. H. Roberts [Salt Lake City: Deseret Book Co., 1912], 6:497)

On that same day, wrote Joseph Grafton Hovey in his reminiscences, Smith assembled the Nauvoo Legion, and "at 11 o'clock the General in his uniform came on the field with his escort and part of the Twelve for the last time. The day was beautiful. After the usual ceremonies had taken place, we marched with our beloved general to his mansion and there we were ordered to file in close compact in order to hear the word of our Chiefta[i]n" (Joseph G. Hovey, "Autobiography," p. 20, Archives, Harold B. Lee Library, Brigham Young University, Provo, Utah). Before a crowd estimated at ten thousand, Smith ordered the Nauvoo Legion to be drawn up in line across from his home, where he stood on a platform hastily made from planks thrown over a house foundation. Dressed in full uniform as lieutenant general of the Nauvoo Legion, Smith spoke publicly to his followers for the last time. Hovey recalled that Smith said:

I lift up my hand to heaven this day and may it be sealed in the archives that we will not give up our rights and privileges to those cursed mobs. May the thunder and forked lightning, war and pestilence come down upon those ungodly men that seek my life and your brethren. I am ready to be offered, for what can they do, only kill the body. Stand firm my friends and seek not to save your lives for he that is afraid to die for the truth will lose his life. Hold out until the end and we shall be resurrected like gods and reign in kingdoms and principalities and power. . . . Therefore, you are blessed and I love all of you. May the God of Israel bless you and the power of God rest down upon the people. (Hovey, "Autobiography," 20–21)

Another member of the legion, Edward Stevenson, remembered that Smith "looked like a noble leader, surrounded by a noble lot of brave men." He added:

I felt proud to form one of the number of the Nauvoo legion on that occasion. . . . I very well remember one special stranger saying never again will my voice be heard speaking against that man. Joseph spoke with great power, so much so that many tears were shed by the multitude who were assembled around that memorable frame building; his speech occupied about one and one-fourth hours. . . . His words carried conviction to every heart, and his power held the entire audience seemingly spell bound. (Edward Stevenson, *The Autobiography of Edward Stevenson, 1820–1897*, ed. Joseph G. Stevenson [Provo, Utah: Stevenson's Genealogical Center, 1986], 101–2)

Following is a text of this last speech by Smith, as reconstructed from several sets of notes made at the time. It captures the seriousness and desperation felt in Nauvoo after the *Expositor* incident, and it is deeply mythic. Avoiding any reference to the Mormon behavior that had aroused widespread opposition, Smith calls upon the "innocent" chosen people to oppose the "ungodly" followers of the devil, who thirst for the blood of believers in the gospel. And he employs American myth as well, portraying the Saints as descendants of Revolutionary War ancestors, fighting for "the rights of freemen" against "lawless marauders." Thus, he transforms the Saints' resistance into a sacred act. And he presents himself as a Christlike sacrificial figure willing to die for the Saints, leading them to celestial glory. No wonder they said "Amen" at the end of his speech. The address was published in Joseph Smith, Jr., *History of the Church of Jesus Christ of Latter-day Saints*, 6:498–500.

It is thought by some that our enemies would be satisfied with my destruction but I tell you that as soon as they have shed my blood they will thirst for the blood of every man in whose heart dwells a single spark of the spirit of the fullness of the Gospel. The opposition of these men is moved by the spirit of the adversary of all righteousness. It is not only to destroy me, but every man and woman who dares believe the doctrines that God hath inspired me to teach to this generation.

We have never violated the laws of our country. We have every right to live under their protection, and are entitled to all the privileges guaranteed by our state and national constitutions. We have turned the barren, bleak prairies and swamps of this state into beautiful towns, farms and cities by our industry; and the men who seek our destruction and cry thief, treason, riot, &c., are those who themselves violate the laws, steal and plunder from their neighbors, and seek to destroy the innocent, heralding forth lies to screen themselves with the just punishment of their crimes by bringing destruction upon this innocent people. I call God, angels and all men to witness that we are innocent of the charges which are heralded forth through the public prints against us by our enemies; and while they assemble together in unlawful mobs to take away our rights and destroy our lives, they think to shield themselves under the refuge of lies which they have thus wickedly fabricated.

We have forwarded a particular account of all our doings to the Governor. We are ready to obey his commands, and we expect that protection at his hands which we know to be our just due.

We have taken the counsel of Judge [Jesse B.] Thomas, and have been tried before a civil magistrate on the charge of riot—not that the law required it, but because the Judge advised it as a precautionary measure, to allay all possible pretext for excitement. We were legally acquitted by Esq. [Daniel H.] Wells, who is a good judge of law. Had we been before the Circuit, the Supreme, or any other court of law in the state or nation, we would have been acquitted, for we have broken no law.

Constable [David] Bettisworth came here with a writ requiring us to go before Mr. [Thomas] Morrison, "or some other justice of the peace of the county," to answer to the charge of riot. We acknowledged ourselves his prisoners, and were ready to go before any magistrate in any precinct in this part of the county, or anywhere else where our lives could be protected from the mob who have published the resolutions for our extermination which you have just heard read. This is a privilege the law guarantees to us, and which the writ itself allows. He broke the law and refused us the privilege, declaring that we should go before Morrison in Carthage, and no one else, when he knew that a numerous mob was collected there who are publicly pledged to destroy our lives.

It was under these circumstances that we availed ourselves of the legal right of the ancient, high, and constitutional privilege of the writ of *habeas corpus*, and were brought before the Municipal Court of this city and discharged from the illegal detention under which we were held by Constable Bettisworth. All mob-men, priests, thieves, and bogus makers, apostates and adulterers, who combine to destroy this people, now raise the hue and cry throughout the state that we resist the law, in order to raise a pretext for calling together thousands more of infuriated mob-men to murder, destroy, plunder and ravish the innocent.

We are American citizens. We live upon a soil for the liberties of which our fathers periled their lives and spilt their blood upon the battlefield. Those rights so dearly purchased, shall not be disgracefully trodden under foot by lawless marauders without at least a noble effort on our part to sustain our liberties.

Will you all stand by me to the death, and sustain at the peril of your lives, the laws of our country, and the liberties and privileges which our fathers have transmitted unto us, sealed with their sacred blood? ("Aye!" shouted thousands.) He then said, "It is well. If you had not done it, I would have gone out there (pointing to the west) and would have raised up a mightier people."

I call upon all men, from Maine to the Rocky Mountains, and from Mexico to British America, whose hearts thrill with horror to behold the rights of freemen trampled under foot, to come to the deliverance of this people from the hand of oppression, cruelty, anarchy and misrule to which they have long been made subject. Come, all ye lovers of liberty, break the oppressor's rod, loose the iron grasp of mobocracy, and bring to condign punishment all those who trample under foot the glorious Constitution and the people's rights. (Drawing his sword, and presenting it to heaven, he said) I call God and angels to witness that I have unsheathed my sword with a firm and unalterable determination that this people shall have their legal rights, and be protected from mob violence, or my blood shall be spilt upon the ground like water, and my body consigned to the silent tomb. While I live, I will never tamely submit to the dominion of cursed mobocracy. I would welcome death rather than submit to this oppression; and it would be sweet, oh, sweet, to rest in the grave rather than submit to this oppression, agitation, annoyance, confusion, and alarm upon alarm, any longer.

I call upon all friends of truth and liberty to come to our assistance; and may the thunders of the Almighty and the forked lightnings of heaven and pestilence, and war and bloodshed come down on those ungodly men who seek to destroy my life and the lives of this innocent people.

I do not regard my own life. I am ready to be offered a sacrifice for this people; for what can our enemies do? Only kill the body, and their power is then at an end. Stand firm, my friends; never flinch. Do not seek to save your lives, for he that is afraid to die for the truth, will lose eternal life. Hold out to the end, and we shall be resurrected and become like Gods, and reign in celestial kingdoms, pri[n]cipalities, and eternal dominions, while this cursed mob will sink to hell, the portion of all those who shed innocent blood.

God has tried you. You are a good people; therefore I love you with all my heart. Greater love hath no man than that he should lay down his life for his friends. You have stood by me in the hour of trouble, and I am willing to sacrifice my life for your preservation.

May the Lord God of Israel bless you for ever and ever. I say it in the name of Jesus of Nazareth, and in the authority of the Holy Priesthood, which He hath conferred upon me.

(The people said "Amen.")

———— •••• 4 •••• ————

"The Condition of Affairs in Nauvoo Were Very Critical"

The following account by Edward Stevenson (1820–97), a young convert to Mormonism who had been born in Gibraltar, Spain, a colony of Great Britain, exemplifies the feelings in Nauvoo at the time of Joseph Smith's arrest and removal to Carthage for trial. Smith tried desperately to avoid leaving Nauvoo because he was convinced, rightly as it turned out, that he was not safe as a result of the backlash from the *Expositor* incident. But once he realized that he had to turn himself in, or lose the confidence of some Mormons, he prepared his followers to view him as a martyr in the event of his death. Stevenson's account shows the influence of that effort. This recollection describes the events of June 1844 in vivid and mythic terms, revealing that Smith's dichotomous vision had been thoroughly accepted by the author. Stevenson produced a kind of sacred narrative, designed to "testify" that Smith was a "prophet sent of God." It was first published in Edward Stevenson, *The Autobiography of Edward Stevenson, 1820–1897*, ed. Joseph Grant Stevenson (Provo, Utah: Stevenson's Genealogical Center, 1986), 99–107.

———— •••• ● •••• ————

The condition of affairs in Nauvoo were very critical. Joseph's enemies are increasing; apostasy enlarging its numbers. Polygamy is trying many and is understood only by a few in its true light and character. [John C.] Bennett, the [Chauncy and Francis M.] Higbees, [William and Wilson] Laws and others take advantage of their knowledge, using it illegally, making evil of what God designed for salvation and exaltation hereafter. . . . Joseph's enemies howl like a pack of wolves. Light has turned unto darkness, and Satan leads them captive at his will. . . .

On 7 June 1844, the Nauvoo *Expositor*, a foul, slanderous newspaper, made its appearance, one number only, before it was abated as a city nuisance (by order of the city of Nauvoo council) on 10 June 1844. It was removed by the city marshall. The press and type, with all of its fixtures, was removed into the street and destroyed. This spoiled the game of the apostates who became very angry and they threatened vengeance.

On the following day, the mayor issued a proclamation setting forth the course taken by the *Expositor* to destroy the peace of the city as well as the true liberty of the people, and it had been destroyed as a nuisance by order of the city council in accordance with the city charter. He called upon all honorable citizens and officers to use all honorable means to maintain the public peace and good order of the city, and to be wise in preventing the promulgating of false statements, libels, and slanders. (For this was the object of this most malicious paper.) He also recommended them to be ready to suppress the gathering of mobs, for there was a daring set of apostates and wicked men who would dishonor themselves, our city, the state and good society. The apostates tried to raise a mob out in the country and finally went to Carthage, swore out a warrant against Joseph Smith and 17 others that they had committed a riot, alleging that, with force and violence, they had broken into the Nauvoo *Expositor* printing office and unlawfully burned and destroyed the printing type and other property of the same. 12 June [1844] Squire [Thomas] Morrison sent a constable with a writ to Nauvoo to arrest Joseph.

The writ stated that the officer was to bring him the person charged in it "before me (Morrison) or some other justice of the peace to answer the premises, and further to be dealt with according to law." Joseph said, "We are ready to go before Esquire [Aaron] Johnson or any justice in Nauvoo." The constable became very angry and swore he would carry them to Carthage. Joseph asked him if he intended to break the law and called upon all present to witness that he then offered himself to go immediately before the nearest justice of the peace. His brother Hyrum offered to do the same. Joseph stood his trial. It was "decided by the court that Joseph Smith had acted under proper authority in destroying the establishment of the Nauvoo Expositor on the 10th Inst; that his orders were executed in an orderly and judicious manner, without noise or tumult; that this was a malicious prosecution on the part of Frank M. Higbee; and that said Higbee pay costs of suit, and that Joseph Smith be honorably discharged from the acquisition of the writ, and go hence without delay." The other brethren were tried also and with the same result.

On the 17th [June 1844] they submitted to a rearrest on the same charge [and were] tried before D. [Daniel] H. Wells who at that time was not a member of the Church, but was a justice of the peace, and after a long and close examination, they were again acquitted.

The apostates were determined to fan a flame of persecution and to drive the Saints once more from their hard-earned homes. One of the leading mobbers was a Baptist preacher, a colonel of militia of Hancock County. His name was Levi Williams. Those mobbers, like Paul in his wicked ways, thought it God's service to rob, mob, or exterminate the D——M—— Mormons. . . . They were looking for help from Missouri to more fully drive the Mormons out of the country, but first of all, to kidnap Joseph over into Missouri. . . . Joseph kept cool and advised us to be ready, vigilant, on guard in the city and on the banks of the river. . . . I spent considerable time in Nauvoo as I owned a lot in the city and was preparing to build a frame house, getting out the frame in Iowa. But nearly all our thoughts were absorbed in the perilous times we were in, for everything foreshadowed serious trouble was near at hand. . . .

The Prophet sent Edward Hunter, Philip B. Lewis and John Bills with letters to Governor Ford, desiring him to come to Nauvoo in person with his staff and investigate the condition of things in the city of Nauvoo without delay. With the brethren, Joseph sent affidavits. If the governor had complied with this reasonable request, peace could have been easily made. The governor either lacked the moral courage and manhood or had become one of the general mob voice of the whole state of Illinois, which shortly afterwards proved true by their acts of violence. Finally, the governor became merely a tool for the mob and they managed him, keeping their plans a secret from him, suiting him to their own purposes, for they had secret plans, and secret enemies within who were working a deep tragedy who had combined with the outside mob, and had secretly covenanted to murder the Prophet at all cost and at all consequence. This is what Joseph meant when he previously publicly said there was a secret Brutus, etc. . . .

The affidavits set forth in clearness the acts of the mob and their plans to annoy the citizens of Nauvoo. Dr. Willard Richards in the meantime, prepared additional documents which were sent the next day by the hand of Lucius Woodworth. Joseph wrote another letter to Governor Ford and sent it by him, making explanations, repeating his request for the governor to come to Nauvoo. If he would come there, the mayor and city council would make all things plain and clear, laying the whole matter before him. But if they had to go to Carthage to do this, they would expose themselves to the power of a mob filled with fury and a "desire to shed blood, a part of whom had already fired shots upon the people of Nauvoo." The governor replied, that nothing short of their submitting to be tried by the same officers who had already officiated previously would satisfy the people at large. Joseph sent forth in another reply, showing that our constitutional law expressly says that no man shall twice be put in jeopardy of life and limb for the same offense. Joseph reminded him that he had promised him protection, but expressed fear as to being able to control the mob, in which case we should be left (said Joseph) to the mercy of the merciless. Blood-thirsty villains were combining and mingling with the mob at Carthage, only waiting an opportunity to take the Prophet's life, and Joseph well knew that if they got him at Carthage, it meant martyrdom and he so expressed himself. Only one hope could be entertained and that was if his work was not already done, God would do as he had done in the past, deliver him from his enemies.

At the closing of Joseph's appeal to the governor, he entreated him to disperse the mob and secure to himself and friends their constitutional privileges, that their lives might not be endangered when they were on trial. The governor was surrounded by our bitter apostates and the mob. The communications were read in their presence; threats, curses and disturbances occurred and the bearers of the letters were insulted while explaining by the vile crew—what could Joseph expect of such a vile crowd, but death. 22 June 1844, Joseph called Hyrum Smith, Willard Richards, John Taylor, W. W. Phelps and some others into his upper room, where he read a letter from the governor.

After it was read through, Joseph remarked, "There is no mercy—no mercy here." Hyrum said, "No; just as sure as we fall into their hands we are dead men." Joseph replied, "Yes; what shall we do Hyrum?" He replied, "I don't know." Joseph's countenance brightened up and he said, "The way is open. It is clear to my mind what to do. All they want is Hyrum and myself; then let everyone attend to their business. They will come and search for us. Let them search; they will not harm you in person or property, and not even a hair of your head. We will cross the river tonight and go away to the west." He arranged for their families to go down the Mississippi and up the Ohio River on the steamboat, *Maid of Iowa.* Joseph told Stephen Markham that if he and his brother Hyrum were ever taken again, they would be massacred, or he was not a prophet of God. Hyrum met Reynolds Cahoon and told him that the Lord had warned Joseph to go to the Rocky Mountains. Joseph parted from his family in tears and about 2:00 A.M. they were crossing the Mississippi River in a leaky boat, bailing it with their boots and shoes, to prevent it from sinking. About daybreak they were in Iowa.

Early in the morning of the 23rd [June 1844] there was a posse after Joseph to arrest him. Not finding him, all but one of the posse, Mr. Yates, returned to Carthage. 1:00 P.M., Emma, Joseph's wife sent over Orrin Porter Rockwell, and Reynolds Cahoon accompanying him, with a letter entreating Joseph to come back and give himself up. These messengers found Joseph, Hyrum and Willard in a room by themselves having flour and other provisions on the floor ready for packing. Reynolds Cahoon, L[orenzo] D. Wasson and Hiram Kimball accused Joseph of cowardice, stating that the governor had pledged his faith and the faith of the state to protect him while he underwent a legal fair trial.

Joseph said, "If my life is of no value to my friends, it is of none to myself." He said, "We shall be butchered." Daniel C. Davis (one of the members of the Pontiac Michigan branch where I received the gospel) was directed to have his boat ready to take them back (to the slaughter). Joseph fell back with Rockwell; the others shouted come on. His reply was, "It's no use hurrying, for we are going back to be slaughtered." Joseph tarried overnight at the mansion.

Brothers [Theodore] Turley and [Jedediah M.] Grant returned from Carthage about 4:00 A.M., having rode in the night as they were not allowed to remain in Carthage. At first the governor thought to allow Joseph an escort but the apostates, Laws, Fosters, Higbees, Joseph H. Jackson, lawyer Skinner and others interfered, saying it was an honor not given to any other citizen. So the governor was again overruled by the mob influence, showing that the governor was ruled by the murderous element; no stability, only a tool for the enemy; and Joseph well knew it for he said, "I have agreed to go." Accompanied by 18 brethren, June 24 [1844] all of whom were accused by Frank M. Higbee of riot in destroying the

Expositor. Passing the temple, Joseph looked with admiration upon that building, and then the city. (Which temple was on a high hill overlooking the city and beautiful river and over into Iowa.) After gazing on the lovely scene he said, "This is the loveliest place and the best people under the heavens; little do they know the trials that await them." He called upon D. H. Wells, not in the Church. On parting he said, "Squire Wells, I wish you to cherish my memory, and not think me the worst man in the world either." Four miles from Carthage, they met 60 mounted militia, commanded by Captain Dunn. On seeing them, Joseph said to his brethren, "Do not be alarmed, brethren, for they cannot do more to you than the enemies of the truth did to the ancient Saints. They can only kill the body." Dunn presented an order from the governor, for all the state arms in possession in the Nauvoo legion. This order Joseph signed.

He also addressed a letter to the governor, stating that he had met Captain Dunn, learned his errand, and had concluded to return to Nauvoo with him to see that the delivery was properly made, after which he should accompany him to see Carthage and cheerfully submit to any requisition of the governor's. He then turned to his traveling companions and said, "I am going like a lamb to the slaughter, but I am calm as a summer's morning. I have a conscience void of offense toward God and toward all men. If they take my life, I shall die an innocent man, and my blood shall cry from the ground for vengeance, and it shall yet be said of me, he was murdered in cold blood."

The Prophet well knew what was intended by giving up our arms and it was with great reluctance that the brethren gave up their arms. Of course, anything Joseph required would be done, but the trap was too visible. I, with others, saw the sad effect of it in the state of Missouri. Joseph solemnly twice bid his family farewell (truly for the last time). Joseph looked solemn; his face was pallid and thoughtful, with mental suffering and grief, which increased the sympathy of his near friends all the more. He knew that he was going to certain death. For himself he expressed that he was willing to lay down his life for his friends and the cause of truth but here was his family, the Saints and the lonely home of the Saints with the future hopes and prospects of a temple and the future work to be performed for the dead, and worst of all, a wicked, bloodthirsty, murderous mob to rob the Saints of all their liberties, lives and homes. Having witnessed the arms given up and bid his family farewell, he turned his face toward Carthage, passing the Masonic Hall. Joseph said to his brethren, "There, boys, if I don't come back take care of yourselves and the Saints. I am going like a lamb to the slaughter."

Arriving at Carthage while passing through the public square, shouting, cursing and swearing with shouts of "shoot him," he has seen the last of Nauvoo. The most uproarious were the Carthage Greys. The governor, hearing these expressions, said, "Gentlemen, I know your great anxiety to see Mr. Smith, which is natural enough, but it is quite too late tonight for you to have the opportunity; but I assure you, gentlemen, you shall have the privilege tomorrow morning, as I will cause him to pass before the troops upon the square, and now I wish you, with this assurance, quietly and peacefully to return to your quarters." At the hotel where Joseph and his company stopped were the bitter apostates, who had threatened that Joseph should be killed, law or no law.

The following morning, 25 June [1844], Joseph and his brethren gave themselves voluntarily up to be tried according to the laws of his county, having nothing to fear as far as justice was concerned. The governor called the troops together in a hollow square on the public grounds. The governor stood on a table with inflamed prejudice by the lies which he had suffered himself to hear from apostates and enemies. With these feelings in his breast, he gave vent to them in a way which was calculated to fan the flame of passion instead of calming the wicked mob spirit already burning.

5

Non-Mormon Preparations

Using the *Warsaw Signal* as a means of stirring up anti-Mormon sentiment after the destruction of the *Expositor*, Thomas C. Sharp kept up constant pressure in Hancock County for action against Joseph Smith and the Mormons. The illegal way in which the Nauvoo City Council had handled the *Expositor* incident certainly contributed, for it served as a major new rallying point for the non-Mormons. Joseph Smith had violated the law, and ultimately he would be forced to answer for it by legal authorities of the state. If he would not surrender peaceably, he would be forced to submit. That was clear within a few days of the press's destruction. In "The Preparation," *Warsaw Signal,* 19 June 1844, p. 2, Sharp describes the sense of injustice felt by many in Hancock County and the growing commitment to force Smith to surrender to authorities outside of Nauvoo. The article also reveals that people were convinced that violence was about to erupt.

Our town in the last weeks has been in a constant state of excitement. Business has been almost entirely suspended, and every able bodied man is under arms and almost constantly in drill. . . .

On Monday last about 150 men mustered in this place under the command of General Knox. The attention paid by every man, and the anxiety manifested to acquire knowledge of military movements, is a full guarantee for the good conduct of our men in the coming emergency.

In Carthage and Green Plains, the citizens are all in arms, and as far as we can hear, throughout the county, every man is ready for the conflict.

We have assurances that our neighbors in Missouri and Iowa will aid us. In Clark County, Mo. we understand that many are holding themselves in readiness to march as soon as wanted. From Rushville we have just learned by express that 300 men have enlisted for the struggle. McDonough County, is all alive and ready for the word of command. From Keosaqua, Iowa we have just received intelligence by a resident of that place, that the citizens are in arms in our behalf, and only wait our call. From Keokuk and the river towns we learn that all are arming. Gen. Stapp of this Brigade, is requested to call out the Militia, and hold himself in readiness.

Joe is evidently much alarmed, but he has gone too far to back out. He must toe the mark, or run. Compromise is out of the question. The delegates sent to the Governor have not yet returned. If they fail to procure his interference, a day will be set forthwith, for a general rally as a *posse*, to assist the officers of justice. As soon as this is done, we will issue a handbill giving notice of the fact. Our friends in surrounding communities, who desire to aid us, will please hold themselves in readiness for this general order. When the word is given, every thing depends on promptness.

Captain [William] Grover last week obtained from Quincy 59 muskets. Men and arms are promised from St. Louis, and every thing betokens the prosperity of our enterprise.

To our friends at a distance we say come! We are too weak in this county, without aid to effect our object. Come! you will be doing your God and your country service, in aiding us to rid earth of a most Heaven daring wretch.

6 o'clock P.M.—D. W. Mathews, who was sent last Saturday to St. Louis, has just returned, by the Die Vernon. He has succeeded in procuring cannon; and has brought up a good supply [of] ammunition.

Mr. Simpson and Mr. Thompson have just returned from their trip to Missouri, and report all is right, and ready.

A Gentleman who conversed with Gov. Ford last week, reports that his excellency said, that he would do all he could in case Joe again defied the laws to bring him to justice. This was before the news of our present difficulties reached him.

We expect a six pounder to morrow night from Quincy.

8 o'clock P.M.—We have just learned that Joe has ordered all his followers into Nauvoo. The settlements around are with all despatch obeying the order.

At Lima a company was formed to day and reported themselves in readiness for orders.

T. A. Thompson, Esq. who saw Gov. Ford last week, states that an order has been granted by His Excellency, to try Joe Smith by Court Martial, for unofficer-like conduct.

——••••• 6 •••••——

The Last Letters of the Prophet to His Family

The relationship of Joseph Smith, Jr., to his wife, Emma Hale (1804–79), was often stormy but always passionate. In some instances they mixed like fire and water, clashing over such things as family finances and debts. They also never agreed on plural marriage, Emma railing against it privately, denying it publicly, and in at least one instance with the Relief Society, organizing women in Nauvoo to combat it. Yet the Smiths had a magnetic attraction to each other, expressed through mutual tenderness and deep respect.

On Monday, 24 June 1844, Joseph Smith, his brother Hyrum, and several others rode into Carthage and surrendered to the state militia under the command of Governor Thomas Ford. Emma Smith remained with her children in Nauvoo. These two letters to her, written by the prophet while incarcerated in Carthage, show something of their relationship. They also reveal that Smith was unsure about the future but that he was optimistic that the differences between him and the state could be worked out. He commented that Thomas Ford was working hard to treat him well and manage the situation. Smith was also trying to keep the Nauvoo Saints under control and asked Emma to make sure that the legion was committed to peaceful activities.

The two short letters, written on 25 and 27 June 1844, provide an intimate look at the situation as Smith understood it. They are published from the microfilm of the originals held by the Library-Archives, Reorganized Church of Jesus Christ of Latter Day Saints, Independence, Missouri. The original letters are housed with the Joseph Smith, Jr., Papers, Church of Jesus Christ of Latter-day Saints Archives, Salt Lake City, Utah, and have been previously published in *The Personal Writings of Joseph Smith*, ed. Dean C. Jessee (Salt Lake City: Deseret Book Co., 1984), 603–4, 611–12.

——••••◉•••••——

Carthage June 25, 1844

Dear Emma—I have had an interview with Gov. Ford & he treats us honorably. Myself & Hyrum have been again arrested for Treason because we called out the Nauvoo Legion but when the truth comes out we have nothing to fear. We all feel calm & composed.

This morning Gov. Ford introduced myself & Hyrum to The malitia [*sic*], in a very appropriate manner as Gen. *Joseph Smith & General Hyrum Smith*. There was a little mutiny among the "Carthage Greys"; but I think the Gov. has & will succeed in enforcing the laws. I do hope the people of Nauvoo will continue placid pacific & prayerful.

N.B. Governor Ford has just concluded to send some of his malitia to Nauvoo to protect the citizens, & I wish that they may be kindly treated. They will co-operate with the police to keep the peace. The Governors orders will be read in hearing of the police & officers of the Legion, as I suppose.

P.S. 3 O'clock. The Governor has just agreed to march his army to Nauvoo, & I shall come along with him. The prisoners, all that can be will be admitted to bail.

I am as ever
Joseph Smith

Carthage Jail Jun. 27th, 1844,
20. Past 8. A.M.

Dear Emma

The Gov continues his courtesies, and permits us to see our friends. We hear this morning that the Governor will not go down with his troops to day to Nauvoo as was anticipated last Evening but, if he does come down with his troops you will be protected, & I want you to tell Bro Dunham to instruct the people to stay at home and attend to their own business and let there be no groups or gathering together unless by permission of the Gov—they are called together to receive communications from the Gov—which would please our people, but let the Gov. direct.—Bro Dunham of course, will obey the orders of the Government officers, and render them the assistance they require. There is no danger of an "exterminating order." Should there be a mutiny among the troops, (which we do not anticipate, excitement is abating,) a part will remain loyal, and stand for the defence of the state & our rights; There is one principle which is Eternal, it is the duty of all men to protect their lives and the lives of their households whenever necessity requires. and no power has a right to forbid it, should the last extreme arrive,—but *I anticipate no such extreme*,—but caution is the parent of safety.—

Joseph Smith

PS Dear Emma,

I am very much resigned to my lot knowing I am Justified and have done the best that could be done. give my love to the children and all my Friends, Mr Brower and all who inquire after me, and as for treason I know that I have not committed any and they cannot prove one apearance [*sic*] of any thing of the kind. So you need not have any fears that any harm can happen to us on that score, may God bless you all. Amen

Joseph Smith

P.S. 20 mi[n] to 10—I just learn that the Governor is about to disband his troops, all but a guard to protect us and the peace,—and come himself to Nauvoo and deliver a speech to the people. This is right as I suppose.

——————•••• *7* ••••——————

An Official Explanation
of the Trouble in Hancock County

It had been difficult to achieve the arrest of Smith and other Mormon leaders, and Governor Ford had personally pledged to protect them. When the Smith brothers were murdered three days later, he felt betrayed and injured by the non-Mormon residents of Hancock County. Not only had they caused him to violate his personal honor, something that he highly prized, but the mob had acted while he was in Nauvoo making a speech to the Latter Day Saints. He had purposely not taken a large militia with him to Nauvoo because he neither wanted to needlessly intimidate the Saints nor have with him an angry military force that might not accept his orders in the Mormon stronghold. Ford was convinced that non-Mormons would not act against the Smiths while he was in Nauvoo because the Saints could easily exact retribution from him.

The Mormons, of course, blamed Ford for their leaders' deaths just as surely as if he had been a member of the lynch mob. Gilbert Belnap ("Autobiography of Gilbert Belnap," p. 36, Archives, Harold B. Lee Library, Brigham Young University) expressed the feelings of many of the Latter Day Saints by calling Thomas Ford a "cowardly, would-be-great man." Mormon Joseph Grafton Hovey also portrayed Ford in less than complimentary terms: "June 27, 1844 the governor left those of our brethren in prison with only eight men to guard them while he, the governor, went to Nauvoo with three to four hundred men to guard him. When he arrived at Nauvoo, he gave an insulting speech and drove away" (Joseph G. Hovey, "Autobiography," p. 21, Archives, Harold B. Lee Library, Brigham Young University, Provo, Utah).

The non-Mormons also laid the blame for the conflict at Ford's feet. They thought he had been too weak in handling the situation from the start. John Hay ("The Mormon Prophet's Tragedy," *Atlantic Monthly* [December 1869]: 673), a small boy living in Hancock County at the time, recalled that anti-Mormon leaders "protested against 'being made the tools and puppets of Tommy Ford'" and decided they had to take matters into their own hands. The attack on the Carthage jail was the response. Ford found himself in an impossible position. He tried to uphold the law and keep the peace but found that his moderation could not be sustained as extremists on both sides of the controversy became increasingly strident in their demands for redress of grievances, both real and imagined.

The Smiths' murders destroyed Ford's political career. Born in Uniontown, Pennsylvania, in 1802, he had grown up around St. Louis where he read law in the office of his stepbrother, George Forquer, and then entered practice. He early became interested in Democratic Party politics and before the age of thirty was appointed state's attorney for the Fifth Judicial District near Quincy, Illinois. He subsequently served as circuit court judge (1835–37, 1839–41) and Illinois Supreme Court justice (1841–42) before being elected governor in 1842. Once in office, Ford worked hard to return Illinois from a position of near bankruptcy, the legacy of an aggressive internal-improvement program in the 1830s. With the exception of the Mormon war, his governorship was successful. Even so, and in part because of his tarnished reputation from handling the Mormon conflict, Ford was turned out of office in 1846. He retired to his home at Peoria in a nearly destitute condition.

While suffering from the consumption that took his life in 1850, he wrote *A History of Illinois, from its Commencement as a State in 1818 to 1847* (Chicago: S. C. Griggs and Co., 1854), an excellent book. It was a vivid and personal statement, reflecting on his career as a public official, as well as a history based on research. Much of it, understandably, was given over to an explanation of his actions during the Mormon conflict. At the end of that book, Ford remarked that he felt "degraded by the reflection, that the humble governor of an obscure State, who would otherwise be forgotten in a few years, stands a fair chance, like Pilate and Herod, by their official connection with the true religion, of being dragged down to posterity with an immortal name, hitched on to the memory of a miserable impostor" (360).

Thomas Ford summarized in his history of Illinois the lessons to be learned from the vigilante murders of the Smiths:

> In framing our governments, it seemed to be the great object of our ancestors to secure the public liberty by depriving government of power. Attacks upon liberty were not anticipated from any considerable portion of the people themselves. It was not expected that one portion of the people would attempt to play the tyrant over another. And if such a thing had been thought of, the only mode of putting it down was to call out the militia, who are, nine times out of ten, partisans on the one side or the other in the contest. The militia may be relied upon to do battle in a popular service, but if mobs are raised to drive out horse thieves, to put down claim-jumpers, to destroy an abolition press, or to expel an odious sect, the militia cannot be brought to act against them efficiently. The people cannot be used to put down the people. (240)

The document printed here describes how he tried to maintain order and uphold the law and how extralegal activities prevented that. It was first published as Thomas Ford, *Message from the Governor, in Relation to the Disturbances in Hancock County* (Springfield, Ill.: Walters & Weber, Public Printers, 1844), 3–21.

On the seventeenth day of June last, a committee of a meeting of the citizens of Carthage, presented themselves to me, with a request that the militia might be ordered out to assist in executing process in the city of Nauvoo. From the affidavits presented at the same time, I judged that an occasion had arisen of considerable difficulty and perplexity; and from their statements, I could be of no other opinion than that great excitement existed in the minds of the people. I therefore determined to visit, in person, that section of the country, and examine for myself the truth and nature of their complaints; and being on the ground, I would be the better enabled to judge of what ought to be done, under the actual circumstances existing. Therefore, no order for the militia was made; and I arrived at Carthage on the morning of the twenty-first day of the same month.

Upon my arrival I found an armed force assembled, and hourly increasing, under the summons and direction of the constables of the county, to serve as a posse comitatus to assist in the execution of process. The General of that Brigade, had also called for the militia, en masse, of the counties of McDonough and Schuyler, for a similar purpose. Another assemblage to a considerable number, had been made at Warsaw, under the command of Col. Levi Williams.

The first thing which I did on my arrival, was to place all the militia then assembled or which were expected to assemble, under military command of their proper officers.

I next despatched a messenger to Nauvoo, informing the Mayor and Common Council of the nature of the complaint made against them; and requested that persons might be sent to me, to lay their side of the question before me. A committee was accordingly sent, who made such acknowledgments, that I had no difficulty in concluding that the following facts were perfectly true.

It appears that a certain portion of the citizens of Nauvoo became dissatisfied with the conduct of some of the leading men of the place; and established a newspaper press, as the organ of their peculiar views. Those persons were ex-communicated from the church called, "The Latter day Saints," but more familiarly known as the Mormon Church; and their printing press and materials were destroyed, by order of the Common Council.

It appeared that previous to the destruction of the press, a very curious trial was had before the Common Council, which resulted in a judgment of that body, that the press was a public nuisance and ought to be abated. It does not appear that any person was tried, or that any of the owners of the property had notice of the proceeding, or were permitted to defend in any particular. The proceeding was an ex-parte proceeding *in rem* against the property. No jury was called or sworn, and most of the witnesses were permitted to give their evidence, without being under oath. It appeared further, that there existed no general ordinance of the city, defining such a press to be a nuisance; and further, that the Common Council possessed legislative authority, only; and could, under no pretence, sit in judgment as a court.

The press, however, was declared a nuisance; and the Mayor was ordered to see it abated as such; and if necessary, to call to his assistance a portion of the Nauvoo Legion. The Mayor made his warrant to the Marshal of the city, who, aided by a portion of the Legion, executed his warrant, by destroying the press and scattering the type and other materials of the office.

The owners of the property proceeded to Carthage and took out warrants from before a justice of the peace, against the Mayor and members of the Council and others engaged in the outrage, for a riot. . . .

The whole proceedings of the Mayor, the Common Council, and the Municipal Court, were irregular and illegal, and not to be endured in a free country. . . .

In addition to these causes of excitement, there were a great many reports in circulation, and generally believed by the people. . . .

It was asserted that Joseph Smith, the founder and head of the Mormon church, had caused himself to be crowned and anointed King of the Mormons; that he had embodied a band of followers, called Danites, who were sworn to obey him as God, and to do his commands, murder and treason not excepted; that he had instituted an order in the church, whereby those who composed it were pretended to be sealed up to eternal life, against all crimes, save the shedding of innocent blood or consenting thereto. That this order was instructed that no blood was innocent blood, except that of the members of the church; and that these two orders were made the ministers of his vengeance, and the instruments of an intolerable tyranny, which he had established over his people, and which he was about to extend over the neighboring country. The people affected to believe, that with this power in the hands of an unscrupulous leader, there was no safety for the lives or property of any one who should oppose him. They affected likewise, to believe, that Smith inculcated the legality of perjury, or any other crime, in defence, or to advance the interests of the true believers; and that himself had set them the example, by swearing to a false accusation against a certain person, for the crime of murder. It was likewise asserted, to be a fundamental article of the Mormon faith, that God had given the world and all it contained, to them as his saints; that they secretly believed in their right to all the goodly lands, farms, and property, in the country; that consequently, there was no moral offence in anticipating God's good time to put them in possession by stealing, if opportunity offered; that in fact, the whole church was a community of murderers, thieves, robbers, and outlaws; that Joseph Smith had established a Bogus factory in Nauvoo, for the manufacture of counterfeit money; and that he maintained about his person, a tribe of swindlers, blacklegs, and counterfeiters, to make it, and put it into circulation.

It was also believed, that Joseph Smith had announced a revelation from heaven, sanctioning polygamy, by some kind of spiritual-wife system, which I never could well understand; but at any rate, whereby a man was allowed one wife in pursuance of the laws of the country, and an indefinite number of others, to be enjoyed in some mystical and spiritual mode; and that he himself, and many of his followers, had practiced upon the precepts of this revelation, by seducing a large number of women.

It was also asserted, that Joseph Smith was in alliance with the Indians of the Western Territories; and had obtained over them such a control, that in case of a war, he could command their assistance, to murder his enemies.

Upon the whole, if one half of these reports had been true, the Mormon community must have been the most intolerable collection of rogues ever assembled; or, if one half of them were false, they were the most maligned and abused.

Fortunately for the purpose of those who were active in creating excitement, there were some truths which gave countenance to some of these accusations. . . . It is a fact also, that his municipal court, of which he was chief justice, by writ of habeas corpus had frequently discharged individuals accused of high crimes and offences against the laws of the State; and on one occasion had discharged a person accused of swindling the Government of the United States, and who had been arrested by process of the federal courts. Thereby giving countenance to the report, that he obstructed the administration of justice; and had set up a government at Nauvoo, independent of the laws and government of the State. This idea was further corroborated in the minds of the people, by the fact that the people of Nauvoo had petitioned the last session of Congress for a territorial government, to be established at Nauvoo, and to be independent of the State government. It was a fact also, that some larcenies and robberies had been committed, and that Mormons had been convicted of the crimes; and that other larcenies had been committed by persons unknown, but suspected to be Mormons. Justice, however, requires me here to say, that I have investigated the charge of promiscuous stealing, and find it to be greatly exaggerated. . . . It is probable, however, that the Mormons sometimes erred in protecting members of their community from prosecution and punishment, who were accused of offences, under a belief that the accusation against them, was a persecution of their enemies on account of their religion.

I have reason to believe too, that the report of an alliance with the Indians, was a groundless calumny. . . .

But the great cause of popular fury was, that the Mormons at several preceding elections had cast their vote as an unit; thereby making the fact apparent that no one could aspire to the honors or offices of the country, within the sphere of their influence, without their approbation and votes. It appears to be one of the principles by which they insist upon being governed as a community to act as a unit in all matters of government and religion. They express themselves to be fearful that if division should be encouraged in politics, it would soon extend to their religion, and rend their church with schism, and into sects.

This seems to me to be an unfortunate view of the subject, and more unfortunate in practice, as I am well satisfied that it must be the fruitful source of excitement, violence, and mobocracy, whilst it is persisted in. It is indeed unfortunate for their peace, that they do not divide in elections, according to their individual preferences or political principles, like other people.

This one principle and practice of theirs, has arrayed against them in deadly hostility, all aspirants for office who are not sure of their support, and all who had been unsuccessful in elections, with all their friends and influence.

These also were the active men in blowing up the fury of the people; in hopes that a popular movement might be set on foot, which would result in the expulsion or extermination of the Mormon voters. For this purpose public meetings had been called; inflammatory speeches had been made; exaggerated and unfounded reports had been extensively circulated; committees had been appointed, and rode night and day to spread the reports, and solicit the aid of the neighboring counties. And at a public meeting at Warsaw resolutions were passed to expel or exterminate the Mormon population. This was not however, a movement which was unanimously concurred in. The county contained a goodly number of inhabitants in favor of peace, or who at least desired to be neutral in such a contest. These were stigmatized by the name of "*Jack Mormons*," and there were not a few of the more furious exciters of the people, who openly expressed their intention to involve them in the common expulsion or extermination. . . .

As my object in visiting Hancock was expressly to assist in the execution of the laws, and not to violate them, or to witness or permit their violation; as I was convinced that the Mormon leaders had committed a crime in the destruction of the press, and had resisted the execution of process, I determined to exert the whole force of the State, if necessary, to bring them to justice. But seeing the great excitement in the public mind, and the manifest tendency of this excitement to run into mobocracy, I was of opinion that before I acted, I ought to obtain a pledge from the officers and men to support me in strictly legal measures, and to protect the prisoners in case they surrendered. For I was determined, if possible, that the forms of law should not be made the catspaw of the mob, to seduce these people to a quiet surrender, as the convenient victims of popular fury. I, therefore, called together the whole force then assembled at Carthage, and made them an address, explaining to them what I could, and what I could not, legally do; and also adducing to them various reasons why they as well as the Mormons, should submit to the laws; and why, if they had resolved upon revolutionary proceedings, their purpose should be abandoned. The assembled troops seemed much pleased with the address; and upon its conclusion the officers and men unanimously voted, with acclamation, to sustain me in a strictly legal course, and that the prisoners should be protected from violence. Upon the arrival of additional forces from Warsaw, McDonough and Schuyler, similar addresses were made, with the same result.

It seemed to me that these votes fully authorized me to promise the accused Mormons the protection of the law in case they surrendered. They were accordingly duly informed that if they surrendered they would be protected, and if they did not, the whole force of the State would be called out, if necessary, to compel their submission. A force of ten men was despatched with the constable to make the arrests and to guard the prisoners to Head Quarters.

In the meantime, Joseph Smith, as Lieutenant General of the Nauvoo Legion, had declared martial law in the city; the Legion was assembled and ordered under arms; the members of it residing in the country, were ordered into town. The Mormon settlements obeyed the summons of their leaders, and marched to his assistance. Nauvoo, was one great military camp, strictly guarded and watched; and no ingress or egress was allowed, except upon the strictest examination. In one instance which came to my knowledge, a citizen of McDonough, who happened to be in the city, was denied the privilege of returning, until he made oath that he did not belong to the party at Carthage; that he would return home without calling at Carthage; and that he would give no information of the movement of the Mormons.

However, upon the arrival of the constable and guard the Mayor and Common Council at once signified their willingness to surrender, and stated their readiness to proceed to Carthage next morning at eight o'clock. Martial law had previously been abolished. The hour of eight o'clock came, and the accused failed to make their appearance. The constable and his escort returned. The constable made no effort to arrest any of them; nor would he or the guard delay their departure one minute beyond the time, to see whether an arrest could probably be made. Upon their return they reported, that they had been informed that the accused had fled and could not be found.

I immediately proposed to a council of officers, to march into Nauvoo with the small force then under my command, but the officers were of opinion that it was too small, and many of them insisted upon a further call of the militia. Upon reflection I was of opinion that the officers were right in the estimate of our force; and the project for immediate action was abandoned. I was soon informed however, of the conduct of the constable and guard, and then I was perfectly satisfied that a most base fraud had been attempted; that in fact it was feared, that the Mormons would submit; and thereby entitle themselves to the protection of the law. It was very important that many of the bustling active spirits, were afraid that there would be no occasion for calling out an overwhelming militia force; for marching into Nauvoo; for probable mutiny when there; and for the extermination of the Mormon race. It appeared that the constable and the escort were fully in the secret, and acted well their part, to promote the conspiracy.

Seeing this to be the state of the case, I delayed any further call of the militia, to give the accused another opportunity to surrender; for indeed I was most anxious to avoid a general call for the militia at that critical season of the year. The whole spring season preceding, had been unusually wet. No ploughing of corn had been done, and but very little planting. The season had just changed to be suitable for ploughing. The crops which had been planted, were universally suffering; and the loss of two weeks, or even of one, at that time, was likely to produce a general famine all over the country. The wheat harvest was also approaching; and if we got into a war, there was no foreseeing when it would end, or when the militia could safely be discharged. In addition to these considerations all the grist mills in all that section of the country had been swept away, or disabled, by the high waters; leaving the inhabitants almost without meal or flour; and making it impossible then to procure provisions, by impressment or otherwise, for the sustenance of any considerable force. I was totally without funds belonging to the State, with which to purchase at more distant markets; and there was no manner of certainty that such purchases could have been made on the credit of the State, considering the embarrassed condition of the treasury. I was also desirous of avoiding the expense of a great armament; and of a war, the duration and expense of which, could not be foreseen; if they could be honorably avoided.

In the meantime I made a requisition upon the officers of the Nauvoo Legion, for the surrender of the State arms in their possession. It appeared that there is no evidence in the Quarter Master General's Office, of the number and description of the arms with which the Legion had been furnished. On this subject I applied to Gen. Wilson Law, for information. He had lately been the Major General of the Legion. He had seceded from the Mormon part; was one of the owners of the proscribed press; had left the city, as he said, in fear of life; and was one of the party asking for justice against its constituted authorities. He was interested to exaggerate the number of arms, rather than to place it at too low an estimate. From his information I learned that the Legion has received three pieces of cannon and about two hundred and fifty stand of small arms and their accoutrements. Of these, the three pieces of cannon and two hundred and twenty stand of small arms, were surrendered. These arms were demanded because the Legion was illegally used in the destruction of the press, and in enforcing martial law in the city, in open resistance to legal process, and the posse comitatus.

I demanded the surrender also on account of the great prejudice and excitement which the possession of these arms by the Mormons, had always kindled in the minds of the people. A large portion of the people, by pure misrepresentation, had been made to believe that the Legion had received of the State as many as thirty pieces of artillery, and five or six thousand stand of small arms, which in all probability would soon be wielded for the conquest of the country; and for their subjection to Mormon domination. I was of opinion that the removal of these arms would tend much to allay this excitement and prejudice; and in point of fact, although wearing a severe aspect, would be an act of real kindness to the Mormons themselves.

On the 23d or 24th day of June, Joseph Smith, the Mayor of Nauvoo, together with his brother Hyrum, and all the members of the council, and all others demanded, came into Carthage and surrendered themselves prisoners to the constable, on the charge of riot. They all voluntarily entered into a recognizance before the Justice of the Peace for their appearance at court to answer the charge. And all of them were discharged from custody, except Joseph and Hyrum Smith, against whom the Magistrate had issued a new writ, on a complaint for treason. They were immediately arrested by the constable, on this new charge, and retained in his custody, to answer it.

The overt act of treason against them, consisted in the alleged levying of war against the State by declaring martial law in Nauvoo, and in ordering out the Legion to resist the posse comitatus. Their actual guiltiness of the charge, would depend upon circumstances. If their opponents had been seeking to put the law in force in good faith, and nothing more, then an array of a military force in open resistance to the posse comitatus, and the militia of the State, most probably would have amounted to treason. But if those opponents merely intended to use the process of the law, the militia of the State, and the posse comitatus, as cats-paws to compass the possession of their persons for the purpose of murdering them afterwards, as the sequel demonstrated the fact to be, it might well be doubted whether they were guilty of treason.

Soon after the surrender of the Smiths, at their request I despatched Captain Singleton with his company from Brown county, to Nauvoo, to guard the town; and I authorized him to take command of the Legion. He reported to me afterwards, that he called out the Legion for inspection; and that upon two hours notice, two thousand of them assembled, all of them armed; and this after the public arms had been taken away from them. So, it appears that they have a sufficiency of private arms, for any reasonable purpose.

After the Smiths had been arrested on the new charge of treason, the Justice of the Peace postponed the examination, because neither of the parties were prepared with their witnesses for trial. In the meantime he committed them to the jail of the county, for greater security.

In all this matter the justice of the peace and constable, though humble in office, were acting in a high and independent capacity, far beyond any legal power in me to control. I considered that the executive power, could only be called in to assist, and not to dictate, or control their action; that in the humble sphere of their duties, they were as independent, and clothed with as high authority by the law, as the Executive Department; and that my province was, simply, to aid them with the force of the State. It is true, that so far as I could prevail on them by advice, I endeavored to do so. The prisoners were not in military custody, or prisoners of war; and I could no more legally control these officers, than I could the superior courts of justice.

Some persons have supposed, that I ought to have had them sent to some more distant and friendly part of the State, for confinement and trial; and that I ought to have searched them for concealed arms; but these surmises and suppositions are readily disposed of, by the fact that they were not my prisoners; but were the prisoners of the constable and jailer, under the direction of the justice of the peace.

The jail in which they were confined, is a considerable stone building; containing a residence for the jailer, cells for the close and secure confinement of prisoners, and one larger room, not so strong, but more airy and comfortable than the cells. They were put into the cells by the jailer; but upon their remonstrance and request, and by my advice, they were transferred to the larger room; and there they remained until the final catastrophe. Neither they nor I, seriously apprehended an attack on the jail through the guard stationed to protect it. Nor did I apprehend the least danger on their part to escape. For I was very sure that any such an attempt would have been the signal of their immediate death. Indeed if they had escaped, it would have been fortunate for the purposes of those who were anxious for the expulsion of the Mormon population. For the great body of that people would most assuredly have followed their prophet and principal leaders, as they did in their flight from Missouri. Since their death, no one has arisen of influence enough to lead them in a similar manner.

The force assembled at Carthage amounted to about twelve or thirteen hundred men; and it was calculated that four or five hundred more, were assembled at Warsaw. Nearly all that portion resident in Hancock, were anxious to be marched into Nauvoo. This measure was supposed to be necessary, to search for counterfeit money, and the apparatus to make it; and also, to strike a salutary terror into the Mormon people, by an exhibition of the force of the State; and thereby prevent future outrages, murders, robberies, burnings and the like, apprehended as the effect of Mormon vengeance, on those who had taken a part against them. On my part, at one time this arrangement was agreed to. The morning of the 27th day of June was appointed for the march; and Golden's point, near the Mississippi river, and about equidistant from Nauvoo and Warsaw, was selected as the place of rendezvous. I had determined to prevail on the Justice to bring out his prisoners, and take them along. A council of officers however, determined that this would be highly inexpedient and dangerous; and offered such substantial reasons for their opinions, as induced me to change my resolution.

Two or three days' preparation had been made for this expedition. I observed that some of the people became more and more excited and inflammatory, the further the preparations were advanced. Occasional threats came to my ears, of destroying the city and murdering or expelling the inhabitants.

I had no objection to ease the terrors of the people by such a display of force; and was most anxious also to search for the alleged apparatus for making counterfeit money; and in fact to enquire into all the charges against that people, if I could have been assured of my command against mutiny and insubordination. But I gradually learned to my entire satisfaction, that there was a plan to get the troops into Nauvoo, and then to begin the war, probably by some of our own party, or some of the seceding Mormons, taking advantage of the night, to fire on our own force, and then laying it on the Mormons. I was satisfied that there were those amongst us fully capable of such an act; hoping that in the alarm, bustle, and confusion of a Militia camp, the truth could not be discovered, and that it might lead to the desired collision.

I had many objections to be made the dupe of any such, or similar artifice. I was openly and boldly opposed to any attack on the city, unless it should become necessary, to arrest prisoners legally charged and demanded. . . .

Besides this, if we had been ever so much disposed to commit such an act of wickedness, we evidently had not the power to do it. It was well assured that the Mormons, at a short notice, could muster as many as two or three thousand well armed men. . . .

Having ordered the guard, and discharged the residue of the militia, I immediately departed for Nauvoo, eighteen miles distant, accompanied by Col. Buckmaster, Quartermaster General, and Capt. Dunn's Company of dragoons.

After we had proceeded four miles, Col. Buckmaster intimated to me, a suspicion, that an attack would be made on the jail. He stated the matter as a mere suspicion, arising from having seen two persons converse together at Carthage, with some air of mystery. I, myself, entertained no suspicion of such an attack; at any rate none before the next day, in the afternoon. Because it was notorious, that we had departed from Carthage, with the declared intention of being absent, at least two days. I could not believe, that any person would attack the jail, whilst we were in Nauvoo; and thereby expose my life, and the lives of my companions, to the sudden vengeance of the Mormons, upon hearing of the death of their leaders. Nevertheless, acting upon the principle of providing against mere possibilities, I sent back one of the company, with a special order to Capt. Smith, to guard the jail strictly and at the peril of his life, until my return.

We proceeded on our journey four miles further. By this time I had convinced myself that no attack would be made on the jail that day, or night. . . .

Having made these arrangements, we proceeded on our march, and arrived at Nauvoo about four o'clock, of the afternoon, of the 27th day of June. As soon as notice could be given, a crowd of the citizens assembled, to hear an address, which I proposed to deliver them. The number present, has been variously estimated, from one, to five thousand.

In this address I stated to them, how, and in what, their functionaries had violated the laws. Also the many scandalous reports in circulation against them, and that these reports, whether true or false, were generally believed by the people. I distinctly stated to them the amount of hatred and prejudice, which prevailed every where against them, and the causes of it, at length.

I also told them plainly and emphatically, that if any vengeance should be attempted openly or secretly against the persons or property of the citizens, who had taken part against their leaders, that the public hatred and excitement was such, that thousands would assemble for the total destruction of their city; and the extermination of their people; and that no power in the State would be able to prevent it. . . .

A short time before sun down, we departed on our return to Carthage. When we had proceeded two miles, we met two individuals, one of them a Mormon, who informed us, that the Smiths had been assassinated in jail, about five or six o'clock of that day. The intelligence seemed to strike every one with a kind of dumbness. As to myself, it was perfectly astounding and I anticipated the very worst consequences from it. The Mormons had been represented to me as a lawless, infatuated, and fanatical people, not governed by the ordinary motives, which influence the majority of mankind. If so, most likely, an exterminating war would ensue, and the whole land would be covered with desolation. . . .

---•••● *8* ●•••---

A Mormon Woman's Reflections
on the Smith Murders

Vilate Kimball (1806–67) was a young Latter Day Saint living in Nauvoo during the *Expositor* affair and its aftermath in June 1844. The wife of apostle Heber C. Kimball, at the time in the eastern states on a missionary trip, she was a keen observer and careful reporter of events in the city in two letters to her husband. She began her first letter to Heber Kimball on 9 June, just after the appearance of the first and only *Expositor* issue but before the press had been destroyed. She added a section on 11 June reporting on the destruction of the press, and a second section on 24 June describing the arrest of Joseph and Hyrum Smith. On 30 June she wrote a second letter to Kimball, this time describing the impact of the murders.

Both of these letters have a vitality and immediacy missing from most other accounts. They capture the intensity of the *Expositor* situation and the concern for the church and its future in the postmartyrdom era. The numerous misspelled words reflect Kimball's limited education, which was typical of most women, and many men, on the Illinois frontier. Her reference to the mysterious phenomenon of blood on the drums of the Nauvoo Legion shows her conviction—no doubt shared by many—that the Mormons were facing inevitable, violent conflict.

The originals of these letters are part of the Kimball Family Collection in the Church of Jesus Christ of Latter-day Saints Archives, Salt Lake City, Utah, and were previously published in Ronald K. Esplin, ed., "Life in Nauvoo, June 1844: Vilate Kimball's Martyrdom Letters," *Brigham Young University Studies* 19 (Winter 1979): 231–40.

---•••●◉●•••---

Nauvoo June 9th 1844

My Dear Companion,

It is one week yesterday since I closed a letter to you. Although I have not spoken to you for a week, yet you have not ben out of my mind many moments at a time when I was awake; and when I am asleep I often dream about you. . . .

June 11th . . . Nauvoo was a scene of confusion last night, some hundred of the Brethren turned out and burned the printing press, and all the aparatus perrtaining to the office of the oposite party. This was done by order of the City Councel. They had only published one Paper, which is concidered a public nucence. But I donot know whether it will be considered so in the eyes of the Law or not. They have sworn revenge, and no doubt they will have it.

June 24th My *Dear Dear* Husband, various have ben the scenes in Nauvoo since I comenced this letter; I should have sent it before now, but I have ben thrown into such confusion I knew not what to write. This is not all. The mails have not come regular, eather on account of bad roads and high water or less they are stoped by mobs. I have not had a letter from you since the one you wrote back by the Ospry. I know your anxiety to hear from us must be very great, as you will no doubt hear of our trouble by report. Nothing is to be heard of but mobs collecting on every side. The Laws and Fosters, and most of the decenting party with their Families left here a day or two after their press was destroyed. They are sworn to have Joseph and the city councel, or exterminate us all. Betwene three and four thousand brethren have ben under arms here the past week. Expecting every day they would come, the brethren were calld in from all the branches round to help defend the city. Joseph sent word to the Governor if he and his staff would come here, he would abide their decision. But instead of his comeing here, he went to carthage, and there walked arm in arm with Law and Foster, untill we have reason to feer he has cought their spirit. He sent thirty men in here dabefore yesterday to take Joseph and sent him a saucy letter, saying if these could not take him thousands could. He ordered the troops here to deliver up their arms, and dispers.

Yesterday morning (although it was sunday) was a scene of confusion. Joseph had fled and left word for the brethren to hang on to their arms and take care of themselves the best way they could. Some were tryed almost to death to think Joseph should leve them in the hour of danger. Hundreds have left the city since the fuss commenced. Most of the merchants on the hill have left. I have not felt frightened amid [it all,] neither has might heart sunk within me, untill yesterday, when I heard Joseph [wrote] and sent word back for his family to follow him, and Br Whitneys family were packing up, not knowing but they would have to go, as he is one of the city councel. For a little while I felt bad enough, but did not let any body know it, neither did I shed any tears. I felt a confidence in the Lord, that he would presurve us from the ravages of our enemies. We expected them here to day by thousands but before night yesterday things put on a different aspect.

Joseph went over the river out of the United States, and there stoped and composed his mind, and got the will of the Lord concerning him, and that was, that he should return and give himself up for trial. He sent a messenger imediately to Carthage to tell the Governor he would meet his staff at the big mound at eight o'clock this morning in company with all that the ritt demanded. They have just passed by here, on their way thare. My heart said Lord bless those Dear men, and presurve them from those that thirst for their blood. Their giveing themselves up is all that will save our city from destruction. The Governor wrote if they did not do so, our city was suspended upon so many caggs of powder, and it needed only one spark to tulch them off, so you can see how he feels. What will be the fate of our dear Brethren the Lord only knows, but I trust he will presurve them.

If you were here, you would be sure to be in their midst. This would increase my anxiety of cors. . . .

Nauvoo June 30th 1844

My Dear Dear Companion

Never before, did I take up my pen to address you under so trying circumstances as we are now placed, but as Br Adams the bearer of this can tell you more than I can write, I shall not attempt to discribe the scene that we have passed through. God forbid that I should ever witness another like unto it. I saw the lifeless corpes of our beloved brethren when they were brought to their almost distracted families. Yea I witnessed their tears, and groans, which was enough to rend the heart of an adamant. Every brother and sister that witnessed the scene fe[lt] deeply to simpathyze with them. Yea, every heart is filled with sorrow, and the very street[s] of Nauvoo seam to morn. Whare it will end the Lord only knows.

We are kept awake night after night by the alarm of mobs. These apostates say, their damnation is sealed, their die is cast, their doom is fixed, and they are determined to do all in their power to have revenge. Law says he wants nine more, that was in his quorum. Some time I am afraid he will get them. I have no doubt but you are on[e]. What makes me feer, is from a circumstance that took place when the legion was first called out to defend the city. There was several Drums found with blood on; no one could account [for how they] got it. They examined to see how many there was; they found tenn, and while they were examining the eleventh there came a large drop on that. Wm has seen them; he says with all the drums have ben use the blood is yet plain to be seen. He has got two; if he gets the nine more it will make eleven. But I try to submit all things into the hands of God.

I have felt oposed to their sending for you to come home at present and did not know as they would untill brother Adams called here a few moments ago, and told me he should start in about two hours. If I wanted to write I must sent it to the mantion house within that time. So I have not time to say much, neither is it nesaceray as he can tell you all. My helth is geting better, the children are all well. I mailed a letter to you last monday directed to Baltimore. The letters you sent from Washington all came to gather last wednesday, and a paper. The mail had not ben in before for fore weeks. The letter you sent from Pistburg I have never got. . . . The children all remember you in love. Now fare you well my love till we meet, which may the lord grant for his sons sake Amen.

Vilate Kimball

———•••• 9 ••••———

The Official Mormon
Rendition of the Murders

Within days of the assassinations at the Carthage jail on 27 June 1844, several accounts of the episode appeared in the press. The *Times and Seasons*, the official religious newspaper of the Latter Day Saints at Nauvoo, was one of the first to prepare a full account. It included a brief description of the last four days of Joseph Smith, essentially from the time of his surrender to Governor Ford on the morning of Monday, 24 June 1844, until his death in the late afternoon of 27 June. Signed by Willard Richards, John Taylor, and Samuel H. Smith, the announcement deplores the tragedy and counsels caution. It also ignores the actual causes of the conflict and claims that the Smith brothers were simply "shot by a Mob for their religion" and "fell as Martyrs." The article also includes a statement by Hugh T. Reid, one of the attorneys for the Smiths. He reviews the situation in Carthage as he perceived it after arriving from Fort Madison, Iowa, on 24 June.

Highly didactic in its tone, the account captures the seriousness of the situation in Hancock County at the time of the murders. It appeared in the newspaper, bordered in black, as "Awful Assassination of Joseph and Hyrum Smith!—The Pledged Faith of the State of Illinois Stained with Innocent Blood by a Mob!" *Times and Seasons* 5 (1 July 1844): 560–65. While the residents of Nauvoo had already learned of the murders by the time this article appeared, it was the first official notification to the Latter Day Saints outside the Mormon stronghold.

———•••◉•••———

On Monday the 24th inst., after Gov. Ford had sent word, that those eighteen persons demanded on a warrant, among whom were Joseph Smith and Hyrum Smith, *should be protected*, by the militia of the State, they in company with some ten or twelve others, started for Carthage. Four miles from that place, they were met by Capt. Dunn, with a company of cavalry, who had an order from the Governor for the "*State Arms.*" Gen. Smith endorsed his acceptance of the same, and both parties returned to Nauvoo to obtain said arms. After the arms were obtained, both parties took up the line of march for Carthage, where they arrived about five minutes before twelve o'clock at night. Capt. Dunn nobly acquitting himself, landed us safely at Hamilton's Hotel.

In the morning we saw the Governor, and he *pledged the faith of the State*, that we should be protected. Gen. Smith and his brother Hyrum were arrested by a warrant founded upon the oaths of H. O. Norton and Augustine Spencer for *treason*. Knowing the threats from several persons, that the two Smiths should never leave Carthage *alive*, we all began to be alarmed for their personal safety. The Gov. and Gen. Deming conducted them before the McDonough troops and introduced them as *Gen. Joseph Smith and Gen. Hyrum Smith.* This manoeuvre came near raising a mutiny among the "Carthage Greys," but the Governor quelled it.

In the afternoon, after great exertions on the part of our counsel, we dispensed with an investigation, and voluntarily gave bail for our appearance to the Circuit Court, to answer in the case of abating the Nauvoo Expositor, as a nuisance.

At evening the Justices made out a mittimus, without an investigation, and committed the two Gen. Smiths to prison *until discharged by due course of law,* and they were safely guarded to jail. In the morning the Governor went to the jail and had an interview with these men, and to every appearance all things were explained on both sides.

The constable then went to take these men from the jail, before the Justice for examination, but the jailor refused to let them go, as they were under his direction *"till discharged by due course of law"*; but the Governor's troops, to the amount of one or two hundred, took them to the Court House, when the hearing was continued til Saturday the 29th, and they were remanded to jail. Several of our citizens had permits from the Governor to lodge with them, and to visit them in jail. It now began to be rumored by several men, whose names will be forthcoming in time, *that there was nothing against these men, the law could not reach them, but powder and ball would!* The Governor was made acquainted with these facts, but on the morning of the 27th, he disbanded the McDonough troops, and sent them home; took Captain Dunn's company of Cavalry and proceeded to Nauvoo, leaving these two men and three or four friends, to be guarded by *eight men* at the jail; and a company in town of 60 men, 80 or 100 rods from the jail, as a corps in reserve.

About six o'clock in the afternoon the guard was surprised by an armed Mob of about 150 to 250, painted red, black and yellow, which surrounded the jail, forced in—poured a shower of bullets into the room where these unfortunate men were held, "in durance vile," to answer to the laws of Illinois; under the solemn pledge of the faith of the State, by Gov. Ford, *that they should be protected!* but the mob ruled!! They fell as Martyrs amid this tornado of lead, each receiving four bullets! John Taylor was wounded by four bullets in his limbs but not seriously. Thus perishes the hope of law; thus vanishes the plighted faith of the state; thus the blood of innocence stains the constituted authorities of the United States, and thus have two among the most noble martyrs since the slaughter of Abel, sealed the truth of their divine mission, *by being shot by a Mob for their religion!*

Messengers were dispatched to Nauvoo, but did not reach there till morning. The following was one of the letters:

12 o'clock at night, 27th June,
Carthage, Hamilton's Tavern.

To Mrs. Emma Smith,
and Maj. Gen. Dunham, &c—

The Governor has just arrived; says all things shall be inquired into, and all right measures taken.

I say to all the citizens of Nauvoo, my brethren, be still, and know that *God reigns. Don't rush out of the city*—don't rush to Carthage; stay at home, and be prepared for an attack from Missouri mobbers. The Governor will render every assistance possible—has sent out orders for troops—Joseph and Hyrum are dead, but not by the Carthage people—the guards were true as I believe.

We will prepare to move the bodies as soon as possible.

The people of the county are greatly excited, and fear the Mormons will come out and take vengeance—I have pledged my word the Mormons will stay at home as soon as they can be informed, and no violence will be on their part, and say to my brethren in Nauvoo, in the name of the Lord—be still—be patient— only let such friends as choose come here to see the bodies—Mr. Taylor's wounds are dressed & not serious—I am sound.

Willard Richards,
John Taylor,
Samuel H. Smith.

Defend yourselves until protection can be furnished as necessary, June 27th, 1844.

Thomas Ford, Governor
and Commander in chief. . . .

The Governor, as well as the citizens of Carthage, was thunderstruck! and fled.

The Legion in Nauvoo, was called out at 10 A.M. and addressed by Judge Phelps, Col. Buckmaster, of Alton, the Governor's aid, and others, and all excitement and fury allayed and preparations were made to receive the bodies of the noble martyrs. About 3 o'clock they were met by a great assemblage of people east of the Temple on Mulholland street, under the direction of the city Marshal, followed by Samuel H. Smith, the brother of the deceased, Dr. Richards and Mr. Hamilton, of Carthage. The wagons were guarded by 8 men. The procession that followed in Nauvoo, was the City Council, the Lieut. General's Staff, the Major General and staff, the Brigadier General and staff, commanders and officers of the Legion and citizens generally, which numbered several thousands, amid the most solemn lamentations and wailings that ever ascended into the ears of the Lord of Hosts to be avenged of our enemies!

When the procession arrived the bodies were both taken into the "Nauvoo Mansion"; the scene at the Mansion cannot be described; the audience was addressed by Dr. Richards, Judge Phelps, Woods and Reed Esqs. of Iowa, and Col. Markham. It was a vast assemblage of some 8 or 10,000 persons, and with one united voice resolved to trust to the law for a remedy of such a high handed assassination, and when that failed to call upon God to avenge us our wrongs! Oh! widows and orphans:—Oh! Americans weep for the glory of freedom has departed!

——•••• 10 ••••——

Willard Richards's Eyewitness Account from Carthage Jail

At the time of the double assassination at the Carthage jail, Willard Richards and John Taylor were both in the company of Joseph and Hyrum Smith. After the assassination they wrote narratives of their experiences. Richards published his description of the event within weeks of the murders in the *Times and Seasons* as "Two Minutes in Jail," 6 (1 August 1844): 598–99. Richards was an apostle in the Mormon Church when the Smith brothers were killed and had long been one of its leaders. (See the biographical sketch in Part III, Document 14.) His article is a vivid and detailed account of the mob violence and has been frequently reprinted.

Interestingly, Richards emphasizes the importance of the bullet in John Taylor's pocket watch that saved his life and fixed the exact time of the attack, while John Taylor's more famous description of the event, entitled "The Martyrdom of Joseph Smith" and published in Joseph Smith, Jr., *History of the Church of Jesus Christ of Latter-day Saints*, ed. B. H. Roberts (Salt Lake City: Deseret Book Co., 1932), 7:99–108, says little about this aspect of the episode. Richards's detailed account not only relates what happened in the jail but also conveys the enormous impact of the bloodshed from the perspective of a devout Mormon who fully believed the Saints were being persecuted for righteousness' sake.

——•••◉•••——

Possibly the following events, occupied near three minutes, but I think only about two, and have penned them for the gratification of many friends.

Carthage, June 27th, 1844.

A shower of musket balls were thrown up the stair way against the door of the prison in the second story, followed by many rapid footsteps. While Generals Joseph and Hyrum Smith, Mr. Taylor, and myself, who were in the front chamber, closed the door of our room against the entry at the head of the stairs, and placed ourselves against it, there being no lock on the door and no ketch [*sic*] that was useable. The door is a common panel, and as soon as we heard the feet at the stairs head, a ball was sent through the door, which passed between us, and showed that our enemies were desperadoes, and we must change our position. Gen. Joseph Smith, Mr. Taylor, and myself sprang back to the front part of the room, and Gen. Hyrum Smith retreated two thirds across the chamber directly in front of and facing the door. A ball was sent through the door which hit Hyrum on the side of his nose, when he fell backwards extended at length without moving his feet. From the holes in his vest, (the day was warm and no one had their coats on but myself,) pantaloons, drawers and shirt, it appears evident that a ball must have been thrown from without, through the window, which entered his back on the right side and passing through lodged against his watch, which was in his right vest pocket, completely pulverizing the crystal and face, tearing off the hands and mashing the whole body of the watch, at the same instance the ball from the door entered his nose. As he struck the floor he exclaimed emphatically: *"I'm a dead man."* Joseph looked towards him, and responded "O dear! *Brother Hyrum!"* and opening the door two or three inches with his left hand, discharged one barrel of a six shooter (pistol) at random in the entry from whence a ball grazed Hyrum's breast, and entering his throat, passed into his head, while other muskets were aimed at him, and some balls hit him. Joseph continued snapping his revolver, round the casing of the door into the space as before, three barrels of which missed fire, while Mr. Taylor with a walking stick stood by his side and knocked down the bayonets and muskets, which were constantly discharging through the door way, while I stood by him, ready to lend any assistance, with another stick, but could not come within striking distance, without going directly before the muzzle of the guns. When the revolver failed, we had no more fire arms, and expecting an immediate rush of the mob, and the door way full of muskets—half way in the room—and no hope but instant death from within, Mr. Taylor rushed into the window, which is some fifteen or twenty feet from the ground. When his body was nearly on a balance, a ball from the door within entered his leg, and a ball from without struck his watch, a patent lever, in his vest pocket, near the left breast, and smashed it in "pie," leaving the hands standing at 5 o'clock, 16 minutes, and 26 seconds—the force of which ball threw him back on the floor, and he rolled under the bed which stood by his side, where he lay motionless, the mob from the door continuing to fire upon him, cutting away a piece of flesh from his left hip as large as a man's hand, and were hindered only by my knocking down their muzzles with a stick; while they continued to reach their guns into the room, probably left handed, and aimed their discharge so far around as almost to reach us in the corner of the room to where we retreated and dodged, and then I re-commenced the attack with my stick again. Joseph attempted as the last resort, to leap the same window from whence Mr. Taylor fell, when two balls pierced him from the door, and one entered his right breast from without, and he fell outward exclaiming, *"O Lord My God!"* As his feet went out of the window my head went in, the balls whistling all around. He fell on his left side a dead man. At this instant the cry was raised, *"He's leaped the window,"* and the mob on the stairs and in the entry ran out. I withdrew from the window, thinking it of no use to leap out on a hundred bayonets, then around Gen. Smith's body. Not satisfied with this I again reached my head out of the window and watched some seconds, to see if there were any signs of life, regardless of my own, determined to see the end of him I loved; being fully satisfied, that he was dead, with a hundred men near the body and more coming round the corner of the jail, and expecting a return to our room I rushed towards the prison door, at the head of the stairs, and through the entry from whence the firing had proceeded, to learn if the doors into the prison were open.—When near the entry, Mr. Taylor called out, "*take me*"; I pressed my way till I found all doors unbarred, returning instantly, caught Mr. Taylor under my arm, and rushed by the stairs into the dungeon, or inner prison, stretched him on the floor and covered him with a bed in such a manner, as not likely to be perceived, expecting an immediate return of the mob. I said to Mr. Taylor, this is a hard case to lay you on the floor, but if your wounds are not fatal I want you to live to tell the story. I expected to be shot the next moment, and stood before the door awaiting the onset.

WILLARD RICHARDS

————•••• *11* ••••————

"Such an Excitement I Never Witnessed in My Life"

I n contrast to the perspective from within the jail offered by Willard Richards, the following letter, written by a non-Mormon eyewitness, depicts the scene in Carthage before and during the killings. Samuel Otho Williams (?–1844) was a second lieutenant in the Carthage militia and left a detailed account of the events which took place in June 1844. Although he did not much like the Latter Day Saints, Williams did not consider himself an anti-Mormon and denied any involvement in the conspiracy to murder the Smith brothers. He wrote this seven-page letter from Carthage to a friend, John Prickett, on 10 July 1844. The original manuscript can be found in the Mormon Collection of the Chicago Historical Society. This letter is published here for the first time.

————•••••••••————

Carthage July 10/44

My Dear John

I have just this moment received your letter of the first inst. and hasten to answer it. I proceed to give you a history of our difficulties with the *Saints*. About a month ago a paper was started in Nauvoo called the Nauvoo Expositor owned by some of the seceding *Saints* which had for its purpose the exposure of the *Smith's* and all *villainy* practised by them and in the City under their direction.

The first number of the paper was issued and the way it let out on *Jo* was a *sin*. He called the City Council together and after much deliberation and talk the new paper was declared a *NUISANCE* and they passed an ordinance requiring the Marshal of the City to destroy the press, pie the type and if any resistance was offered to destroy the house. The Mayor of the City (Jo) accordingly issued his writ to the Marshal commanding him to do the work, which he did. He with his posse (the Marshal) threw the press into the street and broke it up with a Sledge Hammer and barut [?] the type. The Mormons also tried to catch the owners of the press but they escaped; several of them came here. Complaint was made here before a Justice of the peace who issued a warrant and sent a Constable to bring them (Jo and all the others concerned, about 20 in number) to this place for trial. The Constable arrested them and Jo was discharged by the Municipal Court of the City of Nauvoo and afterward Jo discharged the balance on writs of *Habeas Corpus*—these patent writs were entered on the record, honorably discharged. As soon as we heard of the press being destroyed a meeting of the old citizens was called and was in session at the time the officer returned from Nauvoo, without the prisoners of course. Such an excitement I never witnessed in my life—there was about seven hundred of the old citizens assembled here and I tell you we all felt that the time had come where either the Mormons or old citizens had to leave. The meeting determined to call for volunteers to rendezvous at four places in this County and when a sufficient number had assembled the Constable that arrested Smith [and] the others were to call on us as a *posse cum status* [*sic*] to help him arrest the accused.

Our Brigadier General in the mean time called out the forces under his command. The meeting also appointed two persons to go to the Governor and get him to issue a call for the Militia. They repaired to Springfield and returned with his Excellency. When the Gov arrived here he found about 300 men armed and drilling four hours each day and standing guard at night. Our Company the Carthage Grays, as soon as the arresting civic [official came] to the conclusion, was dispatched [with] our tents on the public square and went to work. The Gov soon after his arrival made a speech to the troops and announced his determination to see the law executed and immediately dispatched a messenger to Nauvoo to Smith telling him the consequences if he did not immediately surrender himself for trial—this was on Friday. On Sunday a whole Regiment marched into town from McDonough County and on the next Tuesday a Battalion from Schuyler County which made the forces here amount to about 1400 men. As the different forces marched into town they pledged themselves that no violence should be offered to the prisoners if they did come to Carthage. On Tuesday the Gov sent Capt Dunn of the Warsaw Dragoons of this County to Nauvoo with an order for the State arms with wagons & horses to bring them here.

On the road between this place & Nauvoo they met Smith and the others accused coming to this place to give themselves up for trial. They returned to Nauvoo with Capt Dunn and about 70 of the State Arms delivered to Capt Dunn, and the two Smith's, Jo & Hiram came out here with Capt Dunn with the arms.

On Wednesday Morning the McDonough troops requested the Gov to bring Jo Smith along their lines, many of whom had never see him. The two Smiths were after breakfast brought to the Head Quarters of the Brigadier Genl and our Company stationed at the door as a guard. Your Humble Servant had command of the Grays at this time. I brought the company up to the house and formed a square of three sides in front of the house with their muskets at a "*charge*" and even then had some difficulty in keeping the crowd back so great was the anxiety to see the Smiths, & we stood in this position about ½ an hour when I received orders from the Brig Genl to form the Grays into a Hollow square and guard the Smiths and the Gov. & the Genl to the right of the 57th Regt which was formed about 300 yards from the Genls quarters—which was accordingly done, and when we arrived there, I opened the square and let them out and marched the Grays back to their "quarters." I was about to discharge the Company when the Smiths in company with the Brig Genl came past our quarters. The company [was] in line at "order arms" when the Grays commenced hissing and sarming [?] and making all sorts of *hellish* sounds. I tried to stop it but could not. I was about to dismiss the Company again when several of them requested me to march out and drill awhile. I accordingly marched out and started down a street on which the Tavern stands that Jo was stopping at. On the way we passed the Brig Genl and the Grays. . . . and arrived in a few minutes afterwards out on front of the tavern where I was when the same scene was enacted. Hissing, groaning and all kinds of discordant sounds. I all the time tried my utmost to preserve silence but had no more command over them than I would have had over a pack of wild Indians. At this demonstration of feeling on the part of the Grays Jo *actually fainted*. I will now tell you the reason of all the hissing &c. The Grays thought we were ordered to escort Smith and that it was intended as an honor to be conferred on him, and the Genl always has been what we call a *Jack Mormon*. I believe I have told you what that is and therefore won't stop to explain now. A few days before at our Anti-Mormon meeting he attempted to make a speech and was hissed down. Well to resume, when we arrived at our quarters I was informed that our company was ordered under "*Arrest*." A number of the Company immediately mounted a wagon and made a speech to the troops and the remainder loaded their muskets with *Ball* cartridges and swore that they would die sooner then give up their Arms. A considerable number of the troops say one half swore that the Arms of the Grays should not be taken from them. If you had been here to see the excitement at this time you would have been astonished. I never saw any thing equal it. The Brig Genl had insulted the McDonough troops by introducing the Smiths in this way: "Gentlemen, officers of the 57th Regt, I introduce to you Joseph & Hiram Smith, Generals of the Nauvoo Legion." . . . At this state of the proceedings the Gov came on the ground and stated that no honor was intended to be conferred on the Smiths, that it was done at the request of the 57th Regt that they might see him, that he disapproved of the way of introducing the prisoners and rescinded the order of arrest. At this the shout of the residue ascended to the heavens. We cheered the Gov for about 2 minutes and we made "some advise"; this settled all things for the present.

The same day an order was issued to all the troops to march on Friday into Nauvoo, the whole to rendezvous on Thursday night at Goldens point about 5 miles below Nauvoo. On Thursday morning a council of the officers was called and the former order of march was revoked. The Gov thinking that if we once got into Nauvoo that he could not restrain the troops and that we would burn the place. On Friday morning all the troops except the Warsaw Dragoons, Carthage Grays, and the Carthage Riflemen (the last a Militia Company) were disbanded and left for home. Jo & Hiram [were] all this time in Jail. I forgot to say that 10 of those concerned in destroying the press came forward and gave bail for their appearance at the next term of the Circuit Court without an examination and immediately afterward Jo & Hiram were arrested on a charge of Treason and the examination was postponed until Saturday the 29th inst, which time they were destined never to see. On Friday about 11 oclock A.M. the Gov under the escort of the Warsaw Dragoons started for Nauvoo to address the People there, leaving our Company and the Militia company to protect the prisoners, they being under a pledge to do so. All was quiet at this time, a Guard of six men was placed in the Jail with a Sergeant to command it which was retired about every 3 hours. When the Gov had been gone about 2 hours he sent back a messenger to Capt Smith stating that he was afraid some violence would be afforded against the prisoners and that he expected him to do his duty. The same messenger was sent back to the Gov [to reply] that we would. About 5 oclock PM our look out on the Court House cried out. "There is about 400 Mormons coming down the fence to the Jail." I cannot explain to you the situation of the Jail and our encampment on paper—but when I see you which I hope will be soon I will show you. As soon as the alarm was given our Company and the militia company was immediately formed and started for the Jail which was about 500 yards from our quarters. At the time the alarm was given the *Mob* were in about 200 yard of the Jail. We marched double quick time and when we got to the Jail both the Smiths were Killed and the mob running off. When the Mob came up in front of the Jail our guard challenged them—the mob demanded the prisoners—they were told that if they did not retire the guard would fire on them. The Mob raised a shout and commenced jumping over the low fence in front of the Jail when our guard fired at them—the guard were immediately overpowered and the mob rushed into the Jail and did their work.—The guards were not hurt except some bruises. One of the guard who was the Sergeant in command lost his sword and another his musket. The Guard—also in return the Guard captured a Musket and a rifle.—The Mob all had their faces blacked.—When we were marching to the Jail about 150 yards from the Jail we saw Jo come to the window and turn back, and in about a second or two afterwards he came to the window and tumbled out. He was shot several times and a bayonet run through him after he fell.—From all the information I can get the Mob were about 250 strong.—The forces left to guard the prisoners about 60 or 65 strong.—A messenger was immediately dispatched to the Gov who returned here about 12 oclock that night and advised us to evacuate the town. After the Smiths were killed all the women and children were removed from town and the men were determined to stay and protect their property but when the Gov came in and stated that he believed our town would be in ashes before morning we all left and deserted the town—stop—there were six men in town at daylight Saturday morning.—I was not one of them.—I left Carthage about ½ past one and travelled all night through mud & water knee deep in some places. I arrived at Augusta about 7 oclock Saturday morning having travelled 18 miles, and considering the roads [that] was tolerably good walking. The Gov was badly sawed and stopped in this place but a few minutes and left for Augusta—arrived there about day light and left there directly after breakfast for Quincy where he now is.—What will be the result of the death of the Smiths, I am entirely unable to say.—The Mormons are very badly scared and I dont think they will do anything at present—the citizens of this place have nearly all returned.—

I think I will be in Edwardsville soon—any how as soon as I can leave.—Our Company is still under orders and I cant leave just yet.—My family I sent off to Rushville 50 miles from here as soon as they could start after the Smiths were killed and I returned with them yesterday. . . .

Your Friend Saml Williams

━━━━•••• 12 ••••━━━━

"The Work of Death Has Commenced"

A different view of the murders of the Smiths, a typical non-Mormon position, appears in the contemporary account of David Wells Kilbourne (see the headnote to Part III, Document 12). Kilbourne was certainly not sympathetic to the Latter Day Saints, as shown in this set of letters to a Reverend T. Dent of Billington, near Whalley, Lancashire, England, with whom he corresponded. Kilbourne was a resident of Fort Madison, Iowa Territory, about twelve miles north of Nauvoo on the Mississippi River, and took no part in the actual events.

This letter, written by a literate and well-informed individual near the action, offers an intimate account of the opinions held by non-Mormons around Nauvoo at the time. Kilbourne reports some information that was mostly rumor, but his thoughtful perspectives on the dramatic events taking place in nearby Hancock County include an awareness that Joseph Smith's murder allowed him to escape prosecution and will enable his followers to declare him a martyr. A letter-book copy of this 29 June 1844 letter is contained in the David Wells Kilbourne Papers, State Historical Society of Iowa, Des Moines. It is published here for the first time. A short narrative of the murders has been omitted, for it merely summarizes what others have already described firsthand.

———————●●●●◗◗◗●●●●———————

Fort Madison
June 29th 1844
7 O Clock P.M.

Revd. T. Dent
Billington
near Whalley Lancashire England
My dear Sir

I hasten to inform you of the wonderful events which have taken place at Nauvoo since my last letter to you a few days ago. The work of death has commenced. The *Mormon Prophet* Joe Smith & his brother *Hyrum* are no more. I have just returned from Nauvoo & I this day looked upon the lifeless remains of these two men—the great heads & leaders of Mormonism. Their work of infamy is finished & their *dupes* about two hours since committed their remains to the silent grave. . . .

There is but one feeling throughout this country in regard to this last tragedy, & that is, that merited venge[a]nce has fallen on the right men; at the same time all regret that it happened while he was a prisoner & had a right to expect protection. It is regretted because his followers will now claim that he died a martyr when if he could have been tried on the charges & convicted he would have died a felon.

On Thursday morning I determined to go to Carthage 18 miles distant for the purpose of seeing for myself & learning the true state of the case—but after I got over the river I concluded to go down to Nauvoo. There I found Mr Ford & his company & heard him make his speech. The Gov invited me to go to Carthage with them that evening & about sunset we set out when about 4 miles out we met a messenger with the intel[l]igence that Joe & Hyram were dead. The Gov fearing to have the inte[l]ligence go to Nauvoo took the man in charge & proceeded on towards Carthage.

As it was after dark I turned about myself unnoticed & went back to Nauvoo & put up at Joes tavern where several of my friends from this place were stop[p]ing over night, which circumstance made me feel more secure.

I soon retired without mentioning the circumstances to any one for I could hardly believe it. About 4 O Clock the next Friday June 28th the same messenger arrived at Joes tavern confirming the news. I immediately dressed & went down, saw Joes wife & children about the house, but saw no manifestations of grief on the part of any one save Joes mother who made her appearance at the door in the course of the morning & enquired who had killed her sons.

The Mormons were told by their principal men to be quiet, to be calm, to make no threats—and to remain quiet in the City, as the only possible means of preventing their entire extermination. I remained there until this evening—they are still in a great state of alarm—& I doubt not they have reason to be. The troops are rallying at Carthage & the people at Warsaw, Quincy & other towns. The people say that they must scatter—that there are 12 men yet in Nauvoo who must be brought to Justice. Every body who is able to get away is doing so. I do not myself think that there will be any further hostilities at present—but there may be.

13

A Youth's Recollection of the Smith Murders

Wilⁱlliam R. Hamilton was one of the youngest members of the Carthage Greys at the time of the Smith murders in 1844. Later a judge in the county, he was the son of Artois Hamilton, who owned the hotel in Carthage where the wounded John Taylor was taken and cared for. Hamilton's letter to Foster Walker (see the biographical sketch of Walker in Part II, Document 2) provides a unique perspective on the activities that took place during the assassination. Walker, a resident of Pontoosuc, in Hancock County, sought recollections from many non-Mormons on this subject near the turn of the century.

Hamilton's account accurately depicts the lack of preparation for the attack and the less than spectacular response from the militia stationed in town. This letter is reprinted from Walker's, "The Mormons in Hancock County," *Dallas City* (Ill.) *Review*, 29 January 1903, p. 2, available at the Illinois State Historical Library, Springfield, Ill.

Carthage, Ill., Dec. 24, 1902

FOSTER WALKER,—

It would be a long and, I presume, an uninteresting story to relate all I saw of the Mormons and know of their actions and that of the Antis; therefore I shall confine myself to what I know transpired on the day of the killing of the Prophet and Patriarch—that is Joseph and Hyram Smith—by the mob, without entering into any kind of statements as to causes which had incited the mob to take their lives—which was done at the jail in Carthage at about 4:40 o'clock P.M. on June 27, 1844.

There had been about 1200 troops—state militia—summoned as a "posse comitatus" by a civil officer to assist in arresting them. Charges, writs and legal proceedings are matters of record in the courts. Governor Thomas Ford was here in command. The Smiths had surrendered two days before, and had been kept at my father's hotel until that morning. The governor, presuming all danger of trouble over, ordered the troops to return home and disband except two companies, which he retained—the Carthage Greys and the Augusta Dragoons [as then called]. The cavalry company he took as an escort and went to Nauvoo, leaving the Carthage Greys to Guard the Smiths. This company was commanded by Captain Robert F. Smith, who in the war of the Rebellion was colonel of the 16th Ill. Inft. I was the youngest member of that company and had not as yet fully learned the lesson of red tape and complete obedience to all orders. Still, in the company I had the name of doing quite well for a boy.

A little after 7:00 A.M. the troops broke camp and left for home. The Governor, with his escort started for Nauvoo, and the Smiths were taken to the jail—there kept under guard by a detail of six men from the company, with an officer in command; the company remaining in camp at the public square. About 11 o'clock A.M., myself and another young man were ordered by the captain to go on top of the court house and keep a sharp lookout for and see if a body of men were approaching the town from any direction; and, if any were seen, to immediately report to the captain personally, at his quarters. We had a large field glass and could clearly see in every direction save due north for several miles. We were especially ordered to keep a strict outlook over the prairies towards Nauvoo. Nothing suspicious was discovered until about 4 P.M. when we saw a body of armed men in wagons and on horses approaching the low timber, a little north of west from the jail, and about two miles distant. This was at once reported to the captain, when we were ordered to keep a strict watch and at once report if they came through the timber. In about a half hour after, a body of armed men—about 125—came out of the woods on foot and started in a single file, behind an old rail fence, in the direction of the jail. They were then about three-fourths of a mile distant. This we at once attempted to report, but could not find the captain; and (not being "muzzled," as soldiers of late date) told another officer, who after considerable delay found the captain who ordered the company to fall into line. By this time the mob had reached the jail and had commenced shooting. I there forgot all about orders to put on accoutrements and fall into line; but immediately started on double quick for the jail.

To digress: For one of the best drilled and equipped companies in the state at that time—on that occasion we would have taken the prize for the best exhibition of an awkward squad in existence. I have always thought the officers and some privates were working for delay. The company finally reached the jail, but not until after the mob had completed their work and left in the direction from which they came. When about fifty yards away I saw Joseph Smith come to the window and fall out. One of the men went to him and partially straightened his body out beside the well curb. Just at this time I got up amongst the men and heard him say, "he's dead," when all the mob immediately left. I went to where Smith was lying and found that he was dead without doubt. I then went up to the room where they had been quartered, where I found Hyram Smith lying upon the floor on his back, dead. No person was in the room, or came while I was there. He was stretched out on the floor, just as he had fallen after being shot.

The shot that killed him was fired through the door panel by one of the mob, while in the hall, and struck him in the left breast, he falling backward. There were in the room at that time four persons—the two Smiths and Elders Taylor and Richards. Taylor was wounded, being hit several times—all flesh wounds—and was the same night taken to my father's house, where he was cared for until able to be taken to Nauvoo. Richards was not hurt and immediately after the mob left the hall, carried Taylor into the cell department of the jail, which was done just before I went upstairs. The room in which they were is about 16 x 16 feet and had one window in the east side, two in the front or south end, and the door opening from the hall, just at the top of the stairs almost directly opposite the east side window out of which Smith fell. There was a bedstead in the southeast corner of the room, under which Taylor was after the shooting was over. The door opened in such a manner that when forced open it formed a recess in the corner, so that a person there was hid from sight. Richard's position bought [sic] him into the corner. There was no lock, bolt or even latch upon the door, and when the mob started upstairs, those in the room shut the door and attempted to hold it. After those in the hall had tried several times to push it open, Smith having shot at them by putting the muzzle of his old English pepperbox revolver through the opening at the side of the door (made by their efforts) and firing four shots into the hall, one of the men placed the muzzle of his rifle against the door and fired, which shot killed Hyram Smith, he being behind the panel in a position to do most of the work in keeping the door shut, he falling backward, leaving the door which flew open and hid Richards in the corner. At the same time others in the hall fired into the room, wounding Taylor, who rolled under the bed. Smith, in attempting to escape out of the window was shot from the outside falling outward.

The approach of the mob was made from the rear or north, dividing part to the east and west, meeting at the front, thus completely surrounding the jail. The guards were quietly sitting in front and in the hall below, all of whom were captured without much trouble or danger. Just a little suspicion might be attached to the officer in command. Yet it might be presumed he thought his only duty was to keep the Smiths from coming downstairs. After I had satisfied my curiosity, seen and been among the mob, seen the prophet shot, and seen the dead men, it occurred to me I ought to go home and tell the news. When about 200 yards from the jail I met the company coming ready for business. Nothing was to be done but to "about face," return to camp and be disbanded; which was promptly done in good order, as their prisoners were dead and not likely to run away.

The bodies of the Smiths, after the coroner's inquest, were taken by my father, Artois Hamilton, to his hotel. He had boxes (not coffins) made out of pine boards, in which they were taken to Nauvoo the next day. The news of their death having been sent to Nauvoo, early the next morning two of their brothers, with two other men, came after their bodies in a wagon. The body of Joseph was placed in theirs and that of Hyram in father's wagon, who with two of my brothers went with them.

This is a true statement of what occurred on that day, so far as the doings of the troops and killing of the Smiths. There are many facts and names of persons connected with that tragedy, which are now lost to the world—where it seems best to let them remain.

Wm. R. Hamilton

14

"An Authentic Account of the Massacre"

George T. M. Davis was the non-Mormon editor of the *Alton Telegraph and Democratic Review*, published about eighty miles south on the Mississippi River in Illinois (see Part II, Document 13). He had not been an eyewitness to the Smith brothers' murders, but he went to Carthage immediately and wrote an account of the entire affair soon afterward, based on personal observations and numerous interviews. No friend of the Mormons, Davis justified the killings as an expedient measure to resolve the problems in Hancock County. While he was biased against the Saints, much of his version of events has been substantiated by later writers, both eyewitnesses and scholars. This pamphlet was first published as George T. M. Davis, *An Authentic Account of the Massacre of Joseph Smith, the Mormon Prophet, and Hyrum Smith, His Brother, Together with a Brief History of the Rise and Progress of Mormonism, and All the Circumstances Which Led to Their Death* (St. Louis: Chambers and Knapp, 1844), 24–26.

[After the killing of Joseph and Hyrum Smith] the consternation that pervaded the entire community at Carthage, can better be imagined than described. When the attack was first made upon the jail, and the quick successive reports of the rifles heard, the bells of the taverns were rung, and an alarm was raised throughout the town, that the Mormons had surrounded the jail, and were rescuing the prisoners from the custody of its keeper. Many, crediting the report, supposed the vengeance of the followers of Joe would, as soon as he was released, be turned upon the citizens, and that indiscriminate massacre of life, and conflagration of property, would ensue. A few moments, however, only transpired, before the knowledge of the death of the Smiths disabused the public mind, as to the rumor that the Mormons had attacked the jail, though it by no means lessened the consternation and fear of the inhabitants in general. They supposed that as soon as information could be conveyed to Nauvoo, of the death of their two principal men, and the dangerous wounding of the third, the inhabitants of that city would rush, in a spirit of revenge, with the malignity of fiends, upon the towns of

Carthage and Warsaw, and that, ere the rising of the morning sun, the "blackness of ashes" would alone mark where they stood, and all of their inhabitants who should fall within their grasp, would meet the same fate which had been visited upon the Smiths. A messenger was immediately despatched to Gov. Ford, to inform him of what had transpired, and to enable him to escape, while the citizens, with but very few exceptions, were fleeing in every direction, from what they regarded as inevitable destruction if they remained. The messenger despatched to the Governor, met him about three miles out of the city, on his way back to Carthage, who was requested to return with the escort, and the whole made all convenient haste for the scene of consternation. A despatch, however, was sent to Capt. Singleton, and his company, who were supposed to have remained in Nauvoo, to inform them of what had occurred, with instructions to march without delay to Carthage. He was met a short distance out of Nauvoo, and increasing the march of his men, arrived the next morning at Carthage. The Mormons did not that evening hear of the catastrophe that had befallen their leaders, nor was the information imparted to them, until about daylight the next morning. The Governor and his escort reached Carthage between ten and eleven o'clock that evening. What he did, on his arrival, I prefer giving in his own language, as taken from his address, "*To the people of the State of Illinois,*" under date of June 29th, 1844. In it he says: "*Many of the inhabitants of Carthage had fled with their families; others were prepared to go. I apprehended danger to the settlements, from the sudden fury and passions of the Mormons, and sanctioned their movements in this respect. Gen. Deming volunteered to remain with a few troops, to observe the progress of events, to defend property against small numbers, and with orders to retreat if menaced by a superior force. I decided to proceed immediately to Quincy, to prepare a force sufficient to suppress disorder, in case it should ensue, for the foregoing transactions, or from any other cause.*" The result was a total abandonment of the town of Carthage, during that night, by men, women, and children, saving the handful of persons remaining with Gen. Deming, as sentinels. The public records of the county were all removed to the neighboring town of Augusta, whither the Governor, as well as most of the citizens, repaired that evening. In the rapid flight that ensued, the cannon, arms, and ammunition of the citizens, were all left at Carthage, and the property of those escaping from imaginary danger, left to chance for its preservation.

Upon the arrival of Captain Singleton's company, at the county seat, their apprehensions were greatly increased by Gen. Deming's information imparted to them; and they, too, conceiving that "*distance lent enchantment to the view,*" proceeded with all convenient haste for their homes in Schuyler county. The captain concluded to repair at his ease to Quincy, whither he directed his steps, and reported himself to the commander-in-chief.

At Warsaw, a somewhat different state of things existed. I reached there about midnight of the same day upon which the killing of the Smiths took place. Col. March, of Alton, and myself, left Nauvoo immediately after the Governor had concluded his speech to the Mormons, and started for Keokuk, by wagon, on the opposite side of the river, in hopes of reaching the packet Boreas, previous to her departure from that place. The roads being bad, we did not reach Keokuk until half-past ten o'clock at night, and found the boat gone. We had been there but a few moments, when I heard the report of a cannon in the direction of Warsaw, and at once supposed it was intended as a signal of triumph, and that the event had occurred, which I felt convinced would take place twenty-eight hours previous to its occurrence. Anxious to learn the facts, and somewhat in hopes that the Boreas might not have left Warsaw, we procured a skiff and hired a couple of men to row us down the river to that place, a distance of about five miles. We reached our place of destination about midnight, not without, however, being required to *"stand"* several times and report who we were and what was our business, by sentinels placed upon the outskirts of the town, as well as the most commanding point on the banks of the river. Here, too, I found consternation and alarm pervading, to some extent, the entire community. The events of the tragic scene at Carthage were soon imparted to me. The troops who had marched from Golden's Point, to Carthage, and back again, that day, had but a short time previous returned, were very much fatigued, and were partaking of some refreshments which had been prepared for them by a portion of the citizens. Those having families were congregating the women and children together, on the banks of the Mississippi, with a view of removing them to the little town of Alexandria, on the opposite side of the river. The Boreas lay on the opposite side, and was crowded with families destined for Quincy, as a place of refuge, and determined there to remain, until the result should be known whether Warsaw would be the scene of renewed acts of violence, and their homes laid waste by the torch of an infuriated and unrelenting adversary. The ferry boat was soon crowded with women and children, with what scattering articles of wearing apparel they could collect together in the hurry and excitement of the moment, accompanied by a few of the male citizens, who were sent along to provide them with such accommodations as the place of their refuge would afford. Most of the men remained at their posts in Warsaw, and at once commenced placing their town in as formidable a state of defence, as their numbers, and the quantity of their fire-arms, would admit of. The streets were patrolled by a vigilant guard; sentinels were placed at every point of ingress, on the outskirts of the town; the few pieces of cannon, they had, were stationed at those points, where, it was believed, they would do the most signal service in case of an attack. Several of the merchants had their goods in wagons, ready for a retreat, in the event of the Mormons attacking them with an overpowering force. And all that remained there were kept constantly under arms, anticipating every moment a visitation from the Mormons.

—————•••• *15* ••••—————

A View from Warsaw

George Rockwell (1815–?), a Warsaw druggist, was a Connecticut native who came west in the early 1840s. He was an active member of the anti-Mormon group in Hancock County during the summer of 1844, and this letter to his father, Thomas H. Rockwell of Ridgefield, Connecticut, contains a vivid description of the activities taking place in the area. It conveys clearly the various fears that the Mormons aroused in the wider populace. Rockwell assesses the nature of the conflict, emphasizing Mormon self-righteousness, separatism, bloc voting, and militarism as central ingredients. His letter explicitly shows, from inside one man's head, why otherwise law-abiding citizens would become part of mob action. It also verifies the ideals of republicanism, condemning Mormonism as anathema to the larger cultural ideology.

A typescript copy of this correspondence is in the George Rockwell Letters, Kansas State Historical Society, Topeka, Kansas. The letter is reprinted from "The Mormon War in Hancock County," *Warsaw Bulletin*, 13 March 1925, p. 5.

—————••••◉••••—————

Warsaw, Ill., Aug 3rd, 1844.

Dear Parents:

You have probably received the Warsaw Signal which I have regularly sent you since the commencement of the Mormon troubles. From it you will learn about as true a history of our difficulties as I would be able to give you.

The situation is a deplorable one, but nothing more than I have been looking for two or three years. The Mormons were increasing fast in the County. Their political influence was seen and felt by the whole State, and indeed, it had been so guided by imagined revelation that it bid fair in a few years to sap the very foundations of our government.

They voted almost to a man in accordance with Joe's and Hiram Smith's revelations, and demagoguas [*sic*] and base politicians, seeing this influence of their leader, were ever ready to fawn and flatter for the purpose of benefitting themselves. Joe knowing well how to use the influence he possessed, made use of these men in acquiring powers which he believed necessary to carry out his designs. He acquired these powers from the State Legislature in a Charter for the City of Nauvoo, for the Nauvoo Legion, etc. But these same powers of which he boasted, have probably been the means of shortening his days. Not being content with the extraordinary powers which had been vested in him, he took the responsibility of enlarging them until he had rendered them obnoxious to the surrounding country. The laws of the State were ferquently [*sic*] violated, but if they, or any of their followers in Nauvoo, were arrested, they were immediately released from custody by a writ of habeas corpus.

The state laws had ceased to afford us any protection in any matter of controversy with a Mormon, whether civil or criminal.

This fact we had long known, and felt, and have taken pains to publish it to the world long since. But of late so frequent had the gross and daring violations of the law become that the good citizens, not feeling willing to sacrifice their property, and leave it in the possession of such a lawless banditti, met together in the largest meeting ever assembled in the County out of Nauvoo, and resolved that they would compel them to submit to the laws, or drive them from the State. As the result of this meeting 2,000 men were in arms called out by the officers who had been resisted at Nauvoo in trying to arrest Joe and others on various charges made against them. Joe had his Legion of 3,000 or 4,000 men under arms to protect them, and this was the position of affairs when Gov. Ford arrived in the county. Immediately on his arrival Gov. Ford ordered the posse out in military capacity, placing himself at their head. In spite of the loud protestations which he made when he first came, his actions and conduct, to say the least of them, have been looked upon as puerile in the extreme, and he now makes the humiliating admission, that his honor and the faith of the sovereign State of Illinois had to be pledged to Joe Smith before the murderer, robber, counterfeiter, seducer and blasphemous wretch would place himself in the power of the law.

Joe, receiving the promise, and being threatened with the whole State if he made further resistance, gave himself up, and entered into bonds for his appearance at court. Joe and Hiram were then immediately arrested on a charge of treason against the State. Their counsel, for sundry reasons, had their examination continued from day to day, and all this time they were not confined in jail, but permitted by request of the Governor to remain in the debtor's room, a room occupied by the jailor's family as a parlor, with neither lock or bolt to the doors or shutters or grates to the windows. They had every possible chance for escape, and several circumstances transpired which led the people to suspect them. They were well armed, and his friends whom the Governor had permitted to visit him were detected by the guard in trying to smuggle in old clothes for a disguise.

On the 25th of June the Governor gave his orders to the military to march to Nauvoo on the 27th, but instead of marching them there (to break up their counterfeiting establishment, and make further arrests), he disbanded them on the morning they were to have marched, and went himself with one Company to Nauvoo.

The Regiment stationed at Warsaw, composed of citizens and volunteers from Adams County, Illinois, Missouri, and Iowa, had commenced their march for Nauvoo agreeably to orders, and had gone some 6 or 8 miles, when they were met by a messenger from the Governor, with orders to disband forthwith.

They were accordingly disbanded by their officers, but they were at liberty to go where they pleased. Being within 10 miles of Carthage, and their suspicions being aroused that this disbanding was a plan to let the prisoners escape as they frequently had done before, and feeling unwilling to be trifled with any longer, they determined to take the matter into their own hands, and execute justice before they should succeed in making their escape.

I regret as much as any one the necessity which compelled them to resort to that summary process of executing justice.

That they were bad men, and deserved death I have not the least doubt. They taught their followers that the revelations of God through them were paramount to the laws of man.

It is fully proven that it was to procure the fulfillment of one of Joe's revelations, that "Gov. Boggs of Missouri should die a violent death, and go to hell and be damned" (which revelation was publicly made by Joe at one of the large meetings).

I. N. Jackson and D. R. Foster were severally applied to in the name of the Lord to fulfill that revelation, and money offered them to assassinate Gov. Boggs.

They taught the doctrine of plurality of wives—that it was right in the sight of God, but it was necessary to keep the practice from the knowledge of the Gentile world, as if known it would subject them to persecution and prosecution under the laws of the State. I have frequently conversed with Mormons on this doctrine, and they defend it and proved it to be correct from the Bible, and they say that if it was right in David's and Solomon's time, it is right now, and some have told me that if Joe was to have a revelation that he was to have their wives and daughters, they would freely give them up to him. It was Joe's revelation to Law's wife that caused the division in the church a few months since. Law and his wife would not submit to it. This caused the difficulty between Joe and Law. Perjury to protect a brother is taught by them to be no crime. The Court of record, and the testimony of the best lawyers in the County, is a strong evidence of that fact. They state there has not been for three years a suit between a Mormon and an old citizen, but that the Mormon has gained the case. But Mormon evidence had for the last year or two been looked upon by the old citizens on the jury with distrust. When an important case comes up for trial, the Sheriff, who married a niece of Joe's, fills up the panel of jurors from among the Mormon bystanders whenever an old citizen is challenged by the counsel of the Mormons interested in the case, and they always bring a verdict for the Mormons. I could relate some interesting cases if I had time and space. Stolen property has frequently been traced to Nauvoo, and the thief arrested. But they have proved the property to be their own, and they were discharged by their Mormon magistrates. To obviate this difficulty, warrants have been obtained from other magistrates in the County, and the offenders after being arrested, have been released by writs of habeas corpus issued by the Municipal Court of which Joe is the head.

Long before you read this you will have learned that Joe Smith has poorly paid for his crimes with his life; he was shot at Carthage on June 24 [sic], 1844. This was slight punishment for a man who founded a religion on lies, wrote a new Bible (the Book of Mormon), which he claimed Divine and palmed off on deluded fanatics, a man who was responsible for many murders and much lawlessness, who taught polygamy, and himself claimed other men's wives.

I did not happen to be present when he attempted to escape from the window of the Sheriff's sitting room in the second story of the jail, and was shot by the guards, but I fully approve of it.

If the people of the United States understood our true situation, I am sure that instead of calling it a "cold blooded murder," they would hold public meetings, and express their thanks to men who dared (in spite of the strongest oaths that bound a lawless band together) to execute justice upon two of the vilest men that ever lived.

16

A Heroic Poem of the Martyrdom

Eliza Roxey Snow (1804–87) was one of the most gifted poets in the early Mormon Church, and a leader of Latter Day Saint women, both at Nauvoo and the Great Basin. Her poem recounting "The Assassination of Generals Joseph Smith and Hyrum Smith" offers a heroic image of the Mormon leaders and presents their slaying by an unrighteous world as an event of cosmic significance, second only in spiritual importance to the death of Christ. And it views America as not a locus for Zion but an ungodly place of wickedness from which the Saints must flee. A deeply mythic poem, it was first published in the *Times and Seasons* 5 (1 July 1844): 575, and is reprinted here from Snow's *Poems, Religious, Historical, and Political* (Liverpool, England: F. D. Richards, 1856), 142–45.

The Assassination of Generals Joseph Smith and Hyrum Smith,
First Presidents of the Church of Jesus Christ of Latter-day Saints;
Who Were Massacred by a Mob, in Carthage, Hancock County
Ill., on the 27th of June, 1844.

"And when he had opened the fifth seal, I saw under the altar the souls of them that were slain for the word of God, and for the testimony which they held.

And they cried with a loud voice, saying, How long, O Lord, holy and true, dost thou not judge and avenge our blood on them that dwell on the earth?

And white robes were given unto every one of them; and it was said unto them, that they should rest yet for a little season, until their fellow servants also, and their brethren, that should be killed as they were, should be fulfilled."—*Rev.* 6:9, 10, 11.

Ye heavens attend! Let all the earth give ear!
Let Gods and seraphs, men and angels hear—
The worlds on high—the Universe shall know
What awful scenes are acted here below!
    Had nature's self a heart, her heart would bleed;
At the recital of so foul a deed;
For never, since the Son of God was slain
Has blood so noble flow'd from human vein
As that which now on God for vengeance calls
From "freedom's" ground—from Carthage prison walls!
    Oh! Illinois! thy soil has drunk the blood
Of Prophets martyr'd for the truth of God.
Once-lov'd America! what can atone
For the pure blood of innocence thou'st sown?
    Were all thy streams in teary torrents shed
To mourn the fate of those illustrious dead,
How vain the tribute, for the noblest worth
That grac'd thy surface, O degraded Earth!

    Oh wretched murd'rers, fierce for human blood!
You've slain the Prophets of the living God,
Who've borne oppression from their early youth,
To plant on earth the principles of truth.

    Shades of our patriot fathers! can it be,
Beneath your blood-stain'd flag of Liberty,
The firm supporters of our country's cause,
Are butcher'd while submissive to her laws?
Yes, blameless men, defam'd by hellish lies
Have thus been offer'd as a sacrifice
T'appease the ragings of a brutish clan,
That has defied the laws of God and man!
    'Twas not for crime or guilt of theirs, they fell:
Against the laws they never did rebel.
True to their country, yet her plighted faith
Has prov'd an instrument of cruel death!

Great men had fall'n, mighty men have died—
Nations have mourn'd their fav'rites and their pride;
But TWO, so wise, so virtuous, and so good,
Before on earth, at once, have never stood
Since the creation—men whom God ordain'd
To publish truth where error long had reign'd;
Of whom the world itself unworthy prov'd:
It KNEW THEM NOT; but men with hatred mov'd,
And with infernal spirits, have combin'd
Against the best, the noblest of mankind!

Oh, persecution! shall thy purple hand
Spread utter destruction through the land?
Shall Freedom's banner be no more unfurl'd?
Has peace indeed, been taken from the world?

Thou God of Jacob, in this trying hour
Help us to trust in thy Almighty power—
Support thy Saints beneath this awful stroke,
Make bare thine arm to break oppression's yoke.
We mourn thy Prophet, from whose lips have flow'd
The words of life, thy Spirit has bestow'd—
A depth of thought, no human art could reach
From time to time roll'd in sublimest speech,
From thy celestial fountain, through his mind,
To purify and elevate mankind:
The rich intelligence by him brought forth,
Is like the sun-beam, spreading o'er the earth.

Now Zion mourns—she mourns an earthly head:
Her Prophet and her Patriarch are dead!
The blackest deed that men and devils know
Since Calv'ry's scene, has laid the brothers low!
One while in life, and *one* in death, they prov'd
How strong their friendship—how they truly lov'd:
True to their mission until death they stood,
Then seal'd their testimony with their blood.
All hearts with sorrow bleed, and every eye
Is bath'd in tears, each bosom heaves a sigh,
Heart-broken widows' agonizing groans
Are mingled with the helpless orphans' moans!

Ye Saints! be still, and know that God is just—
With steadfast purpose in His promise trust:
Girded with sackcloth, own His mighty hand,
And wait His judgments on this guilty land!
The noble Martyrs now have gone to move
The cause of Zion in the Courts above.

NAUVOO, JULY 1, 1844.

PART V

THE TRIAL AND THE VIOLENCE

Governor Thomas Ford. Courtesy of Archives and Special Collections, Western Illinois University Library, Macomb.

---··•• PART V ••··---

INTRODUCTION

With the deaths of Joseph and Hyrum Smith, a détente between the two factions in Hancock County occured and lasted several months. For their part, the anti-Mormons were afraid that the Mormons would call out the Nauvoo Legion and lay waste to Carthage and Warsaw. Moreover, the reaction to the murders of the Smiths was almost universally negative. The press castigated the lynching, the state's leadership was appalled, and Governor Thomas Ford pledged to bring the ringleaders to justice. In this situation the anti-Mormons felt that the best course was to lay low. At the same time, they tried to convince those on the outside why vigilante justice had been necessary. The anti-Mormons also hoped that the deaths of the Smith brothers would resolve the "Mormon question" through the collapse of Nauvoo in a leadership vacuum.[1]

The Mormons, for their part, were extremely cautious not to do anything that would excite further violence. They had internal problems to deal with, notably the debate over leadership and the direction of church affairs in the summer of 1844. In fact, the anti-Mormon appraisal was nearly accurate, for the summer of 1844 was one of the most tumultuous in the history of the church as various leaders came forward to assume leadership. No fewer than fifteen different groups surfaced in Mormonism during the succession crisis of 1844, each legitimately claiming one or more of eight proofs of succession.[2] Indeed, Sidney Rigdon, who had been a leader in the church since 1830 and who had broken with Joseph Smith over the attempted seduction of his daughter into plural marriage (Part III, Document 1), returned to Nauvoo in August 1844 to challenge for church leadership. In a climactic public meeting on 8 August, Brigham Young was able to secure control of the administrative machinery in Nauvoo.[3] Internal problems did not end there. For example, Brigham Young and the Quorum of Twelve Apostles clashed with the widow of Joseph Smith and other members of the family for control of resources and a say in church policy and governance.[4]

Ironically, just about the time Young gained administrative control of Nauvoo and was trying to reassert strong leadership in the fall of 1844, difficulties again arose outside. Partly in reaction to the August election in which several pro-Mormon officials had been elected to county offices, in September some anti-Mormons organized what they called a "wolf hunt" to intimidate the Mormons. Ford, fearing that a pogrom was afoot, journeyed from Springfield to Carthage with a force under the command of General John J. Hardin to ensure that order was maintained. He arrived on 25 October, the wolf hunt organizers fled to Iowa, and the immediate problem of violence was averted.

Ford withdrew most of the troops in November, in part because the men were quickly infected with local hatred after non-Mormons told them what had been going on in the county, but Hardin and a small force remained throughout the winter and maintained reasonable order.[5] While in Carthage, Ford had five men arrested for the murders of the Smiths. Although he had warrants for eight men, three ran away and did not stand trial. The remaining five—including Thomas C. Sharp, newspaper editor; Levi Williams, militia officer; and Franklin A. Worrell, commander of the detachment of the Carthage Greys charged with guarding the Smiths—were indicted and bound over for trial for conspiracy to commit murder.

In January 1845, the state legislature abolished the Nauvoo Charter. Illinois leaders were irate at the way the Saints had used its legal mechanisms to prevent the arrest and trial of loyal Mormons outside the municipality, notably the contortions Joseph Smith had worked in trying to keep from being tried in Carthage in June 1844. They also resented the role of the local authorities in silencing the *Expositor*, which they considered a notorious abuse of chartered governmental structure. But most of all, they were incensed at the merger of executive, legislative, and judicial functions under a single head that had resulted from Mormon theocratic control. While some of the more moderate elements, notably Thomas Ford, favored modifications to the charter to guard against abuses, most disagreed, and the city of Nauvoo ceased to exist as a legal entity when the charter was repealed on 29 January 1845.[6] Ironically, one of the complaints that non-Mormons always had expressed was that Mormons had little respect for the property of others (see Part II, Documents 1–3), and without the legal mechanism to make and enforce laws, it was even more difficult to keep order.

In another ironic move, Brigham Young countered the repeal of the Nauvoo Charter with another governmental system that was anathema to non-Mormons. He simply substituted ecclesiastical for civil authority, organizing Nauvoo into congregational units called wards and appointing people to keep order. Deacons were employed as a police force to maintain order, using methods up to and including "whistling and whittling brigades" to secure the public peace. In such an environment civil liberties were violated and democracy was nonexistent, but loyal Mormons believed this was an acceptable trade-off for association with the Saints. Such theocratic tendencies were all too evident to non-Mormons, however, and this, too, became a source of contention in Hancock County.[7] Part of the problem was alleviated on 16 April 1845, when Ford approved the incorporation of a one-mile-square section of Nauvoo under provisions in state law for organizing towns, as opposed to cities. In the midst of this situation, the five accused murderers of Joseph and Hyrum Smith were tried, but as most had predicted, they were acquitted.

Violence erupted again during the second half of 1845. It was triggered by several incidents. First, in May John Miller and his son-in-law were killed in Lee

County, Iowa Territory, by three men from Nauvoo during an attempted robbery. Two Hodges brothers were captured in Nauvoo, brought to trial, and eventually hanged for the crime. The Hodges brothers admitted the robbery but always maintained their innocence of murder, which they claimed had been committed by an accomplice. Although they were not members of the Mormon church, others in their family were, and the violence verified already-existing beliefs about Mormon depredations on nearby non-Mormons.[8] Additionally, in late June 1845, Dr. Samuel Marshall, a bitter anti-Mormon, attacked Sheriff Minor Deming, a Mormon sympathizer. During the fight Deming killed Marshall. Although he claimed self-defense, Deming was arrested for manslaughter and held in the Carthage jail. He died of natural causes not long thereafter and was never brought to trial. Finally, the whole issue of Mormon theft came up in a big way when Brigham Young suggested that it was wise to gather into Nauvoo during the early fall and bring in all the grain and livestock from outlying Mormon farms. Indiscriminate collection of these commodities exacerbated the tensions.[9]

Lawlessness became the norm during September 1845 after a group of anti-Mormons decided to rid the area around Green Plains, in the southwest part of the county, of Mormons and attacked a settlement. After a single incident, in which the Saints fought back, the anti-Mormons roused some three hundred men to repulse Mormon "aggressors." They moved into the Green Plains area and began systematic raids on Mormon farms. On 15 September 1845, Brigham Young reported that forty-four buildings had been burned and numerous crops destroyed in the fields. Terrified Mormons sought refuge in Nauvoo, and Young sent 134 wagons to outlying settlements with armed escorts to help with the evacuation. As this was taking place, the new county sheriff, Jacob B. Backenstos, another Mormon sympathizer, raised a posse of Mormons from Nauvoo to "restore order." If the anti-Mormon raiders were little more than a mob, so was Backenstos's posse. The two groups rode throughout the county in September 1845, chasing each other, bandits, and real and imagined mobbers. As scholar Robert Bruce Flanders has noted, "Civil war had begun in earnest." In the process, Backenstos's posse shot and killed Franklin A. Worrell on 16 September 1845, further exciting animosities.[10]

Ford took action to end this deadlock in late September by asking Hardin to raise another force to come into Hancock County and disarm and separate the two sides. When Hardin arrived in Carthage with about three hundred men, he found the town occupied by a Mormon force under Backenstos's command. Hardin ordered this unit to withdraw within fifteen minutes and went about reestablishing civil authority. He quickly found that anti-Mormon and especially Mormon irregulars were plundering the county at will and put a stop to it by prohibiting any group of more than four persons from either side to assemble.[11] He then proceeded to negotiate a truce and a withdrawal of the Mormons from the territory. The documents in Part V describe the events that followed the murders in Carthage and led to the negotiations for the exodus of the Saints.

Notes

1. This activity is described in Robert B. Flanders, *Nauvoo: Kingdom on the Mississippi* (Urbana: University of Illinois Press, 1965), 306–41. On the press reaction, see Paul D. Ellsworth, "Mobocracy and the Rule of Law: American Press Reaction to the Murder of Joseph Smith," *Brigham Young University Studies* 20 (Fall 1979): 71–82.

2. On this issue, see D. Michael Quinn, "The Mormon Succession Crisis of 1844," *Brigham Young University Studies* 16 (Winter 1976): 187–233.

3. This is one of the pivotal events of Mormon history. It has been recorded from the perspectives of the two chief protagonists in biographies. See F. Mark McKiernan, *The Voice of One Crying in the Wilderness: Sidney Rigdon, Religious Reformer, 1793–1876* (Lawrence, Kans.: Coronado Press, 1971), 125–31; Leonard J. Arrington, *Brigham Young: American Moses* (New York: Alfred A. Knopf, 1985), 113–17.

4. For a discussion of this issue, see Linda K. Newell and Valeen T. Avery, "The Lion and the Lady: Brigham Young and Emma Smith," *Utah Historical Quarterly* 48 (Winter 1980): 81–97; Roger D. Launius, "Joseph Smith III and the Mormon Succession Crisis, 1844–1846," *Western Illinois Regional Studies* 6 (Spring 1983): 5–22; E. Gary Smith, "The Patriarchal Crisis of 1845," *Dialogue: A Journal of Mormon Thought* 16 (Summer 1983): 24–35; Irene M. Bates, "William Smith, 1811–93: Problematic Patriarch," *Dialogue: A Journal of Mormon Thought* 16 (Summer 1983): 12–23; and Paul M. Edwards, "William Smith: Persistent Pretender," *Dialogue: A Journal of Mormon Thought* 18 (Summer 1985): 128–139.

5. Thomas Ford, *A History of Illinois from its Commencement as a State in 1818 to 1847* (Chicago: S. C. Griggs and Co., 1854), 364–66; Thomas Ford, *Message from the Governor, in Relation to the Disturbances in Hancock County* (Springfield, Ill.: Walters & Weber, Public Printers, 1844); Dallin H. Oaks and Marvin S. Hill, *Carthage Conspiracy: The Trial of the Accused Assassins of Joseph Smith* (Urbana: University of Illinois Press, 1975), 30–63.

6. On the charter, see James L. Kimball, Jr., "The Nauvoo Charter: A Reinterpretation," *Journal of the Illinois State Historical Society* 64 (Spring 1971): 66–78; Flanders, *Nauvoo*, 324–25.

7. Flanders, *Nauvoo*, 325–26. Much can be learned about the law-enforcement issue in Juanita Brooks, ed., *On the Mormon Frontier: The Diary of Hosea Stout* (Salt Lake City: University of Utah Press, 1964), 1:1–118.

8. This event has been discussed at length. See *Illinois State Register* (Springfield, Ill.), 23 May 1845, p. 2; *Niles National Register* (Baltimore), 26 July 1845, p. 2; Edward Bonney, *The Banditti of the Prairies* (Chicago: n. p., 1850); Col. J. M. Reid, *Sketches and Anecdotes of the Old Settlers and New Comers, The Mormon Bandits and Danite Band* (Keokuk, Iowa: n. p., 1876); Elnathan C. Gavitt, *Crumbs from My Saddlebags; or Reminiscences of Pioneer Life* (Toledo: n. p., 1884).

9. Flanders, *Nauvoo*, 326–28; Susan S. Rugh, "Conflict in the Countryside: The Mormon Settlement at Macedonia, Illinois," *Brigham Young University Studies* 32 (Winter/Spring 1991): 149–74.

10. Flanders, *Nauvoo*, 329. On the Worrell killing, see Harold Schindler, *Orrin Porter Rockwell: Man of God, Son of Thunder* (Salt Lake City: University of Utah Press, 1966), 145; *Warsaw Signal* (Warsaw, Ill.), 17 September 1845, p. 2.

11. Ford, *A History of Illinois*, 410–11; Robert W. Johannsen, ed., *The Letters of Stephen A. Douglas* (Urbana: University of Illinois Press, 1961), 124–26.

———•••• *1* ••••———

Thomas Sharp on the
Hancock County Conflict

Thomas C. Sharp (see Part II, Document 5) wasted little time in mobilizing the *Warsaw Signal* to explain to non-Mormons in Illinois what had happened in Carthage on 27 June 1844. While few people in the state sympathized with the Mormons, fewer still thought mobocracy was a solution for grievances. Sharp tried to convince them otherwise. Contrary to the narratives of John Taylor and Willard Richards, which emphasized the innocence of the Saints and their persecution by an unrighteous society, or even the nonplussed tone of the Samuel Williams letter, Sharp tried to convey the image of a law-abiding community acting after careful consideration to preserve democratic institutions and the rule of law.

In this article he appeals to the strong sense of republicanism and liberty in his society to justify the anti-Mormon actions in Hancock County in June 1844. In so doing, he is engaging in myth making as surely as many of the Mormon eyewitnesses, but with an opposing purpose. Smith is viewed as a guilty "tyrant," whose "victims" were descendants of the nation's Revolutionary War "forefathers." Hence, by killing Smith the violent non-Mormons were acting out their democratic heritage and affirming their identity as Americans. As with so many documents included here, this one by the leading anti-Mormon reveals the power of myth to shape perceptions of reality and direct behavior. It appeared as "To the Public: Mormon Difficulties in Illinois" in the *Warsaw Signal*, 10 July 1844, p. 2.

———••••◉••••———

The summary execution of two of the Mormon leaders, Joseph and Hiram Smith, at Carthage, on the 27th of June, has excited a deep unrest abroad as well as at home; and has brought upon us the severest invective of nearly the whole newspaper press, as far as we have yet heard. . . .

We hold it to be a self evident proposition, that laws are enacted for the safety and protection of the rights, lives and property of those who are to be governed by them. We hold, moreover, that so long as those laws can afford such protection, it is the duty of every good citizen to abide by their direction and to uphold their supremacy; but that whenever, by a train of circumstances, which our legislators never could have anticipated, the law is rendered ineffectual and cheated out of efficacy, there is an impulse planted by God and Nature in every bosom, which prompts men to throw themselves, for protection, on their reserved rights. The law owes us *protection*, in consideration of which we owe it *allegiance*. If it fails to perform its offices towards us, we are, to the extent of that failure, absolved from its requisitions.

In every age, and in every nation, it has been the highest crime known to the law, for one man to take the life of another, but wherever such an act is done in self defence it is justified; and why: Because in such case the law could afford no protection to the life of the individual threatened; therefore, God and Nature says to everyman, "Protect thyself." What is true in relation to individuals, we hold equally true when applied to communities.

The public may not be generally aware of the peculiar situation in which the people of Hancock County, Illinois, have been placed for the last four years. On the one hand, we beheld a body of men bound together by all the strong bands of superstition and knavery—acknowledging the dictation of one man as supreme in all matters, both spiritual and temporal—committing the most aggravated aggressions on the rights and property of their neighbors, harboring and protecting counterfeiters, horse thieves and blacklegs—having in their employ a sworn band of assassins, who in more instances than one, have attempted the lives of persons obnoxious to them—by their threats, rendering inept the laws. . . .

But of them as a religious sect, we have nothing to do. Absurd and loathsome as is their creed, it might forever have been enjoyed without molestation from any of us. We may have ridiculed, pitied and despised the infatuated credulity of such as put their faith in it, but we have never persecuted. When in the name of the Lord they oppressed us, it was the *oppressor*, and not the *priest* we resisted—when the doom of destruction was pronounced, it was the Demon of destruction, not the *Seer* that we rose to combat—it was the murderer, the robber, the adulterer, and not *the heaven daring blasphemer*, that we wished to punish.

From their first organization as a distinct community, they have been going from one extreme to another—from one atrocity to another, modifying their ridiculous creed to suit their peculiar condition.

A circumstance that tells strongly against them, may be found in the facts that they have brought serious difficulties upon *every* community in which they have lived. Thrice, in the short space of ten years, have they been forced to remove their quarters—once from Ohio, and twice from different portions of Missouri. All the dark spirits of crime, have attended their steps, and scourged every land where they have sojourned. Ohio and Missouri were blamed for driving them off. The cry of "religious persecution,"—the sure key to the sympathies of an unwary public, was raised in their behalf; and we among others, were bitter in our denunciations against Missouri for expelling them, from her borders. We took them in, gave them shelter, supplied their wants. Five years have passed, and the helpless band of exiles that sought our hospitality in the inclement season of winter, have become the most powerful people that ever organized in a distinct community, under our republican institutions. We have had plenty of leisure to study their character; and long since have learned enough to justify their expulsion from Missouri, and to cause us to blush for our own credulity in suffering ourselves to be so easily duped. We nourished a *viper*, and it had no sooner warmed into life than, true to its nature, it turned to destroy its preserver.

Since their appearance among us, the arrogance of their leader had greatly increased. He brought with him political power and influence, and a disposition to make that power and that influence tell on the destinies of his people; and there were found selfish and unprincipled politicians in both parties willing to aid his designs. All the tact, talent and cunning profligate [k]navery could command, were set at work. . . .

It may be known, that Joe Smith was indicted at the last term of the Circuit Court for *adultery* and *perjury*. It is further known here, that there was *evidence enough* to indict him in any other County, for many other heinous offences. These indictment[s] were found in May, more than a month previous to the commencement of the war. Yet up to that time, our kind Clerk, had neglected or refused to issue writs on either of these indictments; and it is extremely doubtful whether they were issued at the time of Smith's death. This omission of the Clerk, however, is in its effect of but small importance, for if the writs had been issued, Joe would immediately have given bail, and if he had lived to stood his trial, there is not a sensible man conversant with the facts, who doubts but that he would have been *honorably* acquitted by a jury of his own packing. If this fact is not made sufficiently clear it can and will be done.

We will now refer more particularly to events of recent occurrence. During the last spring, many of the most respectable of the brotherhood, having satisfied themselves of Joe's unprincipled rascality, but still adhering to the *principles* of the Mormon creed, seceeded [*sic*] from the Church, and established a press in Nauvoo to expose Joe's iniquities. His *saintship*, fired with holy indignation, resolved that those men should be put down. Even before the press was established, he said that no paper opposed to his interests, should be published in Nauvoo. The seceeders, however, dared to beard the lion in his den, and brave his wrath. One number of the Expositor was issued. It boldly attacked the prophet and other leading saints—exposed their foul deeds and designs, and sustained its charges by proof.

The tyrant saw that the axe was laid at the root of his power. His impostures would be exposed—his dark deeds of crime would be published, and his influence over his deluded victims lost. All was at stake—the press must be destroyed or he must fall. The council was called together, & after two days *solemn* deliberation the press was declared a *nuisance*, and the *Legion* ordered out to abate it, which was done. Writs were issued for all the leading actors in this outrage, and they refused to submit to the law. The public is already advised of the results. The civil officers summoned the *posse comitatus*, and Joe fortified himself in the city—declared martial law and put himself in open defiance of the civil authority. The Governor was applied to—the Military called out, headed by his Excellency in person—at last resistance became hopeless and he yielded. Without standing a trial on the charge of riot, he gave bail to appear before the Circuit Court. . . . Though guilty of almost every crime known to the law, though they had followed robbery, swindling and counterfeiting for a livelihood—though the seduction of virtue and innocence was with them a pastime; though blood was upon their skirts, yet the law had in every instance in which it had been tried, proved utterly ineffectual to bring these robbers, seducers and murderers to justice.

If we are to judge of the future by the past, what conclusion could we have come to, under the circumstances, other than that Joe and Hyrum Smith would, although in the custody of the officer of the law, have escaped as in every instance heretofore? The fact was demonstrated—the conviction was universal. Under such circumstances, what could have been done? Should we have laid quietly down, and suffered the tyrant to rivet the chains that had already galled us to madness? Should we have submitted passively to be robbed of property and liberty and knowing from the sad experience of the past, that there was no legal redress, spaniel like, licked the hand of our chastizer, and besought his forbearance? Such questions are insulting to free men. No man through whose vein courses one drop of that noble blood, which promoted our forefathers to throw off the yoke of British oppression, will ask his fellow freeman to kneel at the nod of a tyrant, nor condemn him for asserting his liberty, even if in so doing he is obliged to commit a daring violation of law.

We claim, that the community in which we live, is a law abiding community, and that it will go as far to maintain the supremacy of the law as any other in the nation. Our citizens have regretted, and still regret the necessity that existed for taking the law in this particular instance, into their own hands; but that it would sooner or later have to be done, no one acquainted with the facts of the case, could deny. It was inevitable, and the only question was as to the proper time. In relation to this, we will remark, that Joe and Hiram Smith were regarded as the only individuals that could hold together the Mormon community. They were the instigators and authors of all our troubles. The only alternative then was, whether the guilty cause, should be removed and in the natural course of things suffer the evil to eradicate itself; or whether, we should have waited until renewed aggressions, had so far aroused a feeling of hostility, as to provoke the surrounding country to a general war of extermination. . . .

The Mormons could not be expelled as a people without the cooperation of the Governor. True, he had no clearly expressed Constitutional right to drive them off; no one supposed such a right existed; yet the people thought the necessity of the case would justify it; and they still think so. But this could not be done. Joe and Hiram Smith, their acknowledged heads, were in the custody of the law—so far all was well, they had the promise of the Governor's protection; this was not well, and we think was not generally known, until his Excellency proclaimed it after the catastrophe. But what satisfaction could it afford the old citizens of Hancock, to know that Joe was in jail? They know, and the world must know for reasons before given, that they never could be convicted of any crime. We had taken a great deal of trouble to assert and maintain the supremacy of the *law*, but if the matter rested here, justice might have despaired of his cause. It was this conviction that compressed their execution. Did they deserve death? There can be no doubt in the mind of any intelligent person acquainted with their history.—

Evidence enough to damn them fort[y] times over, has been published. Read the history of the Missouri investigation—Bennet's, Harris', Howe's and Tucker's works, the multitude of affidavits which have been published. But this, we think will not be questioned. It is not their death, but the times and the manner—we plead the *necessity* of the case—we had nothing more to hope from the Executive, until violence on the part of the Mormons demanded his imposition—the law could not reach them—they would soon have been at large. More arrogant and self-sufficient than ever. The late difficulties have added greatly to the two [*sic*] jealousy and hatred of the two parties. All confidence was lost. The old citizens felt that this one-man power must be destroyed, *now*, or they themselves, must quietly surrender all their dearest rights and leave the county. They chose a better alternative—one revolting to their own sensibilities, but prompted by a high sense of duty to themselves and their County. As to the time and manner, it had to be done then and thus, or not at all. It was supposed that a rescue would be attempted that night, or the next. Circumstances that have since come to light have placed that matter above suspicion, and there is not room for a reasonable doubt that if attempted it would have been successful.

—•••• 2 ••••—

The Mormons Call for Calmness

While Thomas C. Sharp and other anti-Mormons in Hancock County defended the murders and sought continued action against the Saints, the Mormon leaders in Nauvoo took a conciliatory stance. They urged the Mormons in the county to try to rebuild their lives, to continue their activities, and to live peacefully. Isaac C. Haight (1813–86), a Mormon living outside of Nauvoo, recalls in his autobiography that "the mob, having accomplished their purpose, began to disperse and peace began to be restored and the Saints to return to their different occupations, harvesting having now commenced. I began to harvest and all became quiet without." Another Latter Day Saint, Joseph Grafton Hovey, remarks in his autobiography, "In a few weeks the excitement was pretty much down among ourselves. Also with our enemies, for the governor had ordered about four or five hundred men to come to Nauvoo and protect the Mormons. They came sometime in September, when our Legion muster was on" (Joseph G. Hovey, "Autobiography," pp. 22–23, Archives, Harold B. Lee Library, Brigham Young University, Provo, Utah).

A non-Mormon observer living a few miles above Nauvoo at Fort Madison, Iowa Territory, David W. Kilbourne (see Part IV, Document 12), confirms this assessment of the atmosphere in Hancock County. He wrote a correspondent in England on 29 July 1844: "There have been no further hostilities since I last wrote you. They are perfectly quiet in Nauvoo & in the surrounding country. The

Mormons are much more decent in their deportment—not insolent as formerly." He added that "they have been taught a lesson which I think they will not soon forget. They will hereafter be afraid to interfere at all with the rights of the people" (David Wells Kilbourne Papers, State Historical Society of Iowa, Des Moines).

The quiet of the Mormons was in large part due to apostles John Taylor and Willard Richards, who had seen both the determination and might of anti-Mormon wrath in the county and wanted to calm the situation. They, as well as several other leaders in Nauvoo, signed an epistle to church members in July 1844 promoting this policy. In it they ask that the membership avoid trouble, reject vengeance, and carry on as best they can. They reassure their readers that the church plans to go on as before, and urge the gathering of as many Saints as possible to Hancock County to infuse the community with new resources and support the church's development program. This article first appeared as "To the Saints Abroad" in the *Times and Seasons* 5 (15 July 1844): 586–87.

Dear Brethren;

On hearing of the martyrdom of our beloved prophet and patriarch, you will doubtless need a word of advice and comfort and look for it from our hands. We would say, therefore, first of all, be still and know that the Lord is God; and that he will fulfill all things in his own due time; and not one jot or tittle of all his purposes and promises shall fail. *Remember,* REMEMBER that the priesthood, and the keys of power are held in eternity as well as in time; and, therefore, the servants of God who pass the veil of death are prepared to enter upon a greater and more effectual work, in the speedy accomplishment of the restoration of all things spoken of by his holy prophets.

Remember that all the prophets and saints who have existed since the world began, are engaged in this holy work, and are yet in the vineyard, as well as the laborers of the eleventh hour: and are all pledged to establish the kingdom of God on the earth, and to give judgement unto the saints; therefore, none can hinder the rolling on of the eternal purposes of the Great Jehovah. And we have now every reason to believe that the fulfil[l]ment of his great purpose are much nearer than we had supposed, and that not many years hence, we shall see the kingdom of God, coming with power and great glory to our deliverance.

As to our country and nation, we have more reason to weep for them, than for those they have murdered; for they are destroying themselves and their institutions and there is no remedy; and as to feelings of revenge, let them not have place for one moment in our bosoms, for God's vengeance will speedily consume to that degree that we would fain be hid away and not endure the sight.

Let us then humble ourselves under the mighty hand of God, and endeavor to put away all our sins and imperfections as a people, and as individuals, and to call upon the Lord with the spirit of grace and supplication; and wait patiently on him, until he shall direct our way.

Let no vain and foolish plans, or imaginations scatter us abroad, and divide us asunder as a people, to seek to save our lives at the expense of truth and principle, but rather let us live or die together and in the enjoyment of society and union. Therefore, we say, let us haste to fulfill the commandments which God has already given us. Yes, let us haste to *build the Temple of our God*, and to GATHER together thereunto, our silver and our gold with us, unto the name of the Lord; and then we may expect that he will teach us of his ways and we will walk in his paths.

We would further say, that in consequence of the great rains which have deluged the western country, and also in consequence of persecution and excitement, there has been but little done here, either in farming or building this season; therefore there is but little employment, and but little means of subsistence at the command of the saints in this region—therefore, let the saints abroad, and others who feel for our calamities and wish to sustain us, come on with their money and means without delay, and purchase lots and farms, and build buildings, and employ hands, as well as to pay their tyhings [*sic*] into the Temple, and their donations to the poor.

We wish it distinctly understood abroad, that we greatly need the assistance of every lover of humanity whether members of the church or otherwise, both in influence and in contributions of our aid, succor, and support. Therefore, if they feel for us, now is the time to show their liberality and patriotism towards the poor and persecuted, but honest and industrious people.

Let the elders who remain abroad, continue to preach the gospel in its purity and fullness, and to bear testimony of the truth of these things which have been revealed for the salvation of this generation.

P. P. Pratt
Willard Richards
John Taylor
W. W. Phelps

3

Thomas Ford to the People of Warsaw

Governor Ford (see Part IV, Document 7) was enraged by the murder of the Smith brothers while in the custody of the state, and he moved during the dog days of summer to stabilize the situation in Hancock County. Always a legalist due to his background in the judicial system, he deplored what had happened in Carthage on that June afternoon when the Smiths were shot. He fully believed that Joseph Smith and the Mormons were dangerous elements in the state, and he was convinced of the illegality of their actions in silencing the Nauvoo *Expositor,* but he was appalled by the vigilantism of the non-Mormons in the county. Moreover, Ford felt personally insulted by the actions of the mob; he had sworn his personal protection to the prisoners, and the murderers had breached his honor. There did not seem to be the slightest remorse about the murders, either, and justifications like Thomas C. Sharp's article (see Part V, Document 1) only intensified his animosity.

In contrast, Ford was very impressed by the patience and caution exercised by the Latter Day Saints (see Part V, Document 2). Most non-Mormons in Hancock County had fully expected the Mormons to respond to the murder of the Smiths by sending the Nauvoo Legion on a campaign of burning and murder, but the Saints did not take revenge. The Mormons petitioned the governor for protection and legal redress, and Ford was committed to seeing that they received them. Not only was this action the morally right thing to do, he believed, but legal proceedings against the mobbers would help vindicate his behavior during the Mormon war.

Fed up with the constant excitement seething in Hancock County, the justifications for what were clearly illegal actions, and the continued threats against the Mormons, Ford sent an epistle to the anti-Mormons, most of whom were in Warsaw. In it he told them to submit to the laws of the state and cease any activities against the Mormons. It was published in both newspapers in the county. It first appeared as "To the People of Warsaw, in Hancock County," *Warsaw Signal,* 25 July 1844, p. 2. The version printed here, virtually identical to the *Warsaw Signal,* appeared as "Thomas Ford to the People of Warsaw in Hancock County, 25 July 1844" in the *Nauvoo Neighbor,* 31 July 1844, p. 2.

I am continually informed of your preparations and threats to renew the war and exterminate the "Mormons." One would suppose that you ought to rest satisfied with what you have already done.

The "Mormon" leaders, if they ever resisted the law, have submitted to its authority. They have surrendered the public arms, and appear to be ready to do anything required to make atonement for whatever wrong may have been done.

Since the assassination of their two principal leaders, under circumstances well calculated to inflame their passions and drive them to excesses for the purposes of revenge, they have been entirely peaceful and submissive, and have patiently awaited the slow operation of the law to redress the wrongs of which they complained. There has been no retaliation, no revenge, and, for anything I can ascertain, there will be none.

Those of your people who are charged with being the most hostile to them have lived, if they knew it, in perfect security from illegal violence.

I am anxious for a pacification of your difficulties. You cannot drive out or exterminate the "Mormons." Such an effort would be madness, and would not be permitted by the people of the state. You cannot be sustained in it either by force or law. You are binding yourselves to your weakness, and keeping up an agitation which must fail of the purpose intended and recoil with terrible energy upon your own heads.

I exhort you to reconsider your infatuated resolutions. Try your "Mormon" neighbors again, and if you cannot dwell together in amity, you may at least refrain from injuring each other.

From the moderation of the "Mormons," under what they conceive to be the deepest injury, you might well hope that if they ever entertained designs inconsistent with your liberty and happiness, that those designs have been abandoned. They are also interested in preserving the peace.

It is not natural to suppose that they, any more than yourselves, wish to live in continual alarm. They hope for quietness, and will be peaceful and submissive in order to enjoy it. But you are continually driving them to desperation by an insane course of threatening and hostility, and depriving yourselves of peace by the same means used to disquiet them.

If I have said anything severe in this address, I pray you attribute it to my deep conviction that your course is improper and unwarrantable. Such is the opinion of the people at large in the state and all over the country.

From being right in the first instance you have put yourselves in the wrong, and there are none who sustain you. As men of sense you are bound to see, if you will open your eyes, that you cannot effect your purposes. Nevertheless, you are still training and drilling, and keeping together, and threatening a renewal of the war.

I have said to you often that you cannot succeed; by this time you ought to see it yourselves. What can your small force do against two thousand armed men, entrenched in a city, and defending themselves, their wives and their children?

Besides, if you are the aggressors I am determined that all the power of the state shall be used to prevent your success. I can never agree that a set of infatuated and infuriated men shall barbarously attack a peaceful people who have submitted to all the demands of the law, and when they had full power to do so, refrained from inflicting vengeance upon their enemies. You may count on my most determined opposition—upon the opposition of the law, and upon that of every peaceful, law-abiding citizen of the country.

This is not spoken in anger. God knows I would do no injury unless compelled to do so to sustain the laws. But mob violence must be put down. It is threatening the whole country with anarchy and ruin. It is menacing our fair form of government, and destroying the confidence of the patriot in the institutions of his country.

I have been informed that the "Mormons" about Lima and Macedonia have been warned to leave the settlements. They have a right to remain and enjoy their property. As long as they are good citizens they shall not be molested, and the sooner those misguided persons withdraw their warning and retrace their steps, the better it will be for them.

Thomas Ford
July 25, 1844

—•••• *4* ••••—

Isaac and Sarah Scott on the
Aftermath of the Murders

I saac and Sarah Scott (see Part III, Document 15) were living in Nauvoo during the summer of 1844 and wrote an insightful series of letters about their experiences. Members of the Latter Day Saints for several years, they began to dissent from the main body of the church in early 1844 and were in sympathy with the Laws and Fosters in the publication of the *Expositor*. They comment on the manner in which the Saints at Nauvoo are dealing with the death of their leaders and the question of succession, noting the internal schisms that have emerged. Both also apparently believed that Joseph Smith had become a "fallen prophet" by teaching improper theology and that God had allowed his death. Hence, in their letter of 22 July–9 August 1844, they challenge the established Mormon concept of leadership by revelation by pointing out that the prophet's death has contradicted his own prophecy. They also debunk the emerging myth of righteous suffering by the persecuted Saints in Hancock County by asserting that the famous "lamb to the slaughter" prophecy and others are Mormon creations, developed to sanctify Smith's death and preserve the faith.

Their letter offers a significant insider perspective during a critical period when the future of Mormon belief was being shaped by the way in which Smith's followers responded to his traumatic death. It is reprinted from a collection by George F. Partridge, ed., "The Death of a Mormon Dictator: Letters of Massachusetts Mormons, 1843–1848," *New England Quarterly* 9 (December 1936): 583–617, this letter is from pp. 597–600. Sarah wrote most of the letter to her in-laws, but her husband added the last few paragraphs.

—•••◉◉•••—

Nauvoo, Illinois
July 22, 1844.

My Dear Father and Mother:

Having an opportunity to send to the East by way of brother Eames, who expects to return in a few weeks, I thought I would improve it and send to you a few lines. I suppose you received our letter and was somewhat prepared, when you heard of the dreadful murder of Joseph and Hyrum Smith in Carthage jail. Little did we think that an event like that would ever transpire. The Church believed that he would be acquitted as he had been on former occasions, and Joseph prophesied in the last *Neighbor* that was published before his death that they would come off victorious over them all, as sure as there was a God in Israel. Joseph also prophesied on the stand a year ago last conference that he could not be killed within five years from that time; that they could not kill him till the Temple would be completed, for that he had received an unconditional promise from the Almighty concerning his days, and he set Earth and Hell at defiance; and then said, putting his hand on his head, they *never* could kill his Child. But now that he *is* killed some of the Church say that he said: unless he gave himself up. My husband was there at the time and says there was not conditions whatever, and many others testify to the same thing.

I suppose you have heard from Mr. Haven and Martha before this and have learned their mind concerning Joseph and Hyrum, but I can not help believing that had they been innocent, that the Lord would not have suffered them to fall by the hands of wicked murderers. I believe they would have been living men to-day, had they been willing for others to enjoy the same liberties they wish for themselves.

The governor visited Nauvoo the day that Joseph and Hyrum were killed and made a speech. He told the people of Nauvoo the burning of that press was arbitrary, unlawful, unconstitutional, and that they had hurt themselves more than ten presses could have injured them in ten years.

The governor was met on his return to Carthage by a messenger informing him of the assassination. Many of the Mormons blame the governor for not bringing them with him and others do not. I think it looks strange his leaving a guard of only eight men with them and taking so many with himself. I have no doubt however but he was afraid of his own life or he would not have taken the number of men he did with him. I heard there were three hundred. The governor did not dare to stop in Carthage that night, and men, women, and children fled from there. I believe there was only three or four men that stopped in the place that night. I think the people of Carthage so far have suffered more than the Mormons. Who the vile murderers were I suppose never will be known till the day when all flesh shall stand before God to answer for the deeds done in the body. Many of the Mormons lay it on the Missourians, others to the apostates, as they call them. If it is apostasy from Mormonism to come out against the doctrines of more Gods than one, more wives than one, and many other damnable heresies that they have taught, I hope and pray that I and all the rest of the Church may become apostates.

Mr. Haven told me last spring before I was married that those doctrines tried his faith very much till he heard Hyrum Smith explain them and now or then he thought it was right. But a few weeks before the murder Hyrum denied that he and Joseph had the revelation concerning it but said that it referred to ancient times; and it was published [so] in the *Neighbor*. After I saw it I said to Mr. Haven: "What do you think of that? Is it not a plain contradiction to what you told me? What do you think of it?" He said that he supposed Hyrum saw what a disturbance it was making and thought he would say it on account of there being much excitement.

When the news reached the governor of the destruction of the press and of the trouble in Nauvoo, he hastened here as fast as possible just in time to save an attack upon the city of Nauvoo. Writs were then issued for the Smiths and others to bring them before the proper authorities for trial. When they were taken to Carthage, it was with difficulty the governor saved their lives. The repeated outrageous laws they had made, made the inhabitants hate the very sight of them. One example: whoever was heard speaking against the city council, charter, or ordinances should be fined five hundred dollars.

It is very warm here and quite sickly; for my part I wish I was in a healthier place. Those that have left the Church and reorganized have settled at a town called Hampton in this state, one hundred miles up the river. It is said to be a healthy place.

When I was teaching school last winter, I used to often think of what you used to tell me about school days. I had some come to school a mile and a half across the prairie with nothing but a bonnet and a little handkerchief around their necks; some bare-headed, some bare-footed, and any way. I have never got all my pay yet, only two-thirds of it, and don't suppose I shall get any more of it, but they who are owing me are good Mormons, and I suppose it's no matter.

Dear Mother: I have seen some sorrowful days since I left you and some happy ones. But I can tell you it is a sorrowful time here at present. Those that stood up for Joseph before his death are getting divided among themselves.

I have since learned that it was a mistake concerning the governor leaving only eight men with Joseph, but that he left a large company. Willard Richards and John Taylor were in jail with them.

August 9: Yesterday I attended a conference in Nauvoo. I supposed Martha will give you the particulars of it. The twelve were appointed to take charge of all the concerns of the Church both spiritual and temporal. Brigham Young said if he had been here, he wouldn't have consented to give Joseph up and he would be damned if he would give himself up to the law of the land. He would see them all in hell first; the Church, and then he said he would see all Creation in Hell before he would. These statements are correct, and they needn't any [of them] attempt to deny them. If they do, they are ignorant of the matter or they are willful liars.

Why don't you write to me? I haven't had a letter from one of you since I left. I am obliged for the newspaper and think you might afford time to write to *me* once in a while. Mother, I wish I had a piece of your brown bread; I have not seen a bit since I came home. I suppose I may wish again before I will get any. I wish we were a little nearer together but I suppose it's all right or it wouldn't be so. I hope there will be a change for the better here soon. I am going to have some graham bread before long; we have got a lot of nice wheat we raised this year.

Sarah Scott

At my wife's request I write a few words. We would like to drop in and talk about the past, present, and future. The present appears to be a wonderful period in the history of mankind. Joseph and Hyrum Smith are murdered; Samuel is dead and buried. The Smiths are all gone the way of all the earth except William, and why all this murder and death in the Smith family? I believe it is because they taught the people of God to transgress His holy laws as did the sons of Eli of old; they taught the people to break the laws of God, for which God revoked the covenant which He had made with Eli and gave him another promise which was that there should not be an old man in his house for ever. Mr. Haven and Mr. E——— have been here to-day. We have had quite a discussion of our "religious differences." Elder H——— tries hard to uphold his old Apostate Church, but when we bring him to the law and the testimony, he can't bring anything to prove his *Sublime Heavenly doctrines*.

You will likely hear a great deal about Joseph's innocence such as: "I go like a lamb to the slaughter, and if I die, I die an innocent man." All these statements, I believe, are false and got up for the purpose of reconciling the minds of the Church. I believe they had not the least idea that they were going to be murdered. Hyrum said the last time I heard him preach, which was only a few days before he and Joseph were taken to Carthage, that their enemies could not kill brother Joseph, for he had a great work to accomplish yet. There was also considerable said in Carthage which proves beyond dispute that they did not expect death. They blame the apostates, as they term them, with being accessory to the murder of the Smiths. This is not the case: the Laws and Fosters were not in the state at the time the murder was committed, and if they had been here, they would have been the last to stain their hands with human blood!

Remember me to all your family in the kindest manner. I wish you would write us a letter. We would be happy to hear from any of our brothers and sisters and answer any questions you or they may think proper to ask.

Yours respectfully,
Isaac Scott

———•••● 5 ●•••———

John Hay on the Trial of the Smiths' Assassins

John Hay (1838–1905) was born in Salem, Indiana, but moved as a small boy with his family to Warsaw, Illinois, in 1841. His father, Charles Hay, was a physician there, and although he apparently did not participate in the mob violence, it was undoubtedly from his father that the younger Hay got much of his information about the Mormon conflict. Dr. Hay tutored his son in Latin and Greek and then sent him to a private school in Pittsfield, Illinois State University (now Concordia College) in Springfield, and eventually to Brown University, where he received a master's degree in 1858. Hay became one of Lincoln's private secretaries, and after the president's assassination, served as a diplomat in Paris, Vienna, Madrid, and London. He later was secretary of state for presidents William

McKinley and Theodore Roosevelt and was responsible for the Open Door policy that initiated free trade with China. Also a noted literary figure, Hay's most famous works are a series of dialect poems called *Pike County Ballads* and a multi-volume life of Lincoln, coauthored with John G. Nicolay.

Hay was living in Warsaw in 1844 and 1845, viewing the Mormon conflict through the lens of a non-Mormon child near the action. He used his literary talent to illuminate the conflict, writing this story about the events in 1869. It is a curious mixture of personal recollection, family and community memoirs, and research. As a non-Mormon account by someone who felt close to the event but was not an eyewitness, it offers valuable insights, especially into the trial of the Smiths' murderers. Hay paints Thomas Ford as the tragic figure in this morality play. The Illinois governor was obsessed with bringing the murderers to justice. For reasons both psychological and legal, he had to succeed in at least bringing them to trial. With the help of troops he sent to Hancock County, the accused murderers were arrested and civil authorities from outside the area placed them on trial. The tense and perjury-ridden trial revealed only that the court could not be effective in Hancock County. This account comes from John Hay, "The Mormon Prophet's Tragedy," *Atlantic Monthly* (December 1869) 671–78.

The reaction now began. . . .

It was impossible that the matter should be allowed to pass entirely unnoticed by the law. Besides, Governor Ford, who considered the murder a personal disrespect to himself, was really anxious to bring the perpetrators to justice. Bills of indictment were found at the October [1844] term of court against Levi Williams, Mark Aldrich, Jacob C. Davis, William N. Grover, Thomas C. Sharp, John Willis, William Voorhees, William Gallagher, and one Allen. They were based on the testimony of two idle youths, named Brackenbury and Daniels, who had accompanied the expedition from Warsaw to Carthage on the 27th of June, and had seen the whole affair. Having a natural disinclination to work, they lived as long as they could by exploiting this rare experience. Their evidence being worse than useless in Warsaw, they went to Nauvoo, professed Mormonism, and had their board paid by the faithful, to secure their attendance at the trial. Brackenbury formed an alliance with a sign-painter, who executed in the highest style of Nauvoo art a panorama of the prophet's Death and Ascension, which they exhibited to the great edification of the Mormons and to such profit that the artist soon died of the trembling madness, and Brackenbury fell heir to the canvas and the fees. Daniels collaborated with a scribbler named Littlefield on a most remarkable pamphlet on the subject, stuffed full of miracles, and inventions more stupid than the truth.

Murray McConnell, who appeared in behalf of the governor to prosecute (and who was himself mysteriously assassinated twenty-four years later—as if a taint of blood were on all connected with this drama), made an arrangement with the defendants' counsel, by which the defendants agreed to appear voluntarily at the next May [1845] term, the State not being ready with its evidence. But toward the end of November, the vote of Davis becoming inconvenient to the leaders of the Seat, this convention was violated, and orders made for writs *instanter* against Davis and the rest. They were treated with contempt. Davis kept his seat in the Senate, and when the sheriff came to Warsaw he was received with that jocose discourtesy which so often in the West indicated a most sinister state of public feeling. He could find no trace of the men he was looking for. Nobody had seen or heard of them for weeks. In every shop he entered, he saw a loaded rifle, or a man oiling a gun-lock or moulding bullets. In the morning, when he mounted his horse to ride away, he found his mane and tail shaved bare as the head of a dervish. Hurrying out of the hostile neighborhood, he passed a crowd of grinning loungers.

"My horse was in bad company last night," he said, with a wretched attempt at good-natured indifference.

"Most generally is, I reckon," was the unfeeling retort; and the chief executive officer of the county left the mutinous town to itself.

The next May, all the defendants appeared, according to agreement, to stand their trial. They began by filing their affidavit that the county commissioners who selected the array of jurors for the week were prejudiced against them; that the sheriff and his deputies were unfitted by prejudice to select the talesman that might be required. They therefore entered a motion to quash the array of jurors, to set aside the sheriff and his deputies, and to appoint elisors to select a jury for the case. After argument, this was done. The elisors presented ninety-six men, before twelve were found ignorant enough and indifferent enough to act as jurors.

A large number of witnesses were examined, but nothing was elicited against the accused from any except Brackenbury, Daniels, and a girl named Eliza Jane Graham. The two first had been lying so constantly for some months professionally, the one in his pamphlet, the other in his rare-show, that they had utterly forgotten where they started from, and so embroidered their original facts with more recent fictions, that their evidence went for nothing. Besides, the showman Brackenbury thought that the pamphleteer Daniels had received more attention than himself from the polite world of Nauvoo, and was consequently stung by jealousy to contradict in his evidence all that Daniels had sworn to. The evidence of Miss Graham, delivered with all the impetuosity of her sex, was all that could be desired—and more too. She had assisted in feeding the hungry mob at the Warsaw House as they came straggling in from Carthage, and she should remember where every man sat, and what he said, and how he said it. Unfortunately, she remembered too much. No one accused her of willful perjury. But her nervous and sensitive character had been powerfully impressed by the influence of Smith, and, brooding constantly upon his death, she came at last to regard her own fancies and suspicions as positive occurrences. A few *alibis* so discredited her evidence, that it was held to prove nothing more than her own honest and half-insane zeal.

The case was closed. There was not a man on the jury, in the court, in the county, that did not know the defendants had done the murder. But it was not proven, and the verdict NOT GUILTY was right in law.

And you cannot find in this generation an original inhabitant of Hancock County who will not stoutly sustain that verdict.

—— ⦁⦁⦁ 6 ⦁⦁⦁ ——

The Anti-Mormons
Demand an Investigation

While the pretrial activities were taking place, and the defendants were out on bail, on 21 December 1844, Governor Thomas Ford delivered a *Message from the Governor, in Relation to the Disturbances in Hancock County* that charged the anti-Mormons in Hancock County with religious persecution. He called the assassinations of Joseph and Hyrum Smith the most vile deed ever committed in the state and demanded that order be restored and the law upheld. Ford's statements infuriated the non-Mormons of Hancock County, who believed that they had been upholding the republican virtues and laws of the United States against those who would subvert them. They especially wanted to prove that their opposition to the Saints at Nauvoo was not motivated by religious bigotry but solely resulted from the criminal behavior and political clannishness of the Mormons. They organized an information-collection project and petitioned the governor for the right to tell their side of the story.

Charles Hay, father of John Hay and a physician in Warsaw, is the author of the first document in this section. He was a member of the Central Committee working to rid Hancock County of Mormonism, and he asks for a compilation of illegal acts committed by Mormons to use as justification for anti-Mormon actions. The letter, located in Archives and Special Collections, Western Illinois University Library, Macomb, is published here for the first time. It shows the scrupulous nature of the effort of these non-Mormons to document criminal behavior by some Mormons. Hay also tries to shift the focus of the debate about Mormonism in Hancock County from religion—the position of the Mormons, and accepted at least for a time by Governor Thomas Ford—to the criminality of the Saints.

The second document is a memorial to the state legislature responding to allegations made by Governor Ford that Hancock County residents opposed the Mormons solely because they disliked their religion. County leaders took pains to establish the political and legal reasons for their opposition and demanded a full investigation—which they never got—by the state's leaders to prove them innocent of religious persecution. This petition was first published in the *Warsaw Signal* on 8 January 1845, p. 1, a copy of which is available in Archives and Special Collections, Western Illinois University Library.

———————•••◦◦●◦◦•••———————

Warsaw, January 3, 1845

Gentlemen

In behalf of the Central Committee I address you in order to impress on your minds the importance of an immediate organization of your precinct. The necessity for some organization and for action [is rendered] more apparent than ever before by the appearance of the Governors special message to the Legislature relative to our difficulties.

Statements have gone forth to the world over the signature of the Executive, and with the sanction of his official honor, well calculated, not only to mislead the public mind in relation to what has already transpired in the County, but also to blast the reputation of the old settlers. These statements must be met by the facts, and in order that there may be no delay in the collection of these facts, and that they may be set forth in a proper manner before the public, it is necessary that each precinct should immediately appoint Committees to whom this duty shall be assigned. To set our grievances fairly before the public every act of thieving that has or may be found in your precinct should be properly reported. In doing this, care should be taken not to report anything that cannot be fully substantiated; for the publication of any erroneous statements will injure rather than benefit our cause. The reports should be made giving the names of the persons who had lost the property and the time when taken. No item should be omitted, no matter how trifling the value. These reports should extend back to all the thieving operations that have taken place in your precinct since the Mormons came amongst us. We conceive that this cause will do us more good than any other, and will serve the purpose of discrediting Governor Ford's statements.

If there are any facts within your reach contradictory of any of Ford's statements let them be properly authenticated by affidavits and transmit the same to the Central Committee for Publication. A memorial, the object of which is to ask of the Legislature an investigation of the charges so grandly made by the Executive against us, will be transmitted herewith for the signature of your citizens. Will you please to appoint a committee immediately to attend specially to this memorial, making it their duty to obtain all the signatures in your precinct with the least possible delay.

If there are any cases in which Counterfeit money has been passed on any of your citizens please report the same. If any of your citizens have been maltreated by the Mormons let the facts be known, and if anything comes to your knowledged in relation to the Holy Brotherhood get the facts in an authentic form and transmit them forthwith.

We must go to work in earnest. The case requires prompt and energetic action. In this place we are determined to leave no stone unturned. Will you second our efforts in the good work?

> Resfy Yours
> Chas. Hay
> Chairman, Central Committee
> Wm. Y. Patch
> Secretary

Memorial

To the Honorable, the Senate and House of Representatives of the State of Illinois, in General Assembly convened.

The undersigned, citizens of Hancock county, respectfully represented to your Honorable Body, that they have read with mingled feelings of surprise and mortification, a communication made to your body on the 23d of December last, by His Excellency, the Governor of the State.—In this communication are charges of a serious and grave character—charges, the half of which, if true, would render us entirely unworthy [of] the society and confidence of honorable men, and stamp us as fit associates of the lawless and abondoned [sic].

Feeling in our hearts that these charges are false—knowing that they have no foundation in truth—and believing that they are the offspring of the ignorance, prejudice and malevolence of our enemies, we, a portion of your constituents, most respectfully invite your attention to an investigation of them. We cannot remain silent, while foul aspersions and deadly slanders are thus permitted to go forth from the Executive chamber, to do their insidious and intended work in blasting our names, and destroying our reputation in the estimation of men. Heretofore, when similar charges have been brought against us, by individuals in private life, it has been sufficient, in order to disarm any prejudice that a plain statement of facts should be made. But now the case is changed. These charges have been endorsed by the Executive, in an official communication to your body. They are now before you and before the world, by an official act of the Governor of the State.

As an act of justice to ourselves, we now ask an investigation into these charges, by a committee of your Honorable body. We challenge our enemies to produce before you the evidence on which they have founded their malignant slanders.

We demand the evidence of the charge that even a portion of our hostility to the Mormons has arisen from religious considerations:

We demand the evidence on which it is asserted by his Excellency, that our antipathy to the Mormons proceeds from a political source:

We demand the proof of the statement made by his Excellency, that our people have maliciously reported thefts and larcenies without foundation:

We demand the proofs on which his Excellency founds the charge that the people of Warsaw passed resolutions unqualifiedly to exterminate the Mormon population:

And finally, we demand the evidence on which is founded the charge of a design on our part to get up a civil war in October last, and which led to the military campaign of that month.

All these charges, and many similar ones, which it is unnecessary to detail preferred against us by his Excellency, we pronounce false; and we demand the evidence upon which they are founded.

We therefore ask your honorable body to appoint a committee to visit our county, or to hold their sessions at the seat of Government, as your body may think best, to take into consideration the charges and statements contained in the Message of his Excellency, and the evidence on which such charges and statements are founded.

7

The Mormon Reaction

The Mormons at Nauvoo did not sit quietly by while non-Mormon groups tried to gather information about their supposed crimes. The Nauvoo City Council met on 13 January 1845 to decide what action was best to stave off this attack. It passed a series of resolutions that were just as strong and demanded just as much action on the part of state authorities as had the Warsaw group.

The document published here, "The Voice of Nauvoo! Proceedings of the City Council. Preamble," *Times and Seasons* 15 (January 1845): 773–74, clearly reflects the concern of the Mormons that the church not be linked to criminal behavior. It was signed by Daniel Spencer (1794–1868), the mayor of Nauvoo elected after Joseph Smith's death. He had joined the Latter Day Saints in 1840, leaving a successful mercantile business on the East Coast and settling in Nauvoo. There Spencer was active in civic and religious affairs until the Mormon exodus. In 1846 he traveled west with the first Mormon companies and settled in Salt Lake City, where he died more than two decades later.

It is with feelings of deep and inexpressible regret that we learn that the inhabitants of various parts of this state are seeking to accumulate all the real and supposed crimes of the whole community for the secret or ostensible purpose of raising a tide of influence against the Mormon community that shall sweep them into irrevocable ruin. This course of conduct, originating with our mortal enemies and gathering in its wake other men that would revolt at the idea of lending a hand to oppress a long abused people that are struggling against foes within and foes without, is at the present time almost insupportable to our feelings. We have scarcely laid by our weeds for murdered men, whom we promptly surrendered up to the state of Illinois for an equitable trial—and now we see in embryo another campaign to spill yet more blood and effect an utter extermination and massacre. We sought to rid our city of counterfeiters and blacklegs; these together with our foes without and within, had established a printing press of unparalleled rancor and malignity. But our efforts to obtain freedom from such vicious monsters cost us much tribulation and precious blood.

The impunity thus far granted the murderers by the senate and other authorities of the State of Illinois, has emboldened them and their apologists to set on foot a series of other exciting causes that they hope will either destroy this community, or prevent their criminals from being brought to punishment. We have not so much fear that our enemies will succeed in their fiendish designs against us, as we have that the peace and good order of this people of this state will be disturbed, and fearful anarchy and bloody misrule will ensue among those who listen to and countenance the fell designs of those who are stealing from quiet citizens of the state and palming upon them a spurious and false currency, and charging to the Mormons their own crimes. If they shall succeed, the citizens will be involved in continual larcenies and neighborhood broils, and crimes the end of which cannot now be foreseen. We deprecate such evils and calamities because we desire the good of all mankind, as the gratuitous labors of the greater portion of our citizens in spreading truth throughout the world under much poverty and suffering, abundantly prove.

As for us, our course is fixed, and while we are peaceable and loyal to the constitution and laws of our country, and are ever willing to join hands with the honest, virtuous, and patriotic in suppressing crime and punishing criminals, we will leave our enemies to judge, whether it would not be better to make Nauvoo one universal burying ground, before we suffer ourselves to be driven from our hard earned and lawful homes, by such high-handed oppression, and it may yet become a question to be decided by the community, whether the Mormons will, after having witnessed their best men murdered without redress, quietly and patiently, suffer their enemies to wrench from them the last shreds of their constitutional rights; and whether they will not make their city one great sepulchre, rather than be the humble devotees at the shrine of mobocracy. But for the satisfaction of all concerned, we reiterate in the following resolutions, sentiments that we have always expressed in all places as occasion demanded.

Resolved, That the greater part of the thefts which have been complained of, are not in our opinion, true in fact, but have been trumped up by inimical persons, in order to cover their aggressive doings, with plausibility, and entice honest and unwary citizens to unite with them in the same uncompromising hostility against this people.

Resolved, That we defy the world to substantiate a single instance, where we have concealed criminals, or screened them from justice; but, on the contrary, always have been, and now are, extremely anxious that they should be ferreted out and brought to justice; and to this end would esteem it a favor, that if any person should lose property, or have good and sufficient reason to suspect any place of containing apparatus for making bogus or counterfeit money, that such person would follow up, trace out, and make diligent search, for all such property and apparatus, and if they can trace it into this city, we pledge ourselves to assist them legally, to the extent of our abilities in so laudable an undertaking.

Resolved, That it is our opinion that very many scoundrels, such as thieves, robbers, bogus makers, counterfeiters, and murderers, have been induced from reports published in the Warsaw Signal, to flock into this county in order to carry on their evil practices, knowing that it would be immediately charged upon the Mormons, and thereby they escape—and although we think that the reports of thefts have been very much exaggerated, yet we know from dear bought experience that such things do exist, and further we doubt not there may be some such characters prowling in and about our city.

Resolved, That we are extremely anxious to ferret out and bring to justice, all such persons, if any, that are within the limits of our city, and for this purpose we have authorized our mayor to enlarge the police, to any number, not exceeding five hundred, and we also pledge ourselves to double our diligence, and call upon our citizens to assist in ridding our city and country of all such infamous characters.

Done, in Council, this 13th day of January, 1845.

D. Spencer, Mayor.

W. *Richards*, Recorder.

8

The Repeal of the Nauvoo Charter

At the same time that these events were taking place in Hancock County, the Illinois State Legislature was meeting in Springfield and considering the propriety of repealing the Nauvoo city charter. The legislators were incensed at the way the charter had been used repeatedly by Joseph Smith to subvert the law and serve his own purposes. The most blatant abuse was the city council's destruction of the Nauvoo *Expositor* in June 1844. The legislature saw the charter as a tool that had been willfully exploited by the Saints; the Mormons, of course, viewed it as a legal bulwark to defend their rights. When the legislature began to consider repealing the charter, Governor Ford thought they were going too far. While Ford had little use for the legal schemes the Mormons had enacted using the charter, he told the legislature, "I do not see how ten or twelve thousand people can do well in a city without some chartered privileges," and he advocated a revision that clearly circumscribed individual authority and ensured separation of powers.

The next document clearly reflects concern about the legislature's repeal of the Nauvoo Charter on 29 January 1845 (by a vote of 25–14 in the senate and 75–31 in the house). Without legal authority to pass and enforce ordinances, what used to be the city of Nauvoo became even more attractive to lawless elements, and as a result, the county took an even more serious step into chaos. On 1 February 1845, for example, Brigham Young wrote to Daniel Webster, asking the Massachusetts senator's help in resolving the plight of the Saints in Illinois, specifically addressing problems created by the charter's repeal. Petitions to other political figures followed. A letter sent to various governors in the United States by the Mormons follows. It is taken from the diary of John Taylor, Mormon apostle and later church president. Originally published in Dean C. Jessee, ed., "The John Taylor Nauvoo Journal," *Brigham Young University Studies* 23 (Summer 1983): 1–96, the section here comes from pages 36–44.

<hr>

Nauvoo, Illinois, March 1845.

Honorable Sir,

Suffer us, sir, in behalf of a disfranchised and long afflicted people to prefer a few suggestions for your serious consideration, in hope of a friendly and unequivocal response, at as early a period as may suit your convenience, and the extreme urgency of the case seems to demand.

It is not our present design to detail the multiplied and aggravated wrongs that we have received in the midst of a nation that gave us birth. Some of us have long been loyal citizens of the state over which you have the honor to preside; while others claim citizenship in each of the states of this great confederacy. We say we are a disfranchised people. We are privately told by the highest authorities of this state, that it is neither prudent nor safe for us to vote at the polls: still we have continued to maintain our right to vote, until the blood of our best men has been shed, both in Missouri and the state of Illinois with impunity.

You are doubtless somewhat familiar with the history of our extermination from the state of Missouri; wherein scores of our brethren were massacred, hundreds died through want and sickness occasioned by their unparalleled suffering, some millions of our property were confiscated or destroyed; and some fifteen thousand souls fled for their lives, to the then hospitable and peaceful shores of Illinois;—and that the state of Illinois granted to us a liberal charter, for the term of perpetual succession, under whose provisions private rights have become invested, and the largest city in the state has grown up numbering about twenty-thousand inhabitants.

But sir, the startling attitude recently assumed by the state of Illinois forbids us to think that her designs are any less vindictive than those of Missouri. She has already used the military of the state, with the executive at their head to coerce and surrender up our best men to unparalleled murder, and that too under the most sacred pledges of protection and safety. As a salve for such unearthly perfidy and guilt, she told us through her highest executive officer, that the laws should be magnified, and the murderers brought to justice; but the blood of her innocent victims had not been wholly wiped from the floor of the awful arena, where the citizens of a sovereign state pounced upon two defenseless servants of God, our Prophet and our Patriarch, before the senate of that state rescued one of the indicted actors in that mournful tragedy, from the sheriff of Hancock County and gave him an honorable seat in [the] Hall of Legislation. And all others who were indicted by the Grand Jury of Hancock County for the murder of Generals Joseph and Hyrum Smith, are suffered to roam at large watching for further prey.

To crown the climax of these bloody deeds, the state has repealed all those chartered rights by which we might have defended ourselves against oppressors. If we defend ourselves hereafter against violence whether it comes under the shadow of the law or otherwise, (for we have reason to expect it both ways), we shall then be charged with treason, and suffer the penalty; and if we continue passive and non-resistant, we must certainly expect to perish, for our enemies have sworn it. And, here, sir, permit us to state that General Joseph Smith, during his short life was arraigned at the bar of his country about 50 times, charged with criminal offenses, but was acquitted every time by his country, his enemies almost invariably being his judges: and we further testify that as a people, we are law-abiding, peaceable, and without crime; and we challenge the world to prove the contrary: And while other less cities in Illinois have had special courts instituted to try their criminals, we have been stripped of every source of arraigning marauders and murderers who are prowling around to destroy us, except the common magistracy.

With these facts before you, sir, will you write to us without delay, as a father and friend, and advise us what to do? We are many of us, citizens of your state, and all members of the same great confederacy. Our fathers, nay some of us, have fought and bled for our country; and we love her constitution dearly.

In the name of Israel's God, and by the virtue of multiplied ties of country and kindred, we ask your friendly interposition in our favor. Will it be too much to ask you to convene a special session of your state legislature, and furnish us an asylum where we can enjoy our rights of conscience and religion unmolested? Or will you in a special message to that body when convened, recommend a remonstrance against such unhallowed acts of oppression and expatriation, as this people have continued to receive from the states of Missouri and Illinois? Or will you favor us by your personal influence, and by your official rank?

Or will you express your views concerning what is called the Great Western Measure of colonizing the Latter-day Saints in Oregon, the North Western Territory or some location, remote from the states, where the hand of oppression shall not crush every noble principle, and extinguish every patriotic feeling? And now honorable sir, having reached out our imploring hands with deep solemnity, we would importune with you as a father, a friend, a patriot, and a statesman; by the constitution of American liberty;—by the blood of our fathers, who have fought for the independence of this republic; by the blood of the martyrs which has been shed in our midst; by the wailings of the widows and orphans; by our murdered fathers and mothers, brothers and sisters, wives and children; by the dread of immediate destruction, from secret combinations now forming for our overthrow, and by every endearing tie that binds men to men and renders life bearable, and that, too, for aught we know, for the last time, that you will lend your immediate aid to quell the violence of mobocracy and exert your influence to establish us as a people in our civil and religious rights, where we now are, or in some part of the United States, or at some place remote therefrom, where we may colonize in peace and safety as soon as circumstances will permit.

We sincerely hope that your future prompt measures towards us will be dictated by the best feelings that dwell in the bosom of humanity; and the blessings of a grateful people, and of many ready to perish, shall come upon you.

We are sir, with great respect, Your obedient servants

[Committee]: Brigham Young, Willard Richards, John Taylor, George Miller, W. W. Phelps, Orson Spencer, L. R. Foster.

In behalf of The Church of Jesus Christ of Latter-day Saints, at Nauvoo, Illinois.

P.S. As many of our communications post marked at Nauvoo, have failed of their destination, and the mails around us have been intercepted by our enemies, we shall send this to some distant office by the hand of a special messenger.

———••••• *9* •••••———

Sheriff Minor Deming and the Resumption of Violence

After the deaths of the Smith brothers, an immediate concern for most non-Mormons in Hancock County was the August 1844 local election. The year before, the Saints had emerged as a central political force in electing individuals friendly to them to county office. Nearly all non-Mormons wanted to reverse this trend, but they faced an uphill battle. The murder of the Smiths had prompted many in the county, even those who disagreed with the Mormons, to condemn the violence. They were little inclined, therefore, to vote for anyone identified with anti-Mormonism.

At this critical juncture, Minor R. Deming (?–1845), a general in the Illinois militia and a sympathetic non-Mormon, stepped forward and was elected sheriff on 6 August 1844. A "law and order" candidate, he ran on a platform that called for the arrest of all the members of the group which had killed the Smiths. Deming was both sensitive and religious, and it disturbed him that the area where he had lived since 1838 would be remembered for what he considered a heinous crime. Even though he personally disliked the attitudes and activities of Joseph and Hyrum Smith, he believed they should have received a fair trial before being punished for any crimes they might have committed. His election was a boon to the Saints, but as sheriff, Deming had the ability to make the lives of anti-Mormons very uncomfortable.

Deming analyzed the situation in Hancock County at the time of his election in a letter to his parents on 22 August 1844, housed in his papers at the Illinois Historical Survey, University of Illinois Library:

> We have had war, murder, politics and animosity bitter and desperate in Hancock, without stint for the last three months. . . . The exterminators [anti-Mormons] are of the two, more fanatical than the Mormons and less regardful of the law. They threaten death to all who have enough daring or humanity to oppose them. . . . The Mormon question since the murder of the Smiths has become political and the venum [*sic*] of party spirit breathes in detraction. . . . There were some 2 or 300 engaged in the murder and they with their friends and the alliance of the Whig party in the county, who mean to sustain and protect the murderers, make a strong party that by threats, violence & desperation aim at supremacy above the law and justice.

He understood that his work would be difficult, but he was prepared to restore order in Hancock County. With the support of Governor Ford, Deming took judicious steps to ensure that the Mormon conflict did not erupt into large-scale violence. He was relatively successful, and the détente in the county essentially coincided with his term as sheriff.

Even so, Deming made many enemies while sheriff in 1844–45, and that led directly to his death. On 24 June 1845, during the trial of Smith's accused murderers at Carthage, Deming had an altercation with one of the local anti-Mormons, Dr. Samuel Marshall, who picked a fight with him, supposedly over a land deal turned sour. Deming, who had just started wearing a gun, had come to court armed and killed Marshall during the altercation. He believed that Marshall's attack had been premeditated, and that the fight over land was merely a pretext to attack him. The day after the shooting, a local grand jury indicted Deming for murder. He was released on five thousand dollars bail, raised by his Mormon constituency, and the trial was set for October. Because of this situation, in July Deming resigned as Hancock County sheriff, forcing a special election that brought to office Jacob B. Backenstos, an ardent pro-Mormon whose policies were partly responsible for the conflict's escalation in the fall of 1845. Before Deming could be brought to trial, however, he died of consumptive fever on 10 September 1845 at his home at St. Mary's—ironically the same day when the first widespread violence since the death of the Smiths in June 1844 erupted in the county. A week after his death, Brigham Young spoke to the Saints in Nauvoo and praised Deming's uprightness, commenting that "if you die—die like Deming in the defence of your country's rights" (*Nauvoo Neighbor*, 15 September 1845).

The letter that follows describes the fate of Deming in the summer of 1845. It was written by his father-in-law, Peter Barnum of Danbury, Connecticut, to his son Ezra Starr Barnum. The Abigail mentioned in the letter is Deming's wife. The letter, dated 31 July 1845, is located in the Archives and Special Collections, Western Illinois University Library. It is printed here for the first time. The letter is especially significant as a statement from a person far removed from the scene about the state of affairs in Hancock County in the summer of 1845.

Danbury July 31, *1845*

Dear Son Ezra, Having got nearly through with hay & harvest, I take my pen to inform you how we are &c. We have enjoyed good health thus far this season, though somewhat worn by hard labor. We are full of anxiety about Minor & Family. You may have seen in the papers some account of M. killing a man, (called Dr. Marshall) of Warsaw. M. & Abigail have both written us since the affray. It is difficult to form an opinion of it without knowing the state of society there. I was aware that M. would be exposed to very much danger in attending to the office of High Sheriff as he would be employed to take some of those concerned in the murder of the Smiths which would arouse the fury of all that was glad they were dead, & that is a large number of the people. The affray took place at a time of Court, when some of those supposed to be engaged in the murder of the Smiths were to be tried. It was in a large room of the Court house with 15 or 20 men in it. Marshall was a very large stout man of violent temper, had several times before abused M. when doing business, in short was his sworn enemy. At this time they were talking about some land that had been sold at Sheriff Sale to pay taxes. Marshall had bought it, (this was done in June some weeks before). Marshall claimed there was an error in the sale & wanted to get it entered on the Clerk's book. M. said he believed there was an error, he would examine his books & see about it. Marshall became enraged. M. says, why this flurry, Dr. I have sent for my books, they will be here in a moment & I will examine & find out the error or something to this amount. M. seeing he was getting high withdrew some distance from him. The Dr soon declares with an oath, you are the meanest rascal out of hell & seized him by the collar near the throat with both hands & pushed him back through a door, at which time M. drew his pistol & shot him. He instantly released his hold & died in a few minutes or within half an hour—M. resigned himself, gave up his pistol, requested the Judge who was not far off to summon a grand jury—he did so & they were not M.['s] friends. They found a bill against him for murder.—M. was put in jail under keepers from Tuesday to Saturday when he was bailed for his appearance at Court in the sum of 5000 dollars. When he will be tried we dont know. We think he is much more likely to be assassinated than to be condemned by the Court.—His friends feared he would be killed the first night; he was used harshly by the guard who refused to let Abigail speak with him, unless they could know what she said. He has his liberty & I suppose is attending to his business. He made known his intention to resign his office as soon as he could get his business settled which he thought would be about the 15 of August.—

M. has carried a six shooter (as they call it) & bowie-knife all the time while on his office away from home. They removed to Carthage last Sept., when he entered the duties of his office, into the jail & which also contains a hall for Court, being a large stone building, the same in which the Smiths were killed. . . .

Your Affectionate Father
Peter Barnum

•••• 10 ••••

The Attack on the Durfee Settlement

Although the overall situation in Hancock County had been relatively quiet for several months, when it became clear that the Saints were not going to leave the area, anti-Mormons in the county began to reassert themselves. Indeed, in "An Epistle of the Twelve, to the Church of Jesus Christ of Latter Day Saints in all the World," appearing in the *Times and Seasons* 6 (15 January 1845): 779–80, Brigham Young stated that the church was stable and committed to building up Nauvoo as a Mormon stronghold. He invited

> all the young, middle aged, and able bodied men who have it in their hearts to stretch forth this work with power to come to Nauvoo, prepared to stay during the summer; and to bring with them means to sustain themselves with, and to enable us to forward this work; to bring with them teams, cattle, sheep, gold, silver, brass, iron, oil, paints and tools; and let those who are within market distance of Nauvoo bring with them provisions to sustain themselves and others during their stay.

This sense of permanence was a significant force in rekindling anti-Mormon sentiments in the county.

As the summer of 1845 ended, an increasing number of isolated instances of violence began to be complained about by the Mormons. These incidents ensured the return of open hostilities. It began on 10 September 1845 at the home of Edmund Durfee near the Mormon community known as Yelrome, or Morleytown. Accounts of the violence reveal the pro-Mormon or anti-Mormon bias of those involved. Several different accounts were recorded in the diary of John Taylor, Mormon apostle, and the ones printed here are excerpted from this source. The first is a letter from Solomon Hancock, who lived near Durfee and reported the attack to church authorities in Nauvoo. The second is an affidavit by Sarah Ann Evarts, another Mormon resident near Morleytown. Both have been published in Dean C. Jessee, ed., "The John Taylor Nauvoo Journal," *Brigham Young University Studies* 23 (Summer 1983): 89–90, 93–94.

Yelrome, Illinois, September 13th, 1845

Dear Brother,

I will agreeably to your request send you some of the particulars of what has been done, on the other side of the branch; it is a scene of desolation. On Wednesday the 10th all of a sudden, the mob rushed upon Edmund Durfee and destroyed some property, and set fire to both of his buildings, they then dispersed; Brother Durfee with his family then put the fire out. The same day in the evening they shot at our guard and missed them, the mob then fled a small distance and soon set fire to the house of John Edmondson, and in a few minutes the house was in flames.

On the morning of the 11th they again set fire to the buildings of Edmund Durfee, and fired upon some of his children without hitting them; they then proceeded to the old shop of Father Morley's and set fire to both his shops, firing at the same time upon J. C. Snow, as they supposed, and thought they had killed him; it proved however to be Clark Hallett who escaped unhurt; they then set fire to J. C. Snow's house, and fled home to Lima.

In the afternoon the mob came on again and set fire to Father Whiting's chair shop, Walter Cox, Cheney Whiting and Azariah Tuttle's houses; at evening they retreated back again.

On the morning of the 12th we held a council and selected two men to go and make proposals to sell, but got no particular answer. Last evening they set on fire three buildings, near Esquire Walker's; and this morning we expect them to renew their work of destruction. Williams and Rosevelt were in Lima yesterday. The mob is determined to destroy us; some of the teams have arrived. Do for us, what you think is best; we will do as you tell us.

Yours in Haste,
Solomon Hancock

To President Brigham Young. . . .

State of Illinois, County of Hancock (S. S.)

Be it remembered that on the seventeenth day of September, A.D. 1845, personally came before me, Daniel H. Wells, an acting Justice of the Peace within and for said county, Sarah Ann Everts, who, being duly sworn according to law, deposeth and saith that on the night of the fifteenth inst. [September], a number of men came to the residence of this deponent about the hour of midnight, and ordered this deponent, who was laying sick at the time with the ague and fever, together with the balance of the family including five persons, two of whom, besides myself, being sick, to get up immediately and leave the house, and immediately commenced carrying the furniture and things [out] of the house. She remonstrated with them; told them she was sick; that she could not safely get up and go out; but all to no purpose; they assisted her out and immediately set fire to the house, and also the barn which were burned to the ground; also about four hundred bushels of wheat thrashed out and stacks of grain were burned; and this deponent further states that one [Michael] Barnes, was one of the persons concerned in the said crime of arson, and this deponent further states that the said Michael Barnes is guilty of the fact charged, and further this deponent saith not.

Sarah Ann Evarts.

Sworn to and subscribed before me this 17th day of September, A.D. 1845. Daniel H. Wells, J. P.

━━━━●●●● *11* ●●●●━━━━

Thomas Sharp on the Killings of Worrell and McBratney

It did not take long for the house burnings, robberies, and other acts of intimidation to turn deadly and escalate beyond the point where they could be contained. Thomas C. Sharp, the anti-Mormon agitator who edited the *Warsaw Signal*, wrote an unpublished history of the Mormon war in the fall of 1845 designed to express the opinions of those opposed to the presence of the Saints in the county. The first portion of that history dealt with the killings of Franklin A. Worrell—the commander of the Carthage Greys detachment that had been guarding the Smith brothers at the time of their murder and an ardent anti-Mormon— on 16 September 1845 and of another anti-Mormon named Samuel McBratney two days later. McBratney's corpse was mutilated. Both killings were assumed to have been commited under the orders of Sheriff Jacob Backenstos.

Accounts of the Worrell killing vary. According to Mormon sources, Backenstos was driving a carriage from Warsaw to Carthage when several riders began to chase him. Backenstos issued a proclamation on 16 September 1845 describing what occurred from his perspective, and it was published in the 15 October 1845 *Warsaw Signal*, p. 2. He explains:

> The chase lasted for a distance of about two miles, when I fortunately over-took three men with teams. I immediately informed them that armed men were pursuing me, evidently to take my life. I summoned them as a posse to aid me in resisting them. I dismounted and took my position in the road, with pistol in hand. I commanded them (the mobbers) to stop, when one of them held his musket in a shooting attitude, whereupon one of my posse fired, and, it is believed, took effect on one of the lawless banditti. We

remained and stood our ground, prepared for the worst, for about ten minutes. The mobbers, retreating some little distance, made no further assault, but finally retreated. I then made my way to the city of Nauvoo, where I am at this time.

The shooter was Orrin Porter Rockwell, a Mormon enforcer. Worrell, whom Rockwell recognized as the leader of the non-Mormon group, made a ready target at a hundred yards and was hit by Rockwell in the chest. He died as the non-Mormons retreated to Warsaw.

Backenstos acted as if he had not ordered the shooting, but according to Thomas L. Barnes, a young physician in Carthage, he admitted that "he had it done," as Barnes recalled in a letter of 9 November 1897 to his daughter, Miranda Barnes Haskett, available in the Santa Rosa, California, Public Library, with photostatic and typescript copies in the Illinois State Historical Library, Springfield. Because of this comment, Backenstos was later arrested for the murder of Worrell, and as Barnes recalled, "I was summoned as a witness for the prosicution [sic], and under oath repeated the conversation giving the time, place and circumstances and who was present." But Mormons whom Backenstos called in his defense refuted Barnes's testimony, and the sheriff was released.

The account by Sharp printed here is strikingly different. Written sometime after 22 October 1845, but probably before the middle of 1846 when he stopped publication of the *Warsaw Signal*, it is part of an overall history meant to be the definitive non-Mormon defense of the conflict. Sharp intended to publish it in his newspaper, and it offers the reasons for the conflict during the fall of 1845 according to the non-Mormons. The original is housed in the Thomas C. Sharp and Allied Anti-Mormon Papers, Coe Collection of Western Americana, Bienecke Library, Yale University, New Haven, Connecticut. It was originally published in Roger D. Launius, ed., "Anti-Mormonism in Illinois: Thomas C. Sharp's Unfinished History of the Mormon War, 1845," *Journal of Mormon History* 15 (1989): 27–45. With the Worrell killing, the contest had turned decidedly deadly, and several additional killings, including that of McBratney, would take place before it ended.

On Tuesday morning the 16th of Sept. [1845] Franklin A. Worrell, a merchant of Carthage and a Lieutenant in the company of Carthage Greys, started from Carthage, with eight or ten other citizens of Carthage, intending to visit Warsaw and the Camp of the burners, in order to inform themselves of the real state of affairs. Mr. Worrell, with three or four others, was on horseback, with their guns strapped over their shoulders, while the remainder of the Company rode in a wagons. They had reached a distance of about ten miles, when the horsemen, being a mile or more ahead of the wagons, saw a man at some considerable distance, in a buggy, driving at a rapid rate, northwardly on the Nauvoo road, and crossing their route. Not knowing the cause for such haste, and believing that it was some one through fear endeavoring to avoid them, or some one from the camp of the burners, with news, they immediately left the road and started in pursuit. Being on horseback, while the stranger was in a buggy, they gained on him; and on arriving near the Rail Road Shantee, they perceived that there were men in the bushes. A moment before the firing, Mr. Worrell exclaimed—"It is Backenstos!" Backenstos (for it was he) was then some distance off, in the bottom of the ravine, and his men were nearer, on the roadside in the bushes. On observing the fire, one of the party exclaimed, "There is a shot from the bushes!" "Yes," said Mr. Worrell, "and I have got it!" They then attempted to ride away, but had not proceeded more than a few paces, when the wounded man slid from his horse to the ground. One of the party now rode forward & beckoned to their companions in the wagons. On arriving at the place, Mr. W. was taken up into the wagon, & supported by his friends until he breathed his last, which he did in about half an hour in great bodily pain. His remains were carried to Warsaw, where he was interred the next day.

The party who were in company with Mr. W. saw quite a number of men in the bushes, not far off, and on the opposite side of the ravine, at the Shantee, were a number of wagons & horses, as if in encampment. They were a *posse* of Mormons whom the Sheriff had lying in ambush, it is thought, for the purpose of intercepting those who might be passing between Carthage & Warsaw, in order to gain intelligence of the movements of the Anti-Mormons.

In one of his proclamations, Backenstos says that being pursued by Worrell & his party, he called upon three travellers whom he overtook in the road, to assist him, and that one of them shot one of the assailants, as he was in the act of raising his gun to fire. It is said that the notorious Or[r]in P. Rockwell was the man who fired the fatal shot. . . .

As a party of burners, and others about 12 or 15 in number, were riding along the road, leading through the Bear Creek settlement, on —— day, the — — of September, —— days after the murder of Lieut. Worrell, they suddenly fell in with the Mormon *Posse*, under the Sheriff and General Bishop George Miller. As soon as the posse discovered them, they dashed forward among them, with weapon in hand, and fired. Two men were shot; one but slightly, and not so badly injured but that he was able to make his escape. The other, Mr. Samuel McBratney, a young man, then resident of Warsaw, but formerly of Marquette Co. was shot through the back, overtaken and killed. His body was not discovered & brought in till next day. The party was pursued for three or four miles over the prairie, but the remainder succeeded in making their escape.

The massacre of McBratney, was one of the most atrocious acts ever perpetrated in a civilized community. When found the next day, he was lying on his back, his clothes torn open in front, and his body pierced through with a sword or knife, a sabre cut on the top of his head, and his throat cut through from ear to ear. The grass was much trodden and beaten down, where the body lay, indicating that there had been a struggle.

From the position & circumstances in which the body was found, the presumption is strong that he was alive at the time the sword wounds were given. The cut on the top of the head, indicated that he was in a standing or sitting posture when it was given; and the stabs about the breast & throat seem to have been given while his arms were held at length and his bosom torn open. The rifle ball could not have killed him instantly: if so, what need of further cutting & slashing upon a body already dead.

When it is recollected that the duty of a Sheriff & his *posse* is to *arrest* & not to kill, offenders, this case seems doubly barbarous. Had McBratney been found in the very act of committing arson, the Sheriff would not have been justified in firing upon him, even, until he had been summoned to surrender, or an attempt made to take him; much less to butcher a wounded and helpless man, after he was completely in their power. But they had no knowledge that McBratney had been engaged, or was intending to engage, in the burning. He was found on horseback, away from any house or farm, and set upon in the manner above described. It is unnecessary to say what the law will do in Illinois, in such a case as this. Time will probably show. But one thing is certain—in any State east of the Ohio, the dastardly perpetrators of such a deed would soon be made to dangle between earth & heaven, an example to all Sheriffs and sheriff's *posses*. . . .

12

The Disappearance of Phineas Wilcox

On 16 September, the same day that Franklin Worrell was killed, non-Mormon Phineas Wilcox went to Nauvoo with a load of wheat to be milled. While waiting for it, he stayed at the home of Ebenezer B. Jennings, a Mormon friend. Apparently there were people in the community who believed that Wilcox was an anti-Mormon spy, and Mrs. Jennings warned Wilcox of danger. Wilcox did not believe her, however, and the next morning Wilcox and Jennings went to visit the temple, then being constructed on the hill above the city. Wilcox was captured at the temple, apparently taken to the Masonic Hall, and never seen again.

In this affidavit published in the *Warsaw Signal* on 22 October 1845, p. 2, Orrin Rhodes gives a detailed account of the disappearance of his stepson, Wilcox, at Nauvoo on 16–17 September 1845. Rhodes's account was corroborated by another affidavit, by Mormon Ebenezer Jennings, which appeared in the same issue. The account by Rhodes is interesting because in searching for his stepson he stumbled upon a group of prisoners being held in the stable of Joseph Smith's Mansion House, and he was also threatened. Apparently the Mormons lived in fear of mob violence, and in the absence of recognized police and courts—because of the repeal of the Nauvoo Charter earlier in 1845—they had resorted to a kind of vigilantism to keep order.

General John J. Hardin, the state militia commander sent to Hancock County to restore order, went to Nauvoo in search of Wilcox—as well as an anti-Mormon named Andrew Daubenheyer who had disappeared on 18 September on the road to Carthage—on 30 September 1845, but he found nothing. Hardin reported his investigation of the disappearance in a letter of 4 October, which appeared in the *Illinois State Register* (Springfield) on 17 October 1845. While in the city, according to the diary of Hosea Stout, Hardin's men specifically searched the Mansion House stable, including the hay, and were told by Stout's men that "they were fools to suppose that we would hide dead men in the Hay &c when the river was so near . . ." (Juanita Brooks, ed., *On the Mormon Frontier: The Diary of Hosea Stout* [Salt Lake City: University of Utah Press, 1964], 78). This led the non-Mormons to believe that Wilcox and Daubenheyer had indeed been killed. They later found Daubenheyer's body buried near a campsite on the Carthage road "with a musket ball through the back of his head" (Thomas Ford, *History of Illinois*, 409). What happened to Wilcox is still unknown.

••••◉••••

Mr. Rhodes' Affidavit

State of Illinois, Hancock county:

Orrin Rhodes, being first duly sworn, deposes and says, that on Tuesday the 16th day of September, A.D. 1845, he went with Phineas Wilcox, deponent's step-son, to the city of Nauvoo, where they went together, to the house of E. B. Jennings, a Mormon living there, where they arrived at about 10 o'clock at night. Deponent then left said Wilcox and went about 3 miles out of the city, in company with his brother, to his mother's farm, and stayed there that night. He returned next evening to the said Jenning's house, and could not find Wilcox and was then told by said Jennings that Wilcox had gone with him to the Temple, and that he (said Jennings) was in a few moments called away from Wilcox, and was told by the man who called him away, that he [Wilcox] was a spy, and was accused of harboring him as such; to which he replied, No! Jennings further stated that said Wilcox came to the city to mill, in the first place, and that shortly after he left him at the Temple, "I saw him with three men going toward the Masonic Hall" and then he afterward saw nothing of him. Deponent further states, that he remained in Nauvoo until Saturday morning the 20th inst., and made every enquiry for said Wilcox possible but could find nothing of him and returned home. He went back to Nauvoo on Monday morning, afterward, searching for Wilcox until the next Friday, when being able to find nothing of him, deponent went home. That on Tuesday before he left, he was taken by some Mormons to the Mansion Stable, where deponent hoped to find Wilcox, that on arriving there, he found 6 or 7 men there, to deponent unknown, guarded by 10 or 15 men well armed, that deponent was threatened by the Mormons there, that those men at the stable were prisoners.—Deponent further states that he could not find Wilcox there, nor any place else in Nauvoo, after the most diligent search, that he then left on Friday, after threats of personal violence to him, and that he believes from all these facts that said Wilcox has been murdered by said Mormons.

Subscribed and sworn to before me, this 1st day of October, 1845.

FRANKLIN J. BARTLETT, J. P.

•••• 13 ••••

Jacob Backenstos and his Proclamations

For a brief period in 1845, the most controversial figure in Hancock County was Jacob B. Backenstos. He had come to the county in 1843, perhaps with the backing of Stephen A. Douglas, to fill the office of circuit clerk. A non-Mormon, he quickly associated himself with the Mormon majority for political reasons. The very next year, he was elected to the state legislature on the strength of the Mormon plurality in the county. Of course, his pro-Mormon political opportunism aroused non-Mormon resentment, which increased in January 1845, when Backenstos made a speech to the legislature opposing revocation of the Nauvoo Charter—and denouncing the anti-Mormons in the process. In short, he became a divisive force in the county, and unfortunately, in August of 1845, Mormon voters elected him sheriff—to fill the position vacated by Minor Deming. The Mormons could not have chosen a man more widely hated among non-Mormons to be the chief law-enforcement officer in Hancock County; his election virtually guaranteed civil conflict.

When an anti-Mormon mob began burning Mormon houses in the southern part of the county—at Morleytown and later Green Plains and Bear Creek—supposedly in retaliation for depredations by Mormon thieves, Sheriff Backenstos tried to stop them. But his tactics were both foolish and repressive, and all he ultimately succeeded in doing was escalating the conflict. On 13 September, in the first of several proclamations, he demanded that the mobbers stop their house burning and called upon all law abiding citizens to join a "posse comitatus" to bring those responsible to justice. While no non-Mormons volunteered, vast numbers of Mormons did. So he issued another proclamation, dated 16 September, in which he asserted that the mobbers were out to kill him, recalling the episode in which Franklin A. Worrell was killed, and then issued a countywide call to arms. He wrote:

> I hereby call upon, and likewise command, every able bodied man throughout the county, to arm themselves in the best possible manner, and to resist any and all further violence on the part of the mob, and to permit no further destruction of property, and to arrest all those engaged in this wicked proceeding and destruction of

property, and threatening of lives, and I further command that the posse comitatus repair to the nearest points, invaded by the rioters, and to defend at the point of the bayonet, and at all hazards, the lives and property of the peaceable citizens.

In these words Backenstos legitimized military action by the Mormons, who became his "posse comitatus," riding throughout the county in search of non-Mormon mobbers. The posse quickly became part of the problem, roaming the countryside with no authority other than its own to maintain order. Many non-Mormons fled the county. According to one newspaper report, nearly half of the population of Carthage and Warsaw had left by late September. When some non-Mormons at Carthage threatened Mormon sympathizers, Backenstos took possession of the city with his posse and resorted to arbitrary arrests, unwarranted and unlawful searches, and intimidation. He then issued his third and fourth proclamations, trying to justify his actions.

Backenstos's third and fourth proclamations are published here. While it is clear from these documents that he wanted to put down the anti-Mormon mob, it is also apparent that he had started a civil war. What he should have done, of course, was seek outside assistance from Governor Thomas Ford. Instead he specifically asks to handle the situation himself and use extensive military operations to restore order, unsuccessfully, as it turned out. It is clear from the language in these proclamations ("detachments," "expedition," "artillery," "infantry," "forced march," "enemy," etc.) that Backenstos thought of himself as a military leader and took pride in commanding such a large force. Small wonder that those who did not accept his approach to resolving the situation often fled the county. In view of all this, his proud declaration, in Proclamation Four, that he had brought peace to Hancock County contradicted the facts.

These proclamations are from the 15 October 1845 *Warsaw Signal*, p. 2. All of Backenstos's proclamations appear together in that issue, including the first, second, and fifth, dated 25 September 1845, in which he rightly blames newspaper editor Thomas Sharp for encouraging the mobocratic activities of the non-Mormons.

<hr />

Proclamation 3

To the citizens of Hancock County, and the surrounding country:

Whereas the community at large may and do expect at my hands, a fair and impartial statement of facts, with regard to the riot which has been raging, and is still continuing its ravages with the firebrand and otherwise; since the issuing of my second proclamation the mob have become more infuriated then ever.

The Post Master at Carthage, Chauncy Robinson, Esq., who is also County Recorder, was compelled to flee from Carthage with his family, in order that their lives might be spared. Capt. Rose the Treasurer and Assessor of Hancock county, was also expelled from his residence in Carthage, and obliged to flee to some secure place with his family for safety.—At Warsaw Edward A. Bedell, Esq., Post Master of that place, and a Justice of the Peace of the Warsaw Precinct, was obliged to flee to save his life, giving him but a half minute time to prepare to go.—These gentlemen have been driven from their homes by force of arms, and threats of immediate death, if they offered any resistance.

Messrs. Bedell & Robinson, are well known with very many citizens of the adjoining counties, and they are favorably known too and are among our very best citizens in Hancock (and if there be merit in it they rank amongst the oldest settlers in the county). Capt. Rrose [sic] is much respected by all honorable men with whom he is acquainted. On the night of the 16th, I raised an armed force of mounted men to march to Carthage, to rescue my family and others threatened. On entering the town we were fired upon by some of the mobbers, who instantly fled. My heart sickens when I think of the distressed situation in which I found my family, in the hands of a gang of black hearted villains, guilty of all the crimes known to our laws. It is however due to say, that there were a few of the Carthagenians and Warsaw people, who have heretofore acted with the mob faction, who are opposed to this riot, yet, up to this time, they have not joined the standard of law and order; the families which I designed to rescue had all fled, with the exception of Mrs. Deming, the widow of the late Gen. Deming, who was of opinion that she might escape their vengeance, inasmuch as the death of her husband so recently, it was thought had appeased their wrath against the family.

After we had entered the town persons were seen running about with fire brands. Anticipating their intention of firing their own buildings, in order to charge the same upon the posse comitatus, under my command, we immediately took steps to prevent this, by threatening to put to the sword all those engaged in firing the place. We then directed our march towards Warsaw, and on reaching a point midway to that place, I was informed of new depredations by the mob. I sent my family to Nauvoo for safety, under a small guard, and took up a line of march in the direction of the rising smoke. On reaching a point about three miles from the rising flames, I divided the posse comitatus in order to surround those engaged in the burning; we were discovered by them.—On our approach the mobbers took flight, the posse pursuing with directions "to arrest them if possible, and to fire upon them if they would not be arrested." The house burners retreating towards one of their strong places at the speed of their horses, a part of the posse, pursuing at full speed, and firing upon them, killing two, and wounding, it is believed others. This occurred on Bear Creek, about two o'clock this after noon.

I commanded one of the detachments in person, and authorized the person who commanded the other. As I was then satisfied that the burners had fled from that place, we directed our line of march northwardly, when we were informed of the approach of a reinforcement of mounted men, who were ordered to reconnoitre, raised the people to defend, and aid them in defending the settlement against the depredations of the mob. We then directed our course to Nauvoo, performing a forced march of about 65 miles in the space of 20 hours. This expedition is the first effort at resistance to mob violence in the county, since the outbreak. I have now a posse comitatus, numbering upwards of 2000 well armed men, firm and ready to aid me in suppressing the riot, and in arresting them. I am happy in informing the citizens that 2000 additional armed men hold themselves in readiness to be called out when necessary.

To those honorable and worthy citizens in the adjoining counties, who have proffered their aid in quelling this disgraceful mob, I will say, after returning my grateful acknowledgements for the kind interest which they have manifested in defence of the rights of American citizens, the Constitution and the laws of our beloved country, that, as yet, we have confidence that I can command force sufficient within this county, to arrest or if that fails, to put to the sword every villain engaged in this inhuman outrage; I am sanguine of success, whether my life be spared or not. Gladly will we receive aid from any of the adjoining counties, for the suppression of the rioters, in the event of the force in this county be insufficient. If no considerable number of mobbers gather from without Hancock, success will crown our efforts. I am well advised that no considerable number from any of our adjoin[in]g counties, will come and act with any mob; and I now declare, that if the mob shall fire their own buildings, grain or other property, for the purpose of charging the same on my posse, I shall deal the same with them as tho' they destroyed the property of others, and arrest or put to the sword all such incendiaries.

Since my last proclamation, I have learned further particulars of the scoundrels, who were in pursuit of me on the highway on the 16th inst., the fact of which we fully set forth in said proclamation so far as was in my possession.—I now inform the public that Franklin A. Worrell was one of the four, who, on that occasion persued [*sic*] me; was shot by one of my posse, who I summoned on the spot to protect my life. Worrel[l] died the same day.

J. B. Backenstos.
Sheriff H. Co., Ill.

Hancock County, Ill.,
September 17th A.D. 1845

Proclamation 4

Since issuing proclamation No. 3 new things have transpired in which the community at large feel a deep and abiding interest, who expect from me, a fair, full and unvarnished statement of facts as they exist with regard to the rioters, if within my knowledge, as well as all my proceedings in attempting to suppress the same, with all the important facts as they occur during my progress.

On the evening of the 18th instant, I proceeded with 200 well armed mounted men, for the second time to the south-west part of the county, which had sustained nearly all the suffering and destruction by the mob, joining the detachment which I had previously detailed to reconnoitre, make arrest and prevent further burning. My intention was to attack the encampment of the rioters, on the following day and rout them. I received intelligence that they had changed their position, which caused me to countermand a previous order for a reinforcement of eight hundred infantry, and two pieces of ordnance. I also received intelligence that the mob were encamped in the bottom near the Mississippi river, below Warsaw, with at least eight hundred men and one piece of artillery. As I had previously determined to march into the camp of the rioters, and arrest or disperse them, I again ordered a reinforcement of four hundred infantry and one piece of artillery, with the intention of attacking the camp; this gave me the command of a posse with seven hundred men and one piece of ordnance.

Knowing the courage, bravery, and skill of the forces under my command, I was willing to make an attack upon the enemy entrenched behind their fortifications. I then took up a line of march to Carthage, the county seat of Hancock, the residence of nearly all of the notorious Carthage Greys, and the head quarters of a band of the most infamous and villainous scoundrels that ever infested any community, who have, for the last two years abandoned labor and the ordinary avocations of good citizens; they are generally poor, a few have been trading upon borrowed capital; but they are selfish and will not even trust their own mob friends. Many of those have considerable large families; they must live and do live;—how, I would ask do such men get a living? men without means and with families, too, and who do nothing but brawl about grog shops, cursing and abusing better citizens than they can be; men who are openly upholding mob violence, aiding and abetting the extermination of the very best and oldest settlers in this county, forsooth they have the independence of differing with them in opinion. Did not the community in this and the surrounding counties already know the names of those heaven daring land pirates, I should give their names at full length. I entered the town of Carthage about the setting of the sun, as I had a large number of writs for the arrest of those accused of burning houses, barns and stacks of grain. I ordered my posse to surround the town and permit none to escape, but to bring every man to the Court House in order that I might arrest such persons as I had writs against, and detain such other persons in custody as are accused by respectable persons until writs could be procured, that they might be dealt with according to the law. All those against whom I had writs fled before I could have them surrounded except one Anthony Barkman.

Col. Gettis, was arrested on suspicion of being one of the ring leaders; he is charged with having ordered out his regiment in order to join the mob, orders signed by him, directing to and commanding the Captains of companies under his command, requiring them immediately to call out their respective companies; this Col. Gettis admits, but claims that he was commanded to do so by a superior officer, viz: Col. Levi Williams, who claims to hold and have command of this brigade, comprising Hancock, McDonough and Schuyler counties, by virtue of seniority by commission; Col. Gettis agreed to remain until morning, when I informed him that he would not be detained, as I was unable to get positive testimony that he was engaged in burning; or that he advised others so to do, however, several suspicious circumstances connected with the conduct and acts of Col. G., for several days previous to my entrance into Carthage; for instance, Col. Levi Williams, John McCauly, a notorious advocate of the mobbers, several others of the same gang and this same Col. Gettis, held a secret meeting in Carthage on the 16th inst. Col. G. is a strong advocate for the extermination of a portion of the community of this county. Some of the law and order citizens of Carthage and vicinity felt disposed to censure me for not putting him under arrest, as it is believed he is a co-operator of the notorious Levi Williams.

After the posse was put in motion in the direction of Carthage, I addressed a communication to Col. Levi Williams and others, in the words and figures following to wit:

2 o'clock P.M., Sept. 18th, 1845.
Head Quarters of the Sheriff of Hancock county, commanding the posse comitatus of the Southern detachment in said county.

To the Mob gathered in the s.w. part of Hancock county, Ills., commanded and directed by Col. Levi Williams and a few others, who as it is said have a strong force under their influence and guidance, and who are also strongly fortified as I am informed, and who have as I *know* destroyed much property with force of arms, by going about this county shooting at, and compelling peaceable citizens to leave their homes, and applying firebrands to their buildings, grain, &c, and otherwise by all manner of inhuman treatment to the sick, and helpless women and children. It is unnecessary for me again to remind you of the magnitude of the crimes of which you already stand charged. Some of the sick women and children who were compelled to leave their sick beds under your wicked and fiendish fiat, have since died as it is believed in consequence of exposure to the inclemency of the weather and the rays of the scorching sun, thus adding murder to the lesser crime of arson. My duty as an officer is defined by law. Your mob proceedings require of me an effort to quell you in your mad career if possible without the shedding of blood. You will all do me the justice to say that I have spared no pains in endeavoring to accomplish such a desirable result; I issued proclamations, and took pains that copies were sent to your mob camps—you know my duty. You were advised openly of my determination and policy which were fully set forth in my proclamations. You have not desisted in your depredations, but on the other hand you became more emboldened than before.

In the mean time I have raised a posse comitatus in order to arrest all engaged in this riot if possible, and in case they should not submit to law and be arrested, to fire upon them or put them to the sword.

The painful necessity of firing upon a party of your depredations, became apparent on the 16th inst., at which time several of the burners were killed; we caught them in the act of burning buildings. I will close this communication by again appealing to you in the name of humanity, the law, and the good of yourselves and our country that you instantly desist your mobbing and burning; deliver yourselves into my hands to be dealt with according to law, that is to say, you the leaders; and to surrender into my hands the ordnance which you procured through fraud and deception; and that you also deliver into my hands all the State arms which you have twice heretofore refused to surrender upon the demand of the Executive of the State by his authorized agent; and forthwith disperse each all of you to your homes and pursue ordinary avocations of good peaceable citizens. Such a course will be honorable to you, and will save the shedding of much blood.

I am authorized to receive and take charge of all the public arms in this county.

It is expected that you will comply with the above reasonable requests. I hereby pledge myself to protect you in all your constitutional rights, and that you shall be dealt with according to the laws of our country. Should you see fit to submit to the laws and requirements as set forth above, you will on the part of the mob, communicate to me in writing at the Chapman place, midway between Carthage and Warsaw, on to-morrow at 12 o'clock M. Should you not submit or refuse to reply, your silence will be taken as a refusal to surrender to the laws, when you must expect to meet the consequences.

Respectfully yours, &c.,

J. B. Backenstos

Sheriff of Hancock county, Illinois

P.S.—I send by the bearer hereof my last proclamation, No. 3.

On the following day Mr. Calkins, the express, returned, and stated that Colonel Williams had crossed the river into the State of Missouri, whither he had fled with the following communication in reply to my letter of yesterday:

September 19th, 1845.

J.B. Backenstos.—Sir:—I received a communication yesterday, thro' the hand of Mr. Calkins, addressed to me in the character of the "leader of the mob." I entertain no communication, neither will I make any reply in that character.—Your communication bespeaks the character of its author, and meets from me that indignant contempt it so richly deserves. If you were worthy the notice of a gentleman, sir, I would meet you on any field, but as you occupy a station so far beneath the dignity of a *man* that I shall not condescend to have anything to do with you in any manner, shape or form. You can pursue what course with the "mob" that you please. I answer not for them, but rest assured that they are at all times ready for you.

Levi Williams.

I am directed by Gov. Ford to collect the public arms which have been demanded in vain twice before from the mobbers to wit: the arms of the Carthage

Greys and the arms in the hands of Capts. Grover and Davis at Warsaw; under this order and instruction I directed my posse at Carthage to collect all the public arms which were so unfortunately placed in the hands of officers and privates who have on many occasions used them as means to terrify, insult and abuse the peaceable citizens of our County. I have collected nine stands and a part of the accoutrements and will endeavor to get the balance.

I have them in my possession subject to the order of the Commander-in-Chief of the Illinois Militia; they are not and shall not be used by the posse under my command, as I have no authority from the Governor for so doing.

The posse under my command have been prompt and obedient to all my orders, with the exception of one order in relation to the collection of the State arms at Carthage. I ordered the posse to ask for and receive from any person in possession of any arms of the Carthage Greys, and deliver them to me at the Court House. This order was disobeyed or misunderstood, by two of the posse by bringing three guns, the private property of citizens, and one man quarrelled with a lady and used in her presence, ungentlemanly language. I ordered the three men immediately under arrest, placed them under guard, sent them home, and returned the guns.

After leaving a sufficient force to defend the place against the mobbers both within and without the town of Carthage, at about 12 o'clock on the 20th inst., we took up our line of march to the place of rendezvous at the Chapman place, between Warsaw and Carthage, thence to proceed against the mob encampment with a design to arrest or rout them from their hiding place. Before I reached midway to Warsaw, I received positive intelligence that the mob had fled the county and state by crossing the Mississippi river at Warsaw with all their arms, cannon, &c., to Missouri. I marched the posse to Warsaw for the purpose of making arrests; remained a short time:—when I directed the infantry and artillery northwardly on the prairie road with the mounted forces. I am now on the bank of the Mississippi river near Montebello.

Since the firing upon the mob at Bear Creek on the 16th inst., there has been no burning of any houses, barns, grain, stacks, nor any thing else that has come to my knowledge. The mobbers, rioters, and other outlaws have principally fled without the limits of this county. Peace and quiet, law and order, has again been restored in Hancock county.

Therefore, I, Jacob Backenstos, Sheriff of Hancock county, hereby proclaim the county in peace; that the rioters have dispersed and gone to their homes, or fled this county and State. Let all good citizens who were expelled by the mobbers, from their homes, and those who fled from the county for security against mob violence, return to their homes, and they shall be protected. I have an armed forced stationed in the Court House at Carthage, for the protection of the officers of the county, who are compelled by law to reside at the county seat, and for the protection of all persons having business at, or who may desire to visit Carthage, and also to protect from insult and mob violence the inhabitants of Carthage and the surrounding country. I have a number of small scouting parties reconnoitering the county to keep the peace and protect the settlements and make arrests of those who are known to be guilty of the riot, in whose hands writs have been placed. I desire that the citizens will aid them in ferreting them out, that they may be arrested and brought to justice.

J. B. Backenstos,
Sheriff of Hancock county, Illinois

Bank of the Mississippi River, near Montebello,

Sept. 20, A.D. 1845

P.S.—The Warsaw Signal Extra of the 18th Sept., contains its usual amount of willful and malicious falsehoods. It is unnecessary for me to deny any one statement; I pronounce the entire Extra a tissue of lies from beginning to end, so far as they purport to give the news of the killing of Worrell and McBratney, and the balance set forth in relation to the difficulties in our county, and I hold myself responsible to prove the same false, by men of the best standing.

J. B. B., Sheriff

•◗◗● *14* ●◖◖•

An Eyewitness Account of the Military Occupation of Carthage

The effort by Sheriff Backenstos to control Hancock County by means of a Mormon posse seemed to many non-Mormons a realization of their deepest fear—loss of liberty through Mormon domination. One man who shared that view was Jason H. Sherman (1813–?), a native of Maine who had moved to the county in 1841 to practice law. He was a resident of Carthage until after the Mormons left for the West and served as Hancock County school commissioner from 1847 to 1851. Sherman later moved to Ithaca, New York, where he became a judge and, toward the end of his life, wrote a ten-part series entitled "Reminiscences of the Mormons in Illinois" for the local newspaper. This excerpt is from number seven of his series, which appeared in the *Ithaca Journal* on 4 May 1886, p. 2. (An earlier, less elaborate version of the same episode, the Backenstos takeover of Carthage, was given by Sherman as an affidavit, published in the *Warsaw Signal*, 22 October 1845, p. 2.)

On 19 September 1845, Sherman witnessed the activities of Sheriff Backenstos and his Mormon posse in Carthage, and he was brought in for questioning at the courthouse along with the rest of the male population. His account captures the enormous fear that gripped the citizens of Carthage at that time—until Governor Ford sent General John J. Hardin into the county, at the head of 300–400 troops, to free the occupied town and restore civil rights. Hardin was part of a four-man commission appointed by Ford to deal with the situation. The others were Congressman Stephen A. Douglas, Attorney General James A. McDougall, and Supreme Court Clerk W. B. Warren.

The next night [18 September 1845] there was another panic in Carthage. About sunset two spies approached near town on the Nauvoo road, and, after reconnoitering a few minutes, hastily departed. At dark sentinels were placed out on that and the road toward the west, whence invasion was apprehended, with instructions to discharge pistols and both run in if danger threatened. At 11 o'clock the sentinel on the west road was approached by two horsemen, who, on being challenged, galloped back. Imagining that these might be scouts in advance of a large body, the sentinel fired and put spurs to his horse. The writer was doing military duty that night as sentinel on the north-west or Nauvoo road, with a rusty horse-pistol that had been loaded ever since dangers began to thicken, and mounted upon a powerful white charger, in comparison with which Zachery [*sic*] Taylor's "old whitey" (as I can testify) was but a common animal. Famous for intelligence, as well as powerful and swift, some said he knew about as much as his master,—but that, of course, was only a strong form of compliment to the horse, without any sinister squint whatever. When he heard the sentinel's shot, Old Jim (for that was his name) raised his head high and stood all alert. Holding my rusty piece aloft and athwart the road, I let it belch, and it kicked itself off into the darkness, with a spiteful spring that would have been fatal to any near-by Mormon in that direction. That was the only time I ever pulled trigger for warlike purposes; and that resulted in filling the town with consternation. Instantly, scarcely waiting for the word, Old Jim darted homeward with a speed rarely surpassed, and a thunder of hoofs, never. The road was smooth and hard as iron; and in the stillness of the hour the reverberation of his foot-falls was like that of a troop upon a race. The citizens heard the pistol and were alarmed. They heard the sound as of many horses' feet on the Nauvoo road and thought the Mormons were upon them. On reaching the public square, I found a scene of indescribable terror. "What does this mean," I asked, "have they come in from the west?" "No, it is on the Nauvoo road!" "Not a Mormon there," said I. "We heard cavalry coming upon the full run!" "It was only Old Jim and I," I said, beginning to comprehend the situation, and hastening to allay the excitement as well as I could. No hostile force came. The horsemen seen by the sentinel belonged, as was afterwards ascertained, to a party out robbing farmers in that neighborhood.

After dispersing the rioters (in the hinterland) Backenstos returned with his troops to Nauvoo. Next day he went back with increased forces, but finding nobody to attack, left a body of infantry in camp, and came to Carthage. This was September 19th. We had no warning of his coming till troops came galloping into town from the west and south a little after sundown. The chronic danger, and frequent alarms, had caused removals of women and children till there were not scarcely twenty families left, with perhaps fifty men. Some of these upon discovery of the invasion started to fly, but were mostly overtaken and brought back. A few, special objects of Mormon hatred, got away. It was scarcely five minutes after the first sight of them before horsemen thronged the streets and surrounded every house, and a guard environed the town. Parties were sent out to the nearest surrounding settlements, and men taken from their terrified families and driven in. At length orders were passed around to bring the prisoners to headquarters, when we were all driven to the Courthouse in such haste that some who were standing outside their doors without their hats were not permitted to get them. Guards were left at our houses during our absence with an omenous [*sic*] display of weapons. At the Courthouse all were detained more than an hour, surrounded by hundreds of sinister looking wretches, who brandished with menacing gestures their instruments of human butchery. Backenstos then came and made a speech, in which he lauded the bravery of his tried soldiers, and said he was raking the county for a number of scoundrels, whom he would pursue until he caught them, without limit as to time or space; after which he came round and discharged most of us one by one, and sent us home with well-armed escorts—that is to say, escorts having guns, swords, pistols and bowie-knives—for with less than these a Mormon was but half armed. Some however were detained under guard till the next day, as he was not certain, he said, whether he had warrants for them or not, and had not time to examine his papers to see. It was his intention to arrest, or rather to seize and carry to Nauvoo (for he had no warrants), ten or twelve Carthagenians against whom he had personal ill-will, or who were known as very active anti-Mormons. For such he and his ruffians searched houses, and questioned children, shaking swords over their heads to make them tell where they were. As it happened those persons had either left the county beforehand, or escaped from town as the troops entered.

The next morning Backenstos said he had an order from the governor for the state arms which had been furnished the Carthage Greys, a volunteer company, under the same law by which the Nauvoo legion had been supplied. He produced no order, but, resistance being vain, the arms were surrendered. Professing to believe that some were withheld and secreted, he ordered houses to be searched for them, both of the families remaining and of those who had fled. His men rummaged drawers and trunks and scattered their contents, and left open doors and yard gates of the absent. In some cases they took private arms and other articles of property. Backenstos went away at noon with all his forces but fifty, which he left garrisoned in the court house to keep military possession of the town. These patrolled the streets, spied about houses, and came up to ha[s]ten whenever two or three were seen talking together. They affected to believe we meditated harm against our postmaster, and followed us with drawn swords whenever we went to the postoffice. They had orders to force us into the ranks, put arms in our hands and make us fight against our friends, if any should come to rescue the town; and orders to put us to the sword if found firing our houses—a thing which Mormons say the Missourians did and charged on them.

Leaving Carthage thus garrisoned, the sheriff led his troops to Warsaw, the chief commercial town of the county, situated upon the river below the rapids. He found the place deserted—the citizens having anticipated his coming and crossed the river into Missouri. He then returned to Nauvoo, leaving no garrison at Warsaw, as it might be cut off by an attack from Missouri before he could reach it with assistance from Nauvoo. From that time he kept bands of troopers scouring the county in quest of persons known as openly active anti-Mormons, or who were personally obnoxious to him or to leading Mormons. Other parties, with or without official authorization, were out plundering night and day, taking horses from stables before the eyes of their owners in some instances, and driving cattle from farms into Nauvoo, where they were slaughtered and salted down for the "Church of Jesus Christ of Latter-Day Saints."

Upon information of the condition of things in Hancock county, Gov. Ford called out a force of militia, and dispatched it thither under command of Gen. J. J. Hardin, of Jacksonville, with discretionary power for the restoration of order. While he was on his way, Backenstos issued a proclamation pronouncing the governor's call for militia a forgery, characterizing Gen. Hardin and his troops as a mob, and declaring his determination to treat them as such. The general and his forces, with Stephen A. Douglas and Attorney-General McDougall upon his staff, arrived at 1 o'clock on the 28th, taking Backenstos into custody, and giving his soldiers fifteen minutes to leave town—which they did not overstay. Then ended our nine days' captivity. . . .

15

An Anti-Mormon Plea for Support

In the midst of the conflict in the fall of 1845, while Backenstos's posse was in control of Carthage, some of the non-Mormons in the county drafted a manifesto to residents nearby, explaining why they were opposed to the Mormons remaining there. In strong terms they describe some of the real and imagined crimes of the Mormons and ask for support in ridding Hancock County of them. They also express regret for the killings at Carthage in 1844 and the subsequent house burnings, for which all non-Mormons were unjustly blamed, but they fail to recognize that their approach to Mormon violence is equally unjust. They would force all Mormons from the county rather than hold individual perpetrators responsible for their lawlessness. Of course, they felt that law enforcement itself had become mob rule under Sheriff Backenstos, but their approach could only further polarize the contending forces.

The manuscript published here for the first time is a virtually unknown epistle that clearly shows the efforts of the non-Mormons to enlist public sympathy. It is printed by permission of Archives and Special Collections, Western Illinois University Library, Macomb.

———••••◆••••———

Hancock County, Sept. 20, 1845

To the quiet and honorable citizens of the agoining [sic] counties, the state at large and agoining States. Your fellow citizens the Old Settlers, Antimormons of Hancock county are and have for a line [sic] time been in trouble. We ask and beseach [sic] you at this time to look, examine, ponder and consider well our many difficulties and sore grievances and in candor ask yourselves if you were in our situation what you would do and what course you would pursue.

We humbly ask you to enquire and examine into the history of the Mormon church and a list of our part of our grievances and see if it is not a true history. No band of Mormons wherever they have resided, whether in Ohio Missouri or Illinois, have they not been banded together to protect each other, right or wrong? Have they not armed themselves for that purpose of oppressing their neighbors? Do not the Mormon dupes render implicit obedience to their leadership? Do they not almost daily steal our horses cattle sheep hogs . . . [specific grievances:]

1. Is it not known that they plunder, rob and steal from us daily?

2. Is it not known that they have grossly insulted and abused peac[e]able and quiet citizens of this and other States for no other offence than being caught in Nauvoo on honest and honorable business?

3. Is it not known that they have Whittled and Whistled honest and honorable Peace officers and citizens of the county out of Nauvoo that had to go there on business?

4. Is it not known that officers of this county with sevil [civil] and criminal writs have made arrests in Nauvoo and that the Saints of that place has as frequently rescued said prisoners and compelled the officers to leave the city?

5. Is it not known that they rescued a prisoner from the United States marshal in Nauvoo?

6. Is it not known that they treated the authority of the State Marshal and United States Marshal with utter contempt when in Nauvoo on business?

7. Is it not known that the Mormons have arrayed themselves against the laws of this State and set the authorities thereof at defiance and trampled upon our beloved institutions?

8. Is it not known that they have threatened the lives and the destruction of the property of the Antimormons indiscriminately?

9. Is it not known that they have threatened to poison the wells of the Antimormons to revenge the death of their pretended prophet?

10. Is it not known that they have a bogus factory in Nauvoo which the authorities of this county can not reach?

11. Is it not known that they have repeatedly boasted that this county is theirs, and they would force the old settlers to leave it?

12. Is it not known that the leaders the twelve apostles (as they call themselves) teach and practice poligmy [*sic*]?

13. Is it not known that by perjury they have screened themselves from paying their just and honest debts?

14. Is it not known that they destroyed a printing press and expelled citizens from Nauvoo because they daired [*sic*] expose their hel[l]ish designs?

15. Is it not known that the notorious Backenstos, the pliant tool of Mormonism in the halls of this State branded the old settlers with infamy in order to sustain the Mormon charter?

16. Is it not known that Mormon witnesses at our last term of court perjured themselves in the presence of hundreds in order to procure the conviction of in[n]ocent men?

17. Is it not know[n] that one of the foulest murders on record (and perhaps many others) was committed in Nauvoo by some of the gang of rob[b]ers that make that place their head quarters?

18. Is it not known that the crimes of Perjury, Bribery, Conspiracy, Rob[b]ery, Bigamy, Adultery and Fornication was prefer[r]ed against the Mormons to court?

19. Is it not known that at the last term of our court a majority of the grand jury were Mormons and that they would not receive or hear any evidence against Mormons?

20. Is it not known that the Mormons forcibly took possession of Carthage and drove the defenceless citizens with many others at the point of the bayonet, making the men all prisoners, and broke open houses and plundered, declaring themselves to be the Sheriff's posse and acting under his command?

21. Is it not known that J. B. Backenstos, Sheriff of this county with his posse did commit wilful murder on the open prairie? Read his proclamation then judge for your Selfs.

22. Is it not known that the Sheriff's posse broke open, rob[b]ed and plundered houses, tore down fences to [get] grain, drove off and Butchered cattle and said it was Sheriff's orders (to Justify)?

23. Is it not known that the Sheriff or Mormons have caused writs to be issued against peac[e]able citizens that were at home during the riotous movements in this county to take them prisoners dead or alive for rioters and houseburners because they dared express their opinion against the Mormon church?

24. Is it not known that the whole Antimormon population of this county are implicated by the Mormons as Mobocrats, rioters and houseburners, against whom they have sworn vengeance when it is known but a few were concerned in it?

25. Is it not known that many of our citizens, peac[e]able and quiet farmers have been rob[b]ed of their horses, sheep and cattle, and several of their household goods by the Mormons?

26. Is it not known that several of our old citizens have been to Nauvoo in pursuit of their stolen property and there made prisoner and not allowed to walk the streets, but ordered to leave the city at the peril of their lives and ordered not

[to] look about the suburbs of the city, and ordered to stope [*sic*] and told if they were seen again within five miles of the city their life would pay the forfeit. . . .

27. Is it not known that the Mormons for the last years have controlled the county and elected to office whom they chose, pliant demagog[ue]s or their own dupes?

28. Is it not known that a few base demagog[ue]s succomb [*sic*] to the Mormons for the sake of office and the spoils of the county, calling them selves Jack Mormons, [the] law and order party to cloke [*sic*] themselves from merited odium abroad?

29. Is it not known that this county under Mormon rule and dictation is emersed [*sic*] in a debt of thousands!

30. Is it not known that the Mormon leaders sustain themselves by base fraud and deceit practiced upon their wily and willing dupes?

31. Is it not known that the foregoing is a true outline history and picture of the Mormon church? Humanity weeps and shudders at the thought.

The above and many other outrages are fresh in the recollection and are well known to the old settlers of this county. (The killing of the Smiths and the burning of houses we do not approve.) Have the old settlers not sought the protection of law? Have they not repeatedly appealed to the law for redress? The law has lost its efficacy in this county and the appeal is in vain. Crime stalks the county in the Mormon garb. Is it then Strange or misterious [*sic*] that the Antimormons should be exasperated to madness? Is it to be wondered at that they should violate the law when in the heighth of their passions?

Ask yourselves the question.

Fellow citizens, the crisis is a trying one and on you depends our fate and your doom. We must have assistance to drive the Mormons from amongst us or we must leave the county. Longer together we cannot live!! If we are forced to yield and leave the county. You in a short time will be compelled by the same ruthless band to follow us and leave the fairest portion of this state in the hands of thieves, plunderers, rob[b]ers and assassins.

Resolved that we whose names are hereunto subscribed residents of _____ Precincts in the county of _____ do sympathize with the Old Settlers, Antimormons of Hancock County in their many troubles and difficulties and we verily believe that the strong arm of the Law does not afford them a sufficient protection and g[u]arantee against the increasing evils and depredations of their Mormon neighbors, and for the better protection and assistance of our Antimormon friends in Hancock County we deem it expedient and of the highest importance that we form ourselves into a company for the better and more sure accomplishment of our purposes in cooperating with our friends and neighbors. We therefore agree to hold our selves in re[a]diness at a moments warning to the assistance of the Antimormons of Hancock County, and should the Mormons refuse to leave the county in peace as they found it we agree to use such means as may prove sufficient to remove them, and to this end we pledge our selves each to the other our lives, our bodily pains and sacred Honors.

————— •••• *16* ••••———————

Mason Brayman Assesses the Situation

As violence between the Mormons and non-Mormons was occurring in Hancock County in the fall of 1845, Thomas Ford was not entirely idle. He sent troops into the county once again to restore order and appointed Mason Brayman, attorney for the state, to negotiate a treaty between the Mormons and the old settlers. The treaty quickly turned into a vehicle for the peaceful removal of the Mormons from the state beginning early in 1846.

Brayman spent several weeks in the county in November 1845 and was disgusted with what he saw. Both sides, he found, had become so intransigent that any compromise was nearly impossible. Neither side was innocent, he concluded, and he was clearly upset with the general lawlessness as both sides fought it out for supremacy in the county. Equally important, he recognized that, hidden by this conflict, renegades were flying under the colors of both groups and enjoying an ideal opportunity to rob and pillage while the authorities were otherwise occupied. Brayman had no love for either group and recognized that they had to be separated; accordingly he worked out the Mormon withdrawal from Illinois.

The letter printed here was written by Brayman on 16 November 1845 to an unnamed correspondent, but there is internal evidence that it might have been Governor Ford or some other state official. In it he comments on the lawlessness of both sides, the efforts of the troops sent into Hancock County from Quincy, Illinois, to restore order, and the concerted efforts of the anti-Mormons to expel the Mormons from the county by violence. He also describes the death of Edmund Durfee, a Mormon gunned down by an anti-Mormon mob. The letter is part of the Mason Brayman Papers, Chicago Historical Society. It is published here for the first time.

————————— ••••◉•••• —————————

Carthage Ill
Sunday Night Nov 16, 1845

Dear Sir: —

Depredations on both sides continue, and I am convinced that a general outbreak is intended. Several robberies have been committed by the Mormons during the past week. A [?], a pair of horses, two fat oxen, sheep, hogs, &c., are "among the missing." They continue to send out spies, patrols, and armed companies, prowling about the prairies and interrupting travellers.

On Wednesday night the Anti-Mormons, about 25 in number, burned the house of *Rice*, on the road to Pontoosuc about 12 miles from here, first taking out the family, and after keeping them in custody, until the house was in a blaze, released them and fled. Property mostly saved. This is the house in which the Council is Said to have been held, by which it was voted to murder Daubenmeyer, some weeks since. Maj. Warren and myself with a couple of officers of the Quincy Rifles scoured the Neighborhood yesterday morning and succeeded in identifying part of the burners, and we are waiting for the arrival of an *affidavit* from Nauvoo to commence making arrests. So far, our movements are Secret, but as soon as proper the rascals will be taken.

Today information came, of an attempt to burn the House of one Hancock, a Mormon near Lima during last night—and the Murder of a man named *Durfee* under the following circumstances, as related by a Son of Hancock, who brought the intelligence this afternoon. Hancock's house had been threatened. Last night, a company of men set fire to a stack of straw near the barn. Persons sleeping in the barn came out, and while endeavoring to prevent the fire from reaching the barn were fired upon. They started to go to the House—a general volley was fired, killing Durfee on the Spot. No shots were fired by the Mormons. On firing, the villains fled, setting fire to a crib of some hundred bushels of corn as they went. None were identified, but I *think* they *can and will* be.

Maj. Warren, immediately left with 30 men, and will arrive to-night. I am anxious to learn the result.—Thorough and Severe measures are necessary to put a stop to these outrages.

But I regard this as only the beginning of New and Still more serious troubles. I am in possession of information which convinced me that a Secret but general organization has been in progress in this and the Surrounding Counties for the purpose of depredating upon the Mormons and producing a State of things which will bring on a Collision—to End in their expulsion from the State at once. Military Companies are organizing in various places. At Mt. Sterling, Dr. Singleton was very busy—has two companies (110 men) and what is most Strange and unfortunate, he has just received from Alton Sixty five Stand of *Cavalry Equipments*, pistols swords, &c.—it is said by order of yourself. *How* is *this*? I suspect some mistake—some fraud, for surely, these arms, so much needed by our men here, ought not to be given to Dr. Singleton for the purpose of arming men about to set the laws of the State at defiance. These arms came from Alton to Quincy, to the Care of *A. Jonas* who is chairman of the *Military Committee*. It seems to me that quite enough of the State arms have been disposed of in this mischivous [*sic*] way, and until they are reclaimed, the authorities will be *powerless*. . . .

I write in haste. Most I have written is of a *private nature*, but the general facts respecting the burning, and the Murder may be used to keep the public mind informed on the subject. . . .

PART VI

THE EXODUS AND THE BATTLE OF NAUVOO

Mormon leader Brigham Young. Courtesy of Archives and Special Collections, Western Illinois University Library, Macomb.

Part VI

Introduction

The Mormon conflict ended twice. On 24 September 1845, the Saints agreed to leave Illinois, capitulating to non-Mormon pressure which had expanded well beyond the limits of Hancock County.[1] It was a reluctant exodus, which began in early February 1846 and resulted in the departure of perhaps twelve thousand Latter Day Saints by late spring. The second ending of the conflict was violent. After the exodus had virtually ceased in June 1846, the more aggressive non-Mormons used intimidation and mob action to force the remaining Saints out. That effort culminated in the Battle of Nauvoo, which occurred in mid-September. Several hundred non-Mormon troops—a posse that had redefined its purpose and become a mob—clashed with the city's defenders, who eventually surrendered. A few men were killed and others were wounded. Much of the credit for keeping casualties to a minimum belongs to a committee of men from Quincy, who urged an end to the fighting and worked out the treaty that ended it.[2] The non-Mormon troops then occupied the city and forced the thousand or so remaining Mormons to leave.

The final stages of the Mormon conflict have not generated nearly as much scholarly interest as the earlier ones. The best modern account of events in 1845 and 1846 is still Robert Bruce Flanders's *Nauvoo: Kingdom on the Mississippi*, which was published in 1965, well before the explosion of Mormon scholarship in the 1970s when Leonard J. Arrington, the Latter-day Saints Church historian, threw open the church archives to professional scholars.[3] But Flanders does not even mention such prominent figures as William Pickett and Thomas Brockman, without whom the climactic battle would probably not have occurred.

Aside from the seventh volume of *History of the Church of Jesus Christ of Latter-day Saints*, the most extensive account of the events that closed the conflict is a slim book that is contemporaneous with the Mormon era, Josiah B. Conyers's *A Brief History of the Leading Causes of the Hancock Mob in the Year 1846*, published just at the end of the Mormon withdrawal from Illinois. Still useful, it provides many documents that the author gathered from Illinois newspapers. Conyers recognized that the forcible expulsion of the Saints was an unparalleled act of lawlessness, but he understood little about the underlying causes of the conflict that had culminated in the Battle of Nauvoo.

During 1845 the Mormons' superior numbers allowed them to control Hancock County politically and—under Sheriff Backenstos—militarily, but the non-Mormons received increasing sympathy and support from people in surrounding areas. That is not surprising, for residents outside the county shared the same essential anxiety about the Mormons, whose militant theocracy was inherently threatening to an open, democratic society. Indeed, as the resolutions of the nine-county non-Mormon convention reveal (Part VI, Document 2), the Mormons would have eventually come into conflict with Americans anywhere in the country.[4]

In a sense the Mormons realized that, too, but they expressed their understanding of the incompatibility between their religious goals and American society in mythic terms. Continued non-Mormon opposition was seen as verification of the social wickedness that had caused the Saints to establish a separatist theocracy in the first place. The Mormon myth of persecuted innocence was, in fact, always self-fulfilling, for acting on it—by establishing a protective theocracy within a larger democratic society—inevitably aroused opposition. By leaving the United States, the Mormons would simply be achieving a more complete separation from the unrighteous, prefiguring the profound separation of Israel and Babylon, the children of God and the children of Satan, at the Judgment.[5] As Mormon rank-and-filer Joseph Grafton Hovey said of the exodus,

> We can then shake the dust from our garments and leave this nation. . . . In our patience we will possess our souls and work out a more exceeding and eternal weight of glory. We will withdraw the power and priesthood from the Gentiles for the greater consolation of Israel, when the wilderness shall blossom as the rose and Babylon fall like a mill stone cast into the sea. The just shall live by faith but the folly of fools will perish. . . .[6]

Hovey and other Mormons failed to recognize that the exodus ultimately resulted from the dichotomous Mormon myth itself, which idealized the Saints and demonized the people who actively opposed them as well as those who disagreed with them and their values but were otherwise benign, such as Thomas Ford.[7] The identity of the Saints was symbolized by the expanding separatist theocracy of Nauvoo. Once the myth had divided the county, only two results were possible: the triumph of God's chosen people (i.e., all of America would become the Mormon Zion, as Smith had prophesied), or their temporary defeat and later victory over the wicked through the power of God. Either result would verify Mormon belief, but self-criticism, compromise, and unification with others would not, so those American values were not part of the Mormon mind-set.[8]

Unfortunately, by persisting in their efforts to build a theocracy, the Mormons aroused the fear of despotism in those whom they called Gentiles, and under the pressures of political anxiety and social polarization, myth eventually led to countermyth.[9] The non-Mormons in turn demonized the Saints while viewing themselves as the virtuous defenders of their highest ideal, democracy. The results were a massive failure of tolerance, a loss of commitment to the common good, and a conflict fueled by fear. Comprehension of this unfortunate process, as it occurred in Hancock County 150 years ago, is the most valuable legacy that our pluralistic society can acquire from the Mormon war.

Notes

1. This activity is described in Robert B. Flanders, *Nauvoo: Kingdom on the Mississippi* (Urbana: University of Illinois Press, 1965), 331–36.

2. One of the members of this committee was Henry Asbury. He recounted his perspective on the events in *Reminiscences of Quincy, Illinois, Containing Historical Events, Anecdotes, Matters Concerning Old Settlers and Old Times, Etc.* (Quincy: D. Wilcox and Sons, 1882), 161–68.

3. Flanders, *Nauvoo*, 324–41, devotes about twelve pages of his sizable history to the events of 1845 and only six pages to 1846. The only scholar to pay significant attention to the postmartyrdom period is Annette P. Hampshire, whose article, "The Triumph of Mobocracy in Hancock County, 1844–1846," *Western Illinois Regional Studies* 5 (Spring 1982): 17–37, is drawn from her larger, sociologically oriented study, *Mormonism in Conflict: The Nauvoo Years* (New York: Edwin Mellen Press, 1985). On the importance of Leonard Arrington's role as Mormon history promoter, see Davis Bitton, "Ten Years in Camelot: A Personal Memoir," *Dialogue: A Journal of Mormon Thought* 16 (Autumn 1983): 9–20. It could be argued that Arrington was the catalyst that made possible the "new Mormon history." A good overview of this aspect of Mormon scholarship can be found in D. Michael Quinn, ed., *The New Mormon History: Revisionist Essays on the Past* (Salt Lake City: Signature Books, 1992).

4. This is basically the conclusion of the brilliant analysis by Marvin S. Hill, *Quest for Refuge: The Mormon Flight from American Pluralism* (Salt Lake City: Signature Books, 1989).

5. The Mormons often thought of themselves in distinctive terms as the literal inheritors of ancient Judaism and the new children of Israel. See Melodie Moench, "Nineteenth Century Mormons: The New Israel," *Dialogue: A Journal of Mormon Thought* 12 (Spring 1979): 42–56; Jan Shipps, *Mormonism: The Story of a New Religious Tradition* (Urbana: University of Illinois Press, 1985); Grant Underwood, "Seminal Versus Sesquicentennial Saints: A Look at Mormon Millennialism," *Dialogue: A Journal of Mormon Thought* 14 (Spring 1981): 32–44.

6. Joseph G. Hovey, "Autobiography," pp. 33–34, Archives, Harold B. Lee Library, Brigham Young University, Provo, Utah.

7. This process of dehumanizing the opposition and creating an "us/them" dichotomy was also used in relation to the Haun's Mill Massacre. See Alma R. Blair, "The Haun's Mill Massacre," *Brigham Young University Studies* 13 (Autumn 1972): 62–67.

8. This has been one of the fundamental problems of modern historical writing about Mormonism as well. For example, Edwin B. Firmage and Richard C. Mangrum, *Zion in the Courts: A Legal History of the Church of Jesus Christ of Latter-day Saints, 1830–1900* (Urbana: University of Illinois Press, 1988), accepts at face value the Mormon myth. The authors write that "the story of the persecution Mormons suffered through the institutions of the legal system, and of their efforts to establish their own legal system—one appropriate to Zion . . . illustrates democracy's potential to oppress an insular, minority community. . ." (xiv–xv). They apparently believe that theocracy is both possible and desirable, but the quest for empire that theocracy mandates will always run against the grain of the American mainstream, and the nation's legal institutions by nature will oppose it. Far from democracy's "oppression" of a minority, such opposition will merely be an assertion of the cherished principles of the Constitution against the perceived threat to liberty from a theocracy bent on centralized control. The authors fail to appreciate the inherent tension between democracy and theocracy. They also do not recognize that there may be other equally valid means to attain Mormonism's religious goals.

9. This process has been discussed at length in Mark P. Leone, *Roots of Modern Mormonism* (Cambridge, Mass: Harvard University Press, 1979), 210–26.

———•••• *1* ••••———

The Mormons Decide to Leave Illinois

By mid-September 1845, Mormons and non-Mormons were still raiding, plundering, and intimidating each other, with no end in sight. General Hardin and his troops did not arrive until 28 September 1845 to reestablish order. But support for the non-Mormons was increasing in western Illinois, especially after the repressive tactics of Sheriff Backenstos and his Mormon posse had been widely reported.

One very important meeting of non-Mormons was held at Quincy on 22 September. Delegates from nine counties—which did not include Hancock— deliberated about the conflict, adopted resolutions advocating Mormon departure and contacted the Quorum of Twelve Apostles. The letter which follows was the Mormon response, written by Brigham Young (1801–77), who had emerged as the preeminent leader of the Saints in Nauvoo. A New Englander, Young joined the Mormon Church in 1831 and soon moved to Kirtland, Ohio. After serving on various missions, he moved to Missouri in 1838, where he helped organize the Mormon evacuation from the state. In 1840 he went on a mission to England, but by the summer of 1841, he had settled in Nauvoo, although he was frequently away on missionary activities. There he embraced polygamy and other theological innovations of Joseph Smith. After Smith's death, Young became the chief leader of the church and eventually led the exodus to the Great Basin, where the Mormons established, for a time, a theocratic kingdom like the one envisioned for Nauvoo.

Young's letter was published in the *Quincy Whig* during late September and was later reprinted in Josiah B. Conyers, *A Brief History of the Leading Causes of the Hancock Mob in the Year 1846* (St. Louis: n. p., 1846), 15–17, from which this account is taken. In the letter Young announced that the Mormons would leave the state in the spring of 1846. Although he and the other Mormons leaders undoubtedly were impressed by the resolutions of the multicounty Quincy convention, they had been discussing plans to leave for some time. In another letter, to General John J. Hardin, dated 1 October 1845, Young states, "We had commenced making arrangements to remove from this county previous to the recent disturbances; that we now have four companies organized of one hundred families each . . . preparatory to removal" (Brigham Young Papers, Church of Jesus Christ of Latter-day Saints Church Archives, Salt Lake City, Utah).

———•••◉◉•••———

Nauvoo, Sept. 24, 1845.

WHEREAS, a council of the authorities of the Church of Jesus Christ of Latter Day Saints, at Nauvoo, have this day received a communication from

Messr. Henry Asbury, John P. Robbins, Albert G. Pearson, P. A. Goodwin, J. N. Ralston, M. Rogers, and E. Conyers, committee of the citizens of Quincy, requesting us to "communicate in writing," our disposition and intention at this time, particularly, with regard to removing to some place where the peculiar organization of our Church will not be likely to engender so much strife and contention that so unhappily exists at this time, in Hancock and some of the adjoining counties.

And, whereas, said committee have reported to us the doings of a public meeting of the citizens of Quincy, on the 22d inst., by which it appears there are some feelings in that place concerning us, as a people, and in relation to which sundry resolutions were passed, purporting to be for the purpose of maintaining or restoring peace to the county.

And, whereas, it is our desire, and ever has been, to live in peace with all men, so far as we can, without sacrificing the right of worshiping God according to the dictates of our own conscience, which privilege is granted by the constitution of these United States; And, whereas, we have, time and again, been driven from our peaceful homes, and our women and children been obliged to exist on the prairies, in the forests, on the roads and in tents, in the dead of winter, suffering all manner of hardships–even to death itself—as the people of Quincy well know; the remembrance of whose hospitality, in former days, still causes our hearts to burn with joy, and raise[s] the prayer to heaven for blessings on their heads;—And, whereas, it is now so late in the season that it is impossible for us, as a people, to remove this fall, without causing a repetition of like sufferings; And, whereas, it has been represented to us from other sources than those named, and even in some communications from the executive of the State, that many of the citizens of the State were unfriendly to our views and principles; And, whereas, many scores of our houses in this county have been burned to ashes, without any justifiable cause or provocation, and we have made no resistance, till compelled by the authorities of the county so to do, and that authority not connected with our Church; And, whereas, said resistance to mobocracy, from legally constituted authority, appears to be misunderstood by some, and misconstrued by others, so as to produce an undue excitement in the public mind.

And, whereas, we desire peace above all other earthly blessings; Therefore, we would say to the committee above mentioned, and to the Governor, and all the authorities and people of Illinois, and the surrounding states and territories, that we propose to leave this county next spring, for some point so remote, that there will not need be any difficulty with the people and ourselves, provided certain propositions, necessary for the accomplishment of our removal, shall be observed, as follows, to-wit:

That the citizens of this and the surrounding counties, and all men, will use their influence and exertions to help us to sell or rent our properties, so as to get means enough that we can help the widow, the fatherless, and the destitute, to remove with us.

That all men will let us alone with their vexatious law suits, so that we may have the time, for we have broken no laws; and help us to [get] cash, dry goods, groceries, good oxen, beef cattle, sheep, wagons, mules, horses, harness, &c., in exchange for our property, at a fair price, and deeds given on the payment, that we may have the means to accomplish a removal without the suffering of the destitute to an extent beyond the endurance of human nature.

That all exchanges of property be conducted by a committee, or committees, of both parties; so that all the business may be transacted honorably, and speedily.

That we will use all lawful means, in connection with others, to preserve the public peace, while we tarry; and shall expect, decidedly, that we be no more molested with house-burning, or any other depredations, to waste our property and time, and hinder our business.

That it is a mistaken idea, that we "*have* proposed to remove in six months," for that would be so early in the Spring; that grass might not grow, nor water run; both of which would be necessary for our removal. But we propose to use our influence, to have no more seed time and harvest among our people, in this county, after gathering our present crop; and that all communications to us be made in writing.

By order of the Council,
BRIGHAM YOUNG, Pres't.
Wm. Richards, Clerk

● 2 ●

The Proceedings of the Carthage Convention

After the Quorum of Twelve Apostles had responded to the representatives of the nine-county meeting, the latter held a second gathering at Carthage on 1–2 October 1845. That convention produced a series of resolutions, the first of which accepted the Mormon proposal to leave Illinois in the spring and recommended that other non-Mormons acquiesce as well. The delegates also called for a multi-county military organization—which never materialized—to keep peace in Hancock County until the Mormons left.

But the published proceedings of that meeting, which appeared in the *Quincy Whig* and are reprinted here from Josiah B. Conyers, *A Brief History of the Leading Causes of the Hancock Mob in the Year 1846* (St. Louis: n. p., 1846), 17–21, also had a second purpose. The delegates, who included such talented leaders as future Congressmen Orville H. Browning and Isaac N. Morris, clearly intended to counter the Mormon self-image of persecuted innocence. Hence, they opened their statement by noting that the non-Mormons of Hancock County were as law-abiding as any citizens in the state before the Mormons came, and in fact, they were people of honor and integrity. In short, they were not evil, as the Mormons maintained.

Nor were the Mormons innocent. Indeed their unified separatism placed them above the law originating from outside Nauvoo and, hence, legitimized Mormon lawlessness. The delegates showed insight into the underlying causes of the Hancock County conflict when they pointed out that "no people, however quietly disposed, can live in the immediate neighborhood of the Mormons without being drawn into collision with them." Lacking a modern comprehension of myth, or the vocabulary for expressing it, the delegates nevertheless realized that Mormon beliefs and behavior made conflict with non-Mormons inevitable, and they recognized as well that chalking the Hancock County disturbance up to persecuted innocence failed to acknowledge the essential, complex realities. Hence, they offered this remarkable resolution: "That we utterly repudiate the impudent assertion so often and so constantly put forth by the Mormons, that they are *persecuted for righteousness' sake*. We do not believe them to be a persecuted people."

Agreeably to previous arrangements, the delegates, appointed to meet in convention at the town of Carthage, to take into consideration the state of affairs in Hancock county, assembled at the Court House in said place, at half past eleven o'clock, October 1st, 1845.

On motion of Col. J. W. Singleton, the Convention was called to order, by appointing I. N. Morris, Esq., of Adams county, President. Whereupon, Col. Wm. Ross, of Pike county, was appointed 1st, Gen. James McCallen, of Warren county, 2d, and John Kirk, Esq., of M'Donough county, 3d, Vice Presidents.

Alva Wheeler, of Knox county, was appointed Secretary, and George Robinson, of Schuyler, and Wm. H. Benneson, of Adams, Assistant Secretaries. . . .

8 o'clock, Thursday Morning, Oct. 2.

The Convention met pursuant to adjournment and was called to order by the President.

The committee appointed to prepare a preamble and resolutions, reported, through O. H. Browning, their chairman, which after some able and interesting remarks from Messrs. Browning, [W. H.] Chapman, [A.] Williams and Scott, were unanimously adopted:

Whereas, the county of Hancock, before the settlement therein of the community called Mormons, was as peaceable, orderly, well regulated, and law-abiding, as any county in the State; and no disturbances had ever occurred among the citizens of said county requiring the interposition of the authorities of the State, but they had deported themselves with a degree of propriety and order not inferior to that which has characterized the citizens of other counties; and whereas, since the Mormons have been settled in said county, difficulties and collisions have frequently arisen between them and the other citizens of said county, of so serious and violent a character as to call for the interposition of an armed force, under the authority of the State, to quell and suppress the same; and whereas, from our long acquaintance with the old citizens of Hancock county, and our intimate knowledge of their honor, integrity, and strict observance of the laws of their country, and from our knowledge of the predatory disposition, and lawless course of the Mormons, we are thoroughly convinced that all the disturbances in the county have grown out of the continual and unceasing depredations of the Mormons upon the persons and property of the other citizens of Hancock, and the surrounding counties; and whereas, we are satisfied that no people, however, quietly disposed, can live in the immediate neighborhood of the Mormons without being drawn into collision with them, and without a resort to arms for self protection; and whereas, we, as citizens of the State of Illinois, and as citizens of the counties immediately surrounding, and adjacent to the county of Hancock, are deeply interested in terminating the scenes of violence which have recently been enacted in said county, and in restoring peace and good order therein; and whereas, we believe the difficulties now existing in said county are above and beyond the reach of the laws, inasmuch as the laws can only be administered through the instrumentality of the officers and juries of the county, and inasmuch as the officers of said county whose duty it is to select the juries are either Mormons, or under Mormon influence, having been elected by them; and whereas, no Mormon can be brought to justice in said county, for any offence, however great its enormity, inasmuch as they are banded and confederated together to sustain, protect, and defend each other, in all acts, however daring and lawless;—and larceny, robbery, perjury, and murder, in their most aggravated forms, therefore, go unpunished; and whereas, we are satisfied that peace and harmony can be restored to the county, only, by the separation of the Mormons and the other citizens of the county; and whereas, we are not willing to consent that the old citizens of the county, (who are among the best citizens of the State,) shall be driven out, and a community of thieves, robbers, and assassins retained in their stead; and whereas, the Mormons, have submitted to the citizens of Quincy, a proposition whereby they agree to remove from the State next Spring. Therefore,

Resolved, That it is the settled and deliberate conviction of this convention, that it is now too late to attempt the settlement of the difficulties in Hancock county upon any other basis than that of the removal of the Mormons from the State; and we therefore accept and respectfully recommend to the people of the surrounding counties to accept the proposition made by the Mormons to remove from the State next Spring, and to wait with patience the time appointed for removal.

Resolved, That whilst we shall endeavor by all means in our power to prevent the occurrence of anything which might operate against their removal, and afford them any ground of complaint, we shall expect equal good faith on their part; and if they do not comply with their own proposition, the consequences must abide with themselves; and we now solemnly pledge ourselves to be ready, at the appointed time, to act as the occasion may require.

Resolved, That we recommend to the people of the several counties represented in their convention, and to the people of the military tract, generally, immediately to adopt a military organization, in order to provide for the preservation of peace in said counties; to act in relation to the affairs of Hancock county as future exigencies may require; and to carry out the views expressed in the preceding resolutions.

Resolved, That we expect, as an indispensable condition to the pacification of the county, that the old citizens be permitted to return to their homes unmolested by the present Sheriff, and the Mormons, for any thing alleged against them; and that any attempt on their part to arrest or prosecute such citizens for pretended offences, will, inevitably, lead to the renewal of the late disorders.

Resolved, That as the Mormons are banded together for their mutual protection, and are under the control of a few leaders, and beyond the reach of the law, the whole body should be held responsible for all lawless acts against the persons, or property, of our citizens.

Resolved, That we utterly repudiate the impudent assertion so often and so constantly put forth by the Mormons, that they are *persecuted for righteousness' sake.* We do not believe them to be a persecuted people. We *know* that they are not; but that whatever grievances they may suffer are the necessary, and legitimate consequences of their illegal, wicked and dishonest acts.

Resolved, That this Convention deem it proper to recommend that a small military force be stationed in Hancock county until next Spring, to prevent depredations on private property, and preserve the peace of said county; and that it be respectfully, yet earnestly, recommended to the Executive of the State to furnish the same for the purposes above named.

On motion of J. H. Mitchell, it was *Resolved,* That should the Mormons, between this and their leaving in the spring, continue to commit depredations and outrages upon the property or persons of the old citizens of Hancock, or other counties, that we not give them fair notice, that we will hold ourselves ready at a moment's warning, and pledge that our fellow citizens of the counties we represent will meet with us, *en masse,* immediately upon such facts being made known to us, and march to Hancock, to put a final and summary end to such outrages.

On motion of J. W. Singleton, the following resolution was adopted:

Resolved, That a committee of five be appointed to report to this Convention, an efficient plan for organizing volunteer companies, in compliance with the resolutions of the Convention; and that said committee make a report thereof, at 12 o'clock.

The Convention then adjourned, to meet again at 12 o'clock.

The Convention met pursuant to adjournment.

The committee on Military Organization, made the following report:

The Committee on Military Organization, report to the Convention the Following plan of Organization:

That the counties of the Military Tract hold meetings in the several precincts, on the 3d Saturday of October, instant—and organize into companies, all persons who may volunteer in support of the proceedings of this Convention—

and that said companies elect their officers—and that the Captains of such Companies, when organized, or hereafter to be organized, report by the first day of November, to A. Jonas, Andrew Johnston, J. H. Holton, E. J. Phillips, and Jno. B. Schwindler, constituting a Military Committee at Quincy, Ill., the number in their companies, number and kind of arms, and names of officers elected.

That the Military Committee at Quincy, shall have full power and authority, after receiving the report of Captains herein before provided for, to appoint a time and place for the meeting of all the Company officers, for the purpose of electing field officers; which time and place shall be notified to the Captains of Companies, and the Captains of Companies shall notify all other officers of their Companies, respectively; and that said Committee had full power and authority to order all the reported force into the field, by fixing on a point or rendezvous, when, in their judgment, such an emergency has arrived, as is contemplated by the resolutions and proceedings of this convention.

On motion of A. C. Harding, the following resolution was adopted.

Resolved, That the Military Central Committee residing at Quincy, be requested to act as a committee to procure and superintend the printing of the proceedings of this Convention, accompanied by such a number of the affidavits reported to the Convention, by the committee on evidence, as they may think proper.

O. H. Browning offered the following resolution, which was enthusiastically adopted:

Resolved, That the Hon. N. H. Purple, Judge of this Judicial Circuit, be requested not to hold a Court in Hancock county, this fall; as, in the opinion of this Convention, such Court could not be holden without producing collision between the Mormons and Anti-Mormons, and renewing the excitement and disturbances which have recently afflicted said county.

On motion of O. H. Hewit, the following resolution was adopted:

Resolved, That the papers of this State be requested to publish the proceedings of this Convention, and that three thousand pamphlets, containing the proceedings of this convention, be printed, to be distributed under the direction of the Military Committee, at Quincy, whose duty it shall be to forward each delegate to this Convention with a copy of the same; and that a collection be now taken to defray the expense of said publication.

J. H. Mitchell submitted the following, which was adopted:

Resolved, That the thanks of this Convention be tendered to the President and Vice Presidents, for the able manner in which that have presided; and to the Secretaries, for the faithful and efficient manner in which they have discharged their duties.

A motion was then made that the Convention adjourn, when the President arose and expressed his high gratification at the signal unanimity which characterized the proceedings of the Convention; and, inasmuch as he had no opportunity of participating in its action, he took that occasion to say, that what they had done met his cordial approbation, and had no doubt would meet the approbation of the people, generally; and thanking the members for the efficient aid they had rendered him in discharging his duty, he declared the Convention adjourned, *sine die.*

—— ••• *3* ••• ——

Eliza Snow's Poem "Let Us Go"

O nce the decision had been made to leave Illinois, most Mormons looked forward to heading west. Eliza Snow (see the headnote to Part IV, Document 16) expressed that view in a poem called "Let Us Go," which was written in the fall of 1845 and subsequently published in a collection of her verse, *Poems, Religious, Historical, and Political* (Liverpool, England: F. D. Richards, 1856), 146–47.

The poem is an interesting expression of the Mormon myth of persecuted innocence. Through incantatory repetition ("Let us go, let us go"), the poet urges the virtuous Mormons to flee from "the wicked" who are "seeking our life." Thus a dichotomy is developed through a contrast between two places—America, which is viewed as evil, and the western wilds, the new habitation of the inherently good. Hence, the identification between America and the millennial kingdom of God is transferred to the West. It will be the new Promised Land. Such a mythic way of thinking would help conceptualize the journey from America to the West as an exodus in the image of Moses and the children of Israel.

—— •••◉••• ——

Let us go, let us go to the ends of the earth—
Let us go far away from the land of our birth;
For the Banner of Freedom no longer will wave
O'er the patriots tomb—o'er the dust of the brave.

Let us go, let us go from a country of strife,
From a land where the wicked are seeking our life,
From a country where justice no longer remains,
From which virtue is fled—where iniquity reigns.

Let us go, let us go from a government where
Our just rights of protection we never can share—
Where the soil we have purchas'd we cannot enjoy
Till the time when "the waster goes forth to destroy."

Let us go, let us go to the wilds for a home,
Where the wolf and the deer and the buffalo roam,

Where the life-inspir'd "Eagle" in liberty flies,
Where the mountains of Israel in majesty rise.

Let us go, let us go to a country whose soil
Can be made to produce wine, milk, honey, and oil;
Where beneath our own vines we may sit and enjoy
The rich fruit of our labors, and naught will destroy.

Let us go, let us go where our rights are secure,
Where the waters are clear and the atmosphere pure,
Where the hand of oppression has never been felt,
Where the blood of the Prophets has never been spilt.

Let us go, let us go where the kingdom of God
Will be seen in its order extending abroad—
Where the Priesthood again will exhibit its worth
In the regeneration of man and of earth.

Let us go, let us go to the far western shore,
Where the blood-thirsty "Christians" will hunt us no more;
Where the waves of the ocean will echo the sound,
And the shout of salvation extend the world round.

4

Governor Ford Justifies the Use of Militia

Governor Ford's dispatching of troops to Hancock County, under the leadership of General John J. Hardin, was not appreciated by most Mormons, who had been pleased with the efforts of Sheriff Jacob Backenstos and his Mormon posse. Two Mormon leaders wrote to Ford and criticized his decision. One was Orson Spencer, president of the Nauvoo City Council, and the other was George Miller, a bishop in the church. Spencer's letter was abusive—(see Joseph Smith, Jr., *History of the Church of Jesus Christ of Latter-day Saints*, ed. B. H. Roberts [Salt Lake City: Deseret Book Co., 1932], 7:502), and Ford replied only briefly. He wrote a longer response to Bishop Miller, which is reprinted here from Smith, *History of the Church*, 7:505–8.

Ford's letter reveals his awareness of the broader implications of the Mormon conflict. He points out that non-Mormons would have fled the county if the Backenstos posse had remained in control and that other non-Mormons in surrounding areas would have gotten involved to prevent Hancock County from becoming all Mormon. Ford had to make pragmatic decisions, based on the complexities of a difficult situation. He recognized that anything he did would not please both contending parties and displayed his exasperation at their failure to take "the law for guide." Ford was caught in the middle, but his outside militia restored some order, which remained until the exodus was well under way.

———————•••••◉••••———————

Springfield, October 30th, 1845.

General George Miller,

Sir: The two letters mentioned by you as having been mailed at Quincy by yourself and Mr. Spencer, were received the next morning after you left. Mr. Spencer is a man for whom I have felt a warm personal esteem but really his letter is a most uncalled for philippic containing the most extraordinary charge, that I have exterminated your people. It is true that I have sent troops to Hancock to quell disturbance. They were few in number and not sufficient for the work of extermination if they had been ever so willing. They were successful in everything except in arresting the rioters. This the sheriff's *posse* could not do, because they had run away. It is true also that the sheriff had apparently restored order before the arrival of General Hardin, but that order was not likely to continue. The anti-Mormons had fled from the county and were successfully enlisting forces in the neighboring counties. You may not believe it, but I assure you they would have raised four or five thousand men. Nothing has saved an attack on your city, by that number, but the march of General Hardin by my order. You may have beaten the assailants and a great number of good honest citizens, the dupes of anti-Mormon falsehoods, would have lost their lives; this was not to be permitted; it would have disgraced any government which would have permitted it.

Although neither your people nor the anti-Mormons were in a temper to appreciate the favor, it was no less my duty and that of General Hardin to stop you on both sides; both parties were so enraged that they were, as they said, anxious to be permitted to fight, though as they were forced asunder by their neighbors; and their ardor sensibly abated when the obstacle to a fight should be removed.

It is supposed by your people that if the sheriff had not been interfered with by the state militia he could have kept the peace and preserved order. There are many reasons why this is not so. First, the anti-Mormons would have removed out of the county. The people of the surrounding counties were afraid in that event, that your people would get the whole of Hancock, and would be as troublesome to them as you had been to the antis of Hancock. For which reason they were determined to drive you off before you got stronger. They reasoned thus: these people, the Mormons, have for some cause or other been in difficulty with all the people they ever lived amongst. They were obliged to leave Ohio and Missouri and they have not agreed better with their neighbors of Hancock. If these neighbors move away their places will be occupied by Mormons, and we, the surrounding counties, will be their nearest neighbors and may expect with certainty to have the like difficulties with them. They said therefore we will take time by the forelock and drive them away before they get stronger and more capable of resistance.

Secondly, although the sheriff had put down the house-burners, he had not suppressed stealing and murder on the other side. One man had certainly been murdered between Carthage and Appanoose, another was missing in Nauvoo under circumstances which leave no doubt but that he was murdered in your city and most probably by order of some of your principal men. At least such is and was the popular belief. Stolen property has been traced to your city during the ascendancy of the sheriff, and the owners who came to search were ordered away and fled for fear of their lives. None of the stolen property could be found and in fact the owners did not dare to go to look for it without the aid and protection of the state troops. You may say this is the work of only a few and that your people are not responsible for the few in your city any more than in any other city; this may be true, but its truth does not do away with the necessity for a military force. I have long believed that there are those in Nauvoo who carry on a pretty large business in stealing. Some have alleged that this gang are patronized by the church authorities. This charge, however, I never believed and would not believe it unless proved by the most satisfactory evidence. Be this as it may, the thieves are there and they do steal as is the case in all other cities of ten or twelve thousand inhabitants.

I think it likely that some of your people who were burnt out by the mob, have persuaded themselves that they have a right to indemnify themselves for their losses by taking the property of their enemies. It is also probable that many persons unconnected with the Mormons go to Hancock to steal on their credit. Be this as it may, stealing as well as burning has been done and the stolen property has been traced to your city. Other thieves have been captured whilst taking it there: all these things took place during the ascendancy of the sheriff and was kept secret from him, or if he knew of it he had no power to prevent it. Under these circumstances it was considered advisable by General Hardin, Judge Douglas, Major Warren and Mr. McDougall the attorney-general to leave one hundred men as a permanent guard. General Hardin informs me by letter that your high council expressed a wish that this force might be left. It was also requested, as he says, by all the well disposed persons in the county and particularly by the Reverend Mr. Owen who has never been a mobocrat. I cannot hear that this force has annoyed your people in any other way than once in a while to be marched into your city in quest of stolen property. This must be what Mr. Spencer calls extermination, for I have never heard that the troops have annoyed you in any other way. Mr. Spencer complains that the presence of these troops prevents the Mormons from going on peaceably and quietly in making their arrangements to remove in the spring. I am at a loss to perceive how, unless it be really true that a part of those arrangements are intended to consist in making reprisals upon the property of your enemies to pay you for your losses. This must not be attempted and will not be permitted. A demonstration of your intention to this effect will cause an attempt by the anti-Mormon party to drive you out before spring. If there are more of you in Nauvoo than can live this winter, good sense would say scatter until spring and be making something by labor to live upon. At all events until I am better informed I will hold it to be my duty to continue a military force in Hancock, both to protect you from the attacks of your enemies, as well as to prevent stealing whether by the anti-Mormons on your credit; by the Mormons themselves; by interlopers who come to your city as a place of refuge or by those who have been burnt out and who may be tempted to take this method of indemnifying themselves for their losses; and if the civil law is not strong enough martial law must be resorted to. Because if these things are not put an end to, the surrounding counties will take up the guard and you may be driven in despite of the state, in the dead of winter.

In the course of my official duties I have had a great deal of trouble with both parties in Hancock. I have been called to do both of you some good and some harm. The harm is always remembered; the good is either not understood or is forgotten. I do not expect any gratitude or applause from either party; and you may be sure that the last things that I will think possible to be accomplished will be to please either you or the anti-Mormons, by any moderate conduct which, by taking the law for guide, repudiates the wildness and infatuation of both parties.

My health is bad or I should have started for Hancock on Wednesday morning last to see for myself what the state of things really are.

> I am most respectfully your
> obedient servant,
> Thomas Ford

5

Continued Conflict in the Mormon Kingdom

That society at Nauvoo was a far cry from righteous and innocent is evident from a wide range of documents from 1845. Among them are several important accounts by Mormons. For example, early in 1845 Sidney Rigdon, the only surviving member of the First Presidency and a leader of his own Mormon faction after the death of Joseph Smith, wrote an extensive article for his *Latter Day Saints Messenger and Advocate*, published in Pittsburgh, entitled "The Apostates and Rebellious Spirits at Nauvoo," 1 January 1845, p. 1, which condemns Brigham Young and other Mormon leaders for their immorality, especially polygamy. Similarly, in October 1845 the prophet's brother, William B. Smith, who believed the church's leadership should remain in the family, issued a proclamation in which he expressed his opposition to polygamy and the duplicity which resulted from attempts to keep it secret. He also spoke out against Mormon intimidation and abuse of non-Mormons: "I opposed also the whittling, whistling, and beastly anointing, practiced upon strangers . . ." ("A Proclamation," *Warsaw Signal*, 29

October 1845, p. 1). Whittling and whistling refer to confrontation by an organized band wielding bowie knives and sharpened sticks (see Part II, Documents 2–
3), and anointing was the practice of heaping excrement on someone, as the following document reveals. Smith also decried the murder of Irvine Hodges near the
home of Brigham Young. For voicing such outspoken criticism, he said, "I was
cautioned to look out for my life," and he provided a detailed account of intimidation by armed police at the Masonic Hall.

Perhaps the most detailed Mormon critique of social conditions at Nauvoo
after the death of the prophet was written by Oliver Olney (1796–ca. 1845). He
had joined the church at Kirtland, converted by his father-in-law, John Johnson, a
wealthy farmer and dissenter from the 1838 period. Between 1836 and 1838, he
presided over all the teachers at Kirtland and subsequently traveled to Missouri,
where he and others opposed mobocratic attacks. Olney later settled in Nauvoo,
but he was disfellowshipped in 1842 "for setting himself up as a prophet" (Joseph
Smith, Jr., *History of the Church of Jesus Christ of Latter-day Saints*, ed. B. H.
Roberts [Salt Lake City: Deseret Book Co., 1902–12], 4:552). He had, in fact,
claimed to be in contact with God.

In 1845 Olney wrote a pamphlet entitled *Spiritual Wifery at Nauvoo Exposed*
(St. Louis: n. p., 1845), portions of which were published as an "Extract of a Pamphlet Entitled Spiritual Wifery at Nauvoo Exposed" in the *Warsaw Signal* on 26
November 1845, p. 1. The following excerpts are from that newspaper. Because
some readers would have known that he had been disfellowshipped, Olney begins
by denying that he writes from "prejudice." He offers no criticism of Joseph Smith
but speaks as one who still considers himself a Mormon. He assesses the situation
in Nauvoo and condemns everything unrighteous, for all such acts reveal a falling
away from the innocence that once characterized God's chosen people. And he
clearly views the forthcoming expulsion from Illinois as God-wrought punishment
for failure to keep his commandments. In short, although there is some exaggeration in this document, Olney sounds very much like other Mormon dissenters,
pointing out errors and calling the people back to a pristine Mormonism. At the
same time, his article fueled the anti-Mormon sentiments in the county.

Perhaps some of you my readers may think this to be the overflowings of a
heart full of prejudice, but I assure you I visited Nauvoo with the intention and
expectation of making it my winter's residence, and for the purpose of receiving
blessings and endowments in the Temple. . . . I found Nauvoo a sink of iniquity,
inhabited by a people whose leaders are whoremongers instead of those who I
fondly thought were among the first to condemn vice and foster the germs of virtue and truth, that thereby the Saints might be brought into the bonds of perfect-
ness. Our prophet Joseph said to the people that he did not want any to leave
Nauvoo till the Temple was finished, and then after receiving their endowments

they might scatter abroad upon the face of the land and preach the Gospel, raise up branches, establish stakes and build Temples on all the land of Zion, which he said was the continent of America, knowing as he did that if they kept the commandments of God, they should never cease to prevail. Thus the important question is, will the people of Nauvoo prevail, or are they in transgression, in consequence of which they are to be moved out of their place. . . .

As I before stated, I visited Nauvoo with the strongest assurance that I should find it a place of piety and virtue, but I found it a place where profane language is in common use with all classes; yea, I have heard God's name profaned in the presence and hearing of the twelve, and instead of reprimanding the swearer one of them excused the matter to me by saying that "the person used to be an infidel, but is a *first rate fellow now!"* . . .

As it respects the late troubles in the county I am prepared to say in truth as follows:

The twelve by their unbounded influences over their subjects, and by teaching that the people round about them are gentiles and that the saints are to "suck the milk of the gentiles," have created such a state of feeling in the breasts of their followers that they think it is no sin for them to "suck a little," just now, and in fact, I have heard prominent men such as High Priests and Presiding Officers say that if a gentile comes in their way the best way to do is to put him "out of the way," as quick as possible. Such sentiments thrown out by the people at Nauvoo have not failed to create a response on the part of the settlers, and the feeling has been fanned into a flame that will ere spring (I opine) burn too hot for Mormons. Yea, even to their expulsion from the state, and for this reason.

A stipulation has been mutually agreed to by both Mormons and Anties [*sic*], that hostile operations and maneuvers should cease on both sides, and also that the Mormons should leave Nauvoo as soon as grass grows sufficient for teams to subsist upon.

Yet still the Mormons have been visited by writs to bring some offenders (of which class there are many) to justice; which serves as a pretext for the Mormons to send out armed forces, numbering from 50 up to 200, who on horseback scour the prairie between Nauvoo and Carthage, (as they say) in search of "Prairie Chickens," and latterly as if this was not enough; a body of these men have been to Carthage, and entirely broken up the court which was in session at that place, so I heard one of the men engaged in the transaction declare, so that none of the brethren could be tried at that court if arrested, for Brigham says to the people to "give them what is in their guns first and then use them to the best advantage before they submit to an arrest."

The Judge of the court in company with some of the lawyers of the county, visited Nauvoo to inquire the reason of the breaking up of the court in such a manner, but received nothing satisfactory, except a tirade from John Taylor, one of the twelve, which, he the judge carried away rankling and festering in his own bosom.

Another evidence of their purity and holiness, may be gathered from the fact that at the houses of some of the twelve, I have seen from three to five young females, whose prolific appearance indicates a great increase of posterity in the temporal kingdom, to say nothing of a great number of married women who are sealed to different ones in high standing in the church, and (as I have been taught from their own mouths,) believe it to be their privilege before God to raise up as many children here in the flesh as they can, that they may have a greater kingdom to rule over in eternity; and on being asked how many women it is one's privilege to beget children with, the answer was, "as many as he can maintain." This making it an object among themselves, (except the twelve, the bishops, the Temple committee and some other privileged characters) who help themselves out of Temple funds; to enter largely into speculating engagements, that thereby upon their income they may support (if they have no husbands to support them) those unhallowed and polluted vestiges of humanity, with whom they practise such abominations under the guard of righteousness; [it] must make the heavens weep, and the earth mourn, in witness to the fallen and degraded light of those who are to be "a light unto the world & also the saviors of men." And whose privilege it was to bring in everlasting righteousness, to make the earth bloom as Eden and to gather Israel from the dispersions, preparatory to the coming of the Messiah and establishing of the celestial kingdom of God, when the earth and the ful[l]ness thereof shall be given into the hands of the most High.

Another important item in the present teachings of the twelve, is that "At the time of receiving their washings and anointings of their endowments, all marriages will be declared void, and every person have the privilege of choosing for him or herself, by a mutual agreement, that is, if two choose to remain together it is their privilege to do so, but neither one can retain the other, if he or she chooses to depart and live with another. Oh shame! where is thy blush? Furthermore, it is said by the redoubtable Brigham, that "when the church once gets away from Nauvoo, if any find any fault with the twelve, their heads shall come off, and none shall ever return to tell their tales!" . . .

Another testimony of the purity of that people is the fact that a High Priest of that place told me that he had witnessed the deaths of five mobocrats at the hands of Mormons on the prairie, and also that the catfish of the Mississippi had scraped the bones of some who had better have kept away from Nauvoo.

The "anointing and washing" as it is jocosely called, is practised frequently upon those offenders who are not judged worthy of death, which is covering them from head to foot with filth obtained from the vault of some necessary in the city, and then casting them into the river.

Alas! for the purity of such a people, when their renowned head is upholding them in, and urging them on to deeds of shame and degradation, no where equalled in the annals of history, but which must stand forth in bold relief, as a warning to any who may hereafter be called to stand in as high and holy a calling as where these men who have now sacrificed every honest and virtuous principle at the shrine of female corruption, and justly merited a portion with those who are left without the city, such as (see Rev. 22:16) "Dogs and sorcerers, and whoremongers, and murderers, and idolaters, and whosoever loveth and maketh a lie."

Another heart-rending fact in the present history of Nauvoo is that hundreds of honest h[e]arted females are there, who have no means with which to get away, & scarce any means of subsistence there, except at the expense of virtue, and who are continually subject to the importunities of those fiends in human shape who, after having gratified their passions for lust, will, straightway, upon the public stand, declare before God & Angels, that no system of spiritual wifery is practised or tolerated by them, when perhaps some of their victims are at the very time upon their knees in secret beseeching God to forgive them for yielding in an ung[u]arded moment to their seducers, and to open a way for their escape from the folds of their destroyers, that, perchance, by a life of morality, virtue and piety, they may atone for the weakness of a moment, and at last gain an inheritance with the saints of God.

Think not, my readers, that this is a fancy piece, or the suggestions of an over excited imagination, for it is but a few out of the thousands of the testimonies that might be brought to show that virtue and truth have fled from their midst, and vice, in almost every form, has stalked forth, and holds, unchecked by any pure principle, the sway over almost the entire community, while the publications— "Times and Seasons" and "Neighbor"—would fain make the people at a distance believe that Nauvoo is pure as was Eden at first, and that the people are the innocent but persecuted people which they once were. . . .

6

The Completion of the Temple

While the conflict continued and the Mormons prepared to leave Nauvoo, work on the temple proceeded. The huge stone structure, located on the hill that rose in back of the town, lacked some finishing touches in the interior but was sufficiently complete to be used for meetings starting in early October 1845. More importantly, and the reason why the Saints so diligently worked on the building even though they planned to use it for only a few months, it was the site, beginning in early 1846, for "endowments"—the ritual ceremonies in which the faithful received spiritual blessings, such as the sealing of spouses for time and eternity—that Joseph Smith had instituted in a limited way in 1842. Belief in the spiritual efficacy of these endowments, as well as constant urging by church leaders, prodded the Mormons to keep working on the project through the winter of 1845–46 despite economic hardship, anxiety about mob violence, and division within the church.

A number of Mormons who worked on the temple later wrote memoirs. One of the longest and most interesting is the "Autobiography of Wandle Mace," held at the Church of Jesus Christ of Latter-day Saints Archives, Salt Lake City, Utah, and never published before. Mace (1809–90) had been born in Johnstown,

New York, and worked in New York City as what might be called a mechanical engineer. He redesigned several machines to work more efficiently and accurately tooled items for use in manufacturing. For example, he patented a post-mortising and rail-sharpening machine for fencing and received an award for it from the Mechanic's Institute of New York in 1837. At about that time, he heard of Joseph Smith and the Mormon gospel; he joined the church soon thereafter and moved to the institutional stronghold at Kirtland, Ohio. He later went to Missouri, and after the Mormon expulsion from the state, settled at Montrose, Iowa Territory. In 1842 he moved across the river to Nauvoo.

As his autobiography reveals, Mace was working on the temple when Brigham Young directed him to prepare four old cannons for service in case Nauvoo was attacked by the non-Mormons. He did so and was still in Nauvoo during September 1846, when those cannons were used in an unsuccessful defense of the city. He then headed west with his family.

Mace's autobiography interprets his Nauvoo experience as part of Mormon sacred history. Hence, he refers to remarks by Joseph Smith and Brigham Young that he regarded as prophetic. As the final paragraph suggests, receiving endowments in the temple upon which he had labored was undoubtedly the high point of his life in the church up to that time. The following excerpts are from chapter 24, pp. 188–90, 193–94, of Mace's account.

We had been told by the Prophet Joseph, that the Lord had given sufficient time in which to build the temple, and if we did not do it we would be rejected with our dead. We were therefore very diligent in our labors on the temple. Men were as thick as blackbirds busily engaged upon the various portions, all intent upon its completion: although we were being in constant expectation of a mob. Some old cannons had been brought to Nauvoo from New Orleans which had lain in the salt water until they had become very rusty. I was called upon by President Young to fit these cannons for action.

He told me to take them into the basement of the temple, and rebore them, and get them ready for action. I accordingly called upon two or three of the brethren to help me, and we took them by night into the basement, white washed the windows to prevent observation, and went to work. After much hard labor having to work upon the cannon at night, and superintend the work on the temple in the daytime, thus working day and night with very little time to rest, we had them ready to defend the city.

We placed these four cannons each one on the hind axle of a wagon, the muzzle close against the tail board of the wagon box, which was without bottom. Seats sufficient for eight men was placed on the box. When required for action the men would lift off the wagon box and the cannon was ready for action. As soon as the mobs heard the boom of our cannon and learned we had something to defend ourselves with, we heard no more of the wolf hunt. They tried every means they could devise to bring trouble upon Nauvoo. . . .

Through the vigilance of our brethren who in this way protected the city, we were enabled to continue our labors until the temple was so far completed that a portion was dedicated for the purpose of giving endowments; thus we labored while the wicked raged, the mobs howled, but they could not stop the work on the temple until it was so far completed that it was accepted of the Lord.

While we were energetically performing our labors in the city, our brethren in the southern part of Hancock County was suffering from the malignity of the mob. While harvesting their grain the mob pounced upon them, and whipped some into insensibility, their backs being horribly cut from the lash. The suffering of the people in the outlaying settlements were terrible. In the forepart of September the mob commenced to burn the houses and grain. The sheriff endeavored to stay the mob, but in one week they burned near two hundred buildings and a large quantity of grain, as it was in the sickly season many died from exposure to the scorching rays of the sun and the dews of evening. Doctors, lawyers, statesmen, and Christians of various denominations, as well as military men from colonels down, were engaged in stealing cattle and anything they wanted.

They finally determined to drive the Saints from the country or exterminate them, and delegates were sent to Nauvoo to demand the departure of the Mormons. This delegation was met by the Twelve and answered for the people that the removal should take place as soon as possible.

General Hardin, commander of the state militia, was one of the delegates; he asked of the Twelve, "What guarantee will you give us?" Said President Young to him, "You have our all as guarantee." Senator Douglas, another of the delegation, seemed satisfied with the answer.

These things did not come upon us unexpectedly,—at least to those who were watching the signs of the times—the Prophet Joseph had told us that many of us would live to go to the "Rocky Mountains," and there become a mighty people, therefore we were looking forward to this time. Some of us was afraid we would not have time to finish the temple before these things came upon us, they were coming so fast.

Joseph, when preaching upon the redemption of Zion, read from the Book of Doctrine and Covenants, the parable of the twelve olive trees,—a revelation given through him on the 16th December, 1833. Commencing at the 43rd verse—he explained this parable. He said, "The twelve olive trees were twelve stakes of Zion which should be built up; and thrown down by our enemies," and while we were building the tower of the temple we could count that 12 stakes had been organized, and we were a little fearful we would not accomplish our part of the labor. We did however, although the finish was given, and the final dedication took place after the body of the Church had started from Nauvoo; the 12 stakes were broken down, and the people fled to the Rocky Mountains.

No general conference had been held for the last three years, according to the declaration of our martyred prophet, who said, "There shall be no more baptisms for the dead until the ordinances can be attended too [*sic*] in the font of the Lord's House; and the Church shall not hold another General Conference, until they can meet in said House. For thus saith the Lord!"

Amid the scenes of persecution and trial we have passed through it gives us satisfaction to think that since April 6th, 1841, when the corner stones was laid amidst the most straightened circumstances the Saints can now meet in the Lord's House, temporary floors be[ing] laid in the temple, and pulpits erected; also seats for the people, preparatory for a General Conference. The temple was entirely enclosed in windows, etc.

Conference assembled and the first meeting was held on Sunday the 5th, October 1845. President Young opened the services of the day in a dedicatory prayer, presenting the temple thus far completed, as a monument of the Saints liberality, fidelity, and faith, concluding with, "Lord we dedicate this house and ourselves to thee." The day was occupied in hearing instructions and teachings, and offering up the gratitude of our hearts for so great a privilege as worshiping God within his holy house, its motto, "Holiness to the Lord."

The instructions we received throughout the conference was mostly in relation to our removal from the midst of mobs and strife and taking our journey to the west. President Young moved, "that we take all the Saints with us, to the extent of our ability," which was seconded by Elder Heber C. Kimball, and unanimously carried. President Young then said, "If you will be faithful to your covenants, I will prophecy that the Great God will shower down means upon this people, to accomplish it to the very letter. The time has come sooner than I expected that, that scripture is being fulfilled, 'My people shall be willing in the day of my power,' and I thank God the time has come. . . ."

Conference over, we continued our labors on the temple with renewed diligence completing portions, that the endowments might be bestowed upon the living for themselves and their dead; at the same time wagon companies were organized to make wagons for the journey to the Rocky Mountains.

There was quite a number of such companies, in fact the whole people was interested in some one of them. I was called upon to superintend the one called the Michigan Wagon Company's Shop. I made a boring and mortising machine to facilitate the work. There was much to do and little time to do it. During these labors I was called to the temple to receive my endowments and sealings, as Joseph said, "Those whose names are on the books showing their labors for the temple, shall have the first claim." President Brigham Young and the Twelve were very particular to carry out his instructions; they saw that those who spent their whole time in these labors received the reward of their diligence by giving them a great endowment.

—•••• 7 ••••—

A Mormon Interprets the Last Days of Nauvoo

As previous events had been, the final conflict with non-Mormons and the exodus from Nauvoo were viewed by many Mormons through the prism of myth. The innocent chosen people of God continued to be persecuted by the wicked. Perhaps no document illustrates that perspective more clearly than the memoir of Joseph Lee Robinson (1811–90), a young Mormon living in Nauvoo at the time.

The tendency of myth to gloss over the complexities of history is striking in the opening sentence of Robinson's account of Nauvoo's last days: "And it came to pass that the Devil was mad." No sociological or political factors are taken into account. The conflict between Mormons and non-Mormons is not explained, indeed not explainable, in human terms. Rather, it is an episode in the cosmic struggle between God and the devil, good and evil. Belief made the Mormons "true worshippers of God" and, thus, innocent; and lack of belief made the Gentiles servants of the devil and, thus, wicked.

The memoir is also interesting as an attempt to lend pseudobiblical weight to the Mormon experience through use of the scriptural phrase, "And it came to pass." Robinson obviously regards himself as the author of sacred history, as did many other Saints who wrote their recollections of the Nauvoo era. The vision that he reports, full of division within the church and divine reward for those who follow the Quorum of Twelve Apostles, underlines his conviction that the exodus to the West is a sacred event.

The Robinson memoir also reveals that polygamous relationships were sometimes sanctioned in temple ceremonies in Nauvoo. Both of his wives were sealed to him for time and eternity during January 1846, when many endowments were given at the Nauvoo Temple in preparation for the westward migration. These excerpts printed here are from the unpublished typescript of Robinson's memoirs, pp. 20–22, held by the Utah State Historical Society Library, Salt Lake City.

———••••◉••••———

And it came to pass that the Devil was mad. The people imagined vain things. The wicked raged and gnashed upon us. It was with great difficulty we could keep them from us till we could build the Temple so that we could get our endowments and sealings which the Lord proposed we should receive before we should go into the wilderness for he did truly propose to take this people into a goodly land from under the Gentile yoke where he could plant them and teach and train them to do His liking, preparatory to the redemption of Zion. The Lamanites have to be taught. They have to be baptized and a great army organized and prepared to redeem Zion and avenge the blood of the Prophets which mighty work shall be accomplished as the Lord liveth. . . .

The work on our Temple was pursued with vigor. We will relate a very interesting vision, that one of our brethren had given unto him as he related it to me. He was a laborer upon the Temple. It was manifested unto him a short time before the death of the Prophet Joseph and Hyrum as he was returning from his work one evening sometime before sunset. He had reached his gate that led to his house. The vision opened up before him. He saw our people in commotion, seemingly in trouble. They were in arms and a dark cloud arose. It looked very gloomy and doleful, yea frightful, as the cloud passed over, and when they came out their arms had passed away and so had their Prophet and his brother for he saw them no more, and the people was in great mourning and presently he saw the Twelve with Brigham at their head and they led the Church, and the next he saw the Church moving West. He could see them for hundreds of miles with covered wagons and tents moving West. He saw them settled in a goodly land. They built up cities and temples and spread abroad exceedingly. By and by he saw the dark cloud rising and spreading over this people. It looked gloomy and fearful, dangerous. He saw three iron hoops around this Church and the Twelve and others with little wooden mallets thumping away bright[e]ning up these hoops—three hoops and it still grew more dark and fearful and they kept tightening up the hoops, and it came to pass that the hoops burst and the people went right away directly every way. They were so scared they ran; as near as he could calculate, nearly or quite one-half of the people left the body of the Church and then he said it seemed that before the hindermost of them were fairly out of sight this dark and dreary cloud passed away and the sunbeam of righteousness shined forth and all that were left were exceedingly happy; now with him a time of reflection and inquiry, says he, I came within a hair's breath of leaving also, oh how thankful I am, said he that I did not leave this church. Then an inquiry arose in his mind and he exclaimed, Oh Lord why was it, why was it so that such a dark and fearful cloud and feeling should come over and upon the people? The answer came directly that God had a great blessing to pour out upon His people and that there were a great many that had the name of His people that were not worthy and that in His wisdom he took this method to purge them out. Said the man, the answer that I received perfectly satisfied me. He saw nothing that affrighted ones went to join but that they were so frightened they ran away. Then it came to pass that the authorities of the Church led the saints to a kind of large underground room where tables were set loaded with sweetmeats and all manner of precious things and feasted the people and that they were exceedingly happy. . . .

And it came to pass that the Gentiles that should have been our friends became our bitter enemies, as they had been in Kirtland, Ohio, as also they were in Missouri. Our people had been driven from both of these places and now they meant to drive us from Illinois. They sent a delegation to confer with our leaders to see whether we would leave the State, and when, saying the Mormons had to leave at all hazards. Our leaders counseled with the people and we all agreed to leave the country in the spring. They made arrangements to that effect with the mob. We thought it better for us to leave than to be slaughtered which we should have been, so that we worked with all diligence to prepare for our exit. We did not like the idea of leaving our beautiful Temple until we had received our endowments, washings, anointings, and sealings. Our people made a beautiful Faunt [*sic*] in the basement of the Temple underneath resting upon twelve beautiful oxen and many had been baptized for their dead and many for their health. I have been baptized for some of my dead and had one of my little sons. . . . We prepared some rooms so that the holy ordinances could be performed, so that the saints could receive their blessings, our enemies were so desperate and determined that we should leave the country our brethren were obliged to arm themselves while working on the Temple. We labored with all our might and the Lord helped us so that we commenced giving and receiving our endowments about this time. My first wife, Maria was sealed to me January 13, 1846, and my second wife, Susan, January 31, 1846. It was a hurrying time, a great many thousand people received their endowments in a comparatively short time, but we were thankful to get so great blessings in that holy, holy House. Surely it was a very beautiful, inspiring House. It cost us oh so much labor and so much means, but we never regretted what we had done for we considered ourselves well and amply paid for all we had done. We counted it the Lord's House and we considered ourselves the Lord's also and all that we do we do in the name of and for the Lord and all that we have is the Lord's for it is in Him we live and move and have our being and truly we are a very exceedingly happy people, hated and slandered, belied and persecuted, the most of any people on earth yet we are full of charity towards all men, but more especially for or toward the household of faith, we pray for our enemies. We know they do not realize what they are doing, that they are fighting against God and persecuting their best friends.

July 12, 1846. The Lord gave to the Prophet Joseph a revelation on the eternity of the marriage covenant including plurality of wives but it was not made public so that we do know that the heavy persecutions and murderings and drivings and robbings that was perpetrated upon the Latter-day Saints prior to their being driven into the Rocky Mountains was not on account of polygamy but as it always has been the true worshippers of God were unpopular, drawing down the wrath of their enemies upon them.

And it came to pass the Twelve with many others left Nauvoo in the Winter with their families and set out as exiles to seek asylum in the far West.

———— •••◗ *8* ◖•••————

Brigham Young Describes the Exodus

The Mormons began leaving Nauvoo for the West in early February 1846 under the leadership of Brigham Young (for biographical information, see the headnote to Part VI, Document 1). From 9 August 1844 until the exodus he kept a detailed journal, which includes the following account of his activities and related events on 6–9 February 1846. These excerpts are from the journal at the Church of Jesus Christ of Latter-day Saints Archives, Salt Lake City, Utah and were previously published in Joseph Smith, Jr., *History of the Church of Jesus Christ of Latter-day Saints*, ed. B. H. Roberts, (Salt Lake City: Deseret Book Co., 1932), 7:580–82. As his entries for those four days reveal, he was busy supervising two extensive, important matters at the same time—the temple endowments and the evacuation of the city. Neither activity was without problems and setbacks. In the long entry for 9 February, he describes a temple fire that interrupted the use of the building for endowments and a river accident that resulted in a sunken flatboat, drowned oxen, and lost possessions.

As Young's journal also shows, the Mississippi River was not covered with ice when the Mormon exodus began. The river had frozen over in January, but a period of warmer weather had melted the ice in some places, including the Nauvoo area, so the Saints could use the water craft that Young mentions. However, the weather soon became extremely cold, and the river refroze to a depth of several inches. By later in February, the Saints were crossing on the ice, and perhaps two thousand of them had left the city by early March.

———— •••◗◗●◖◖••• ————

Friday, 6 [February] —Five hundred and twelve persons received the first ordinances of endowment in the Temple.

Bishop George Miller and family crossed the Mississippi river. They had six wagons.

Saturday, 7 —According to G. A. Smith's journal upwards of six hundred received the ordinances; one hundred and twenty-six of which were reported in the Seventies record.

Sunday, 8 —I met with the Council of the Twelve in the southwest corner room of the attic of the Temple. We knelt around the altar, and dedicated the building to the Most High. We asked his blessing upon our intended move to the west; also asked him to enable us someday to finish the Temple, and dedicate it to him, and we would leave it in his hands to do as he pleased; and to preserve the building as a monument to Joseph Smith. We asked the Lord to accept the labours of his servants in this land. We then left the Temple.

I addressed the Saints in the grove and informed them that the company going to the west would start this week across the river.

John Smith, President of the Stake, and family crossed the river, accompanied by his clerk, Albert Carrington, and family.

Monday, 9 —A detachment of the governor's troops came into the city and apprehended a man named Samuel Smith, who soon escaped.

Elder George A. Smith sent his family across the river.

Three-thirty P.M., the roof of the Temple was discovered to be on fire. An alarm was immediately given, when the brethren marched steadily to its rescue. I saw the flames from a distance, but it was out of my power to get there in time to do any good towards putting out the fire, and I said, "If it is the will of the Lord that the Temple be burned, instead of being defiled by the Gentiles, Amen to it."

I went to the Temple as soon as I could; after the fire had been extinguished, the brethren gave a loud shout of Hosannah, while standing on the deck roof.

Willard Richards called on the brethren to bring out all their buckets, fill them with water, and pass them on. Lines inside were formed, and the buckets passed in quick succession. The fire raged near half an hour. It was caused by the stove pipe being overheated, drying the clothing in the upper room. It burned from the west stovepipe from the ridge to the railing, about sixteen feet north and south, and about ten feet east and west on the north side. The shingles on the north were broken in several places.

By the advice of President H. C. Kimball the brethren dispersed.

Several of the troops went to the Temple and attempted to enter, but were prevented by the brethren at the door.

At the same time that the Temple was on fire, a number of brethren were crossing the river in a flat boat, when in their rear a man and two boys were in a skiff in a sinking condition, on account of being overloaded and the unskilfulness of the helmsman. They hailed to the flatboat, which was soon turned, and rendered them assistance. As soon as they had got the three on board the flatboat, a filthy wicked man squirted some tobacco juice into the eyes of one of the oxen that was attached to Thomas Grover's wagon, which immediately plunged into the river, dragging another with him, and as he was going overboard he tore off one of the sideboards which caused the water to flow into the flat boat, and as they approached the shore the boat sank to the bottom, before all the men could leap off. Several of the brethren were picked up in an exhausted condition. Two oxen were drowned and a few things floated away and were lost. The wagon was drawn out of the river with its contents damaged.

The crossing of the river was superintended by the police, under the direction of Hosea Stout. They gathered several flatboats, some old lighters, and a number of skiffs, forming altogether quite a fleet, and were at work, night and day, crossing the saints.

——•••• *9* ••••——

Nauvoo in the Spring of 1846

A s the Mormons began leaving, other people moved to Nauvoo—non-Mormons who were taking advantage of the inexpensive homes for sale. One of these newcomers later wrote an extensive account of Nauvoo and the conflict in 1846. His series of newspaper articles, entitled "Nauvoo—Then and Now," appeared on page 1 of the *Carthage Gazette* from 30 June through 3 November 1875, and from 18 January through 9 February 1876. The author's identity remains unknown because he simply signed the articles "X. Y. Z."

These excerpts are from the 30 June and 7 July installments, and they focus on the appearance and social conditions of the city in the spring of 1846, when Nauvoo still had thousands of Mormon residents, as well as "Jack Mormons" (Mormon sympathizers) and non-Mormon newcomers. By the time X. Y. Z. was writing, thirty years after the conflict, Nauvoo had only about fifteen hundred people, and the Mormon period of the town's history had become legendary. The author made a special effort to depict the community as he had known it, without exaggerated population figures and glorified descriptions. He made it clear that Nauvoo in the mid-1840s was a terribly overcrowded community. And he portrayed the town as overrun with "desperadoes," who took advantage of the departure of Brigham Young and other members of the Quorum of Twelve Apostles in the spring of 1846, the only significant leadership. Since the Nauvoo Charter had been repealed, there was no institutional restraint on behavior. In short, Nauvoo in 1846 was characterized by factions, rowdyism, and fear.

——••••◉◉••••——

The writer arrived in 1846, during the Mormon hegira, and after the temple was completed. Thousands of the Mormons had emigrated west and were on their long journey to Council Bluffs; whilst the western bank of the Mississippi was white with the tent cloths of those who had just expatriated themselves from their proud capitol city, and were organizing themselves into companies, preparatory to their over land march, to the Pacific coast. The city of Nauvoo did not then look like an oriental paradise, or any other sort of a paradise. Thousands of the population had already vacated the city; yet there were no vacant houses. Not only every house appeared to be occupied, but every separate room in each house contained a family. The miserable dilapidated and ruinous looking town, was still overcharged with an excessive population. There was nothing like "gorgeous splendor" in Nauvoo at that time, unless the huge "Mormon Temple," the house constructed without any known model, might be so considered.

We have no time to describe this heavy fortress looking building. The city of Nauvoo, which already had a history "well read of all men," and which outnumbered the Chicago of that day, in population, was really nothing but a straggling village; some good houses there were, but these were comparatively few. The Mormons were, in a great measure, sheltered by temporary buildings, which were eventually to give place to other and better structures. They had contemplated many improvements, but with the exception of the temple, had completed none. They had devised canals around the rapids and dams to secure the current of the Mississippi river, for manufacturing purposes, but nothing had been accomplished; all their energies had been wasted in the erection of the temple. Ordinary improvements, for the conveniences of the people, had not been thought of. There was not a side walk in the city, no street had been reduced to a grade, not a school house had yet been erected, or had even been contemplated. There was not a place in Illinois which had not developed more of the progressive element than Nauvoo.

This was the situation of Nauvoo where we first saw it, and yet we are continually reminded by those who ought to know better, how much Nauvoo has declined, since the expulsion of the Mormons. Nauvoo has vastly less population than it had in Mormon times, but vastly more of material progress, of wealth, and improvements, than it had in the best days of the rule of the Mormon dynasty.

In our last, we noticed the general appearance of Nauvoo in the spring of 1846. As yet there had been no devastation committed. War had not yet been declared in Hancock county. All the buildings which had ever been erected by the Mormons, in their city, were still standing. But now as the city was, having only existed some seven years, it presented a decayed and squalid appearance. It was not a "deserted village"; it still swarmed with population, but it was a population preparing for migration, which had no care for the surroundings of their city. There was nothing done by improving arts to enhance the natural beauty of the locality. Then there were many substantial and comfortable dwellings but the number of rude shanties, hastily erected for the shelter of a rapidly augmenting population, was much larger. Gardens, there were none. Fences had disappeared. There was scarcely an enclosed lot in the city. On the summit of the highest bluff in the city was enthroned the temple; huge and of its own peculiar model; constructed of white lime stone—so white that it glistened in the sun shine. It stood amongst the noted dwellings of the saints like a nightly giant, surrounded by an army of pygmies. It was the only building of modern times modeled and constructed by divine revelation, yet the unregenerated, mocking gentiles would fancy, that buildings vastly more beautiful and grand, had been constructed without any such supernatural assistance. We have not got time or space to elaborate a description of this building, so conspicuous in its day. Sufficient it is to say, that this grand effort of Mormon enterprise has perished—not a stone remains to mark its original site: even its solid foundations have been exhumed and sold for building purposes. The plow share has many times passed over its sacred area.

At the time of which we write the public mind was much excited over the Mormon question. The fact that the Mormons were selling out at very low figures was attracting a large number of strangers to the city. Many came with a view to speculation, others came to secure cheap homes, quite a number came with motives less worthy. It was well understood that the quiet then reigning was not to be trusted, that the Mormons were watched by jealous eyes, that their enemies were determined to enforce the contract for their removal at all hazards, even if violence, to the extent of civil war, should be necessary. The anticipation of civil strife had induced some of the worst class of society to make Nauvoo a temporary stopping place, men who lived by preying upon their fellow men, thieves, robbers and vagabonds, to congregate into the disturbed district for the purposes of plunder. Many of those desperadoes, who had confidence in the success of the Mormon cause, were found swaggering in the streets of Nauvoo—flourishing deadly weapons, revolvers of the old pepper box pattern, bowie knives of pretentious dimensions, of a pattern of which the immortal Bowie had never dreamed—the handy work of Nauvoo black smiths of the Mormon persuasion. These wretches more than any other, gave tone and character to the society of Nauvoo, at this period. They were most noisy and boisterous and most decided in the expression of opinion—were most sincere, and profuse and blasphemous in their denunciations of the d——d mobocrats, who were preparing to make a descent upon the holy city, to plunder the saints of the Most High. Besides, this modern banditti drank more whiskey themselves, and stood treat oftener and more liberally, than any or all others. They were the patrons and pets of the bar keepers of the times; and the bar keeper is always a leading institution in the land in which he is allowed full sway; and if he was not allowed full liberty, at the time of which we write, it was his own fault.

There was really no law in the land in the municipal sense. The legislature, disgusted with the many abuses of the Mormon charter, of the city of Nauvoo, had at one blow swept it out of existence. We have always doubted whether the legislature in this fit of righteous indignation had acted wisely. It has always appeared to us, that if these wise Solons assembled at Springfield, had modified the charter, by striking out its objectionable features and inserting others, which would control the fanatical and despotic tendencies of the wayward sect, that by such a course, they would have manifested more prudence and common sense, clearer judgment and showed wiser and more judicious statesmanship. The effect of the repeal of the Nauvoo charter, was to reduce the Mormon population of Hancock county, to the condition of outlaws, which state they occupied during the whole period of these troublesome times, until their final expulsion.

10

The Battle of Nauvoo

Conflict between Mormons and non-Mormons erupted again in the early summer of 1846 and continued sporadically until mid-September, when a non-Mormon posse seized control of Nauvoo and expelled the last Mormons. The cause for the fighting was that perhaps a thousand Mormons chose not to leave Nauvoo. By June the migration had virtually ceased and the non-Mormons believed, rightly as it turned out, that those who remained intended to stay. Some were Mormon dissenters, such as Joseph Smith's widow and children, who were on the outs with Brigham Young's group, while others simply saw no reason to abandon their property without real pressure. The differences between the Mormon groups were not apparent to outsiders, who tarred all with the same malevolent brush. In September 1846, a company of about three hundred militia rode to Golden's Point, a few miles southeast of Nauvoo, and encamped there, intending to encourage Mormon departure by a show of force. However, the Mormons responded by gathering a company of five to six hundred militia under Jacob Backenstos, and the non-Mormons retreated and disbanded.

Then non-Mormons developed another strategy: trying to keep the Saints bottled up inside Nauvoo. When a small group of Mormons went to Camp Creek to harvest grain during the summer, a non-Mormon mob captured them, whipped them, and sent them back to Nauvoo. That aroused the Mormons, who rallied under the leadership of William Pickett. He was a non-Mormon, a lawyer of southern background who had settled in Nauvoo earlier in 1846, and a "fire eater" with considerable oratorical ability. Hence, he became the leader of the Mormon vigilantes who rode out in search of members of the mob. Pickett's men captured a couple of non-Mormons, one of whom was almost certainly innocent. They later captured thirteen others in a group. All were held at Nauvoo without bail or examination. In retaliation the non-Mormons then seized some Mormons, including Phineas Young. Fortunately, the potentially explosive situation was defused when Pickett's prisoners were released on a writ of habeas corpus issued by the court in Quincy, and the non-Mormons then let their Mormon captives go. However, this episode led to the climactic military clash of the conflict.

The so-called Battle of Nauvoo in mid-September of 1846 was precipitated by the events of June and July. In August writs were sworn out by the non-Mormons, charging William Pickett and others with false imprisonment, and John Carlin was appointed special constable to arrest them. All of the charged men were apprehended except Pickett, who refused to give himself up. He also had the backing of many Mormons. So Carlin issued a proclamation on 17 August, calling for a posse comitatus to form in Carthage on 24 August to assist him in making the arrest. Of course, many non-Mormons—and perhaps Carlin himself—saw the situation as an opportunity to seize control of Nauvoo and enforce the agreed-upon evacuation of the city.

The posse of perhaps six hundred men spent more than two weeks organizing and preparing for the march to Nauvoo, while the Mormons were getting ready to defend their community from what they regarded as mobocratic action. Governor Ford was informed of the impending battle, and he sent Major James R. Parker of Fulton County to command the militia at Nauvoo. When Parker learned that the non-Mormon force was much superior, he left—ostensibly to get reinforcements from another county—and was replaced by Major Benjamin Clifford of Quincy. As this makes clear, by pursuing their plan to attack Nauvoo, the non-Mormon force was going against the authority of the state.

Colonel James W. Singleton, commander in chief of the non-Mormon force, attempted to work out an agreement whereby the Mormons would leave Nauvoo in sixty days but was not supported by the other non-Mormons, so he resigned his position. Unfortunately, his successor was Colonel (not General) Thomas S. Brockman, a Mormon-hating blacksmith and preacher from Brown County, who was more than willing to take command. On 10 September he marched his troops to the vicinity of Nauvoo, and on the following day he moved them to the northeastern outskirts of the city. Then he sent a message to the Mormon commander, asking for the surrender of arms and offering the Mormons thirty days to leave. The latter did not accept, perhaps because they feared surrendering their arms to a hostile force, so on the next day, 12 September, the battle was fought.

Once again, the best available account is by X. Y. Z., who not only witnessed the episode but later interviewed some of the participants. As he points out, cannons were fired on both sides, and at least three Mormons and one non-Mormon were killed. An undetermined number were wounded. The entire engagement lasted for an hour and fifteen minutes, and nothing decisive was accomplished. This article appeared as "Nauvoo—Then and Now" in the *Carthage Gazette* on 19 January 1876, p. 1.

On the following morning, it was thought expedient to try the Mormons with another flag of truce; but the trial resulted in nothing. It only remained to fight for the possession of Nauvoo. An advance was accordingly made by the anti-Mormon force, in a southerly direction. A halt was made on Ripley street, opposite the house now owned and occupied by John Hohl. It was then the property of John J. Brent, and the house situated on the premises was seized upon for a hospital. The troops, both the first and second regiments, were halted in the low ravine or hollow, at the place indicated. The artillery was advanced on the hill, some two or three hundred yards north west, and were playing on the Mormon lines, with what effect no one at the time knew; but as subsequent events proved, without any effect whatever, and here is where the Mormons lost their opportunity. Brockman had advanced his artillery without any support. He had two regiments crowded together in the ravine, which in their present position, could do nothing; but it never occurred to him that that [*sic*] this force, or a part of it, could have been made useful by supporting the artillery. In the mean time, had a single company of the Mormon force, made a dash on the battery, they could have captured every gun, and turned them on their enemies, and effectually prevented any further advance.

Upon remonstrance, however, Gen. Brockman sent a force to protect the batteries. In the mean time, the Mormons, during the preceding night, had gone to work for the first time, in preparing for the defense of the place. They had thrown up, or rather, had constructed of old timbers, breast works, between Mulholland and Knight streets, and between Knight and Young streets. One of these breast works was on the place known as the Park place; then the property of Wm. D. Mildeberger, of New York, and commanded the street running north and south, by the Prentice place, and known as the Carthage road.

A small squad of Mormons was placed behind each of these breastworks and a small force was detailed from the anti-Mormon camp, to assail these works. This movement was more of a feint, than for the purpose of a fight. Whilst this small force was engaging the breastworks on the anti-Mormon right, the main force was advanced on their left, with a view to route the Mormon force on their right, and force a passage into the city on Parley street.

The advance of the army was made under a severe fire, both from the small arms and the batteries of the Mormons, which wounded quite a number of their men. The anti-Mormons took their positions and formed a line of battle; their center resting on a brick house, now owned and occupied by Lewis Stutz, being one block east of the Carthage road. The Mormon line was right across the road or street, and was formed in squads, around some straggling houses, along that road. Some of these troops having no better protection than was afforded by a very shabby and dilapidated old picket fence, which, by the way, is with various patches and repairs, still standing.

The firing of small arms was kept up with spirit, by both parties, whilst the artillery on both sides, was raining down solid and grape shots and slugs. The solid and grape shot, from the anti-Mormon battery, and the slugs from the Mormon. These slugs were an ugly contrivance, produced by smashing up an old steam engine, and whizzed through the air like the shriek of a lost spirit. We never understood that these slugs hurt any body; but that they frightened many brave anti-Mormons almost out of their wits, is beyond question and is not to be wondered at. The anti-Mormons were instructed to watch for the smoke of the Mormon battery, and instantly upon its appearance, to fall flat on the ground, and let the shot pass harmlessly over them. This order was obeyed promptly, and to the letter, leaving no doubt of the admirable discipline of the anti-Mormon army. But one sturdy old farmer, who had not heard the order amid the din and confusion of the battle, when he saw the whole army prostrate before him, instantly formed the conclusions that some luckless shot had finished the whole anti-Mormon force. And that like the numberless Assyrian host, encamped around the city of David, when swept by the wing of the destroying angel, they were all dead corpses. The old gentleman did not wait to see the mystery unraveled, but immediately made the best of his way home, where he reported that the whole army had perished. That all his comrades were lying dead and unburied in Nauvoo, with their feet to the foe, and their sightless eyes towards the sun, and that he alone had escaped to tell the story, that he was the only "reminiscence" of the Mormon war.

Nor was the unsophisticated old man alone in his conclusions, in relation to the havoc caused by these fierce shrieking fragments of an old steam engine. One of the guns of the Mormon battery was served by one Bolander, an old Methodist preacher, who might have been reported to his conference at the time in a "state of falling from Grace." The old gentleman had lost his religious equipoise, and was thus rapidly gravitating towards "the world, the flesh, and the devil." The old man was in much the same condition as the good and pious Bishop Polk, during the war of the rebellion. When he commanded an army corps in the rebel army, the good man would often so forget himself as to swear an oath as round and fierce, as an old salt-water commodore, and so could the Rev. Bolander, and besides this accomplishment, he had the most vigorous and extravagant imagination, and could garnish and decorate a story equal to any romance writer in the land.

The Rev. Bolander, commanded a gun as already stated, and one which was handled with more dexterity and vigor than any other gun of the Mormon battery; and the Reverend Gentleman, long after the battle, informed the writer of this article, that it was all "Bosh" about the anti-Mormon loss, being as trifling as represented in their report. "I myself, at a single shot from my gun, brought down thirty of the rascals, I saw them fall, and their guns fly from their hands." So reported the Rev. Bolander.

The anti-Mormon Batteries, in the meantime, riddled the houses which sheltered the Mormons. Captain Anderson had placed his company behind the Lamareaux' Blacksmith shop, which stood in the corner of Mulholland street and the Carthage road, and which has long since disappeared. This force so situated and protected, was armed with the celebrated Mormon invention, called the fifteen shooting rifle. The idea was to charge their guns, and step out and deliver their fire. Captain Anderson, in thus delivering his fire, was shot dead and his son, a mere lad of 14 or 15 years of age, immediately afterwards suffered the same fate. In the meantime the blacksmith shop, which was a mere shell of brick, was shattered considerably by the solid shot of the anti-Mormon battery. One shot finally passed throught [sic] the frail building, rattling the bricks around the ears of these heroes at such a rate, that they considered that it was time to seek a safer locality, and they accordingly retreated west, down Mulholland street, two or three blocks and took shelter behind a substantial brick dwelling house, then owned and occupied by an old widow lady, known as Mrs. Naggle. This retreat was made without loss, either in killed or wounded; but one poor fellow by the name of Norris, who conducted his retreat on his own hook, who fled south with a view of renewing the fight, under the shelter of the next house, had proceeded but a few steps when he was cut in two, by a solid shot from the anti-Mormon Battery.

Our brave warriors, who were recuperating their exhausted energies, beneath the protecting walls of Mrs. Naggle's house, were a little surprised to see the old lady occupant make her appearance, right amongst them, with a broom stick in her hands. "Cowardly dogs!" she demanded, "What are you doing here, where the mob is fighting their way down into the city?" One fellow insisted that they had been ordered to fall back to that point, to oppose the advancing column of the enemy. "And I order you to the front" she responded, "to prevent the enemy from making any advance; oppose the enemy where they are, and not where they may come," retorted the old woman with flashing eyes and broom stick ready for an assault.

Our exhausted heroes heard the booming of the cannon in front and they heard the rattling of the old woman's tongue in the rear. They didn't known exactly what to do, but finally, slowly and sullenly advanced to the front, considering the cannon balls a less danger than that which threatened them from the enraged and spunky old lady of the broom stick.

In the mean time, as these fellows were nervously wending their way back, to the point of attack, casting many a "longing and lingering look behind," in apprehension of a charge upon their rear from the excited Amazon, who had ordered them around, as if she were a major general in full command, Captain Bolander was plying his artillery, shooting his steamboat at the enemy, in a manner which made things lively. Whilst thus engaged, he was visited by a genteel and dignified old lady, a Mrs. Player, an English lady, the wife of the superintending architect of the Temple, and of the Nauvoo house, whose mansion was contiguous to the battle ground, and with in range of the anti-Mormon batteries. A stray shot, from an anti-Mormon cannon had fallen in her door yard, and the old lady brought it and presented it to Captain Bolander. "Captain" said the polished old lady, "please return this ball to the anti-Mormons with my compliments." Mrs. Player then retired, a shower of musket-balls whizzing in her ears, which appeared to disturb her equanimity no more than the buzzing of so many mosquitoes. Of course the gallant captain returned the cannon ball as requested. Whether the whole anti-Mormon army bowed their thanks to the polite old lady, by falling prostrate on the ground we have not been informed.

The battle was about over. The anti-Mormons had expended their am[m]unition, and like the heroes of Bunker Hill they were compelled to retire; which they did in good order.

The question, as to who commanded the Mormons in this engagement, is an open one. Major Clifford was in chief command but the life of the gallant Major was too precious to be hazzarded [*sic*] on the battlefield. He established his headquarters at the Temple, and placed the masonry of that strong fortress between himself and danger. Major Clifford, it is hardly necessary to state, survived this battle. Col. Johnson, who was to have commanded on the field, did not put in an appearance. He was at home in bed, sick, or pretending to be so. The impetuous and fiery Pickett was on the field; but his fifteen shooter was not half so eloquent as he was. The solution of who commanded is found in the fact that every Mormon who fought at all, did what was right in his own eyes, without taking orders from any body. Anderson directed the movements, until he was killed, and after his death, the fighting was at random.

After the battle the next thing was to give the dead a decent interment, which was not a very difficult or laborious job. The Mormons lost in killed three, and a very few wounded and none of them seriously. The anti-Mormons had a number wounded, and only one mortally. . . .

—••●● 11 ●●••—

The Treaty That Ended the Conflict

As the miniature civil war raged in Hancock County, leaders in Quincy quickly organized a committee to negotiate yet another agreement to end the fighting between the two hostile parties. The committee of a hundred men, formed by Henry Asbury and Isaac N. Morris, and chaired by Andrew W. Johnson, then traveled to Nauvoo, sending word ahead that they were coming to act as mediators. After securing a suspension of the fighting, the Quincy group formed subcommittees to visit the leaders on each side. They eventually worked out an arrangement whereby the Mormons would surrender their arms temporarily to the Quincy committee, and the non-Mormon posse would enter the city. Moreover, the treaty stipulated that the remaining Mormon population of Nauvoo must cross the Mississippi River as soon as possible. That, not the arrest of William Pickett, had become the central objective of the non-Mormon forces.

The text of the treaty is reprinted here from Josiah B. Conyers, *A Brief History of the Leading Causes of the Hancock Mob in the Year 1846* (St. Louis: n. p., 1846), 62. Shortly after it was signed, it also was published in area newspapers.

—••●●◗●●••—

Articles of accommodation, treaty and agreement, made and entered into, this sixteenth of September, A.D., 1846, between Almon W. Babbit, Joseph L. Haywood, and John S. Fullmer, Trustees in Trust for the Church of Jesus Christ of Latter Day Saints of the one part—Thomas S. Brockman, commander of the posse, and John Carlin, special constable and civil head of the posse of Hancock county, of the second part—and Andrew Johnson, chairman of the citizens of Quincy, of the third part—

1. The city of Nauvoo will surrender. The force of Col. Brockman, to enter and take possession of the city to-morrow, the 17th of September, at three o'clock, P.M.

2. The arms to be delivered to the Quincy committee, to be returned on the crossing of the river.

3. The Quincy committee pledge themselves to use their influence for the protection of persons and property from all violence, and the officers of the camp and the men pledge themselves to protect all persons and property from violence.

4. The sick and helpless to be protected and treated with humanity.

5. The Mormon population of the city to leave the State, or disperse as soon as they can cross the river.

6. Five men, including the Trustees of the Church, and five clerks, with their families, (Wm. Pickett not one of the number,) to be permitted to remain in the city for the disposition of property, free from all molestation and personal violence.

7. Hostilities to cease immediately, and ten men of the Quincy committee to enter the city in the execution of their duty as soon as they think proper.

We, the undersigned, subscribe to, ratify, and confirm the foregoing articles of accommodation, treaty and agreement, the day and year first above written.

Almon W. Babitt,	Trustees in Trust for the Church
Joseph L. Haywood,	of Jesus Christ of Latter Day
John S. Fulmer,	Saints.
Andrew Johnson,	Chairman of the Com. of Quincy.
Thos. S. Brockman,	Commanding Posse.
John Carlin,	Special Constable.

12

*A Nauvoo Resident
Who Tried to Stay Neutral*

Among the documents about Nauvoo in 1846 is a letter by a store owner, William Cooper, Jr. (1813–?), a native of Ohio who had moved from Kentucky to the Mormon community in the spring of that year. His wife was apparently from Harrison County, Indiana, and his letter is addressed to the Crozier family there. Cooper describes the same kind of lawlessness in Nauvoo that X. Y. Z. complained about (see Part VI, Document 9), but he also depicts the difficulty in remaining neutral as the conflict between the Mormons and their enemies accelerated. In particular he describes the intimidation of neutrals like himself by Mormon sympathizers (Jacks). Although he names no one, he refers to the man who had recently married Emma Smith, the widow of the Mormon prophet—Lewis C. Bidamon, who had settled in Nauvoo during 1846. Because of his negative experience with both the Mormons—one of whom had robbed his store—and the leading Jack Mormons, Cooper was glad to see the non-Mormons take over the community.

He also mentions that, at the time he was writing, early in 1848, the town was "filling up with Dutch [i.e., Germans] and French." Those were, in fact, the dominant ethnic groups in Nauvoo for generations afterward. However, the city was never repopulated and had only two thousand residents by the turn of the century. It remains a small village today.

Cooper's letter was written from the Warsaw area, where he lived for many years, first as a farmer and tinplate worker, and later as a store owner. It is printed, by permission, from a photocopy in the James H. Lawton Collection, Archives and Special Collections, Western Illinois University Library, Macomb.

———————————•••••◉•••••———————————

Warsaw, Ill. Jan 2, 1848

Much esteemed Friends, *Croziers* all:—We rec'd your letter this morning, Robert, and was truly glad to hear from you, as well as to give us a start to write to you which we have thought of a hundred times or more. We thought, & wanted to hear, and there it ended, in a vague desire to see or hear from some that knew us. This letter is the most gratifying that we have received since we left. For it was only night before last that Almira dreamed of being in the old neighborhood & seeing a good many of her acquaintances. She realized the truth of some of her dream in the receipt of your letter. The asking of questions, the answers in your letter, and her dreams are exactly. (Don't laugh at our credulity.) We believe that dreams sometimes are the precorsair [*sic*] to events, or that we may find parallels to our dreams sometimes. Of ourselves since we left Brandenburg. We went as we intended to Nauvoo where I bought me a house & lot where we lived a most disagreeable life for eighteen months on account of the difficulties that existed between the Mormons and antimormons though not on that account all the time. That lasted about six months after we went there but after those difficulties ceased, the society was of the very worst kind. Drinking, Gambling, Stealing, and Lewdness comprised nine tenths of what was done. Out of 27 cases before the Grand Jury, 20 of them came up from Nauvoo. This has given it a check together with poverty. The want of means to carry on the above branches of debauchery has scattered those concerned hither and thither so that the place is a little better than it was and is filling up with Dutch and French. I thought to have weathered it out, till I was convinced that the population would finally resolve itself into Dutch, French, & some few miserable Americans so I sold out and left. From the continual carousing, Shooting etc kept us in continual dread. There was no business doing there more than merely furnishing the town. The country being all anti-Mormon would not come there to trade and never did trade there much so I did not hold my own. I am worse off than when I went there. I am now in a good place & my prospects are good. Almira don't like it because she is lonesome but I am in hopes that she will get over that when we are properly settled here. The prettiest cite [*sic*] for a town is Nauvoo on the Mississippi and also the most despisable [*sic*] place to me. Let it go.

Warsaw is the first landing below the Rapids on the Illinois side & there is a good deal of trade from a great distance comes here & is quite a commercial point and I have a farm about twelve miles from this place that I exchanged my house and lot for. The Mormons are nearly all gone from the county & those that remain are too poor to go. There are perhaps some good, ignorant well meaning Mormons among the class of them but the Leaders are all villains at heart. Vampires sucking their subsistence from the poor ignorant ones. I cannot give you any idea of what they are; you only can know to see & converse with them and then add to that a little experience.

We have never had a letter from *Mother* since she left us *nor James*. I have written to *James* to come out. I suppose they are about *Milton* in *Wayne County*, Indiana but do not know for certain. We have seen your *brother* and *sisters* that live in Iowa. Her brother was at my house in Nauvoo about 3 months ago. He was at that time engaged in putting the cabin on a steamboat and was on his way down to St. Louis with the boat to finish the job. He is a very pious upright kind of man. I should have tried to have had mother and James with us before, but I had no prospects more than people saying, "Hold on, times will be better," & not wishing to take them to such a place I never could write and to this same cause I may attribute my neglect of writing to any of my friends. Indeed we often thought of the good people about your neighborhood and Brandenberg. At Nauvoo everybody were strangers to one another and then there were Mormons coming from a distance and settling in as new citizens and another class that are termed Jack Mormons which made it but little better for us than being in a foreign country or we may say in among the Mexicans. These Jack Mormons are those who were more or less allied to the Mormons either in their counterfeiting & swindling, and to sustain themselves fight for the Mormons. They are more or less allied to the Mormons. One of the most notorious Jacks has lately married the widow of Joe Smith (within two weeks) and these same Jacks are those Jacks are those [*sic*] who said publickly [*sic*] "If you don't turn out and fight with us, you are against us and shall be the the [*sic*] very first ones to be *shot* when it is convenient." This was said of the neutral party to which I belong. I am an antiMormon in feeling and in deed but don't choose to join in any fight nor did the antis require it for they said to the new citizens "if you can't consistent with your concience [*sic*], come & join us, just lay neutral & you and your property shall be protected." This accorded with my sentiments exactly and I did in that way so when the antis proved victorious & marched into town we found it in that way and all who fought against them were expelled [from] the town but not misused except some few of the worst Jacks were hurried off in double quick time with Bayonets after them. There were some old inoffensive Mormons who were protected by the antis and are there now. Some Mormons who cleared [out] while sick through fear suffered no doubt but none were driven by the antis. The tale gets exaggerated when it gets abroad and entirely misrepresented. Many of the poor had provisions given to them from the antiMormons. I have had frequent opportunities of hearing some of the tales told at a distance and I was there to know what was going on. I being in a neutral position could see and know and do know that the antiMormons were right and mean right and did right. If it was not legal they dont pretend to say it was legal. It was an alternative & the only alternative and the Jacks were as brands kindling discord & encouraging the Mormons to stay. During the time the antiMormons were encamped out on the prairie the threats got so pointed and strong that we got too much alarmed to stay in our house so we put up at the Hotel during which time one of the Mormon families who were trying to sail under the new citizens flag till the antis came too close broke open my shop and stole about sixty dollars worth of groceries. I hope they had enough to take them as far the other side of California as they were this side. There are as I said before some good Mormons. (But you recollect poor Tray.) I am afraid I am consuming too much about Mormonism so drop it. I might say something about the country. It is a delightful country. Perhaps the Des Moines valley is equal to the *Miami Valley* if not superior & it is filling up rapidly. The Des Moines empties into the Mississippi opposite Warsaw and perhaps is a better country than on this side of the river. The Des Moines divides Missouri from Iowa. It is a fact as *Mrs. Holiday* says the young men of America are too slack. They are staying just where they were raised and For-eigners are coming in and taking the cream of the Land & leaving the native born to the old worn out Lands on which they have been raised. There is now as good land in the west here as the world produces for $1.25 per acre. Last fall there was a company of Dutch who bought & settled a Township of Land in Iowa about 100 miles back and next summer there are an other company to come. Excuse me, *Aunt Becky* said it and it is a fact. I am afraid if I dont lengthen my lines I wont have room to finish. I have to talk for Almira too. She has a host to say and I reckon you will have to ask *George* and *Thomas* to give her Love to her old associates; altho she has not written she has often thought of the many pleasures she has enjoyed in that neighborhood and many of the scenes that never will be blotted out of her memory. Remember us to *your Father, Uncle James Holiday* and all our friends.

Wm and Almira Cooper

•••• 13 ••••

A Mormon Woman Recalls
the Battle of Nauvoo

The experience of Mormons who were expelled from Nauvoo in September 1846 is exemplified by the short memoir of Ann Eliza Coffin Garner. Although she was a small child in 1846, she recalls the response of her parents, which must have been typical of many Latter Day Saints. Her father fought the non-Mormons in the battle; her mother hated to see them occupy the temple. And her memoir reveals the hardship and sorrow that the Mormons suffered as they left in haste to begin their long journey to the West.

Garner's memoir also illustrates something about the operation of the Mormon mind. As members of the church in later years looked back on the Nauvoo experience, which was regarded as an episode of sacred history, their recollections were often unconsciously reshaped to verify that sacredness. Hence, Garner asserts that Joseph Smith told her father to fight the mob, that he would not be hurt, and so he wasn't. But of course, Smith had been dead for over two years before the battle—and almost a year before the Coffin family even moved to Nauvoo. The Smith story was spun in Garner's mind as part of an unconscious effort to validate his prophetic ability and, therefore, the truth of the church. Similarly, the dramatic last words of her father, "go on to the valley, this is the true church," sound suspiciously like the kind of thing that is "recalled" when memory becomes the servant of faith.

This memoir is published here for the first time. It is held in the collection of the Utah State Historical Society Library, Salt Lake City.

I, Ann Eliza (Coffin) Garner was born of goodly parents in the state of Indiana, Wayne Co., Richmond on 24 Jan 1839. My parents William Barney Coffin and Abagail Starbuck joined the Church of Jesus Christ of L.D.S. in about 1843 & was with the Saints through all the trials, mobbings, & persecution. They came from N. Carolina to Indiana & on to Nauvoo Ill in the spring of 1845.

I was but a small girl but well do I remember the sufferings & deprivations & sorrows of the Saints. I well remember the army coming into the town of Nauvoo & hearing them shoot their guns when 2 miles away from town & saw the cannon ball roll past our door Then the drive from Nauvoo & the suffering that followed. I well rem[em]ber seeing the mob take possession of the Temple & how they climbed on the outside of the railing that was built around the top about one foot from the edge, & marched around the Temple & the remark of my dear mother when she saw them; she said "I wish the old Devils would fall off from there & break their necks." My father was sick in bed for 2 weeks, he got right up, dressed, shouldered his gun & went right out into battle & fought the mob. During the skirmish the mob was driven across a slough. While father was gone a mob came in disguise & told my mother she would have to leave or get killed. Before father left the Prophet Joseph said, "Go, & not one hair of your head shall be lost." So he went & while out a cannon ball passed over his head & knocked his hat off, but the prophecy of the Lord was fulfilled & not one hair of his head was lost. They returned him to his family with the rest of the brethren & shared with them until driven out of Nauvoo to Mount Rose [Montrose] into Iowa or Council Bluffs in 184——. He died 4 June 1850 at Council Bluffs Iowa & his last words to my mother were "go on to the valley, this is the true church." O what sorrow to us to be left alone without a father & have to lay him down alone & go on. We were too poor to go with the saints & so we had to stay over for 2 yrs until we could get a little better prepared for the hard long journey which lay before us. . . .

14

The Final Evacuation

The Nauvoo treaty, dated 16 September 1846, gave the remaining Mormons five days to leave the city, and a few days later, on 19 September, a correspondent for the *Burlington Hawkeye*, published in Iowa Territory about thirty miles north of Nauvoo on the Mississippi, witnessed this departure and wrote a brief account. He signed the article "CHE MO KO MON," a Sauk term meaning "white man," so his identity is unknown, but he may have been living near Fort Madison. His letter to the editor, entitled "Nauvoo. The Day After It was Evacuated," appeared in the 24 September 1846 issue of the *Burlington Hawkeye*, p. 2.

The article is a very effective piece of writing, largely because of its immediacy. The author apparently wrote it in the very sanctuary of the temple, after witnessing the results of the battle and the still-ongoing evacuation. He caught the eerie quiet of the deserted streets and the incongruity of soldiers and armaments in a sacred building that proclaimed on its wall, "The Lord is our Sacrifice." Also, he conveyed the suffering of hundreds of people by depicting a few cases of distress that came to his attention.

Also notable about this article is that the author does not condemn the non-Mormons for their inhumanity or criticize the Mormons for their fanaticism, but rather suggests that both were responsible for the human tragedy he witnessed. The poor widow from Yorkshire, whom he encountered on the street, was in distress not only because she and her family had to leave but also because her husband "gave all his money to the church." She clearly felt abandoned, if not exploited, by the church and the circumstances of the exodus. And while the author roamed through the defeated and occupied town, he recalled the Mormon prophet, who had ironically reveled there in "military glory." Also, by referring to Nauvoo as a "doomed city," he invites the reader to reflect on the reasons for its downfall. Whoever he was, CHE MO KO MON wrote one of the finest newspaper accounts of the Mormon conflict.

DEAR HAWK—My powers of description are totally inadequate to give your readers any just conception of the "scenes" that now present themselves on every hand in this vicinity. On either shore of the Mississippi may be seen a long line of tents, wagons, cattle, &c., with numberless wretched specimens of humanity. Since the armistice or "treaty" the Mormons are crossing in almost breathless haste. Three or four "flats" are running constantly, both day and night. This morning, Saturday, 19th, at the solicitation of Capt. Vrooman, of the Fort Madison Guards, I crossed the river from Montrose, to take a peek at this City of Desolation. We proceeded to the Mansion House, where we met with a small detachment of soldiers and a number of strangers. From thence we went to the Temple. On entering the vestibule of this renowned edifice, a singular spectacle presented itself. The seats of the High Priests of the "Twelve" and of the "seventy" were occupied by a grim visaged soldiery. Some lay sleeping on their "arms," and others lay rolled up in their blankets. On every hand lay scattered about in beautiful confusion, muskets, swords, cannon balls and terrible missiles of death. Verily, thought I, how are the *holy* places desecrated! I thought of old Oliver Cromwell, when he drove the horses of his army through the "cloisters" of the Worcester Cathedral, and appropriated the Baptismal fount as a manger.

I am penning this scrawl to you in the upper seat of the Sanctuary. Over my head there is an inscription in large gold letters, "The Lord is our Sacrifice"; on my right lie three soldiers asleep, resting on their arms—my feet are resting on a pile of chain shot—and a keg of powder, just discovered, lies at my elbow.

I left the Temple "solitary and alone," to perambulate the desolate city. All was still and hushed as the charnel house.—Not a human being was seen. Houses appeared suddenly deserted, as though the inmates had precipitately fled from a pestilence or the burning of a volcano. Some had windows open and the flowers blooming [in] the casements, but no fair hand was there, and no breath was heard, save the rustling zephyrs of heaven. It appeared as if the vengeance of the Almighty rested upon this doomed city.

I roamed over the vast Parade Ground where, four years ago, I beheld the *soi distant* "Prophet" review his Legion of 3000 strong, in all the "pride and circumstance" of military glory. Where now is the Prophet? Let the Plains of Carthage answer! And where the multitudes that shouted hosannas to his name? Verily, thought I, "truth is stranger than fiction." I returned again through the desolate streets to the Mansion House. One solitary being, with a child in her arms, stood at the corner of a street, and saluted me with an imploring and almost frantic look.

"Pray, sir, are you one of the committee," said she.

When I replied that I was a stranger, her eyes filled with tears. She related her history. Tis soon told, and is the history of hundreds.

"We came from Yorkshire, England, my husband died eighteen months after our arrival. He gave all his money to the church."

"Where are your friends," said I.

"I have none—not one. The soldiers say I must leave in two hours. This child is sick, and my other is a cripple." She had flour enough for but one dinner!

On the Montrose side of the Mississippi, many of the scenes were heart-breaking. I stopped at the door of one tent, arrested by the subdued sobs of a young mother, whose heart was broken with grief. By her side lay her infant, a corpse. She had neither friend or relative to bury her child, nor a mouthful of food to eat.

I was convinced that Gen. Brockman, to his honor be it spoken, conducted [the evacuation] with marked distinction and humanity; and the night the army took possession of the city, not a rail was disturbed or a particle of property molested. Although they encamped adjoining an extensive orchard of choice fruit, not a hand was laid upon it. The boat is leaving for Montrose and I must drop my pen. Perhaps more anon from your faithful chronicler.

CHE MO KO MON.

——————•••• 15 ••••——————

The Empty City

Another well-written description of Nauvoo is set at the end of September, after the evacuation was completed. Like the previous article, it was a letter to the editor of a newspaper—in this case, the St. Louis *Missouri Republican*. The author signed it simply "T. G." ("A Week in Nauvoo—View from the Temple," *Missouri Republican*, September 29, 1845), but since the letter was later reprinted in Thomas Gregg's *The Prophet of Palmyra* (New York: John B. Alden, 1890), 369–74, he was probably the author (see Part II, Document 6).

His account is of interest for several reasons. First, he discusses the sale of Mormon property, providing specific information about how cheaply vacated homes could be acquired. Also, he takes an actual count of the city's buildings from atop the temple, itemizing the vast number of "mere shanties" that reveal Nauvoo's poverty. And he briefly comments on the small occupying force, located at the temple. At the same time, Gregg views the deserted city from a historical perspective, comparing it to the "little town of Commerce" that he knew during his earliest years in the county. He was always outspokenly opposed to violence, but he had deplored much that had gone on in Nauvoo, so it is not surprising that he closes his letter with an example of religious fanaticism—the abandonment of a wounded woman and one small child by her husband, a "rabid Mormon" who wanted to go west.

——————•••• ••••——————

Warsaw, Illinois, Sept. 29th, 1846.

Since my last letter I have spent a week in Nauvoo, and can attest the truth of the remarks of another of your correspondents, in regard to the desolate appearance of the city.

I arrived there on Monday evening of last week. On Tuesday morning I took a stroll through a portion of the now deserted streets, and for miles, I may safely say, I passed nothing but tenantless houses; some of them closed and barred, and others with doors wide open, as if left in haste. All along the city, for miles, wherever I went, might be seen on the doors, or on the walls, some notice that the tenement was for sale, or for rent. Every thing indicates that Mormonism is for ever extinct in Illinois. As a people they are completely subdued. Not one, in my opinion, will ever try to regain a foothold in Hancock. They are selling their little property at very low rates, indeed, almost giving it away—for the sake of raising means to take them away. Horses, cows, oxen, and wagons, are in great demand. Many design to join the expedition, which has gone in advance, to the wilderness of the Far West, while many others have already left for points up and down the river.

There are many instances of individual distress and suffering, and how could it be otherwise in a case like this? Many, doubtless, have left the city with nothing to live upon a day in advance. Many have crossed the river, who were entirely destitute of the means to sustain their families before, and who now have added to their former miseries the want of a house to live in, or a roof to shelter them from the "peltings of the pitiless storm." Many have nothing left them in the wide world but the little hut which they tenanted in the city, and the small patch of ground upon which it stands, and for which, probably, they will not be able to realize the sum of twenty dollars. I was present myself at the sale of two lots of ground, with a log house and a few fruit trees on each, for one of which the purchaser paid a horse, and for the other a cow, and the holders seemed glad to get away with so much. Low as this, doubtless, seemed to them, who had probably paid $200 or $300 each; yet the purchaser had better kept his horse and cow. If all the lots in Nauvoo could be bought at the same rate, I would consider them dearly paid for.

During my stay I took several o[c]casions to look at the city and surrounding country from the top of the Temple. It is, indeed, a grand and imposing scene, and presents the most magnificent view to be found any where on the banks of the Mississippi. There is but one point on the river that exceeds it in beauty, in my opinion, and that is Rock Island. Ten years ago, when all that part of the city which lies east of the Temple was covered with forest trees, and little patches of oak and other timber dotted the flat part of the city nearest the river bank, and the little town of Commerce, with its five or six houses huddled together on the bank, it presented a very different aspect from what it does at present. Then it presented nature in all her loveliness: the placid and broad current of the Mississippi, its islands and sand bars—the far reaching prairies of Iowa—the bold bluff which runs in semi-circular form around the town of Montrose (then Fort Des Moines), with here and there a wreath of ascending smoke, to tell the habitation of some settler—that is the picture it presented ten or twelve years ago. But now how changed is the scene! What a mutation it has undergone! And yet, it is now a thousand times more desolate. The only thing I noticed which had undergone no change since I was familiar with it in 1836 and '7, was Cutler's Grave. It was enclosed with a stone wall, and stood about half a mile from the river near the road which descended the hill from where the Temple now stands—and there it is yet, standing in the midst of all this desolation, looking the same as it did ere the hand of man had wrought all this change around it. GEORGE Y. CUTLER was one of the earliest settlers of Hancock County, and one of its first county commissioners—dying, he was buried at this spot.

I took occasion to ascertain as near as possible the number of houses in the city. From my position on the Temple, I could count a large portion of the city; and from actual count, and estimate based upon count, I think there are at least two thousand houses in the city proper, and in the suburbs five hundred more—making in all two thousand five hundred houses. About one-half of these are mere shanties, built some of logs, some of poles plastered over, and some framed. Of the remaining portion—say twelve hundred houses—all are tolerably fit residences, and one-half are good brick or frame houses. There are probably five hundred brick houses in the city, most of which are good buildings, and some are elegant and handsomely finished residences, such as would adorn any city.

Of these two thousand five hundred houses, I think about one-twelfth are tenanted—some by Mormons who had not yet got away, the remainder by Anti-Mormons, new or old settlers, who have been permitted to stay.

Col. GEDDES, of Fountain Green, in this county, was left in command of a small force, when the army was disbanded, and has been in command during the past week. He has now returned to his home, leaving twenty or thirty men at the Temple, under command of Major McAULEY and Mr. BRATTLE. A small force will probably remain in the city as long at the Mormons remain on the other side of the river.

No event of importance has transpired during the week. A certain Dr. OLIVER DRESSER, who hails from Maine, and who was somewhat conspicuous in the late difficulties, as a friend and companion of PICKETT's, ventured over on Wednesday from the other side. He was taken into custody and kept in the Temple till morning, and then marched to the river in double quick time, between two files of men, where he took passage for Iowa. A few other scenes of similar character, to some of which the ceremony of *dipping* was added, is all that occurred during the week, of an exciting character.

Several cases of deep distress, mostly lone widows and orphans, came to my knowledge during my stay. In all of these aid was freely given. One of these cases is a peculiar one. During the preparations previous to the fight, one of the horsemen of the city, which riding through the street, was thrown from his horse, and his gun discharged, the ball from which entered the body of a Mrs. HAYWOOD, who was in the door at the time. The lady was badly wounded, but not killed; and was unable to be removed from the city, at the time the *posse* entered.

Her husband being a rabid Mormon, ran over the river, leaving her and a young child on this side, where she fell under the notice of the Anti-Mormons. Provision was immediately made for her support—medical aid procured, and every care and attention bestowed which was in the power of the commander or his men. She is now doing well, and will in a few days, be removed to some place in the interior until she will be able to go to her friends in Vermont—as she has decided not to follow her husband into the wilderness. What renders her case more pitiable is, that he has possession of her three children, all under ten years old, and is making use of them to induce her to alter her determination. She never was a Mormons [*sic*] but in that confidence which woman only repose, in the object of her regard, she followed him to Nauvoo. Since that time, her confidence has been shaken, and she has now determined never to cross the Mississippi, to swell the tide of war which Mormonism is destined to carry in its train. This accident, which she doubtless regarded as a most unfortunate one, I regard as one of the most fortunate circumstances of her life. It has been the means of separating an interesting woman from a brutal and fanatical husband who would else have dragged her into the far wilderness to suffer unutterable woes.

Yours, etc.,
T. G.

16

Governor Ford Gets Reinvolved

The takeover of Nauvoo by non-Mormons had an impact on Governor Ford (see Part IV, Document 7). While he was glad to have the troublesome Mormons out of Illinois, he had clearly tried to prevent forcible expulsion, so the action of Colonel Brockman's military unit was yet another blow to his authority and prestige. Afterward Ford felt that he must do something to reassert civil authority in Nauvoo, and he also wanted to restore to their homes some "new citizens" who had been ejected for assisting the Mormons in the battle. He therefore gathered two hundred militia, marched to Hancock County, and accomplished both tasks. Although he was criticized, Ford encountered no overt resistance, and non-Mormons stated that he had been misinformed about the possibility of opposition. In fact he was ridiculed for overreacting.

The following excerpt from Ford's 7 December 1846 message to the Illinois Senate, as printed in the *Warsaw Signal* on 19 December 1846, p. 3, describes his venture into the county, which was the final military effort of the Mormon era in Illinois. Ford made clear in his report that he was disgusted with the lawlessness of the non-Mormons, who had proven to be just as blind to the rights of others as the Mormons had been earlier.

In a few days the main force of the posse was disbanded; Brockman returned home, leaving Col. Geddes, who appeared to be a gentleman, [with] a hundred men who volunteered to remain to prevent the return of those who had been expelled, or who had fled, knowing that they would be expelled and otherwise cruelly treated.

This posse of one hundred was gradually diminished to about thirty men under Major McCall, and continued to exercise all the power and authority of Government in Nauvoo, committing many high handed acts of tyranny and injustice and, as they allege, some acts of charity to the suffering Mormons, until they heard that I had raised a small force and was marching to disperse them, when they disbanded.

I left Springfield on the 20th of October, with seventy men, under the command of Capt. Robert Allen, which force was increased by the time I reached Hancock county to about two hundred. The motive for going over this time was to restore the new citizens not being Mormons to their homes, who had left or been driven away. As to the Mormons, I was well satisfied that they could not be persuaded to come back on any terms. Although I had once sent over a military force to restore the Anti-Mormons to their homes, after being driven or rather frightened away by the Sheriff and his Mormon posse; and although I had now gone over to restore another class of citizens to their homes, who had been driven away by the Anti-Mormons; yet very much to my astonishment I encountered a hostility and bitterness of feeling from the Anti-Mormons which was truly surprising and unlooked for. As soon as it was known that I was coming, Brockman was sent for to Brown county and now commenced a series of vexatious proceedings and conduct, which clearly showed that continued disaffection of many of the citizens. The Anti-Mormons generally could hardly find terms strong enough in which to express their unaffected surprise and astonishment at the impudence of the Governor and the people of other counties, in going over to interfere in the affairs of Hancock, and to see that the laws were executed there. So far had the mob scenes through which they had passed beclouded their judgments, that they really seemed to entertain the opinion that the people of Hancock possessed some kind of government and sovereignty of their own, and that to interfere with this was to invade their sacred rights.

After we arrived in the county, two public meetings were held by the Anti-Mormons, one in Carthage and the other in Nauvoo, at both of which it was resolved that they would do nothing whilst the State forces remained; but believing that such a force would be kept up only a short time, they solemnly determined again to drive out the proscribed citizens, as soon as the volunteers were recalled. They make their calculations that the public opinion and feeling are every where in their favor, and that the force will not be kept up for the protection of the expelled citizens, only during my continuance in office. I am solemnly persuaded that if there is any reliance to be placed upon the solemn resolutions of two Anti-Mormon meetings, the expelled citizens who have been restored to their homes, will be again expelled as soon as the volunteers are withdrawn.

During my stay there, Captain Robert Allen, with parts of his company and others, to the number of forty-four men, volunteered to make a secret expedition in the night to Carthage in search of the State arms, having previously gained intelligence that a large amount were concealed in that village. As Anti-Mormons had stationed a committee near us to watch our movements, and as Capt. Allen's men marched on foot, intelligence of his coming was conveyed to Carthage, and the arms removed to some other place of concealment before his arrival. During his absence, Major George R. Weber, who commanded the battalion, whilst going the rounds out side of the encampment, discovered an Anti-Mormon spy laying upon a wall, looking into our camp, and endeavored to arrest him. Major Weber aimed to make the arrest without the taking of life; and instead of shooting, only struck at the person with his pistol. Writs were now sworn out, not only for the arrest of Major Weber, but also for Capt. Allen for stopping some persons on the streets in Carthage whilst searching for arms. These writs were intended to be made the foundation of another call for the posse, which was intended for our expulsion from the county. . . . The mob party not being able this time to raise a large force, abandoned their design of making these arrests.

After remaining in the county for about seventeen days, and making diligent search for the five pieces of cannon and other arms belonging to the State without success, I disbanded the principal part of the force, and left about fifty men under the command of Major Jackson and Capt. Connelly, to remain until the fifteenth day of this month. The General Assembly being now in session [is left], to judge for themselves of the propriety of keeping up this force.

We did not think it worth while to arrest any one implicated in previous riots knowing as we did, that, as the State could not change the trial to any other county, no one could be convicted in Hancock. In fact the Anti-Mormons made their boasts, that, as they are now in the entire possession of the juries and the civil offices of the county, no jury can be obtained there to convict them. In this respect the administration of justice in that county is yet fully as bad as it ever was under the dominion of the Mormons. This makes the desperate men of the Anti-Mormons rely upon impunity for crime against their enemies, and greatly encourages them to much extravagant behaviour. . . .

—••• 17 •••—

A Tourist Views Hancock County in 1852

After the Mormons were gone, Hancock County returned to a peaceful, law-abiding condition, and despite the sudden decline in population, with the loss of a city of some twelve thousand people, prosperity slowly increased. Indeed, the county had much to offer, including extensive, rich farmland and direct access to the Mississippi River, which had attracted hopeful settlers since the early 1830s.

But after 1846 Hancock County also had one thing that few other places in the state possessed in the mid-nineteenth century—a past. A distinctive era, marked by intimidation and violence, had come and gone, and it would always have an impact on the minds of local residents. The Mormon era—for so it would be called—also held an interest for curious travelers who had read or heard about the sect that had been involved in a miniature civil war that had produced an empty city and started a massive trek to the West.

One such traveler—a forerunner of thousands who would visit the Mormon sites in the twentieth century—stopped at both Carthage and Nauvoo in 1852 and subsequently wrote an article about his experience for the *Cincinnati Gazette*. It was reprinted as "Scenes in Illinois" in the *McDonough Independent* at nearby Macomb on 29 October 1852, p. 2. Like most non-Mormons of that time, he was critical of the religious sect that had once occupied Nauvoo, and his reference to the "unnatural condition of society" indicates that he was fully aware of the Mormon practice of polygamy, which had been publicly unveiled in Utah.

But of greater interest are his remarks about the Carthage jail, which was already something of a tourist attraction, and the still-desolate city of Nauvoo, which then was occupied by only a few hundred French Icarians, which he mentions, and a small number of other residents, among whom were the widow and children of Joseph Smith, Jr. The reference to "Spiritual Rappers" at the jail is a reflection of the mid-nineteenth century fascination with spiritualism. The Mormon temple was in ruins because of a 9 October 1848 fire that had been set by an arsonist—apparently motivated by the fear that it might attract a return of the Mormons—and an 1850 tornado that had knocked down three of its four walls.

The tourist was right about the "moral desolation" symbolized by the ruins of Nauvoo, but he was certainly wrong in associating it with the Mormons alone, as the documents in this volume so clearly reveal. Both sides contributed to the tragedy that engulfed the early residents of Hancock County.

———————•••❁•••———————

On my way from Rushville to Warsaw, Illinois, I stopped a day at Carthage, the county seat of Hancock county, noted for its late Mormon War, and the violent death of Joe Smith and his brother Hiram. The Mormon Prophet could not have selected a richer or more beautiful country for his operation than that in Hancock county; and but little argument could have been necessary to convince his deluded followers that this was indeed the "Promised Land."

Though the desolation which their own hands wrought fell more heavily upon themselves, yet deep traces of it shall remain upon that country which they cursed by their presence. It has been seen in the ruins of Nauvoo, in the confusion of titles and claims to property, in the continual litigation consequent upon these conflicting interests, and above all, in the blots of moral desolation, caused by such unnatural condition of society as existed there eight years ago. From all these ills, however, the county of Hancock is rapidly recovering, and it will soon stand among the first in the State, for its wealth, and as a desirable place of residence.

The jail in which the Mormon leader met his fate, stands on the outskirts of the village of Carthage, and is an object of much interest to the curious traveler. In company with a friend I visited the building, and a little daughter of the jailer very courteously led me into the room where Joe and Hiram Smith were confined on the night of their murder, and pointed out the spot where each of them fell mortally wounded by the bullets of the mob outside. The walls of the room show the marks of many of the bullets, and the door which Hiram was holding shut against the mob, had one solitary bullet hole, through which passed the fatal lead which laid him low.

The room is now occupied as a sleeping apartment by the family of the jailor, and our little guide innocently informed us that the "Spiritual Rappers" were common in that room, and that she believed that they were made by "Old Joe and Hiram." It was about dusk in the evening when we were there, and after the above item of spiritual intelligence had been communicated, my friend was very anxious to return to the hotel *before dark*.

Nauvoo, a busy city of eighteen thousand inhabitants a few years ago, is now probably the most desolate and melancholy village on the continent. The fall grass now hides the lines of former streets and squares, and the broad plain is only here and there broken by a crumbling chimney or the shattered frame of a house. A little cluster of dwellings near the ruins of the Temple is all that remains of the once prosperous and beautiful Nauvoo. Three or four thousand persons, including the French Icarian community, under Mr. Cabet, live very comfortably here by tilling the soil and trading among themselves. The west wall of the Temple is still standing, vast and noble in its architectural proportions, and seeming, amid the graveyard stillness and desolation that surrounds it, to be an appropriate monument to departed Mormonism.

The Mormon Temple in Nauvoo. It was the center of Mormon religious life and a symbol of the conflict of cultures in western Illinois during the 1840s. From Henry Lewis, *Das Illustrirte Mississippithal* (Leipzig, 1848).

BIBLIOGRAPHIC
NOTE

This short bibliographic note describes a few of the most significant book-length secondary materials available for anyone seeking information on the development of the Mormon conflict in Illinois during the 1840s. A more detailed discussion of the historiography of Mormon Nauvoo will be contained in the forthcoming book edited by Roger D. Launius and John E. Hallwas, *Nauvoo in Mormon History: Kingdom on the Mississippi Revisited* (Urbana: University of Illinois Press, forthcoming). For perceptive reviews of the general literature on Mormon Nauvoo, see Richard D. Poll, "Nauvoo and the New Mormon History: A Bibliographical Survey," *Journal of Mormon History* 5 (1978): 105–23, and Glen M. Leonard, "Recent Writing on Mormon Nauvoo," *Western Illinois Regional Studies* 11 (Fall 1988): 69–93.

For anyone beginning a study of the Mormon/non-Mormon conflict in Hancock County, there are several good starting points. The best introduction to the Mormon experience in Nauvoo remains Robert B. Flanders, *Nauvoo: Kingdom on the Mississippi* (Urbana: University of Illinois Press, 1965), although it is now almost thirty years old. David E. Miller and Della S. Miller, *Nauvoo: The City of Joseph* (Santa Barbara, Calif.: Peregrine Smith, 1974) emphasizes the social and religious development of the city. Finally, Samuel W. Taylor, *Nightfall at Nauvoo* (New York: Macmillan Co., 1971), a historical work that employs fictional techniques, contains many insights that should be pondered by serious students of Mormonism and the conflict in Illinois.

Several older works deal with the crisis in a defensive manner while fostering the myth of Mormon innocence and religious persecution. *Joseph Smith, Jr., History of the Church of Jesus Christ of Latter-day Saints*, ed. B. H. Roberts, 7 vols. (Salt Lake City: Deseret Book Co., 1902–32), has gone through several editions since 1932 and contains a wealth of primary source materials but must be used with caution since it takes a decidedly apologetic approach in documenting the history of the church. Synthetic works in this genre are B. H. Roberts, *The Rise and Fall of Nauvoo* (1900; reprint, Salt Lake City: Bookcraft, 1965); E. Cecil McGavin, *Nauvoo the Beautiful* (Salt Lake City: Stevens & Wallis, 1946); Mabel A. Sanford, *Joseph's City Beautiful* (1933; reprint, Independence, Mo: Herald Publishing House, 1976); and Elbert A. Smith, *Timbers for the Temple* (Independence, Mo: Herald Publishing House, 1922). For non-Mormon perspectives, see Thomas Gregg, *The History of Hancock County, Illinois* (Chicago: Charles C. Chapman, 1880); Thomas Ford, *A History of Illinois, from its Commencement as a State in 1818 to 1847* (Chicago: S. C. Griggs and Co., 1854); John E. Hallwas, "Mormon Nauvoo from a

Non-Mormon Perspective," *Journal of Mormon History* 16 (1990): 53–69; and John E. Hallwas, *Western Illinois Heritage* (Macomb: Illinois Heritage Press, 1983).

Two general histories of early Mormonism offer intriguing possibilities for interpreting the Mormon conflict in Illinois. Marvin S. Hill's *Quest for Refuge: The Mormon Flight from American Pluralism* (Salt Lake City: Signature Books, 1989) describes the early Saints as generally destitute and the social and economic policies of the church they embraced as radical, in part because there was little to be lost in a complete restructuring of society. Kenneth H. Winn's *Exiles in a Land of Liberty: Mormons in America, 1830–1846* (Chapel Hill: University of North Carolina Press, 1989) carries some of these same ideas into a study of the use of rhetoric and the theme of republicanism in Jacksonian America.

Specifically on the conflict, see Kenneth W. Godfrey, "Causes of Mormon-Non-Mormon Conflict in Hancock County, Illinois, 1839–1846" (Ph.D. diss., Brigham Young University, 1967); Annette P. Hampshire, *Mormonism in Conflict: The Nauvoo Years* (New York: Edwin Mellen Press, 1985); and Klaus J. Hansen, *Quest for Empire: The Kingdom of God and the Council of Fifty in Mormon History* (East Lansing: Michigan State University Press, 1967; reprint, Lincoln: University of Nebraska Press, 1974).

Polygamy, of course, sparked non-Mormon opposition, and it has been dealt with in Lawrence Foster, *Religion and Sexuality: Three American Communal Experiments of the Nineteenth Century* (New York: Oxford University Press, 1981); Louis J. Kern, *An Ordered Love: Sex Roles and Sexuality in Victorian Utopias—the Shakers, the Mormons, and the Oneida Community* (Chapel Hill: University of North Carolina Press, 1981); Richard S. Van Wagoner, *Mormon Polygamy: A History* (Salt Lake City: Signature Books, 1986); and B. Carmon Hardy, *Solemn Covenant: The Mormon Polygamous Passage* (Urbana: University of Illinois Press, 1992). An important study on the death of the Smith brothers and its aftermath is Dallin H. Oaks and Marvin S. Hill, *Carthage Conspiracy: The Trial of the Accused Assassins of Joseph Smith* (Urbana: University of Illinois Press, 1975). Contemporary accounts can be found in Keith Huntress, ed., *Murder of an American Prophet: Materials for Analysis* (San Francisco: Chandler Publishing Co., 1960).

Several important biographies shed light on the Mormon conflict in western Illinois: Fawn M. Brodie, *No Man Knows My History: The Life of Joseph Smith, the Mormon Prophet* (1945; 2d ed., New York: Alfred A. Knopf, 1971); Donna Hill, *Joseph Smith: The First Mormon* (Garden City, N.Y.: Doubleday and Co., 1977); Linda K. Newell and Valeen T. Avery, *Mormon Enigma: Emma Hale Smith, Prophet's Wife, "Elect Lady," Polygamy's Foe* (Garden City, N.Y.: Doubleday and Co., 1984); Leonard J. Arrington, *Brigham Young: American Moses* (New York: Alfred A. Knopf, 1985); F. Mark McKiernan, *The Voice of One Crying in the Wilderness: Sidney Rigdon, Religious Reformer, 1793–1876* (Lawrence, Kans.: Coronado Press, 1971); and Roger D. Launius, *Joseph Smith III: Pragmatic Prophet* (Urbana: University of Illinois Press, 1988).

Special editions of historical journals have been devoted to the Nauvoo experience. These include *Dialogue: A Journal of Mormon Thought*, Spring 1970;

Journal of the Illinois State Historical Society, Spring 1971; *Brigham Young University Studies*, Summer 1975, Winter 1978, Spring 1979, Winter 1979, Winter/Spring 1992; and *Western Illinois Regional Studies*, Fall 1988. Isolated articles dealing with the Nauvoo experience have appeared in each of these journals at other times, as well as in the *Journal of Mormon History*, the *Utah Historical Quarterly*, the *Journal of the Early Republic*, the *John Whitmer Historical Association Journal*, and *Sunstone*.

In general, there has been an enormous imbalance in scholarship on the Mormon conflict. Mormon biography abounds, but there are no thorough studies of such key non-Mormons as Thomas Ford and Thomas Sharp, and lesser figures like Jacob Backenstos and Levi Williams have received virtually no attention. Furthermore, while Nauvoo has been studied from every angle, the important non-Mormon towns of Carthage and Warsaw have been all but neglected. And, finally, as this documentary history reveals, there is a need for a thoroughgoing study of the critical role which myth played in the experience of the early Mormons.

INDEX

A

Adams, Charles Francis, 44, 45, 46, 47, 49
Adams County, Ill., 19, 88, 235, 305
Adams, George J., 129, 216
Adams, John, 44
Aldrich, Mark, 260–62
Allen, Capt. Robert, 346–47
Allen, James B., 2–3
Allen, Mr., 260–62
Alton, Ill., 67, 103, 219, 232, 296
Alton Telegraph and Democratic Review, 103, 231
American Home Missionary Society, 32–35
American Myth/American Reality, 5
American Prophet's Record: The Diaries and Journals of Joseph Smith, An, 35–38, 156
Anderson, Capt., 332
Anderson, S. H., 24
Anti–Mormon Party, 68, 80–81, 82
Anti–Mormons, 68, 80–81, 82, 97–101, 101–2, 103–7; after the Mormon exodus, 336–38, 342–45, 347–49; and aftermath of Smith brothers' assassinations, 231–32, 243–45; Anti–Mormon Party of, 68, 80–81, 81–82; and arrest of Joseph Smith, 88–90, 91–97, 199–200, 209–13, 214–16, 217–18, 223; and assassinations of Joseph and Hyrum Smith, 70, 79, 103, 178, 196–97, 203–13, 214–16, 217–20, 220–22, 223–26, 227–28, 229–31, 234–37, 256, 258; and Backenstos proclamations, 280–88; and battle of Nauvoo, 1, 299, 329–34, 338–40; Carthage convention of, 304–9; and completion of Nauvoo Temple, 317–20, 321–23;

and defense of Smith brothers' assassinations, 247–51; and demands for a murder investigation, 262–65; and disappearance of Phineas Wilcox, 278–80; and 1842 gubernatorial election, 82–85; and 1843 congressional election, 85–87; and the *Expositor* affair, 1, 3, 111, 113, 139, 142–48, 149–56, 156–59, 159–60, 161–62, 163–65, 167–68, 169–72, 175–78, 181, 185, 186, 190, 198, 205–6, 244; and expulsion of Mormon sympathizers, 282–83; and fear of Mormons after deaths of Joseph and Hyrum Smith, 231–33, 243; and Ford's use of force, 310–13; and gathering of Mormons, 1, 15–17, 20–21, 24–29, 30–31, 34–35, 36–38, 39–51, 61; and general description of Mormon conflict in, 1–8; and John C. Bennett, 115–21, 121–25, 251; and killings of Worrell and McBratney, 275–78; mobbery of, 194–99, 270–73, 274–75; and Mormon decision to leave, 302–4; and Mormon demands for murder investigation, 262–65; and Mormon dissenters, 131–32, 139, 142–48, 149–56, 156–59, 159–60, 161–62, 163–65, 166–68, 313–17; and Mormon exodus, 304–7, 309–10, 324–25, 326–27, 340–42; and Mormon occupation of Carthage, 288–91; and Mormon theft, 70–78, 244, 293, 312; and Mormon use of habeas corpus, 91–97, 167, 176–78, 185, 192–93, 195, 223; and Nauvoo city charter, 21–24, 25–26, 54, 76, 88, 91, 132, 234–35, 244, 267–70; and Nauvoo Legion, 24–29, 46–47,

About the
Authors

John E. Hallwas is a professor of English and director of regional collections at Western Illinois University in Macomb, Illinois. Among his many publications are *Thomas Gregg: Early Illinois Journalist and Author* (Macomb: Western Illinois Monograph Series, 1983); *Western Illinois Heritage* (Macomb: Illinois Heritage Press, 1983); and *Spoon River Anthology: An Annotated Edition* (Urbana: University of Illinois Press, 1992).

Roger D. Launius is chief historian at the National Aeronautics and Space Administration, Washington, D.C. He is the author or editor of *Joseph Smith III: Pragmatic Prophet* (Urbana: University of Illinois Press, 1988); *Differing Visions: Dissenters in Mormon History* (Urbana: University of Illinois Press, 1994); *NASA: A History of the U.S. Civil Space Program* (Malabar, Fla.: Krieger Publishing Co., 1994), and nine other books.